Wissenschaftliche Untersuchungen
zum Neuen Testament

Herausgegeben von
Martin Hengel und Otfried Hofius

79

Faith, Obedience, and Perseverance

Aspects of Paul's Letter to the Romans

by

Don Garlington

WIPF & STOCK · Eugene, Oregon

Wipf and Stock Publishers
199 W 8th Ave, Suite 3
Eugene, OR 97401

Faith, Obedience and Perseverance
Aspects of Paul's Letter to the Romans
By Garlington, Don
Copyright©1994 Mohr Siebeck GmbH & Co.
ISBN 13: 978-1-60608-825-8
Publication date 6/15/2009
Previously published by J. C. B. Mohr (Paul Siebeck), 1994

"This edition reprinted 2009 by Wipf and Stock through special arrangement with Mohr Siebeck Gmbh & Co. Copyright J.C.B. Mohr (Paul Siebeck) 1994".

For Elizabeth, Robert, and Thomas

who have persevered with this book – and with me!

Table of Contents

Abbreviations IX

Introduction 1

Chapter One: Faith's Obedience: The Meaning of ὑπακοὴ πίστεως ... 10
    I. The Function of Romans 1:5 and 16:26 within Their Immediate
        Contexts 11
    II. The Grammatical Options 13
        A. Summary of the Grammatical Options 14
        B. Evaluation of the Grammatical Options 14
    III. "The Obedience of Faith" as the Believer's Total Response to the
        Gospel 15
    IV. Summary 30

Chapter Two: The Disobedience of Israel 32
    I. The Problem of Romans 2:22 32
    II. Ἱεροσυλεῖν as Israel's Idolatry 34
    III. Summary 43

Chapter Three: The Obedience of Faith and the Doers of the Law ... 44
    I. Paul's Dialogue with Israel in Romans 1:1–3:8 45
    II. The Justification of the Doers of the Law: Romans 2:13 .. 56
    III. The Doing of the Law as the Obedience of Faith 61
        A. The Hearing of Faith 62
        B. The Primacy of Love 64
        C. Perseverance 67
    IV. Summary 71

Chapter Four: The Obedience of Christ and the Obedience of the Christian ... 72
    I. Romans 5 within the Scheme of Chapters 5–8 72
    II. Romans 5:1–11: Reconciliation and New Creation 74
        A. The Two Results of Justification by Faith, vv. 1–2 ... 75
        B. The Relation of the Two Results of Justification by Faith, vv. 3–10 . 77
        C. The Two Results of Justification by Faith, v. 11 78

VIII Table of Contents

   III. Romans 5:12–21: Adam and Christ: Disobedience and Obedience ... 79
      A. Structure and Relation to the Preceding 79
      B. Paul's Creation Typology 81
      C. Paul's Dialogue with Israel 82
      D. The Disobedient First Adam and the Old Humanity 84
        1. Adam's Sin as the Gateway of All Subsequent Sin and Death 84
        2. The Reign of Death from Adam to Moses 95
      E. The Obedient Last Adam and the New Humanity 98
      F. Christ, not the Torah, the Source of Life 107
   IV. Summary 108

Chapter Five: The Obedience of Faith as Life Between Two Worlds ... 110

   I. The Approach to Romans 7:14–25 110
        Note on the "I" of 7:14–25 114
   II. Romans 5–8 and the Theology of Creation 114
   III. The Function of Romans 7:14–25 within the Debate of Chapters 6–7 . 115
        Note on Paul, Adam, and Eve 118
   IV. Romans 7:13–25: Two Creations, One Person 119
      A. The Law and Paul's Awareness of Sin, v. 13 120
      B. The Law and Paul's Continuing Struggle with Sin, vv. 14–20 120
        Note on the Present Tenses of 7:14–25 120
      C. Paul's Summary and Conclusion, vv. 21–25 136
        Note on Paul's wretchedness 140
   V. Summary 143

Chapter Six: Reflections 144

   I. "The Obedience of Faith" 144
   II. The Obedience of Faith and the Doers of the Law 146
   III. The Obedience of Christ and the Obedience of the Christian 150
   IV. Justification and Sanctification 151
   V. The Obedience of Faith as Life Between Two Worlds 161

Bibliography 164

Index of Passages 179
   I. Old Testament 179
   II. Jewish Literature 181
   III. Greco-Roman Literature 184
   IV. New Testament 184

Index of Authors 193

Index of Subjects 199

Abbreviations

AB	Anchor Bible
AGJU	Arbeiten zur Geschichte des antiken Judentums und des Urchristentums
AnBib	Analecta biblica
ANRW	*Aufstieg und Neidergang der römische Welt*, eds. Wolfgang Haase and Hildegard Temporini; 21 vols.; Berlin: De Gruyter, 1974-.
ATANT	Abhandlungen zur Theologie des Alten und Neuen Testaments
BAGD	W. Baur, W.F. Arndt, F.W. Gingrich, and F. W. Danker, *A Greek-English Lexicon of the New Testament and Other Early Christian Literature*, Chicago: University of Chicago Press, 1979.
BDF	F. Blass, A. Debrunner, and R.W. Funk, *A Greek Grammar of the New Testament and Other Early Christian Literature*, Chicago: University of Chicago Press, 1961.
BEvT	Beiträge zur evangelischen Theologie
Bib	*Biblica*
BJRL	*Bulletin of the John Rylands University Library of Manchester*
BR	Biblical Research
BZ	*Biblische Zeitschrift*
BZNW	Beihefte zur *ZNW*
CBQ	*Catholic Biblical Quarterly*
CJT	*Canadian Journal of Theology*
CNT	Commentaar op het Nieuwe Testament
CRINT	Compendia Rerum Iudaicarum ad Novum Testamentum
CUOS	Columbia University Oriental Studies
Ebib	Études Bibliques
EKK	Evangelisch-Katholischer Kommentar zum Neuen Testament
ExA	*Ex Auditu*
ExpT	*Expository Times*
FRLANT	Forschungen zur Religion und Literature des Alten und Neuen Testaments
GTA	Göttinger theologische Arbeiten
HNT	Handbuch zum Neuen Testament
HNTC	Harpers New Testament Commentary
HTKNT	Herders theologischer Kommentar zum Neuen Testament
ICC	International Critical Commentary
IDB	*The Interpreter's Dictionary of the Bible*, ed. G.A. Buttrick; 5 vols.; Nashville: Abingdon, 1962.
ISBE	*International Standard Bible Encyclopedia*, eds. Geoffrey W. Bromiley, et al.; 4 vols.; Grand Rapids: Eerdmans, ^{2}1979−88.

JBL	*Journal of Biblical Literature*
JBR	*Journal of Bible and Religion*
JETS	*Journal of the Evangelical Theological Society*
JJS	*Journal of Jewish Studies*
JQR	*Jewish Quarterly Review*
JSJ	*Journal for the Study of Judaism*
JSNT	*Journal for the Study of the New Testament*
JSNTSup	Journal for the Study of the New Testament – Supplement Series
JSPSup	Journal for the Study of the Pseudepigrapha – Supplement Series
JTS	*Journal of Theological Studies*
KBANT	Kommentare und Beiträge zum Alten und Neuen Testament
LCC	Library of Christian Classics
LSJ	H. G. Liddell, R. Scott, and H. S. Jones, *A Greek-English Lexicon*, Oxford: Clarendon, 1968.
MeyerK	H. A. W. Meyer, et al. eds., Kritisch-exegetischer Kommentar über das Neue Testament
MNTC	Moffatt New Testament Commentary
NCB	New Century Bible
NFTL	New Foundations Theological Library
NDT	*New Dictionary of Theology*, eds. S. Ferguson and D. F. Wright; Leicester: Inter-Varsity, 1988.
Neot	*Neotestamentica*
NICNT	New International Commentary on the New Testament
NIDNTT	*The New International Dictionary of New Testament Theology*, ed. C. Brown; 3 vols.; Grand Rapids: Zondervan, 1975.
NIGTC	New International Greek Testament Commentary
NovT	*Novum Testamentum*
NovTSup	Novum Testamentum, Supplements
NTAbh	Neutestamentliche Abhandlungen
NTC	New Testament Commentary
NTS	*New Testament Studies*
OTL	Old Testament Library
OTP	*The Old Testament Pseudepigrapha*, ed. J. H. Charlesworth; 2 vols.; New York: Doubleday, 1983, 1985.
RB	*Revue biblique*
RNT	Regensburger Neues Testament
RTR	*Reformed Theological Review*
SBLDS	Society of Biblical Literature Dissertation Series
SBLMS	Society of Biblical Literature Monograph Series
SBLSP	Society of Biblical Literature Seminar Papers
SBT	Studies in Biblical Theology
SD	Studies in Dogmatics
SE	*Studia Evangelica*
SJT	*Scottish Journal of Theology*
SMB	Serie Monografica di "Benedictina;" Sezione biblico-ecumenica
SNTSMS	Society for New Testament Studies Monograph Series
SNTW	Studies of the New Testament and Its World

Str-B	H. Strack and P. Billerbeck, *Kommentar zum Neuen Testament aus Talmud und Midrash*; 6 vols.; Munich: C. H. Beck, 1924–28, 1956.
TBü	Theologische Bücherei
TCGNT	B. M. Metzger, *A Textual Commentary on The Greek New Testament*, United Bible Societies, 1971.
TDNT	*Theological Dictionary of the New Testament*, eds. G. Kittel and G. Friedrich; 10 vols.; Grand Rapids: Eerdmans, 1964–76.
TDOT	*Theological Dictionary of the Old Testament*, eds. G. J. Botterweck and H. Ringgren; Grand Rapids: Eerdmans, 1974-.
Them	*Themelios*
TLZ	*Theologische Literaturzeitung*
TNTC	Tyndale New Testament Commentaries
TRE	*Theologische Realenzyklopädie*, eds., G. Krause and G. Müller; Berlin: de Gruyter, 1977-.
TrinJ	*Trinity Journal*
TS	Theologische Studien
TTZ	*Trierer theologische Zeitschrift*
TynBul	*Tyndale Bulletin*
TZ	*Theologische Zeitschrift*
UTB	Uni-Taschenbücher
WBC	Word Biblical Commentary
WEC	Wycliffe Exegetical Commentary
WTJ	*Westminster Theological Journal*
WMANT	Wissenschaftliche Monographien zum Alten und Neuen Testament
WUNT	Wissenschaftliche Untersuchungen zum Neuen Testament
ZAW	*Zeitschrift für die alttestamentliche Wissenschaft*
ZNW	*Zeitschrift für die neutestamentliche Wissenschaft*
ZTK	*Zeitschrift für Theologie und Kirche*

Introduction

The present volume is the outgrowth of five articles on the interpretation of Paul's letter to the Romans which have appeared over the course of the past few years. Each has been extensively revised and, with the addition of the final chapter, is now presented as a monograph. The articles were originally published as: "'ΙΕΡΟΣΥΛΕΙΝ and the Idolatry of Israel (Romans 2.22)," *NTS* 36 (1990), 142–51; "The Obedience of Faith in the Letter to the Romans. Part I: The Meaning of ὑπακοὴ πίστεως," *WTJ* 52 (1990), 201–224; "The Obedience of Faith in the Letter to the Romans. Part II: The Obedience of Faith and Judgment by Works," *WTJ* 53 (1991), 47–72; "The Obedience of Faith in the Letter to the Romans. Part III: The Obedience of Christ and the Obedience of the Christian," *WTJ* 55 (1993), 87–112, 281–97; "Romans 7:14–25 and the Creation Theology of Paul," *TrinJ* ns 11 (1990), 197–235. Each is used with the kind permission of the respective periodicals.

The connecting thread of these studies is mirrored in its main title: *Faith, Obedience, and Perseverance*. It is particularly the "Obedience of Faith" series in *WTJ*, now appearing as chapters 1, 3, and 4, which forms the core of this amalgamation of essays. In those pieces, an attempt was made, initially, to explore the significance of Paul's unique phrase "the obedience of faith." By an analysis of the phrase in its respective contexts, I drew the conclusion that it is designed to say more than one thing at the same time; that is, by this particular combination of words Paul gives voice to an obedience which consists in faith in Jesus the Son of God and is the outgrowth of faith's commitment to him. In other words, "the obedience of faith" addresses itself both to the inception of Christian existence and its continuation in the perseverance of the believer, the latter being defined as one's determination to remain faithful to Christ from conversion till death.

This basic conclusion concerning "the obedience of faith" led to an exploration of Rom 2:13, according to which only "the doers of the law" will be "justified" in eschatological judgment. At this stage of the investigation, an earlier impression was confirmed, viz., that the proposition contained in the verse is, in the apostle's perception, far from hypothetical. Quite the contrary, it gives voice to his vision of the realities of final judgment and of the urgency of seeking "glory, honor, and immortality" (2:7) as the precondition of eternal life. There is, in other words, in Paul the idea of a future justification of the people of God, which forms an analogue to their present justification. Attempting, then, to understand Rom 2:13 in light of "the obedience of faith," it was concluded that the link between the two moments of justification is none other than the notion embedded in this phrase which sets the tone of the entire epistle (1:5; [16:26]).[1] Precisely how the link is forged will be the burden of the ensuing volume.

In the final installment of this series, attention was given to Romans 5 and its portrayal of Christ as the obedient last Adam, who ensures "the obedience of faith" of his people. As the following pages seek to establish, the peculiar character of the Christian's obedience is derived from the obedience of Christ himself: he is the most vital link of all between present and future justification.

Chapters 2 and 5 respectively fall outside the "Obedience of Faith" articles proper but are, nonetheless, integrally related to them. Chapter 2 pauses between the contextual study of ὑπακοὴ πίστεως (chapter 1) and its application to Rom 2:13 (chapter 3) to reflect on Israel's disobedience. Since Paul's conception of (faith's) obedience stands in rather stark relief to the (unbelieving) disobedience of his Jewish contemporaries, it is only against the backdrop of his indictment of Israel that aspects of his teaching emerge with tolerable clarity. Thus, attention is turned to Rom 2:22 in order to discern what is intended in the charge of "sacrilege" laid at the doorstep of the apostle's contemporaries.

Chapter 5, an exposition of Rom 7:14–25, approaches "the obedience of faith" from the angle of the Christian's personal, subjective experience, as he contends with the onslaught of the powers of this "present evil age" (Gal 1:4) which seek to reassert their influence over him. The ideals of "the age to come," as set out in chapters 1–4, are thus seen to be tempered by the realism of life as it actually is during this period of overlapping aeons. This means that Rom 7:14–25 makes its direct impact on the one who, in his own person, is a microcosm of salvation history. He is the one who lives in two worlds at the same time and is, by virtue of that fact, simultaneously "flesh" and "spirit." Hence, the relevance of this portion of Romans is that notwithstanding one's many shortcomings (due to "indwelling sin"), there is no condemnation for those who are in Christ Jesus (Rom 8:1). I should add that while this application of 7:14–25 to the Christian is traditional, the approach to the passage is not altogether so, at least to the degree that I have sought to place the text within the perimeters of a theology of creation, which, I believe, forms the substructure of Romans 5–8 as a whole.[2]

---

[1] On the textual problem of Rom 16:26, see n. 1 of chapter one.

[2] Throughout this study, it will be seen that in Romans Paul takes creation (rather than the Torah) as his point of theological departure. For him creation sets the outermost limits of biblical religion. Not least, this ideology of creation bears on his conception of "righteousness," which, as argued effectively by Käsemann, is God's commitment to his creation. Apart from the claim that δικαιοσύνη θεοῦ is a technical phrase taken over by Paul from Jewish Apocalyptic, underlying this exposition are the perspectives of Käsemann's "Righteousness," as reflected in his *Romans* (e.g., pp. 79–80, 154–58). See further de Boer, *Defeat*, 150–56; Beker, *Paul*, 262–64; Motyer, "Righteousness," 53–54; Davies, *Faith*, 36–38.

So, this book is about *Faith, Obedience, and Perseverance* in Romans. However, its subtitle, *Aspects of Paul's Letter to the Romans*, is designed to say something too. The purpose, in other words, is not to address the entirety of the triad of faith, obedience, and perseverance – even in Romans, let alone in Paul generally – but dimensions of the theme which, in my view, are sufficiently noteworthy to call forth a reexamination. Not unexpectedly, then, several of the passages treated are familiar, even well-worn; but they are explored, hopefully, in such a way as to fill some gaps and reinforce their significance for perseverance in Paul. It is because the approach is selective by definition that I have not attempted to construct anything like an overall systematic theology of perseverance. Consequently, apart from the splendid works of G.C. Berkouwer, this study basically bypasses the countless volumes of systematic and dogmatic theology.

Along with this disclaimer, it must be clarified that the book is not cast in terms of whether one can "lose" salvation, à la the historic (and contemporary) Calvinist/Arminian debate.[3] Its intention, rather, is to argue that *"the obedience of faith" in Romans is perseverance in Christ (rather than perseverance in the Torah), a perseverance requisite to eschatological salvation.* Scot McKnight's conclusion respecting perseverance in Hebrews, in my view, is equally applicable to Romans. That is to say, Paul contemplates what Mcknight calls the "phenomenological-true believer" (I prefer "confessing believer"): his warnings against apostasy and encouragements to fidelity are directed to people who genuinely believe but who will, nonetheless, forsake Christ, *if theirs is not a persevering faith*. As McKnight puts it, those who finally apostatize are believers in every observable sense; even so, they can stop believing and forfeit eternal salvation. Hence, what Christian theology calls "true" or "saving" faith is none other than *persevering* faith.[4] Given that "salvation" (in Paul and Hebrews) is dominantly future-eschatological, it is best to speak not of "loosing" salvation but of failing to enter into the salvation which is yet to be.[5] While on the surface this may appear troubling, we shall see in some detail, in agreement with McKnight, that the only sin which can separate "the confessing believer" from final salvation is apostasy.

Recent days have seen the appearance of two important works in English similar to this undertaking. One is Judith M. Gundry Volf's study, *Paul and Perseverance: Staying In and Falling Away*. In light of her volume, it should be stated, again, that the present contribution proposes to fill certain noticeable gaps – to me anyway – in her treatment of passages in Paul relevant to perseverance, in particular Romans 2, 5, and 7. These, I think, are as crucial as any in Paul's letters. Moreover, there are areas, the reader will discern, in which these two approaches to the same topic are in disagreement.

---

[3] See McKnight, "Passages," 21–22, nn. 1–2.
[4] Ibid., 24.
[5] Ibid., 58.

Another fresh publication, more akin to the present one, is that of Glenn N. Davies, *Faith and Obedience in Romans: A Study of Romans 1–4*. In major agreement, as I, with the "new view" of Paul and Judaism (see below), Davies asserts that there is a continuity in God's way of dealing with mankind both before and after the coming of Christ. These two eras respectively can be termed "promise" and "fulfillment." Yet, he says, within the framework of this promise/fulfillment schema, the appropriate response of men and women to God is always faith and obedience, which applies indiscriminately to Jew and Gentile. Hence, obedience as evidence of and expressive for Christian faith is not qualitatively different from that exhibited by believers under the old covenant, although the specific content of that obedience as it relates to the Torah requires some adjustment. Paul's rejection of the Jew/Gentile distinction, therefore, is not temporally dependent on Christ's coming. Rather, according to Davies:

> The distinctions that Paul wishes to emphasize ... are between the righteous and the wicked, believers and unbelievers, the obedient and the disobedient. These are the distinctions which constitute the contours of Paul's gospel, that gospel of God's righteousness with which he had been commissioned to bring about the obedience of faith for Christ's sake among all nations.[6]

With certain qualifications to be voiced throughout, the following study is in accord with Davies' fine work, so that in places I have opted simply to refer the reader to his discussions of various points. Nonetheless, I believe a kindred volume is justifiable for similar reasons as those pertaining to Gundry Volf's monograph, because, in addition to treatments of chapters 5 and 7 of Romans, which do not appear in his book, more space is devoted herein to an exploration of the actual phrase ὑπακοὴ πίστεως and to the pivotal text Rom 2:13 than allotted by him.

It is to be acknowledged from the outset that some of the conclusions may prove to be controversial. Among the most hotly debatable issues, which have been placed on the agenda of Protestant/Roman Catholic dialogue from the Reformation onward, are two: (1) a future (eschatological) dimension of justification which takes into account "works;" (2) the relation of "justification" and "sanctification" as the two, in Reformed theology particularly, have been subsumed under an *ordo salutis*. In both cases, it has appeared to me that adjustments to the customary Protestant/Reformed scheme are in order. This is why, in the last chapter especially, I have sought to interact with modern Reformed scholarship.

In the face of potential criticism, I would plead that oversimplification in any direction is one of the most dangerous enemies of biblical research, to which I would add that the positions herein espoused are not without precedent among Protestants – including the Reformers – as will become evident enough. In any event, I am convinced that while the debate cannot be abstracted from an

---

[6] Davies, *Faith*, 18–19 (quote from p. 19).

awareness of confessional standards, the exegete must be allowed to probe the biblical text, free to draw whatever conclusions are consonant with his/her exegesis. It is fully my conviction that the agenda of scholarship is not to be set by church-historical controversies, with the unspoken – if not spoken! – assumption that certain conclusions are to be avoided at all costs. We do well to listen to Berkouwer: "The way of dogmatic logicism is not that of faith, which always listens, listens,– to the Word."[7]

This book follows upon my *'The Obedience of Faith': A Pauline Phrase in Historical Context* (WUNT 2/38), a revision of a Durham Ph.D. thesis supervised by my esteemed teacher and friend J. D. G. Dunn. The aim of the earlier publication was to develop an insight into Rom 1:5 picked up from Otto Michel, viz., when Paul coins his singular phrase ὑπακοὴ πίστεως, he does so antithetically to Judaism and the kind of Jewish Christianity represented by the "circumcision party."[8] Accordingly, I sought to set the phrase within its historical context in order to determine the nature of the controversy between Paul and his opponents as articulated by that peculiar combination of words. Whereas "the obedience of faith" in Paul's day was commensurate with devotion to the law ("covenantal nomism"), for him a reversal has taken place. The phrase is his declaration that to be acceptable to God as a faithful covenant-keeper it is no longer necessary to become and then remain Jewish: the privileges entailed in Israel's identity as the people of God can be had by virtue of faith alone in the risen Christ, the Seed of David and the powerful Son of God.[9] Several conclusions were drawn by the previous investigation which set the presuppositional framework of this one.[10]

For one, it was Paul's vision of the obedient people of God which most radically drew the line of demarcation between him and first-century Judaism. As intimated immediately above, "the obedience of faith" for Paul's contemporaries was inseparable from the *whole Torah*, especially as emblematized by those aspects of it which came to serve as the boundary marking mechanisms of the chosen people: circumcision, dietary laws, purity regulations, sabbath, and cultus as concentrated in the temple-worship. It is thus the sum and total of the Torah's requirements for covenant life, with the "boundary markers" most pointedly serving as the acid tests of loyalty to Judaism, which form the "works

---

[7] Berkouwer, *Sanctification*, 66. Berkouwer says elsewhere: "Theology is relative to the Word of God. This relativity is decisive for the method and significance of theology. It means that theology is occupied in continuous attentive and obedient listening to the Word of God" (*Justification*, 9).

[8] Michel, *Römer*, 76.

[9] Garlington, *Obedience*, 247. That such associations are attached to ὑπακοὴ πίστεως is argued in detail in the final chapter. Some reviewers, I should say, have paid less attention to the book's main thesis than to certain conclusions which were more secondary to its intent.

[10] See in detail ibid., 254–68.

of the law" required of all of Yahweh's faithful.¹¹ These were to be embraced by all Israelites in response to Yahweh's covenant with them.¹²

Second, Paul's conception of faith's obedience speaks to the heart of his controversy with Second Temple Judaism regarding the law. What was at stake was not "legalism" vs. "grace" in the heretofore conventional understanding of the terms but rather the on-going status of the Torah as defining the people of God. Israel, in its insistence that the law is eternal and unchangeable, demanded that all who would enter Yahweh's covenant must submit to its entrance-rite, circumcision, and thereafter make a commitment to the law, Israel's "constitution,"¹³ as the expression of God's will for his people (cf. Jdt 14:10; Gal 5:3). Given such a scenario, "the obedience of faith" is Paul's battle cry, his manifesto, that, by virtue of the Christ who has received "all" without distinction (Rom 1:5–7; 15:7–12, passim), people of varying descriptions can be reckoned among the faithful – quite apart from circumcision and the particulars of the Mosaic code. From one vantage point, then, the debate about the law can be reduced to Paul's ethnic inclusiveness as opposed to the particularism of his Jewish kinsmen;¹⁴ from another, the dispute revolves around a basic question: What does one think of Jesus of Nazareth as the Christ? Is it he or the Torah which forms the gateway to salvation?

In the third place, organically related to both these points, my earlier historical study of "the obedience of faith" seconded the basic findings of E.P. Sanders' *Paul and Palestinian Judaism*, i.e., the phrase which best describes ancient Judaism as a religion and way of life is "covenantal nomism," meaning that Israel's striving to keep the law was but the outgrowth of a prior covenant relationship rooted in the electing grace of God. Since Sanders' work is well-known by this time, no attempt will be made to summarize it as such. I simply take it for granted that the main lines of his approach to the sources are sufficiently familiar that scholars may now feel free to interact with them apart from the necessity of first expounding them.

In following this "covenantal nomism" model, it is not to be denied that in, most conspicuously, Rom 4:4–5 Paul challenges a works-principle in Judaism. Yet the ensuing context (vv. 9–12) supports the contention that Paul's concern is not with a merit theology but with the works of covenant loyalty subsequent to circumcision (cf. Gal 5:3). That "the one who works" receives a "wage" (v. 4) is not a particular problem, because the "wage" in question is eternal life

---

¹¹ Frequently, scholars on the other side of the debate over the law have alleged that the view propounded here limits Paul's complaint against Israel to an exaggerated emphasis on the "boundary markers." However, precisely the contrary is stated in my *Obedience*, 261–62 (quoting Dunn). Moreover, I have affirmed that there was, in Paul's view, an anthropological failure on Israel's part, for which the law was insufficient (ibid., 260–61).

¹² See Davies' discussion of work(s) in Paul (*Faith*, 115–27).

¹³ Renaud, "Loi," 56, 61; Arenhoevel, *Theokratie*, 15–16.

¹⁴ The expression "ethnic inclusiveness" rather than "universalism" is quite deliberate, because it is arguable that Paul propounds a "new particularism" in that salvation is available only in Christ. See my *Obedience*, 247, n. 68.

bestowed at the end of this age on those who remain faithful to Yahweh, whose will is enshrined in the Torah. Qualitatively, the Jewish position is no different than that embodied in the parable of Matt 20:1–16: the workers in the vineyard receive the wage of their labor, i.e., the eschatological kingdom of God as preached by Jesus.[15] Hence, the works envisaged by Romans 4 (and other passages) are just those demanded by the Torah; they accompany faith and eventuate in the life of the age to come. To be sure, works *are* a condition of "staying in" the covenant. Yet "staying in" is not "getting in." Israel's works are but its response to Yahweh's saving grace: they are tantamount to *perseverance*, not "works-righteousness legalism." As we shall argue throughout, it is in the same sense that "good works" (= perseverance) in Paul's own theology are a condition of "staying in" Christ.

It is in keeping with these perspectives that Paul's opposition to Jewish covenantal nomism can be reduced to his insistence on *Christ-fidelity vs. Torah-fidelity*. The core issue in Romans (and Galatians) is an "either-or:" either *Christ* or *the Torah* as the embodiment of the righteousness of God and the way to salvation.[16] To phrase it otherwise, Where is salvation to be found: in allegiance to Christ or to the law? For Paul the answer was obvious: Christ takes the place of the Torah, and henceforth any faith not directed to him is illegitimate by definition. His thought thus penetrates beyond the "boundary markers" of the covenant to the underlying mindset which came to focus in these boundary marking mechanisms, i.e., the conviction that the law of the Sinai covenant is eternal, unchangeable, and Yahweh's sole provision for the welfare of his people. At the end of the day, from the apostle's perspective, *one must decide between Christ and the Torah*.

Fourth, at the risk of some repetition, notwithstanding my considerable debt to Sanders, my *Obedience* disagrees with him in one important regard and sides with Dunn in his own continuing debate with Sanders. Assuming "covenantal

---

[15] Cf. Bruegemann, *Genesis*, 141–42. Even the ὀφείλημα according to which the wage is reckoned does not pose an insurmountable barrier to a "covenantal nomism" (re)construction of Second Temple Judaism, just because "debt" does not *have* to mean anything more than God's commitment to recompense the endeavors of his people, who zealously "will" and "run" to maintain the covenant (Rom 9:16; 10:2–3). One may wonder, then, What does Paul object to as he pens the words of Rom 4:4–5 (11:6)? For one thing, he takes exception to the proposition that adherence to *the law* ensures justification, because God's grace has now been revealed definitively *in Christ*. Thus, he juxtaposes "grace" not to "legalism" but to grace's preeschatological manifestation in the Sinai covenant: it is being in Christ which counts, not belonging to Israel (see my *Obedience*, 260). Therefore, Israel's "works" are wrongheaded inasmuch as they proceed from the Torah, not from Christ. For another, these covenantal works, were they to be retained, would exclude Gentiles from Christ because of their nationalistically restrictive makeup (cf. Räisänen, *Paul*, 177; Mundle, *Glaubensbegriff*, 99–101). Consequently, given Paul's convictions on both points, "the one who does not work" (v. 5) is the person who disregards the law as "the Jewish gateway to salvation" (Räisänen, *Paul*, 177–91) and simply trusts in Christ.

[16] Cf. Gordon, "Problem;" Donaldson, "Zealot and Convert," 679–80. Donaldson is quite right that in coming to Christ Paul underwent a "paradigm shift," i.e., "a transfer from one set of world-structuring convictions to another" (ibid., 682).

nomism" as his avenue of approach to the Jewish materials, Dunn has repeatedly affirmed, in distinction to Sanders and others, that the picture of Judaism emerging from Paul is not a distortion or misrepresentation; rather, what is required is a readjustment of our conception of the precise bone of contention in the law-controversy. That is to say, what Paul opposed was the too narrowly nationalistic conception of God's purposes in history. Dunn, therefore, in line with various precursors, has defined "works of the law" in Paul not as the compilation of good deeds for the purpose of earning God's favor ("legalism") but as Yahweh's requirements for covenant fellowship with himself.[17] And it was just in the sweep of Jewish history from Antiochus IV onward that these "works of the law" came to be encapsulated in the several "identity markers" of the nation's distinctiveness, so that fidelity to the God of Israel, by Paul's day, had become unthinkable apart from these "badges" of Yahweh's ownership of his favored ones. This implies, among other things, that Israel's "boasting" (Rom 2:17, 23; Gal 6:13; cf. Gal 6:14; Phil 3:3) pertains not to its efforts at self-salvation but to its privileges and possessions as the chosen people.[18]

In sum, the present undertaking proceeds along of the lines of "the Sanders-Dunn trajectory,"[19] i.e., an assessment of Judaism in keeping with Sanders' and an evaluation of the law in Paul consistent with Dunn's findings.[20] Because such a foundation is already in place, the following book must presuppose what has gone before. Practical speaking, this means that at many points I have opted to defer to the first book, with the scholarly literature therein documented, rather than further clutter an already very busy looking collection of notes. For the same reason, the study touches base with only a cross section of the most

---

[17] On the term "legalism," see my *Obedience*, 127–28. As stated there, "nomism" is much to be preferred to "legalism" as a denomination of predestruction Judaism. Writing some years before Sanders, R. N. Longenecker chose to apply to this Judaism the phrase "reacting nomism," i.e., "the molding of one's life in all its varying relations according to the Law in response to the love and grace of God" (*Paul*, 78). "Reacting nomism," for all intents and purposes, is the same as Sanders' "covenantal nomism" (*Paul*, 236, passim). On the related issue of merit, see my *Obedience*, 120 (with literature); Beker, *Paul*, 268.

[18] See further Davies, *Faith*, 127–35. In countering Israel's "boasting," Davies maintains, the apostle intends to exclude glorying without obedience. Once we have defined "obedience," it will be seen that this conclusion is consonant with our own argument.

[19] Silva, "Law," 341.

[20] I would call especial attention to Dunn's *Jesus, Paul*, chaps. 6–9; *Partings*, chaps. 2–7; and throughout *Romans*. Noteworthy as well is B. W. Longenecker's *Eschatology*, a comparison of 4 Ezra and Romans 1–11, which takes advantage of the most recent research relating to Paul and Israel. The "new view" of Paul has been applied to Galatians in the excellent essays of Gordon ("Problem" and "ΠΑΙΔΑΓΩΓΟΣ"). An adequate response cannot here be provided to dissenting reviews of Sanders on Judaism and Dunn on Paul, such as Hübner, "Proprium;" id., *Law*; id., "Werke," Gundry, "Grace;" Silva, "Reconstruction;" id., "Law;" Westerholm, *Law*; Cranfield, "Works;" and the articles of Schreiner. For further literature, see Dunn, *Jesus, Paul*, 234, n. 41. I must qualify, however, that my endorsement of Dunn's overall position does not imply an acceptance of his peculiar treatment of Gal 2:16; 3:10. This is to be conceded to Silva ("Law," 346) and Cranfield ("Works," 92).

relevant (in my view) of the vast and rapidly expanding body of literature devoted to the explication of Paul's letters, including, not least, the law and the ideas of faith, righteousness/justification, obedience, and perseverance in his theology. As though that were not enough, one's frustrations are further compounded by the attempt to set the Pauline epistles against their OT backdrop and within the context of predestruction Judaism. So, I have opted to interact in more depth with a restricted body of secondary sources rather than make only passing reference to a larger company of authors.

As a final word of clarification, this study attempts, in some measure at least, to press beyond scientific exegesis into the realm of pastoral theology. Assuming that scholarship can and ought to have practical consequences, I have endeavored to speak to the issues of faith, obedience, and perseverance as they come to concrete expression in the "in Christ" experience.[21]

To relate some technical matters: (1) documentation of scholarly literature appears only in shortened form in the footnotes, with full information provided in the bibliography; (2) abbreviations of primary sources conform to *JBL* 107/3 (1988), 583−87; (3) for the sake of a wider readership, all quotations from non-English secondary literature have been translated by me; (4) as a rule, English Bible translations are from the RSV.

Before commencing, it is only appropriate to convey once more my indebtedness to professors Martin Hengel and Otfried Hofius and to Mr. Georg Siebeck for their kind acceptance of another work of mine into this series. Not least, an additional word of thanks must go to the staff of J. C. B. Mohr (Paul Siebeck) for their skill and efficiency in turning the manuscript into a book. I think particularly of Mr. Rudolf Pflug, whose labor has been indispensable in the realization of two publications now.

---

[21] A fine precedent has been set by Dunn in "Rom. 7,14−25;" *Jesus*, esp. 301−42; and the "Explanation" sections of *Romans*.

Chapter One
Faith's Obedience: The Meaning of ὑπακοὴ πίστεως

Unique to the whole of pre-Christian Greek literature, and to Paul himself, the phrase ὑπακοὴ πίστεως, occurring in Rom 1:5; 16:26,[1] give voices to the very design of the apostle's missionary labors, i.e., he has been called to summon the nations to a believing obedience directed toward Jesus the crucified and risen Son of God, the king of Israel. Within Romans itself, the phrase is invested with a twofold significance. For one, against the backdrop of faith's obedience in Jewish literature, these words assume a decidedly polemical thrust: the covenant fidelity of God's ancient people (Israel) is now a possibility apart from assuming the identity of that people.[2] Dunn, then, is right that the phrase neatly summarizes Paul's apologetic in the Roman letter.[3]

For another, Rom 1:5 can be looked upon as a programmatic statement of the main purpose of Romans.[4] For this reason, Dunn again is correct in writing: "To clarify what faith is and its importance to his gospel is one of Paul's chief objectives in this letter."[5] In order to appreciate the point, it will be necessary briefly to relate the importance of faith to another purpose of the letter, viz., "to redraw the boundaries which marked out the people of God."[6] Whereas before to be a member of the covenant community was to live within the boundary set by the law, the eschatological people have assumed a new corpo-

---

[1] 16:26 is part of a well-known textual crux. See further Garlington, *Obedience*, 1, n. 1. In my view, the arguments for the doxology's authenticity are sufficiently strong that some consideration must given to it, although the force of the ensuing argument does not by any means depend on the originality of 16:26.

[2] I have argued this at length in *Obedience*.

[3] Dunn, *Romans* 1.18.

[4] Wright, "Messiah," 11. Black likewise remarks that "to win obedience from the Gentiles" is "the main purpose of the Epistle to the Romans" (*Romans*, 175).

[5] Dunn, *Romans* 1.17.

[6] Dunn, "Romans 13:1–7," 61. As he remarks elsewhere (*Romans* 2.580–81), when Paul in Rom 9:30b redefines righteousness (i.e., from righteousness as articulated by the Torah to that of faith in Christ), he is fully aware that in the process he is redefining the covenant. Davies similarly contends: "Paul demands that the people of God, belonging to Abraham, be defined in a new way. The meaning of 'descent' from Abraham has to be radically reconsidered: it no longer has a 'physical' connotation" (*Studies*, 128). Likewise Black: "The whole inspiration of Jewish life was the Law and obedience to it; the inspiration of Christian living is Christ, apprehended by faith, and obedience to the Risen Lord" (*Romans*, 38).

rate identity.⁷ And since there is now "no distinction" between Jew and Gentile (1:16−17; 2:11; 10:12, etc.), Paul endeavors in Romans, particularly in chaps. 6−8 and 12−16, to expound the ethical and social responsibilities of this new corporate entity. Pursuant to this end, the letter's opening paragraph (1:1−7) draws upon concepts evocative of Israel's relationship to Yahweh and applies them to *all* the Romans, the κλητοί of Jesus Christ.⁸ The pivotal point of the introduction is v. 5 − the obedience of faith among all the nations for Christ's name's sake − "A neat and fitting summary of his complete apologetic in Romans."⁹

Actually, these facets of the phrase are two sides of the same coin: Paul's clarification of the significance of faith entails both his denial of Jewish superiority and his reshaping of the covenant community. The recognition of this is vital to our concern, because, as we shall argue later, the relation of faith and works in Paul is illuminated to no small degree by the way in which "the obedience of faith" serves in Paul's hands as a tool for obliterating distinctions between Jew and Gentile.

In light of its significance for Romans, then, "the obedience of faith" is a phrase of no little importance for understanding the Pauline mission as a whole, both in its universal outreach and its ethical dimensions. Nevertheless, because its precise meaning remains a debating ground for commentators on Romans, it will be necessary to explore the meaning of Paul's singular phrase within the setting of his famous missionary epistle.

I. The Function of Romans 1:5 and 16:26 within Their Immediate Contexts

Rom 1:5 occurs in the middle of Paul's opening greeting to the Christians in Rome. He begins by identifying himself as a servant of Christ Jesus and an apostle called and separated to the gospel of God (1:1). This succinct description of his identity and commission leads him to write somewhat more fully of this gospel, which was promised in the OT and has as its subject Jesus Christ, the Son of David and risen Son of God (1:2−4). Thereafter he speaks of his apostolic commission and more particularly of its goal, i.e., to bring about the obedience of faith among all the nations for the sake of the name of Christ (1:5). Thus, the totality of Paul's missionary endeavors is epitomized by the words εἰς ὑπακοὴν πίστεως ἐν πᾶσιν τοῖς ἔθνεσιν ὑπὲρ τοῦ ὀνόματος αὐτοῦ. Comment-

---

⁷ Dunn, "Romans 13:1−7," 61. Kaylor's *Community* approaches the letter from this vantage point.

⁸ In detail, see Garlington, *Obedience*, 233−53.

⁹ Dunn, *Romans* 1.18. Commenting on Rom 15:18, Dunn remarks: "The recall of a key motif from 1:5 [i.e., "the obedience of the Gentiles"] is no doubt deliberate since it ties together precisely a key theme of Jewish covenant self-awareness (obedience) and Paul's outreach to the Gentiles: it is precisely Paul's claim that the obligations of the covenant were being fulfilled in the faith response of the Gentiles" (ibid., 2.868).

ing on "all the nations," Michel rightly observes that we have to do with a comprehensive missionary expresssion which corresponds to faith's obedience.[10] Paul then relates that the Roman Christians are themselves included among the ἔθνη who fall within the scope of his apostolic activities (1:6). Finally, he greets them as God's beloved and called saints, terms evocative of Israel's peculiar relation to Yahweh in the covenant (1:7).

Rom 1:5 thus stands at the pivotal point of the letter's introductory paragraph, i.e., between Paul's statement of his calling and his depiction of the gospel (vv. 1–4), on the one side, and his address of the Roman Christians (vv. 6–7), on the other. Effectively, the verse's expression of the design of Paul's apostleship is also a delineation of the eschatological purposes of God: it is through Paul's preaching that Jesus, the king of Israel, takes the nations in captive obedience to himself (cf. Gen 49:10; Num 24:17–24; Ps 2:8–9). Paul, therefore, portrays his mission as the instrumentality by which the risen Christ in the fullness of time asserts his rule over the new people of God.[11]

Rom 16:26 forms part of the letter's concluding doxology, which ascribes glory to the only wise God for his confirmation of the Romans in the gospel preached by Paul. This gospel is further explicated by the statement beginning with the second κατά of v. 25 and extending through v. 26. Paul's depiction of his gospel takes the form of a contrast between the "silence" of the "mystery" in eternity past and its "manifestation" through the "prophetic Scriptures" at the present time.

As in 1:5, the reiterated ὑπακοὴ πίστεως here in 16:26 assumes a decidedly eschatological coloring.[12] For one thing, it stands in direct relation to the "prophetic Scriptures."[13] Such a connection between faith's obedience and the Scriptures of Israel is to be viewed in connection with Romans 9–11 and 15:9–12, where Paul argues from the OT that it was the divine purpose all along to bring the Gentiles into covenant standing with Israel. In so doing, he explains how the Scriptures have come to fulfillment in the preaching of Christ to all peoples without distinction. Thus, the contact of ὑπακοὴ πίστεως with the "prophetic Scriptures" is significant, because Paul sees in the latter an intention of God to manifest faith's obedience as an eschatological reality.

Second, Paul announces that the "mystery," i.e., the eternal salvific plan,

---

[10] Michel, *Römer*, 76.

[11] "The apostle's preaching was not merely eschatological in its subject matter; it was itself a part of the eschatological drama. The apostle was called, not just to build a group of believers, but to take part in the work of God which is to culminate in a wholly new order of existence" (Beardslee, *Achievement*, 85). See further Beker, *Paul*, 144–45; Garlington, *Obedience*, 234.

[12] On the eschatological character of faith in Paul, see Binder, *Glaube*, e.g., 43, 89; Bultmann, *Theology* 1.329–30; Pathrapankal, *Metanoia*, 167–99.

[13] Cf. 1:5, where the phrase is located within close proximity of 1:2, which speaks of the foretelling of the gospel "through his prophets in the holy scriptures."

has "now"[14] been realized in the preaching of the gospel.[15] Without going into any real detail, μυστήριον in Paul is a salvation-historical concept. By the nature of the case, explains Ridderbos, there is an informational aspect to it, which is preserved by Paul.[16] But there is in addition "a plainly historical connotation: it is that which has not yet appeared, that which still exists in the counsel of God and has not been realized in history as fulfillment of that counsel."[17] And it is just the historical realization of the μυστήριον that Paul envisages in his preaching of Christ.[18] Analogous to 1:5, faith's obedience on the part of the Gentiles is the goal to which the revelation of the mystery looked. Consequently, faith and the obedience of faith assume a distinctively eschatological character. Seen in this light, "the obedience of faith" is to be regarded as a phrase of some significance for the understanding of Paul. It is, in other words, *his own articulation of the design and purpose of his missionary labors*: God is *now* bringing his purposes to pass in salvation history through Paul's gospel, i.e., the preaching of Jesus Christ (v. 25). Paul's commission, therefore, is to be viewed as nothing less than the eschatological actualization of the eternal plan to create faith's obedience among the nations.

This, then, is how Rom 1:5 and 16:26 function within their respective contexts. However, the primary question is yet to be answered: What does ὑπακοὴ πίστεως mean?

II. The Grammatical Options

As noted above, the precise import of the phrase continues to be a matter of dispute among the commentators. Its interpretation is mainly bound up with one's understanding of the genitive πίστεως, although to a certain degree the meaning of "faith" in these texts is involved as well. Simply put, what is the relation of "faith" to "obedience?"

---

[14] The "eschatological νῦν" of v. 26 is an adverb recurring in crucial Pauline passages which announce the arrival of the eschaton, e.g., Rom 3:21; 5:9; 7:6, 17; Eph 2:12–13; Col 1:26–27.

[15] See Cranfield's remarks, *Romans* 2.812.

[16] See further the studies of Brown, *"Mystery;"* Coppens, *"'Mystery';"* Van Elderen, "Parables," 184–86; Williams, "Righteousness," 256.

[17] Ridderbos, *Paul*, 46; cf. id., *Israël*, 57–58. Brown rightly concludes that μυστήριον in Paul is uniformly the (historical/eschatological) realization of God's purpose to unite Jew and Gentile in the body of Christ (*"Mystery,"* 68). See further Kim, *Origin*, 74–99.

[18] As Dunn notes, the schema of a mystery previously hidden and now unveiled by means of the correct hermeneutical key was a familiar one. He cites 1QH 2:13–19; 1QpHab; 4QpPs 37; 1 Pet 1:10–12; 2 Pet 1:19–20 (*Romans* 2.915).

A. Summary of the Grammatical Options[19]

1. Three interpretations assume the objective genitive:

(a) "obedience to the faith" (i.e., faith in the sense of *fides quae creditur*)
(b) "obedience to faith" (i.e., to the authority of faith)
(c) "obedience to God's faithfulness attested in the gospel"

2. Two interpretations are in line with the subjective genitive:

(a) "the obedience which faith works"
(b) "the obedience required by faith"

3. One interpretation calls for the adjectival genitive: "believing obedience."

4. One interpretation invokes the genitive of apposition: "the obedience which consists in faith."

It should be noted that the terminology varies among individual writers. Black, for example, opts for the adjectival genitive; but he defines this as the obedience which springs from faith, thus combining the ideas of adjectival and subjective genitive (or genitive of source).[20] In fact, it will be seen that some of the grammatical options differ in name only.

B. Evaluation of the Grammatical Options

We begin with those based on the objective genitive. Viewed solely in grammatical terms, these interpretations are the least attractive. H. Schlier argues with some plausibility that if the idea conveyed by the objective genitive were correct, Paul would have written something like ἵνα ὑπακούσωσιν τῇ πίστει, in a manner corresponding to ὑπακούειν τῷ εὐαγγελίῳ in 10:16; 2 Thess 1:8; cf. 3:14.[21] Parke-Taylor reasons as well that if "the faith" (i.e., a body of formulated doctrine) had been intended, the definite article would have been used.[22] An additional problem is that 1:5 would be the only instance in Romans where πίστις is used in the sense of *fides quae creditur*.[23]

It is true that this reading of the text is not entirely beyond redemption. As is clear from 2 Thess 1:8; 3:14, there is in Paul the notion that one is to obey the gospel or the word of God. According to Rom 6:17, what characterizes those who walk in newness of life is their obedience from the heart to the τύπος διδαχῆς, the apostolic tradition, to which they have been committed. In fact, Paul's particular problem with Israel is that it has refused to submit to God's righteousness (Rom 10:3), i.e., it has not obeyed the gospel (Rom 10:16). Similarly, the Galatians, under the influence of the Judaizers, were being hindered from obeying the truth (Gal 5:17). As a grammatical category, howev-

---

[19] Drawn from Cranfield, *Romans* 1.66.
[20] Black, *Romans*, 38.
[21] Schlier, *Römerbrief*, 29. Cf. Käsemann, *Romans*, 14.
[22] Parke-Taylor, "Note," 305.
[23] Gal 3:23 demonstrates that Paul could use "faith" in this way, but with the article.

er, "objective genitive" has difficulty standing up to the criticisms brought against it, since ὑπακοὴ πίστεως would be a rather unexpected way of saying "obedience to the (authority of) faith" (or "God's faithfulness attested in the gospel").

The two possibilities categorized by Cranfield as subjective genitive differ little, if any, in effect. The real intention of this line of thinking is that obedience finds its fountainhead in faith. As Black remarks: "The words define the purpose and sphere of Paul's special apostleship: it was to bring the Gentile world to an obedience which springs from faith, in contradistinction to an obedience based on the external observance of the law."[24] Strictly speaking, it might be more appropriate to regard πίστεως thus interpreted as genitive of source rather than subjective genitive, since faith is viewed as the matrix of obedience. Yet "subjective genitive" is not totally without merit, as stress is placed on faith as the active agent in obedience. At any rate, Cranfield's two variations on the subjective genitive can be merged into one, thus simplifying somewhat the options between which one must decide.

The interpretation which takes πίστεως to be genitive of apposition perhaps commands the most respect among commentators.[25] Michel, while taking the genitive as objective, expresses what is at stake in the genitive of apposition as applied to our phrase: "Faith for Paul is in the first instance obedience to the word, and *obedience for him is the fundamental and decisive act of faith.*"[26]

The one category which remains is "adjectival genitive," i.e., ὑπακοὴ πίστεως is "believing obedience," the significance of which is to be determined by Paul's broader statements on the relation of ὑπακοή and πίστις.

The possibilities before us, then, are subjective genitive/genitive of source (used interchangeably), genitive of apposition, and adjectival genitive. These will now be considered in more detail. It should be clarified, however, that our interest lies not in grammatical labels for their own sake but principally in the complex of ideas suggested by these categories.

III. "The Obedience of Faith" as the Believer's Total Response to the Gospel

The (exclusive) genitive of apposition interpretation is most commonly found among the commentators. Taking Cranfield as a representative, the usual argument is that of the analogy of usage in the Roman letter: "The equivalence for Paul of faith in God and obedience to him may be illustrated again and again from this epistle. Paul's preaching is aimed at obtaining from his hearers true obedience to God, the essence of which is a responding to His

---

[24] Black, *Romans*, 38. Cf. the commentaries of Bruce, Lenski, and Hendriksen.
[25] Including Barrett, Cranfield, Calvin, Murray, Käsemann, Ridderbos, Schlier, Sanday/Headlam, and Wilckens.
[26] Michel, *Römer*, 76 (italics mine).

message of good news and faith."²⁷ Murray likewise maintains: "Faith is regarded as an act of obedience, of commitment to the gospel of Christ."²⁸ Such statements illustrate that there is accord among a certain class of exegetes that ὑπακοὴ πίστεως signifies an obedience which is directly identifiable with faith. Sometimes this is set over against the obedience which consists in "works of the law."²⁹

The strength of this position resides in the parallel texts in which faith and obedience are evidently tantamount to each other. The point should be sufficiently clear from the following table:³⁰

1:8:	"your *faith* is proclaimed in all the world"
16:19:	"your *obedience* is known to all"
10:16a:	"but all have not *obeyed* the gospel"
10:16b:	"for Isaiah says, 'Who has *believed* our report'"
11:23:	"if they do not remain in *unbelief*"
11:30:	"by their *disobedience*"
11:31:	"so they now have been *disobedient*"
1:5:	"the *obedience of faith* among all the nations"
15:18:	"to win *obedience* from the nations"

Schlier supplements the list by pointing to 10:21 (λαὸν ἀπειθοῦντα καὶ ἀντιλέγοντα) and 15:31 (τῶν ἀπειθούντων ἐν τῇ Ἰουδαίᾳ), according to which unbelieving Israel is described in terms of disobedience (cf. 2 Thess 1:8). He concludes that obedience is that of faith, so that unbelief can be designated as disobedience.³¹

We may reply that as far as these texts are concerned – with one qualification to be established below – the point is well-taken. V.P. Furnish is correct that obeying the gospel can parallel believing the preached word (Rom 10:16; cf. John 3:36; Heb 3:18–19).³² Furthermore, the obedience character of faith is implied in Rom 10:3, where Paul complains that Israel has not *submitted* to God's righteousness in the gospel, choosing, rather, to maintain (στῆσαι) its own. It would be idle, then, to deny that Paul regarded Israel's unbelief as disobedience, and vice versa.

At this juncture, however, the question arises: Is the significance of ὑπακοὴ πίστεως exhausted by treating it as a genitive of apposition? In answering, it must be appreciated that other factors enter into the picture. Cranfield, for example, having championed the genitive of apposition, seems compelled to add: "It is also true to say that to make the decision of faith is an act of obedience toward God and also that true faith by its very nature includes in

---

[27] Cranfield, *Romans* 1.66.
[28] Murray, *Romans* 1.13–14.
[29] Cf. Michel, *Römer*, 76; Black, *Romans*, 38; Davies, *Paul*, 148.
[30] Modified from Cranfield, *Romans* 1.66, n. 3.
[31] Schlier, *Römer*, 29.
[32] Furnish, *Theology*, 185.

itself the sincere desire and will to obey God in all things."³³ Murray, similarly, has been quoted as saying that faith is an act of obedience, i.e., commitment to the gospel; but, he continues: "Hence the implications of this expression "obedience of faith" are far-reaching. For the faith which the apostleship was intended to promote was not an evanescent act of emotion but the commitment of *whole hearted devotion* to Christ and to the truth of his gospel. It is to such faith that all nations are called."³⁴ In effect, therefore, the obedience which consists in faith cannot be abstracted from the obedience demanded by the gospel.

Thus, there would appear to be some basis for thinking that there is more to the genitive πίστεως than the idea of apposition. The question is whether other data can be brought to bear which would serve to clarify matters. In my estimation, such data are at hand. While conceding that πίστεως is, at least in part, appositional, we come now to argue that there is a place for the genitive of source in our interpretation of Paul's language. In so doing, we shall reason briefly from the broader perspective of faith and obedience in Judaism and Paul and then at some length from contextual considerations in Romans itself.

In the OT and Second Temple Judaism, faith and obedience are virtually synonymous.³⁵ As represented principally by אמונה, "faith" in the Hebrew Bible is two-sided: trust *and* a commitment (to the covenant) resultant from trust. Without going into any real detail, we note, with Edmund Perry:

> the Old Testament does not set trust and obedience in contrast to each other as separate ways of satisfying the demands of God. *'emuna* comprehends the totality of what we commonly mean in the familiar expression "faith and works." Obedience without trust (i.e. obedience not genetically generated from trust) is not the obedience God requires. Only the obedience of trust is reckoned to man as righteousness and everything else is exposed for the sham that it is, "lying wind words," "false lips" and "deceitful ways." Conversely, trust inevitably expresses itself in action. "Trust in the Lord and do good" are two aspects of the same act of will by which man is declared righteous.³⁶

Along similar lines, Bultmann can say that faithfulness is obedience; hence, the law and the commandments are among the objects of faith.³⁷ D. Hill likewise remarks that "Judaism has really no place for a rigid distinction between faith and works: faith can only fully exist when it is embodied in works."³⁸ J. Pathrapankal adds that "The obligation of the people to have faith in Yahweh was precisely an undertaking to remain faithful to the co-

---

[33] Cranfield, *Romans* 1.66–67.
[34] Murray, *Romans* 1.14 (italics mine). Cf. Schlatter, *Gerechtigkeit*, 22.
[35] The following is condensed from my *Obedience*, 9–13.
[36] Perry, "*'emuna*," 255–56. For further literature, see Garlington, *Obedience*, 10, n. 41.
[37] Bultmann, *TDNT* 6.199–200.
[38] Hill, *Words*, 145, n. 1.

venant,"³⁹ while Dobbeler underscores that faith is both the reflex and sign of Israel's election, so that faith is nothing less than the mode of righteousness *par excellence*.⁴⁰ G. Fohrer, consequently, is able to remark that a systematic exposition of faith in Judaism is unnecessary, impossible and even foreign to its idea of faith, because "Faith is action – this holds true for biblical faith as well as for postbiblical Judaism."⁴¹

In a real sense, then, to speak of faith *is* to speak of obedience. "Faith and obedience are one action. Faith has to be proven by obedience."⁴² Further confirmation is provided by the OT's main terminology for obedience, viz., hearing (normally שָׁמַע, as rendered by ἀκούω, ὑπακούω, and εἰσακούω).⁴³ F. W. Young is worth quoting at length.

> To really hear God's word inevitably involves one in an obedient response in action prompted by faithfulness to and faith in the God who is revealing himself in and through particular historical events. Not to respond in obedient action is tantamount to unbelief – and so the prophet chastises his people for their blind eyes and deaf ears (Isa 6:9–10), which betray their faithlessness. This inevitable consequence of failing to hear is rebellion or disobedience. But rebellion is not just the wilful disobedience of one who has heard. Rebellion is the sign that one has not really heard, since *to hear implies a faith-obedience response*.⁴⁴

Of course, it is possible to argue that Paul's ideology of faith represents a radical break with his Jewish heritage. Nevertheless, one of the most striking phenomena of the extant letters is that he nowhere debates the meaning of faith with his opponents.⁴⁵ Faith as such was never a point of controversy; Paul simply assumes the OT conception as the common ground between him and those with whom he disagrees.⁴⁶ Furnish, therefore, is justified in speaking of *faith as obedience* in Paul.⁴⁷ What is radical about Paul, however, is *faith's object*

---

³⁹ Pathrapankal, *Metanoia*, 77.
⁴⁰ Dobbeler, *Glaube*, 160.
⁴¹ Fohrer, *Glauben*, 159.
⁴² Bartsch, "Faith," 51.
⁴³ A linguistic study of "obedience," with the various Hebrew and Greek synonyms, has been provided by Friedrich ("ὑπακοὴ πίστεως," although Friedrich's conclusion that ὑπακοὴ πίστεως means "the preaching of the gospel" and not "the obedience of faith" does not follow from his data) and Deichgräber ("Gehorsam").
⁴⁴ Young, *IDB* 3.580. According to Käsemann, "faith is right hearing" ("Righteousness," 177). On obedience and disobedience in the OT (and NT), see, among others, Büchler, *Sin*, 1–118; Kittel, *TDNT* 1.217–18; Mundle, *NIDNTT* 2.172–75; Garlington, *Obedience*, 11–13.
⁴⁵ The same is true of "righteousness." I would agree with Byrne ("Righteousness," 571), over against Sanders (*Paul*, 502–8), that righteousness in Paul retains its Jewish character as the gateway into eternal life. It is not a matter, Byrne says, of choosing between righteousness and participationist categories, as Sanders holds. Rather, Paul's distinctiveness lies in the way in which the required righteousness is produced; in other words, in his view of how that righteousness is brought about in the eschatological era, due to Paul's divergent view of the present state of relations between God and humanity (Israel).
⁴⁶ Cf. Wilckens, *Römer* 1.89.
⁴⁷ Furnish, *Theology*, 182–88.

III. "The Obedience of Faith" as Total Response to the Gospel 19

– Christ.⁴⁸ Apart from the scandal of a crucified Messiah, the deciding factor, to coin a phrase, was Paul's "christological eschatology."⁴⁹

In like terms, in every other occurrence of "obedience" language in Paul, the reference is to Christian behavior, also in keeping with the precedent set by Paul's Jewish heritage.⁵⁰ In particular, it must be appreciated that the obedience character of faith in Paul entails transfer from one realm into another. As Furnish points out, faith's reference is in the first instance to the God who raised Christ from the dead and is coordinate with the confession that Jesus is Lord. Furthermore, "It is precisely the obedience character of faith which makes it the means of the believer's participation in Christ's death and resurrection and which discloses how this is at the same time a 'walking in newness of life.'" Consequently: "The acknowledgment of Jesus as 'Lord' is not possible apart from the acknowledgment that one resides in the sphere of his sovereign power and is bound over to his service. Faith, therefore, is the acknowledgment that one 'belongs' to Christ, and as such it is an act of commitment to him."⁵¹ In short, any idea of faith as obedience and obedience as faith must reckon with the broader eschatological/ethical dimensions of Paul's thought, in particular transfer of lordship, which lies at the heart of the Pauline "obedience of faith."⁵²

Moving to contextual factors in Romans, the sequence of thought in chaps. 1–8 has something to say. Although interpreters differ as to the chapter and verse divisions of this portion of the letter, it is, nonetheless, true that Paul's discussion of justification by faith is followed by his demand that the justified live the life of the new creation. Therefore, the eschatological revelation of the righteousness of God (1:17; 3:21) can hardly be divorced from the formation of a righteous community modeled on the obedience of Jesus Christ, the last Adam (5:12–19). One may say that the latter-day realization of the δικαιοσύνη θεοῦ has as its intention a covenant-keeping community in the truest sense. In the language of Isa 61:10, the eschatological Israel is to be clothed in a garment of righteousness. Significantly, it is within the cadre of the new creation theology of Romans 5–8 that Paul can depict Christians as those who have become obedient from the heart to the τύπος διδαχῆς to which they have been committed (6:17).⁵³ Paul is, therefore, very much concerned to maintain

---

⁴⁸ This most naturally accounts for Paul's singular phrase πίστις Ἰησοῦ Χριστοῦ, which Hultgren appropriately paraphrases as "Christic faith" (*"Pistis,"* 257. On pp. 259–60, Hultgren shows that the occurrence of the formulation in Rom 3:22, 26 is situated in contexts employing the "eschatological νῦν" of the revelation of the righteousness of God).

⁴⁹ Cf. Ridderbos, *Paul*, 49; Moule, "Jesus," 50.

⁵⁰ Rom 2:8; 5:19; 6:12, 16, 17; 1 Cor 14:34; 2 Cor 2:9; 7:15; 10:5, 6; Eph 6:1, 5; Col 3:18, 20, 22; Phil 2:12; Phlm 21 (Titus 2:5, 9; 3:1).

⁵¹ Furnish, *Theology*, 185.

⁵² Cf. Minear, *Obedience*, 65; Tannehill, *Dying*, 9. Paul's "transfer terminology" has been examined in more detail by Sanders, *Paul*, 463–72.

⁵³ L. Goppelt (*TDNT* 8.250) remarks that τύπος διδαχῆς is "the impress which makes an impression, so that in context the teaching can be described as the mould and norm which shapes the whole personal conduct of the one who is delivered up to it and has become obedient thereto."

the organic relationship between a faith which justifies and a faith which works, as is James (Jas 2:18–26).

Within the immediate context of 1:5 further confirmation is to be had. There is, for one thing, the connection between ὑπακοὴ πίστεως and Paul's greeting of the Roman Christians in 1:6, in which he includes *them* within the scope of the apostolic commission to promote faith's obedience ἐν τοῖς ἔθνεσιν. Were obedience confined solely to the initial act of faith, Paul could not have written as he does, simply because the Roman church was founded by another (15:20). Yet he includes even them within the purview of his labors: it is *their* obedience of faith which he is eager to secure, along with that of the other ἔθνη.

Also, in 1:10–15 Paul relates his concern for the Romans. In particular, he prays that he may be allowed to visit them in order to impart some spiritual gift, specifically the mutual encouragement of his and their *faith*. Thereafter he states that his intentions in coming to Rome were with a view to reaping some harvest among the *believers* there. It is in this connection that he voices his obligation and eagerness to preach the gospel in Rome, an especially significant consideration, as it alerts us to the fact that Paul's preaching had a more comprehensive design than the conversion of non-Christians to the faith. Paul, in other words, proposes to preach the gospel in Rome *for the express goal of contributing to the advancement of those who are already committed to Christ.*[54] Thus, his "harvest" among the Romans and the other ἔθνη (1:13) bears a striking resemblance to the "obedience of faith," which he seeks to engender not only among the nations but also on the part of the Romans (1:5–6). In short, this conjunction of 1:5–6 with 1:10–15 informs us that there is more at stake in faith's obedience than the initial act of credence/trust which responds to (obeys) the gospel as preached by Paul.

In addition to these arguments in favor of a more inclusive reading of ὑπακοὴ πίστεως, the parallels between faith and obedience cited by various commentators could stand some re-examination. No doubt, Rom 10:16; 11:23, 30 (10:21; 15:31) are to be understood in terms of an equivalence between disobedience and unbelief (cf. again John 3:36; Heb 3:18–19). In this regard, Cranfield is justified in stating: "The obedience which God requires is faith. To obey the gospel is to believe it and to believe in Him who is its content; and to believe the gospel and believe in Christ involves obeying it, obeying him."[55] However, as we shall see below, Israel's disobedience is not to be oversimplified. Moreover, the passages which speak positively of faith and obedience possess a comprehensive dimension, which includes not only one's acceptance of Jesus as the Christ but also one's compliance with the (covenant) demands of

---

[54] The same conclusion is drawn by Davies (*Faith*, 26–28). The fact that Paul's gift is conveyed by gospel preaching implies that when, in 1:16–17, he envisages the δικαιοσύνη θεοῦ as being revealed in the gospel, the righteousness in question transcends the forensic category of a "righteous status" and is inclusive of the totality of God's requirements for righteous living in the "eschatological now" (Rom 3:21, etc.).

[55] Cranfield, *Romans* 2.536.

III. "The Obedience of Faith" as Total Response to the Gospel

this Christ. It is not to be denied that the obedience which consists in faith is primary (both logically and chronologically): cause and effect must be kept in proper sequence. Nevertheless, the parallels of phraseology exhibited by 1:5/15:18 and 1:8/16:19 can be read in another light, so as to suggest that more is involved than the bare equation of obedience and faith.

We begin with 1:8 as compared with 16:19, because of the conspicuous similarity of language between the two. In the former, Paul gives thanks for the faith of the Romans, which is proclaimed in all the world, and, in the latter, he rejoices that their obedience is a matter of public record. The principal question is whether obedience in 16:19 is entirely tantamount to faith in 1:8 or can be distinguished from it in some sense.

It will be advantageous to look first at 16:19: "For while your obedience is known to all, so that I rejoice over you, I would have you wise as to what is good and guileless as to what is evil." As might be expected, there is no real uniformity among the commentators respecting the precise import of "obedience" in this verse. On the one side are scholars who take 16:19 to be a repetition of 1:8. For instance, Käsemann maintains that "if its [the Roman church's] faith is characterized as ὑπακοή, this means subjection to the received doctrine, which corresponds again to 6:17."[56] Michel likewise believes that Paul here repeats 1:8. He further compares "obedience" in our verse with its occurrence in 1:5 and interprets it along the lines of his understanding of ὑπακοὴ πίστεως, i.e., as objective genitive. For Michel, the gospel has become a "new law" requiring faith as the fulfillment of its stipulations, as over against the Torah, which required "works" for the satisfaction of its demands.[57] These writers represent the consensus view that 16:19's commendation of the Roman's obedience is *ipso facto* a commendation of their reception of the gospel.[58] 16:19, in their view, is little more than a repetition of 1:8.

However, we proceed to what might be called the "minority report" on "obedience" in 16:19. Black takes it to be Christian obedience, i.e., the obedience of faith, as defined at 1:5.[59] Murray calls ὑπακοή a term characteristic of this epistle and adapted to the subject of which Paul now speaks, i.e., the ability to discern good from evil, so that the body of Christ is not destroyed by controversy.[60] Hodge relates that the language of 16:19 can bear two interpretations: "The word *obedience* may express either their *obedience to the gospel*, their faith... or their *obedient disposition*, their readiness to follow the instruc-

---

[56] Käsemann, *Romans*, 418.
[57] Michel, *Römer*, 481.
[58] See as well the comments of Dodd, Godet, Leenhardt, Cranfield, and Schlatter.
[59] Black, *Romans*, 184 (cf. ibid., 38).
[60] Murray, *Romans* 2.236. Williams remarks that the paraenesis of the concluding chapters is directed to specific conflicts and disagreements: "Within the end-time purpose of God Paul has a responsibility even to the Christians in Rome. That responsibility is met not by compiling a collection of general exhortations but by setting them straight at specific critical points" ("Righteousness," 254). Williams relates the paraenetic materials to Paul's intention to secure Rome as a base of support for the mission to Spain (ibid., 249–54).

tions of their religious teachers." He opts for the latter view, citing as parallels 2 Cor 10:6; Phlm 21.[61]

For the sake of clarification, it should be said that these two assessments of our text are not necessarily antithetical to each other, at least not directly so. It is, rather, a matter of a more limited as opposed to a more expansive range of meaning for "obedience." Those who take the term in the more comprehensive sense would certainly include within the scope of ὑπακοή the primary factor of believing reception of the gospel. The question is, then, How broad are Paul's horizons when he speaks of the obedience of the Romans?

In attempting to resolve the issue, due weight should be given to the flow of thought in which 16:19 is situated, i.e., in the middle of Paul's admonition to his readers to avoid those who create dissensions and stumbling blocks, which run counter to the teaching received by them (16:17–20).[62] In view of τὴν διδαχήν in 15:17, it would be tempting to conclude that the obedience of the Romans consisted solely in their acceptance of a body of teaching. Yet even a cursory reading of 16:17–20 informs us that other issues are very much on the apostle's mind. There is, in other words, more implied in the text than the loyalty of the Roman Christians to a set of propositions, as important as that was for Paul. A thoughtful reading of the paragraph indicates that there is an inseparability of obedience and perseverance in Paul's exhortations at this stage of the letter. At least two data point in this direction.

First of all, the "obedience" of the Romans is a backward glance to Paul's earlier portrait of them; it is they who became "obedient from the heart" to the τύπος διδαχῆς to which they had been committed (6:17). Their present obedience, in other words, is the outgrowth of their initial commitment to Paul's gospel. It is such obedience which is set over against αἱ διχοστασίαι and τὰ σκάνδαλα which were at variance with the received teaching (παρὰ τὴν διδαχὴν ἣν ὑμεῖς ἐμάθετε) (v. 17). The terms chosen have a significance of their own. Αἱ διχοστασίαι, as in Gal 5:20, are particularly heinous because of their devastating effects on the peace and harmony of the church (cf. 1 Cor 1:10–17). They represent, in other words, a return to the chaos of the old way of life (cf. Titus 3:3). Τὰ σκάνδαλα, in the present context, are best taken as "enticements to apostasy,"[63] because it is precisely this which Paul wishes to avoid. Those who create such enticements have as their hidden agenda the seduction of people away from Christ and after themselves. Actually, there is a kind of cause and effect relationship between the divi-

---

[61] Hodge, *Romans*, 450–51.

[62] Contra Sanday/Headlam (*Romans*, 430), 16:17 does imply that dissensions and erroneous teachings had begun to be a feature within the Roman church. Assuming, as he does, the inseparable connection between teaching and practice, Paul makes a special point of exhorting his readers in this regard.

[63] BAGD, 753.

sions in the Roman church (14:1−15:13) and the potential of apostasy. Were the church to disintegrate as a result of its internal strife, as instigated by the "deceivers," the only real alternative would be the abandonment of Christianity altogether.

Second, the obedience of the Romans was to be supplemented with wisdom and guilelessness (v. 19b). Paul rejoices over the well-known obedience of his readers, but he desires that they be σοφοὺς εἰς τὸ ἀγαθόν, ἀκεραίους δὲ εἰς τὸ κακόν. Most likely, 19b stands in an adversative relation to 19a, i.e., the Romans are far-famed in their consistency of Christian commitment, yet Paul desires that such obedience be shored up by the discernment of good and the avoidance of evil. Again, the terms chosen are quite deliberate. "Good" and "evil" are evocative of the choice set before Adam in the Garden of Eden, meaning not "right" and "wrong" in the generally ethical sense but the specific good of keeping faith with God the Creator and the particular wrong of abandoning him in favor of the creature. This very conception of good and evil is taken up by Deut 30:15: "I have set before you this day *life and good, death and evil*." A choice is thus placed before Israel, a choice which epitomizes the alternatives of obedience and disobedience. It the same association of terms which provides a paradigm for Paul's warning to the Corinthians not to desire "evil" and thereby become "idolaters" as Israel's wilderness generation (1 Cor 10:6−7). Therefore, unlike Adam, on whose lips "guile" was found for the first time, and Israel later, who forsook the covenant by disobedience, the Romans are to be both σοφούς and ἀκεραίους, so that the attacks on their faith by the deceivers will not ultimately succeed.

It is these allusions to Genesis 3 which are so suggestive. In v. 18, the false teachers in Rome are likened to the serpent in the Garden, who deceived Eve. What the serpent began to do to the human race is continued by the deceivers in the Roman church, who sought to seduce the unsuspecting.[64] (The same identification is made in 2 Cor 11:3, 14−15, where the "super-apostles" are depicted in these terms.) In v. 20a, the reference to Gen 3:15 virtually identifies the Romans with the seed of the woman, who was to be the instrument of Satan's undoing. Accordingly, it is not stretching the point to see in 19b Paul placing his readers in the position of Adam and Eve, who in paradise were tempted to transgress the will of God. Thus, Paul wants them to be able to discern the good of worshipping and serving the Creator, while avoiding involvement in the evil of renouncing him. Hence, the "obedience" of the Romans is colored by the creation ideal of commitment to the Creator rather than to Satan, and, therefore, belongs very much within the sphere of covenant devotion. That such is Paul's intention is confirmed by Rom 5:12−19, according to which the obedient last Adam has created a new humanity characterized by obedience.

Having considered 16:19 in some detail, it will be necessary to look only

---

[64] The deception motif also occurs in Rom 7:11, where likewise the deceitful tactics of the serpent are in view. See Dunn, *Christology*, 103−4.

briefly at 1:8, in which Paul thanks God for the Romans because their *faith* is proclaimed in all the world. It is incontestable that this verse is in some sense akin to 16:19. The question is, though, How are we to understand the particular relationship of the two?

In answering the question, we must first pause to inquire into the denotation of πίστις in 1:8. One group of commentators is insistent that the reference is not to the "act" but the "state" of faith, i.e., "Christianity," thus placing πίστις entirely within the realm of the objective. Michel and Käsemann for example, maintain that πίστις does not mean so much "coming to faith" (*Gläubigwerdens*) as the "condition of faith" (*Glaubensstand*). Käsemann in particular views 16:19 as a mere repetition of 1:8.[65]

On the other side, Schlier concedes that πίστις could mean the state of being a Christian (*Christenstand*) or Christianity (*Christentum*). "But," he says, "such a translation considerably weakens what is meant here, namely, that which Paul in 1:5 has called ὑπακοὴ πίστεως."[66] This, I think, carries more conviction, because, apart from 1:5, πιστεύω and πίστις in 1:16−17 clearly denote the act of trust whereby one encounters the δικαιοσύνη θεοῦ. It is highly unlikely, consequently, that "faith" in 1:8 would bear a meaning other than its obvious one in the verses which bracket it.

Assuming, then, that πίστις in 1:8 is to be understood in its typical Pauline sense of the act of belief/trust in Christ (or the gospel), we return to the original question, viz., How does 1:8 ("your faith") relate to 16:19 ("your obedience")? Over against those who understand the latter to be a virtual reiteration of the former, the contention here is that the relationship is to be understood otherwise, i.e., the "obedience" of the Romans praised by Paul in 16:19 completes their "faith" (for which he gives thanks in 1:8), simply because of the connotations of perseverance attached to ὑπακοή in 16:19 (in context). Indeed, this phenomenon of faith giving rise to obedience is exactly what one would expect when ὑπακοὴ πίστεως is given its pregnant force of an obedience which springs from faith. Consequently, the similarity of language between 1:8 and 16:19 is accounted for not because Paul says the same thing over again but because in his thinking obedience is the inevitable and indispensable accompaniment of the faith which accepts Jesus Christ in the gospel.

In sum, the conclusion to be drawn from 1:8 and 16:19 is that they do not support the interpretation which views ὑπακοὴ πίστεως as only the obedience which consists in faith. On the contrary, this conjunction of faith and obedience in 1:8 and 16:19 respectively argues strongly for giving Paul's phrase a more inclusive reading.

---

[65] Michel, *Römer*, 80, n. 8; Käsemann, *Romans*, 17. Cf. Sanday/Headlam, who see "faith" as a merger of ideas with stress on πίστις as the state or condition of faith – but with an important qualification: "Here it is practically equivalent to 'your Christianity', the distinctive act which makes a man a Christian carrying with it the direct consequences of that act upon the character" (*Romans*, 19).

[66] Schlier, *Römerbrief*, 36.

III. "The Obedience of Faith" as Total Response to the Gospel

It remains now to give some consideration to the similar-sounding statements of 1:5, "the obedience of faith among all the nations," and 15:18, "the obedience of the nations." Since it is the meaning of 1:5 which is in dispute, our attention will be focused on 15:18 in its context in order to determine what light can be shed by the latter on the former.

In turning to the commentators, we are not surprised to find them divided along the same lines as previously indicated. On the one side, Michel can say that εἰς ὑπακοὴν ἐθνῶν in 15:18 means "to obey, i.e., to come to faith." He cites as parallels 1:5; 6:17; 16:26 and concludes that "the entire Roman letter is occupied with this 'obedience' of faith."[67] Käsemann likewise views the "obedience" of this verse as "identical with acceptance of the gospel."[68] Barrett also sees here a reference to the conversion of the Gentiles.[69] Others, while calling attention to the obvious parallel between 15:18 and 1:5, assume a different position as to the actual sense of ὑπακοὴ ἐθνῶν; that is, ἐθνῶν is taken as a subjective genitive, making the obedience in question that rendered by the Gentiles, their obedience which proceeds from faith.[70]

The context of 15:18 argues in favor of the latter group. The first factor is that 15:7 is a summary of the entire paraenetic section commencing at 14:1: "Welcome one another, therefore, as Christ has welcomed you, for the glory of God." 14:1–15:7 in particular is a plea for harmony and unity among the Roman house-churches, the gist of which is voiced by 15:5–6: "May the God of steadfastness and encouragement grant you to live in such harmony with one another, in accord with Jesus Christ, that together you may with one voice glorify the God and Father of our Lord Jesus Christ." Such obedience is possible because the believers in Rome have presented themselves as "living sacrifice" (12:1). As we have seen, Paul places the highest premium on the unity of the church because it is the surest preventive against the "enticements to apostasy" posed by the deceptive teachers who have made inroads into the congregations.

Therefore, the train of thought begun in 14:1 and climaxing at 15:7 provides the backdrop for our interest in 15:18. Paul's paraenetic goal is seen all the more clearly in the light of two data which precede the summary (15:7) of his exhortations to the Romans. The first is the servanthood of Christ (15:3 as it quotes Ps 69:9); the second is the life of harmony in accord with Christ Jesus to be lived by all Christians (15:5). Christ, then, most notably in his role as the Servant, the one on whose lips no "guile" was found (Isa 53:9; cf. 1 Pet 2:22), is the model for the Romans in their everyday relations with one another, particularly as regards their own "guilelessness" in the presence of evil and their

---

[67] Michel, *Römer*, 459.
[68] Käsemann, *Romans*, 393–94.
[69] Barrett, *Romans*, 276. Cf. Schlatter, *Gerechtigkeit*, 387; Leenhardt, *Romans*, 369; Ridderbos, *Romeinen*, 331; Nygren, *Romans*, 453; Cranfield, *Romans* 2.758 (see n. 2 for the variant ἀκοήν in 15:18).
[70] Black, *Romans*, 175; Lenski, *Romans*, 883; Hodge, *Romans*, 440.

endeavors to maintain the bond of peace (16:17, 19). Hence, this portion of chap. 15 is an analogue of 16:17−20, inasmuch as Paul envisages the obedient Servant of Yahweh who insures the peace and stability of his people. As we shall see later, portions of Isaiah 53 undergird Paul's presentation of Christ as the last Adam (Rom 5:12−21), the one who reverses the work of the original Adam – and here in 15:3, 8, the Servant = Adam equation is strengthened by the connection with 16:17−20. In the case of both Adam and the Servant, obedience was the prime requirement, which, in turn, was to promote the obedience of others.

Second, 15:8−13 grows out of 15:7, i.e., the Romans are to welcome one another because of the mutual position occupied by Jew and Gentile in the purposes of God. In a more explicit statement of the servanthood of Christ (v. 8), Paul indicates that Christ acted on behalf of the "circumcised," in order to confirm God's promises to the patriarchs and thereby to bring about the acceptance of the Gentiles as the people of God.[71] Having supported this contention with biblical proof (vv. 9b−12), he prays that the Romans' faith may be attended with joy, peace, and hope (empowered by the Holy Spirit). The effect of vv. 8−13 is to ground the mutual reception of the Romans (v. 7) in salvation history, i.e., the purpose of God as achieved by Christ is that the nations now have come to share in the promises made to Israel's patriarchs. In this respect, Schlatter is justified in his reference to the Gentiles' former disobedience and their present obedience of believing in Christ.[72] Yet, according to v. 13, Paul's concern goes beyond their reception of the gospel. This statement sufficiently corresponds to v. 5, both in form and content, that the latter is virtually recapitulated by the former. Thus, the work of Christ (v. 8), as anticipated by the OT (vv. 9b−12), was destined to attain its fruition in the harmonious coexistence of the various factions within the Roman congregations (v. 13) (as opposed to διχοστασίαι and σκάνδαλα).

As the thought progresses, the intensity of Paul's paraenesis is not lessened. Therefore, the third contextual datum is that having wished for joy, peace, and hope to be enjoyed by his readers, he confirms his optimism for them by stating his conviction that they are "full of goodness," along with knowledge and the ability to instruct one another (v. 14). Nevertheless, he is aware that in certain regards they need reminding about their obligations as Christians (v. 15a), which Paul is bold enough to do because of his office as an apostle of Christ (vv. 15b−16). Two points in this connection are noteworthy.

(1) It is again to be observed that Paul includes the Romans within the scope of his mission, even though their church had not been founded by him. Therefore, his promotion of their obedience assumes wider dimensions than the

---

[71] "The recall of a key motif from 1:5 is no doubt deliberate since it ties together precisely a key theme of Jewish covenant self-awareness (obedience) and Paul's outreach to the Gentiles: it is precisely Paul's claim that the obligations of the covenant were being fulfilled in the faith response of the Gentiles" (Dunn, *Romans* 2.868).

[72] Schlatter, *Gerechtigkeit*, 387.

III. "The Obedience of Faith" as Total Response to the Gospel

conversion experience. Hence, when 15:18 speaks of Paul's aim to win obedience from the Gentiles, such obedience, by the nature of the case, must be subsequent to their initial response to his gospel.

(2) Vv. 15b–16 are directly reminiscent of 12:1–2.[73] 15:16 draws on the ideology of the OT cultus. Paul is a λειτουργὸς Χριστοῦ εἰς τὰ ἔθνη, who likens the Gentiles to a προσφορά offered by him in priestly service of the gospel (ἱερουγοῦντα τὸ εὐαγγέλιον τοῦ θεοῦ).[74] Earlier, in 12:1, he called on the Romans to present themselves as a "living sacrifice," "acceptable" (εὐάρεστος) to God. Coordinate with this is his appeal to them to be transformed by the renewal of their minds, so that they may discern God's will (12:2).[75] When, therefore, in 15:18 Paul articulates the goal of his mission as the ὑπακοὴ ἐθνῶν, a statement made on the heels of his intention that the προσφορὰ ἐθνῶν be "acceptable" (εὐπρόσδεκτος), "sanctified by the Holy Spirit,"[76] one cannot help but see something more than a forensic dimension to the outcome of his ministry.[77]

From vv. 17–21 a fourth matter of relevance emerges. Paul here reflects on the "sanctified" character of his offering and concludes that he has reason to be proud of his work for God (v. 17), although he qualifies by ascribing the winning of the Gentiles, by word and deed, to Christ (v. 18; cf. 1 Cor 15:10). In addition to word and deed, the power of the Holy Spirit in producing signs and wonders enabled Paul to preach the gospel of Christ "from Jerusalem and as far round as Illyricum" (v. 19). A cursory reading of vv. 18c–19 might leave the impression that the obedience of the Gentiles consisted solely in their belief in

---

[73] If we bring 12:3 into play, the correspondence with 15.15 is enlarged; both speak of the "grace" given to Paul to be an apostle. It is in 1:5 that he speaks for the first time of this "grace," and does so in direct connection with "the obedience of faith."

[74] As over against Jewett ("Letter," 16) and Käsemann (*Romans*, 392–93), Paul's conception of himself as a λειτουργός is sacerdotal in connotation; not literally so, but as he saw his mission as the fulfillment of the symbolico-typological ministry of the Levitical priesthood. In this regard, Käsemann is right that cultic terms and motifs are here used in a "transferred eschatological sense" (ibid., 393), so that Israel's cultic service finds its fruition in Paul's mission to the nations. See further Dunn, *Partings*, 79–81; Hultgren, *Gospel*, 134–37.

[75] 12:1–2 represents the reverse of the sin of Jew and Gentile condemned in chaps. 1 and 2 (Furnish, *Theology*, 102–5; Williams, "Righteousness," 254). The church, as God's new humanity, thus replaces the old humanity comprised of non-Christian Jews and Gentiles.

[76] Ἁγιάζω, as Dunn explains, is used in the OT particularly with respect to the cultus, by means of which the people of Israel were "rendered holy," i.e., set apart and marked off from the nations. Therefore, for Paul to use this verb of the "sacrifice" of Gentiles, the *un*-sanctified by definition, unable to penetrate the Jerusalem temple beyond the court of the Gentiles and outside the bounds of national purity, means that *they* have become the sacrifice (*Partings*, 82–83. Cf. id., *Romans* 2.861)!

[77] Käsemann is correct that in the phrase ἡ προσφορὰ τῶν ἐθνῶν the genitive is epexegetical: "the Gentile world itself is the offering." However, he is wrong in denying a connection between this and "the self-offering of Christians which the apostle brings about" (*Romans*, 393). Surely the one is the immediate effect of the other. Moreover, in both instances, the sacrifice in question is meant to be "acceptable," an OT cultic term signifying the unblemished character of what is offered to Yahweh.

the gospel. But without downplaying the primary importance of their reception of Christ, it is possible to read Paul's *whole* train of thought in another way.

15:14–16 expresses two ideas. On the one hand, there is Paul's assurance of the "goodness" of the Romans and their ability to instruct one another; on the other, he has "written boldly" about areas of concern, which he can do because he has been appointed a minister of Christ to the nations. It is his self-awareness as a λειτουργὸς Χριστοῦ εἰς τὰ ἔθνη which is brought over into his reflection on the success of his missionary work (vv. 17–21). In other words, the obedience of the Gentiles by word, deed, signs and wonders, and the power of the Holy Spirit is traced to its fountainhead in Paul's labor of bringing the gospel to those who have never heard. Hence, in 15:14–21, we encounter the twin ideas of an obedience consisting in faith and an obedience proceeding from faith, only in reverse order.[78] 15:18, then, which speaks of the obedience of the Gentiles, comes at the pivotal point between the effects of Paul's preaching and his account of the preaching itself.

One final contextual consideration emerges from the verses which constitute the remainder of chap. 15, viz., vv. 22–33. For the sake of convenience, this part of the text can be divided into two subsections. The first is vv. 22–29. Here Paul reiterates his desire to visit Rome *en route* to Spain. In this connection, he mentions the offering by the Gentile churches on behalf of the poor in Jerusalem; it is they who have come to share in the spiritual blessings of Israel and ought, therefore, to share with Jewish Christians in material things as a part of their priestly service (λειτουργῆσαι αὐτοῖς). Two matters are particularly noteworthy.

(1) The participation of the Gentiles in Israel's spiritual blessings at least implies that they have come to partake of God's total salvation in Christ. 15:8 speaks of the confirmation of God's promises to the patriarchs; and by way of analogy with the broader Pauline teaching, these promises are inclusive of such items as sonship to God and the gift of the Spirit. These πνευματικά look back to 11:12, where they are called "riches," i.e., the full benefit of being a Christian, which can only be had by the salvation of "all Israel" (11:26). At the very least, we may deduce that Paul envisages a complex state of affairs to which the nations have been admitted, once again centering around the mutual acceptance and respect of Jew and Gentile in one community in Christ. (2) The Gentiles, who are Paul's offering to God, have become priests in their own right: they are now privileged and obliged to serve (as priests) their Jewish counterparts in Jerusalem. This service is integral to their obedience.

Within this same subsection, v. 29 has some bearing on the issue. Paul is confident that when he comes to Rome he will do so in the "blessing" of Christ. Assuming the reading εὐλογίας[79], we are taken back to Paul's previously stated desire to impart some spiritual gift to the Romans (1:11), i.e., the strengthening

---

[78] It is possible to see a chiastic pattern in the construction of 15:7–21 as a whole: vv. 14–21 correspond inversely to vv. 7–13.

[79] *TCGNT*, 537.

III. "The Obedience of Faith" as Total Response to the Gospel

of their faith (1:12).⁸⁰ The obedience of Paul's readers, in other words, will be promoted by the impartation of Christ's blessing. Hence, the blessing of Christ and the obedience of the Romans can be seen in terms of cause and effect.

The second subsection of the remainder of chap. 15 is vv. 30–33. Of particular concern is Paul's request for prayer for himself that he may be delivered from "the disobedient [τῶν ἀπειθούντων] in Judea," who are most naturally Jews who oppose the gospel (cf. 2 Thess 1:8). However, many commentators make a simple cross-reference to 10:16, 21; 11:30–31 in their delineation of these "disobedient."⁸¹ While in basic accord with this procedure, Michel calls attention to two points of interest, although he apparently does not take note of their significance for v. 18 of this chapter. For one thing, he cites 2:8 as a parallel to 15:31. The former verse speaks of τοῖς ἀπειθοῦσι τῇ ἀληθείᾳ. This reference is appropriate because, as W. Mundle reminds us, Paul has in view there the totality of non-Christian humanity as disobedient to the truth.⁸² For another, Michel maintains that the antithesis of ἀπειθοῦντες is self-evidently ὑπακοὴ πίστεως.⁸³

The impact of Michel's observations is that the "disobedient" of 15:31, i.e., unbelieving Jews, are not to be identified solely in terms of their rejection of the gospel. Such, of course, was for Paul a momentous issue. Nevertheless, disobedience to the truth (2:8) entails more than the repudiation of a set of propositions. As the context of 2:8 suggests most plainly – especially 1:18–32 – behavioral patterns hinge on one's acceptance or rejection of the truth.⁸⁴ It is, according to 2:13, only the doers of the law who will be justified (in eschatological judgment). More pointedly, in 2:17–24 Paul charges that his Jewish contemporaries have been guilty of certain ethical infractions, thus nullifying the value of their circumcision (vv. 25–29). Therefore, by the term "disobedient" he reduces them to the level of paganism! It is surely striking that Paul's question about Israel in 3:3, "What if some were *disobedient*," is paralleled in the second clause by "does their *unfaithfulness* [ἀπιστία]⁸⁵ nullify the faithfulness of God?" Consequently, without minimizing the significance of Israel's unbelief for Paul, the disobedient in Judea form the antithesis of the obedient Gentiles (15:18), in the pregnant sense of ὑπακοή.

---

⁸⁰ Jewett wishes to restrict the blessing of Christ to the reconciliation of Jew and Gentile in Rome ("Letter," 18). No doubt, this was much on the apostle's mind; but the blessing in question is certainly more comprehensive. In 1:11–12, Paul spoke of his desire to visit the Romans for the purpose of strengthening their faith. Thus, the blessing of Christ is the totality of what he would do through Paul to further the obedience of faith among the Romans.

⁸¹ E.g., Cranfield, *Romans* 2.778; Schlier, *Römerbrief*, 438.

⁸² Mundle, *Glaubensbegriff*, 30.

⁸³ Michel, *Römer*, 468, n. 19.

⁸⁴ To be sure, in Gal 5:7 "obeying the truth" has to do with the acceptance of Paul's gospel as over against that of the Judaizers. Yet, as the context clarifies, only those who adhere to this gospel can produce the "fruit of the Spirit" as opposed to the "works of the flesh" (5:19, 22). Cf. Barclay, *Truth*, esp. 110–25, 202–15.

⁸⁵ Cf. ἡ ἀδικία ἡμῶν (v. 5) and ἐν τῷ ἐμῷ ψεύσματι (v. 7), both of which carry overtones of covenant infidelity.

The disobedience of the Palestinian Jews, in this light, is precisely the opposite of "the obedience of faith." Thus, more is at stake in the statements of 10:16; 11:23, 30, 31 than is normally granted by the commentators. The nature of Israel's disobedience will be considered in the next two chapters. For the moment, we note only that Israel, in Paul's estimation, though able to fulfill the law on the "nationalistic" level, could not do so on the more profound level demanded by "the obedience of faith." At heart, this is because, notwithstanding its protests to the contrary, Israel's disobedience for Paul is identifiable with its lack of fidelity to God's covenant! In what sense this comprehensible, we shall see.

We deduce, then, from 15:18 and its context that "the obedience of the Gentiles" does indeed form a parallel to "the obedience of faith" in 1:5. Yet it is a "progressive parallelism": Paul envisages not only the believing reception of his gospel by the nations but also their devotion to Christ and to one another. Their obedience (of faith), in other words, stands in contrast to the disobedience (of unbelief) of Israel, commensurate with its rejection of the same gospel.

IV. Summary

In Rom 1:5 (16:26), Paul has chosen to coin an *ambiguous* phrase expressive of two ideas:[86] the obedience which consists in faith, and the obedience which is the product of faith.[87] On the level of the grammatical, although tags can be applied to the genitive πίστεως only with some reservation, the category which best conveys his intentions is "adjectival genitive;"[88] that is, πίστεως is descriptive of ὑπακοή in a manner to be defined by the larger context and in keeping with the most pertinent exegetical data.[89] This means that "genitive of apposition" and "genitive of source," while not inappropriate in themselves, are to be rejected as too restrictive. Consequently, the English "faith's obedience"

---

[86] As an interesting analogy, Przybylski (*Righteousness*, 17–20) discusses the possible translations of the title *moreh tsedeq* in CD. He notes that the Hebrew could be rendered either "teacher of righteousness" (objective genitive) or "righteous or right teacher" (explicative genitive). He opts for the former, yet concedes that "The problem with which we have been dealing may in actual fact be a pseudo-problem arising solely out of difficulties inherent in the process of translating from Hebrew into English." Thus, "It should not be taken for granted that these two ideas are mutually exclusive" (ibid., 20). This is suggestive because it reminds us that Paul's Semitic background could easily account for a flexibility in his Greek usage, permitting more than one meaning to reside in his genitival phrases. Perhaps the most famous of such phrases is δικαιοσύνη θεοῦ.

[87] Cf. Dunn, *Romans* 1.17; Ridderbos, *Paul*, 237. While I am completely sympathetic with Davies' evaluation of the relation of faith and obedience (*Faith*, 28–30), it is not necessary, with him, to restrict ourselves to the subjective genitive/genitive of origin. The parallels of faith in obedience in 10:16; 11:23, 30, 31 do have something to say.

[88] Labeled, however, as "genitive of quality" by Turner (*Grammar*, 212) and BDF, 91.

[89] Cf. Barclay's treatment of Paul's expression ὁ νόμος τοῦ Χριστοῦ (*Truth*, 134).

(or "believing obedience") perhaps as well as any translation preserves the intention (and ambiguity) of the original.⁹⁰

On the plane of the theological and practical, the significance of the phrase's ambiguity is well expressed by Fitzmeyer: "Though that faith begins for Paul as a 'hearing'... it does not stop there. It involves the entire personal commitment of a man/woman to Christ Jesus as 'Lord'.... The word ὑπακοή implies the '*sub*mission' or total personal response of the believer to the risen Lord."⁹¹ It is just the commitment factor which informs us that Paul's principal concern is for the perseverance of the Romans in the Christian faith, particularly in the face of the enticements to apostasy placed in their way by certain teachers. Obedience is thereby brought into connection with the harmony of the church, because for Christians, under the influence of such teachers, to refuse to welcome one another is to sabotage the purpose for which Christ died and came to life again (14:9), and to short-circuit the aim of the Pauline mission: to promote the obedience of faith among *all the nations*.

---

⁹⁰ See Parke-Taylor, "Note," 305, for the various ways in which translators have grappled with the difficulties inherent in our phrase. The German *Glaubensgehorsam* perhaps better conveys the unity of faith and obedience than most of the English renderings.

⁹¹ Fitzmeyer, "*Kyrios*-Title," 132.

Chapter Two

The Disobedience of Israel

We have now argued for a certain understanding of the phrase ὑπακοὴ πίστεως and its attendant theology. But before proceeding to develop these basic findings, it will be necessary to lay a more substantial foundation. That is to say, since Paul's idea of the obedience of faith stands in rather stark relief to his conception of the disobedience of his Jewish contemporaries, it is only against the backdrop of his indictment of Israel that aspects of his teaching emerge with tolerable clarity. In establishing this perspective, we turn to Rom 2:22.

I. The Problem of Romans 2:22

Perhaps one of the most curious, if not perplexing, passages from the pen of Paul is the charge of Rom 2:22 – by way of an accusatory rhetorical question[1] – that Israel is guilty of what he calls ἱεροσυλεῖν. As is commonly known, this verb is capable of a narrower and a broader meaning. In terms of the former, Paul's accusation is that Israel is blameworthy for "robbing temples," while, according to the latter, its culpability has respect to "committing sacrilege" in some unspecified sense.[2] In either case, Paul's charge was seriously intended, thereby raising a real difficulty of interpretation since he was apparently addressing the "typical Jew" of his day, as is evident enough from 2:17–20.[3] How could Israel *qua* Israel have been guilty of the sort of behavior depicted by either sense of ἱεροσυλέω?

---

[1] Cranfield, *Romans* 1.167.
[2] Thus resembling its cognate ἱεροσυλία. See Schrenk, *TDNT* 3.255. Michel (*Römer*, 131, n. 14) finds three distinct applications of the term: (1) rob temples; (2) commit an act of desecration against a sanctuary; (3) misappropriate temple funds. For further references, see BAGD, 373; LSJ, 822. In 2 Maccabees, the verb is used of the desecration of the Jerusalem temple by Lysimachus (2:39, 42), the attempted plunder of the pagan temple in Persepolis by Antiochus (9:2), and the general charge of sacrilege brought against Menelaus and his sort (13:6).
[3] See Wilckens, *Römer* 1.147–48; Dunn, *Partings*, 21–23, 143–46; Garlington, *Obedience*, 146, 159. The identity of the "Jew" militates against Watson's attempt to make Paul's language specially applicable to the Roman Jewish leadership (*Paul*, 114). Paul, no doubt, was sensitive to the Roman situation. Nevertheless, his mode of argumentation in the letter is conditioned by the *whole* of his missionary enterprise.

I. The Problem of Romans 2:22   33

Cranfield is right that in Paul's day "it could be confidently assumed that there was no longer any idolatry in Israel."[4] Yet this historical fact simply intensifies the irony of Paul's complaint that the Jewish people have engaged in the activity denoted by ἱεροσυλέω. To the Jew who is confident of his complete purity in respect of idolatry Paul addresses the accusation: ἱεροσυλεῖς? At the very least, we can agree with Cranfield that the Jew who was so confident in his purity from idolatry was, according to Paul, not free from its taint.[5] But in what sense is this meaningful?

Picking up on the two possible translations of the term, Cranfield relates that some scholars take the reference to be to ἱεροσυλία committed against pagan temples, in contravention of Deut 7:25−26.[6] Alternatively, he notes, others view the Jew's very abhorrence of idolatry, out of loyalty to the true God, to be an act of ἱεροσυλία against him. In the latter instance, Cranfield says, it is best not to assume that Paul envisages the robbing of the Jerusalem temple (e. g., *T. Levi* 14:5; *Pss. Sol.* 1:8; 8:11; CD 6:16) but that he is using ἱεροσυλέω in the broader sense of "commit sacrilege." Accordingly, Paul's field of vision, on this construction, is not to be restricted to obviously sacrilegious behavior: it embraces as well that of "less obvious and more subtle forms of sacrilege."[7]

The difficulty with the first is that although there are recorded instances of Jewish temple-plundering, they are so relatively infrequent that it is unlikely in the extreme that Paul would impute such goings-on to his fellow Jews at large, especially since this would apply only to Diaspora and not Palestinian Jews.[8] The second falters because, as normally set forth, it is too unspecific. What is sacrilegious behavior? Against whom has it been perpetrated? The answer is not clear. Moreover, both proposals fail to explain adequately how ἱεροσυλέω can form the counterpart of ὁ βδελυσσόμενος τὰ εἴδωλα,[9] conformable to the

---

[4] Cranfield, *Romans* 1.169. He notes that such confidence was expressed already in Jdt 8:18.

[5] Ibid.

[6] As illustrated by Str-B 3.113−15. Cf. Acts 19:37; Josephus, *Ant.* 4.8.10 (207). In *Ag. Ap.* 1.249, 310−11, 318−19, Josephus relates and then rebuffs the charges of Jewish temple robbery stemming from the anti-Semites Manetho and Lysimachus; the latter whimsically derived the name of Jerusalem from ἱερόσυλα − "city of temple robbers."

[7] Cranfield, *Romans* 1.170. Barrett (*Romans*, 57) similarly takes the term in its broader signification and interprets the Jew's sacrilege as his exaltation of himself as a judge over his fellow creatures. This insight, as we shall see, brings us close to Paul's intention.

[8] In spite of Michel, *Römer*, 131; Schlier, *Römerbrief*, 86; Zeller, *Römer*, 72; Schrenk, *TDNT* 3.256 (even conceding to Schlier, Zeller, and Schrenk that ἱεροσυλεῖν was one of the worst crimes in antiquity); Wilckens, *Römer* 1.150; Leenhardt, *Romans*, 87; Murray, *Romans* 1.84; Black, *Romans*, 60; Hendriksen, *Romans* 1.105; Watson, *Paul*, 114. To be sure, temple robbery was not unheard of among the Jews. The question, however, is whether it was sufficiently widespread to warrant Paul's accusation in this place (cf. Cranfield's remarks, *Romans* 1.168). Certainly, such an obvious piece of anti-Semitism as that of Manetho and Lysimachus is not to be taken as objective historical evidence that the Jews were characteristically given to pillaging temples. Thus, it is difficult to believe that Paul is chiming in with a Gentile criticism of Judaism (Zeller).

[9] Τὰ εἴδωλα are clearly pagan idols (for references, see Schlier, *Römerbrief*, 86).

pattern of the questions and replies in vv. 21–22.[10] In what follows, therefore, we shall attempt an explanation of Rom 2:22 which seeks to do justice to both the verse's immediate setting and the broader purview of Paul's controversy with Israel over the law.

In providing a framework of interpretation, we wish to challenge the assumption that Paul could not be accusing Israel of idolatry,[11] an assumption which has promoted the equation of ἱεροσυλεῖν with outrages committed against pagan temples. We turn, then, to consider that the idolatry motif of Rom 1:18–32, along with the disobedience theme of 5:12–19, serves to open up Paul's intentions in 2:22.

II. Ἱεροσυλεῖν as Israel's Idolatry

Since the publication of M. D. Hooker's article "Adam in Romans I," scholars have been aware that Paul's depiction of man and his plight is modeled on the fall of Adam in Genesis.[12] By both his choice of language and the sequence of events outlined in Romans 1, we are led to believe that the apostle's thought is rooted in the story of Adam as told in Genesis 1–3. Although it is hardly true that Adam was an idolater in exactly the same way as Paul's pagan contemporaries, he can be justly accused, as Hooker observes, of serving the creature rather than the creator; "and it is from this confusion between God and the things which he has made that idolatry springs."[13] For Paul, then, mankind outside of Christ is an idolater by definition.

---

[10] Stowers shows that each of the four indicting rhetorical questions has a participial phrase describing an activity of the interlocutor followed by a verb which poses a question to the interlocutor about *his own participation in that activity* (*Diatribe*, 97). Wilckens is to be exempted, since he takes ἱεροσυλέω in its broader meaning and refers it to involvement with idolatrous images and temple goods (*Römer*, 150). Similarly, Schlatter (*Gerechtigkeit*, 106) entertains the possibility that the Jew secretly appropriates to himself what is holy to the pagan. Nevertheless, only Diaspora Jews, as a rule, would be liable to such a charge, and even then it hardly seems likely that the practice was so prevalent that Paul would single it out as a fundamental grievance against the Jewish people.

[11] E.g., Zeller, *Römer*, 72.

[12] Cf. Dunn, *Christology*, 101–2; Barrett, *Adam*, 17–20; Wedderburn, "Adam," 413–19; Longenecker, *Eschatology*, 173–74. I agree with Hooker over against Davies (*Faith*, 48, n. 1) and Milne ("Genesis 3") that Romans 1 does concern itself with mankind's solidarity in Adam. The distinction between solidarity with Adam and the Adamic history pressed by Davies and Milne is an artificial one. Contra Bassler (*Impartiality*, 196), Paul's intertwining indictment of Jew and Gentile is predicated precisely on the basis of the fallenness of both groups in Adam: they are equal in sin. Bassler's brief treatment of Rom 1:23 (ibid., 195–97) is flawed in that fallenness is pitted against idolatry. In subsequent chapters, we shall see in some detail that Paul equates the two: human fallenness is none other than its condition of idolatry, of worshipping and serving the creature.

[13] Hooker, "Adam," 301. Contra Bassler (*Impartiality*, 196), who fails to appreciate that the essence of idolatry is to be found in worshipping and serving the creature. What else could constitute idolatry?

Most relevant for our purposes is the fact that Paul does not exempt Israel from the indictment of idolatry. It is true, as Hooker and others have pointed out, that most of the vocabulary of Rom 1:23 is drawn from Genesis. However, the words ἤλλαξαν τὴν δόξαν (τοῦ ἀφθάρτου θεοῦ) are extracted from Ps 106(105):20 and Jer 2:11 (cf. Deut 4:15–18), which have to do with *Israel's* idolatry in the wilderness and later in the land. At the very least, then, it can be said that in the matter of idolatry Paul conceived of an Israel which was at one with the rest of humanity – as startling a notion as that must have been to his Jewish compatriots.

It is at this point that Paul's running debate in the Roman letter with Judaism (and the Jewish Christian missionaries) comes into play, whereby, from his side, there is no longer any distinction between Jew and Greek. Especially noteworthy is the affinity of 1:18–32 with the book of Wisdom. Scholars have long been aware that much of Paul's denunciation of idols and immorality is patterned after Wisdom, and have rightly emphasized the similarities.[14] Paul, in other words, excoriates idolatry and its attendant ills in the precise terms set by Jewish precedents.

However, Hooker is right to insist that the differences are no less important than the similarities.[15] The most striking discrepancy is that whereas in Wisdom the Gentiles and *apostate* Jews engage in idolatry, in Romans 1 Israel as such is implicated in Paul's charge. Paul, in other words, has reduced contemporary Israel to the level of paganism, the Israel which is unswervingly loyal to the Torah and the God of the Torah. The chosen people, no less than the Gentiles, are involved in and repeat the primal sin of Adam.

The argumentation of 1:18–32 finds its counterpart in 5:12–19. Here Paul takes his readers back to the inception of "the present evil age" (Gal 1:4) with the disobedience of Adam and explains that the believer's past existence was the result of his connection with him. His main point, continued into chap. 6, is that it is only by virtue of identification with Christ, the last Adam, that one can make a new beginning and thus succeed in one's endeavor to be obedient to God. It is in pursuing this line of thought that he seeks to qualify the idea that *Israel* represents a new beginning and the realization of God's purposes for mankind as originally created.[16]

Illustrative of this conception is Sir 10:19 and Sirach 17.[17] The former is composed of a series of rhetorical questions:

What race [σπέρμα ἀνθρώπου] is worthy of honor?
 The human race.
What race is worthy of honor?
 Those who fear the Lord.

---

[14] See the literature cited in Garlington, *Obedience*, 68, n. 13.

[15] Hooker, "Adam," 299.

[16] See Wright, "Adam," 360–65. This notion will feature again in the exposition of 5:12–19 below.

[17] See further Garlington, *Obedience*, 58–60 (with literature).

What race is unworthy of honor?
The human race?
What race is unworthy of honor?
Those who transgress the commandments.

According to the scribe, there is a sense in which Israel is to be identified with the whole of humanity: along with the nations, it is the σπέρμα ἀνθρώπου. However, it is equally evident that this nation is to be distinguished from other peoples. While every race ought to fear the Lord and keep his commandments, only one actually does, Israel (cf. 4 Ezra 3:33–36; 7:37). The Jewish people thus fulfill the creation ideal of humanity.

Chap. 17 falls into a broader section of the book commencing with 16:24, which can be designated as "divine wisdom in creation providing the pattern for human wisdom." 16:24–28 eulogize the order, the labor, and the obedience of the inanimate creation. Vv. 29–30 recount the filling of the earth with living beings and thus form the transition into chap. 17, which relates in detail the status and function of man as God's image in the creation.

As in 10:19, there is once more an interplay between humanity at large and Israel. The language of 17:1–10 is couched in general terms which recall humanity's creation in Adam. V. 11, however, seems to mark a turning point, with Israel specifically in view, because it is on this people that God has bestowed knowledge, i. e., "the law of life,"[18] with whom also he established an "eternal covenant" (vv. 11–12; cf. Bar 4:1). Hence, while the portrait of man is painted in generic colors, that of the law and the covenant is not.[19]

Again, these data suggest that Ben Sira saw in his people the realization of the creation intention of God for mankind. What the σπέρμα ἀνθρώπου stemming from Adam failed to be, the σπέρμα ʼΑβραάμ has become by its custodianship of wisdom (1:15), its reception of the "eternal covenant" and "the law of life," its keeping of the commandments, and the fear of the Lord (10:19, passim).[20] This inference is supported by v. 17: given the fall of the first humanity (v. 15), "He appointed a ruler for every nation, but Israel is the Lord's own portion."

All this sets the stage for the polemical impact of Rom 5:12–19 and for the radicalism of Paul's stance toward Israel. The Jewish position was that the people of Israel were God's new beginning and the remedy for the consequences of Adam's disobedience. It was none other than Abraham's obedience to the Lord's command (in a time of testing) which marked the inception of a

---

[18] The phrase also occurs in 45:5 and is derived from Lev 18:5; Deut 30:11–20; cf. Bar 4:1–4. For Ben Sira (and Baruch) the law was directly tantamount to divine wisdom.

[19] Elsewhere, these two are joined in specifically Jewish terms: 24:23; 28:7; 39:1–8; 42:2, 5. In addition, 17:14 probably alludes to the "book of the covenant" (Exodus 21–23).

[20] Cf. *Gen. R.* 14:6: "I will make Adam first: if he goes wrong Abraham will come to restore everything again."

new, obedient humanity, Israel.²¹ But, in complete contrast, what Israel ascribed to itself Paul ascribes to Christ and Christians. On the one hand, humanity outside of Christ – including Israel – is in Adam and, therefore, still participates in the effects of his sin. On the other, he asserts that everyone in Christ – regardless of ethnic identity and commitment to the Torah – has entered the new creation with its blessings.

In all likelihood, Paul would have conceded that there was a legitimate sense in which a new beginning was made with Abraham and later at Sinai. Yet Israel's mistake, for him, was to confine this fresh start to its own people and to exclude any portion of humanity unwilling to become as they. His contemporaries, in short, were insistent that participation in a new creation was possible only within the perimeters of the chosen race and their Torah. Thus, Paul's qualification of the Jewish position is striking – to say the least! As he saw it, if Israel's nationhood marked a new beginning of the human race, it was only that this new beginning might, "in the fullness of the time" (Gal 4:4), find its fruition in the calling of Jew and Gentile without distinction. If it be asked how Saul of Tarsus could have so modified his former convictions as one zealous for the "paternal traditions" (Gal 1:14) of his own people,²² the answer must reside in his christology. For him "all the promises of God" find their "yes" not in Israel but in Christ (2 Cor 1:20). It is this Christ who has summoned all the nations to "the obedience of faith" to himself (see below).

In sum, the combination of Rom 1:18–32 and 5:12–19, against their polemical backdrop, leads us to believe that Paul is denying Israel's claim to being a new beginning after the fall of Adam. Rather, according to him, the chosen people are as much involved in Adam's idolatry as the outside world. Naturally, the question is, How can this be so? If idolatry in Palestine was a thing of the past, and if in the Diaspora only apostate Jews engaged in the worship of other deities than Yahweh, in what sense could Paul's accusation, for him anyway, be meaningful? It is the answer to this question, we propose, that is provided by 2:22.

As Paul continues his argument that "there is no distinction" between Jew and Gentile into chap. 2, he is still concerned to identify Israel with generic humanity (ὦ ἄνθρωπε, 2:1, 3).²³ In vv. 1–16, he develops the proposition that possession of the law in itself means nothing; it is only the doers of the law who will be justified in eschatological judgment, irrespective of national origins (vv. 6–9). Of course, Israel as a distinct entity is implicitly in view; but it is not until vv. 17–29 that he addresses the one who calls himself a Jew (v. 17). From this point through 3:8, he dialogues with Israel along the lines of its national

---

²¹ See Wright, "Adam," 360–65; Watson, *Paul*, 137; Longenecker, *Eschatology*, 211–21 (Longenecker's criticisms of Westerholm are especially apropos).

²² The πατρικοὶ παραδόσεις of Gal 1:14 find their equivalent in the πάτριοι or πατρῷοι νόμοι of 2, 3, 4 Maccabees, Josephus, and Philo. See Garlington, *Obedience*, 157.

²³ Contra Watson (*Paul*, 109–10), the discussion does not take a specifically Jewish orientation until v. 17.

privileges and distinctives and concludes that possession of the law and circumcision are advantageous only if Israel keeps the law (vv. 23–27). Indeed, the "true Jew," from now on, is one whose heart, not flesh, has been circumcised (vv. 28–29).

It is within the subsection of 2:17–3:8 that Paul frames his questions of vv. 21–22 for the Jew, who relies on the law and boasts in God (v. 17).[24] In other words, the person being addressed is, in Jewish terms, the faithful covenant-keeping Israelite: what Paul predicates of him is precisely what he would have claimed for himself. It is of him, ὁ βδελυσσόμενος τὰ εἴδωλα, that Paul asks: ἱεροσυλεῖς? Whatever one makes of the queries respecting the Jew's morality (theft and adultery),[25] it is obvious enough that Paul is implicating his interlocutor in the very thing against which he instructs others. Hence, the Jew, who abominates idolatry, is himself an idolater.

What exactly Paul has in mind is intimated, in the first place, by the Adam/idolatry/disobedience motifs of 1:18–32 and 5:12–19. In both passages, Israel is "in Adam" and part of the problems created by his fall, not their cure. This Paul sets over against the nation's arrogation to itself of the exclusive role of reversing the effects of the first man's sin, which meant, practically speaking, that anyone wishing to escape the ravages of the old creation (sin and condemnation) must join its ranks. Therefore, Paul's Adam theology is aimed specifically at the Jewish nationalistic self-consciousness,[26] implying that in his mind there was a connection between Israel's idolatry and its ethnic, religious, and political self-awareness as the people of God.

In the second place, such an impression is only confirmed by the way Paul introduces his final question in 2:23, viz., ὃς ἐν νόμῳ καυχᾶσαι (v. 23a): the

---

[24] The combination of trust in the law and boasting in God is not surprising in view of Sir 32:24–33:3, where faith in the Torah and faith in God are placed on a par with each other. Similarly, 1 Macc 2:59, 61 commend faith in Yahweh, while 1 Macc 2:64 has Mattathias exhort his sons to "grow strong in the law." The rationale here is simply that the Torah was the divinely given expression of God's will and, with the Lord himself, must be an object of trust. In the words of *2 Apoc. Bar.* 48:22: "In you we have put our trust, because, behold, your law is with us." Lührmann, then, is right that the stem *pist-* designates the relationship of those who devote themselves to God and his law ("Pistis," 34). As contra Nygren (*Romans*, 131–32), the Jew did not stop with merely knowing the law, nor was his mistake that he put his trust in the law. Rather, his boast in God implies faith in God, in keeping with the pattern of God and the Torah as the twofold object of faith. As we shall see below, his mistake, according to Paul, was that he made his distinctive ethnico-religious identity, derived from his reliance on the law and his boast in God, the paradigm for measuring all men's acceptability to God.

[25] Barrett and Moo note that theft, adultery, and sacrilege often appear side by side in lists of vices (e.g., Philo, *Conf.* 163; *Spec. Leg.* 2.13; 4.87). Cranfield, however, senses the problem occasioned by Paul's application of these three sins to Israel and opts for the view that Paul is radicalizing the law in much the same manner as Matt 5:21–30 (*Romans* 1.168–69). Watson (*Paul*, 114), on the other hand, understands Paul literally and thinks that his charges are directed toward immoral Rabbis in Rome. Among others, Räisänen also seems to interpret in actual terms (*Paul*, 98). In view of Paul's stress on the circumcision of the heart (vv. 28–29), I would say that Cranfield's proposal is not at all farfetched.

[26] See Wright, "Adam," 360–65, and chapter 4 below.

perpetrator of ἱεροσυλεῖν is simultaneously the one who "boasts in the law." Combined with his remarks on Adam and Israel, this suggests most forcefully that for Paul *the new idol is the Torah*! The "sacrilege" in question is *Israel's idolatrous attachment to the law itself*. It is the one who commits such sacrilege who, so ironically, dishonors God διὰ τῆς παραβάσεως τοῦ νόμου. No wonder, then, ἱεροσυλεῖν is connected directly with theft and adultery, not as a random example of how the Jew fails to practice what he preaches but as being on a par with and even surpassing both of these serious moral failures. In point of fact, nothing could have touched the national self-consciousness more dramatically than this charge of idolatry, not even theft and adultery.[27]

Intimations of the Torah-idolatry motif can be found subtly (or not so subtly!) in various other places in Paul. One is Rom 10:19–20, which makes use of Deut 32:21 and Isa 65:1–2; another is Gal 4:8–9, a kind of capstone to the anti-Torah polemic of Galatians 3 and 4.

According to Deut 32:21, as placed in service by Rom 10:19: "I will make you jealous of those who are not a nation; with a foolish nation I will make you angry." The quotation appears within the Song of Moses, which as a whole is a defense of Yahweh's faithfulness to Israel, in the spite of its infidelity to him. The tone of the Song is set by vv. 4–5: "The Rock, his work is perfect; for all his ways are justice. A God of faithfulness and without iniquity, just and right is he. They have dealt corruptly with him, they are no longer his children because of their blemish; they are a perverse and crooked generation." Within this setting, v. 21 is Yahweh's threat to provoke Israel with a "non-people," a "foolish nation," i.e., the Gentile power which will take Israel into captivity because of its idolatry (vv. 15–18). Israel will be stirred to jealousy, therefore, when it sees pagans taking away its national treasures into a foreign land. As Paul applies the text, however, the "foolish people" are the Gentiles who believe in Christ and thus provoke the Israel of his generation – the Israel which presently idolizes the Torah. This is the "unbeloved people" (9:25) which has now come into possession of those treasures (privileges) enumerated in 9:4–5, preeminently the Christ. Paul's hope in all this is that his kinsmen will look with envy upon those who have despoiled their goods, abandon their idol and embrace the Christ of his gospel. This desire for Israel is reiterated in 11:11–16.

Isa 65:1–2, quoted in the very next verse, has the same end in view: "I have been found by those who did not seek me; I have shown myself to those who did not ask for me." In its own context, the most obvious aspect of the quotation is that God himself speaks his mind about Israel and the nations. In so doing, he gives voice to a role reversal beginning to take place even in the prophet's day. To any pious Jew, of course, pagan lifestyle was idolatrous by definition. Yet it is precisely God's indictment of Israel's idolatry which is the burden of Isa 65:1–16. Hence, Yahweh expresses his desire that former idolaters embrace

---

[27] However, the mention of adultery in the same breath as idolatry may glance at the equation of the two in ancient Judaism. See Garlington, *Obedience*, 186–91 (esp. pp. 190–91).

him as their God, while Israel is to be rejected for its love of idols. Paul's application of the passage to his mission is clear enough: whereas the nations have thrown off their idols and have come to faith in Christ, Israel continues to cling to its idol – the Torah. This idolatrous Israel is explicitly called by him "disobedient" (ἀπειθοῦντα) and "contradictory" (ἀντιλεγοῦντα, cf. Acts 13:45). (It would appear that as early as the composition of 2 Thessalonians "disobedience" had actually become a technical term to designate Israel [1:8]). Again, the irony is evident: the self-perceived obedient, in Paul's view, are actually the opposite.

Of the many unnerving things Paul says about the Torah in Galatians 3 and 4, the sentences of 4:8–9 are probably the most scandalous. In turning directly to the Gentile segment of the Galatian congregations, he addresses them as those who, at one time, did not know God (cf. 2 Thess 2:8) and were enslaved to those "deities" which they now acknowledge to have no existence. Yet having come to know the true God (in Christ), they want to return again to τὰ ἀσθενῆ καὶ πτωχὰ στοιχεῖα (= τὰ στοιχεῖα τοῦ κόσμου, 4:3), to which again they desire to be enslaved. The shock effect of Paul's protest is that he draws a parallel between their former enslavement to idols and the bondage in which they wish to place themselves under the Torah (cf. 3:23–25; and esp. 4:3). The one form of idolatry is as bad as the other! They might as well have never left paganism!

The rationale for Paul's equation of the Torah with idol-worship is to be sought in his controversy with his Jewish kinsmen regarding the law. Whereas for Israel the law was eternal (e. g., Bar 4:1; Wis 18:4), for Paul it was intended only to be provisional, a παιδαγωγὸς εἰς Χριστόν (Gal 3:23–25):[28] Christ is the law's τέλος (Rom 10:4).[29] Thus, *Israel's idolatry is its tenacious insistence that the Torah is God's definitive provision for eternal life and, therefore, its clinging to the law as an object of trust to the exclusion of Christ.* Or, to say it another way, its joy was in the Torah, not in Christ.

In the final analysis, the basic dispute revolved around eschatology, or better, as far as Paul was concerned, around the complex of eschatology and christology. It was, most pointedly, Paul's "christological eschatology" which was the deciding factor.[30] In the words of C. F. D. Moule, "The all-inclusiveness of Jesus Christ was the conviction that determined Paul's thinking and practice," because "Paul was caught in the explosion that was the person of Jesus."[31] Thus, however valid the law may have been for its time, "*now* the righteousness of God has been manifested apart from the law" (Rom 3:21). Therefore, Israel's problem for Paul was its insistence on remaining on the wrong side of

---

[28] Cf. Lull, "Pedagogue;" Gordon, "Note."

[29] Whether τέλος is "goal" or "termination," the point remains unchanged, although it is not improbable that it means both at the same time. See my *Obedience*, 256, n. 10.

[30] See further Longenecker, "Eschatology;" Ridderbos, *Paul*, 49; Garlington, *Obedience*, 255. By way of corollary, Paul's quarrel was not with his ancestors but his contemporaries. Unlike them, the light of the new creation has dawned on Paul (2 Cor 4:6), convincing him that he should no longer be a "zealot" for the paternal traditions (Gal 1:14; Phil 3:6).

[31] Moule, "Jesus," 50.

II. Ἱεροσυλεῖν as Israel's Idolatry 41

the eschatological divide, commensurate with its rejection of Jesus of Nazareth and its desire to remain within the "fence" of the Torah (*Ep. Arist.* 139–42).[32]

For Paul, however, since the advent of Christ, there is a new covenant (2 Corinthians 3) and a new creation (2 Cor 5:17; Gal 6:15). Far from being the "commandments of life" (Bar 3:9, 14; 4:1), the law for him actually fosters sin, wrath, death, and condemnation (Rom 3:19–20; 4:15; 5:20; 7:1–13; 2 Cor 3:6–7); its real purpose was to point to Christ (Rom 10:4; Gal 3:23–25). And now that Christ has come, circumcision preeminently is no longer one of the commandments of God; it counts for nothing (1 Cor 7:19; Gal 5:6); what is of importance is not circumcision but the new creation (Gal 6:15); indeed, to make Gentiles submit to circumcision is to endanger "the truth of the gospel" (Gal 2:5, 14). Consistent with this is Paul's denial that the special days of Israel (Gal 4:10; Col 2:16–17) and its food laws (Rom 14:2–4; Col 2:16–17) are of any lasting significance: they belong to the "elements of the world" (Gal 4:3, 9; Col 2:20). Since the "law of Christ"[33] (Gal 6:2; 1 Cor 9:21) has jettisoned many of the distinctives of Israelite self-identification, Paul feels no compulsion to make Gentiles "live as Jews" (Ἰουδαΐζειν) (Gal 2:14).[34] Unlike many of his Jewish compatriots (Rom 10:2), he is no longer a "zealot" for the paternal traditions (Gal 1:13–14; Phil 3:6), because a radical reversal has taken place: he is now the persecuted, proof of his zeal for Christ![35] As matter of course, then, his boast is no longer in the Torah, the God of the Torah, and his standing as an Israelite (Rom 2:17, 23; Phil 3:4–6),[36] but in Christ (Gal 6:14; Phil 3:3; Rom 5:2). Henceforth his striving to attain to the resurrection is motivated not by a desire to be one of the vindicated obedient of Israel (2 Maccabees 7; *Testament of Moses* 9) but by a passion to be found in Christ, because he has been apprehended by Christ (Phil 3:5–14).

So fundamental was Paul's break with the law that from now on he is adjudged apostate and heretic by the synagogue,[37] since his new-found convic-

---

[32] Beker remarks that Judaism, otherwise so tolerant in doctrinal matters, could not permit a confession (i.e., of Jesus as Messiah) that undermined its life under the Torah, which was why the pre-Christian Paul considered it simply a scandalous heresy to confess a crucified Messiah (in itself bad enough), who caused his followers to tamper with the Torah (*Paul*, 206–7, 183).

[33] The main lines of debate concerning the phrase have been documented by Barclay (*Truth*, 126–35) and Schnabel (*Law*, 277, nn. 252–254). See further my "Burden Bearing," 173–76.

[34] On Ἰουδαΐζειν, see Dunn, *Jesus, Paul*, 145, 148–58. Dunn does qualify that circumcision was not necessarily included in Ἰουδαΐζειν (ibid., 154).

[35] Pobee, *Persecution*, 93–98.

[36] Boasting is herein understood in terms of its nationalistic dimensions. Israel's boasting, in other words, is commensurate with its pride in covenant privileges (Rom 9:4–5). See Dunn, *Jesus, Paul*, 200–2; id., *Romans* 1.lxx-lxxi, 110–11; Räisänen, *Paul*, 170, 177; id., "Conversion," 410–12; Saldarini, *Pharisees*, 136. Contra Hübner (*Law*, 113–124) and Westerholm (*Law*, 169–73).

[37] See Hengel, *Judaism* 1.307–8, 314; 2.204, n. 305; Gaston, "Paul," 53–57; Dunn, "Heretic," 55–60; id., *Unity*, 241; Michel, *Römer*, 291.

tions in Christ flew in the face of the "paternal traditions" (Gal 1:14) in which he had been nurtured. One of the immediate results of Paul's departure from Judaism was a readjustment of his understanding of "faith's obedience." If, for the most part, Pauline theology rests on the radical reversal of former values and aims through an encounter with the crucified and risen Jesus of Nazareth,[38] it was the apostle's vision of the obedient people of God, we might say, which most radically drew the line of demarcation between him and Second Temple Judaism.

Among the many documents which illuminate this cleavage from the Jewish side, the book of Judith provides us with a classic example of faith's obedience in its pre-Pauline conception.[39] According to Jdt 14:10, Achior the Gentile believed in God with all his heart, was circumcised and joined the house of Israel, remaining steadfast for the entirety of his life. That Gentiles would be circumcised goes virtually without saying.[40] However, Hengel helps us to understand the import of Achior's joining the house of Israel. He remarks that the persecution and then victories of the Maccabean period aroused not only strong religious but also political forces. With Achior's conversion specifically in view, Hengel continues: "In antiquity, to become a Jew was never simply a religious action; it was also a political decision: on his conversion the Gentile became a member of the Jewish 'ethnos'."[41] By contrast, for Paul the obedience of faith was no longer contingent on individuals becoming Achiors; rather, the way into God's (new) covenant was by faith alone.[42]

The purpose of these remarks is to underscore that the polarity between Paul and Israel was widened by definite historical circumstances. In the climate created by the events of some two hundred years earlier,[43] Paul's proclamation of faith's obedience as a possibility for Gentiles *qua* Gentiles was the source of deepest offense for at least three reasons.[44] (1) Theologically, it meant the removal of age-old distinctions, implying that Israel was no longer exclusively the exalted and glorified people of God.[45] (2) Socially, it destroyed the identity and boundary markers which segregated Israel from the nations.[46] (3) Morally, it signified to the Jewish faithful the breakdown of the ethics demanded by the covenant, since, in their view, it invited apostasy from Moses.[47]

---

[38] Hengel, *Paul*, 86.

[39] See Garlington, *Obedience*, 182–83.

[40] This has been disputed, but, in my view, to no effect. See ibid., 88.

[41] Hengel, *Judaism* 1.307.

[42] In the main, Sanders discussion is quite adequate (*Law*, 17–64).

[43] See the penetrating comments of Hengel, *Judaism* 1.303–9.

[44] See further Garlington, *Obedience*, 261–63.

[45] E.g., Sir 50:22; Tob 14:7; Jdt 10:8; 13:4; Wis 3:8; 18:8; 19:22; Add Esth 11:11.

[46] See Dunn, *Jesus, Paul*, 216–19; Sanders, *Law*, 102; and the important discussion of Limbeck (*Ordnung*, 29–50), who shows that the motivation of Jewish zeal for the law was not "legalism" but the preservation of the community.

[47] Cf. *Ep. Arist.* 139–42. Gal 2:15 is indicative of the common Jewish outlook that Gentiles are *ipso facto* "sinners." Moreover, Gal 2:17 reflects the allegation that, given Paul's principles, Christ must be a "minister of sin."

These three factors in combination were sufficient to render the Pauline gospel intolerable to first-century Judaism. Yet Paul's response was equally forthright. For him Israel's refusal to relinquish the Torah, the very emblem of its distinctiveness, was nothing less than an act of idolatry, because God had destined Jesus Christ to be the sacrifice for sins and the gateway of salvation for all races (Rom 3:25–26). "In their rejection of Christ in the gospel," confirms Beker, "the Jews manifest that they have failed to understand the promise and the demand of the Torah. They have construed the Torah as a domain of segregation from the rest of mankind, as a tool that isolates God's grace as if it is the possession of a special people."[48] Since, in Paul's estimation, this is so, for Israel to take an inflexible stance with regard to the "old things" which have now passed away (2 Cor 5:17; cf. Gal 2:18) is for it to exalt the Torah to a status it was never intended to have in the long-range purposes of God; it was to make the law an end in itself rather than a means to an end, viz., the coming of (the) faith (Gal 3:23–25). To phrase it another way, what Israel was seeking in the Torah Paul found in Christ.

III. Summary

In Rom 2:22, Paul questions whether his Jewish kinsmen, who abhor idols, are not themselves guilty of idolatry, i.e., the idolatry of elevating the law of Moses to a position of unwarranted devotion and bestowing on it a permanence it was never intended to have in God's ultimate plan.[49] Over against Israel, which perceived itself as the guardian of the traditions (Sir 1:15; 'Abot 1:1; Rom 3:2) and, consequently, would not loosen its grip on an unmodified Torah,[50] Paul saw in Jesus of Nazareth both the goal and the termination of the law. Hence, the only distinction to survive the resurrection is that of faith and unbelief as respects him, God's Christ.[51] In this light, Israel's preference for the law to the exclusion of Christ could for Paul be nothing less than ἱεροσυλεῖν, an act of sacrilege.[52] It is these respective attitudes, we shall argue, which shape to a considerable degree the discussion of the "the obedience of faith" in the Roman letter.

---

[48] Beker, *Paul*, 336.

[49] According to Beker, the Torah in first-century Judaism was not only a moral code but actually gained "ontological status:" "It summarizes everything that makes Israel 'special' as the people of the election, but it has become as well the first creation of God and the reason for – and pattern of – his creation of the world.... The ontological status of the Torah epitomizes God's exclusive self-revelation to Israel and has universal-cosmic status" (*Paul*, 260–61). See further my *Obedience*, 38 (with literature).

[50] See Davies, *Torah*, 84; Banks, *Jesus*, 67–85 (esp. pp. 79–81); Räisänen, *Paul*, 261.

[51] Minear, *Obedience*, 48.

[52] Paul perhaps chose this verb (in its broader sense) to avoid the connotations of actual idol-worship inherent in the εἴδωλον family of words.

Chapter Three
The Obedience of Faith and the Doers of the Law

The first chapter of this study was an attempt to determine exegetically the meaning of ὑπακοὴ πίστεως within the Roman letter. It was concluded that the phrase is deliberately ambiguous, denoting simultaneously the obedience which is faith and the obedience which is the product of faith, with the prime stress, in the latter instance, falling on perseverance. The second chapter presented the case that faith's obedience stands in contrast to the disobedience of Israel, i.e, its idolatrous attachment to the Torah, whose effect was exclusion from Christ. It is against this backdrop that we come now to argue that the ideology contained in "the obedience of faith" provides an essential clue in resolving a perennial problem in the interpretation of Paul, viz., how he can make what appears to be a quantum leap from present justification by faith alone to future justification which entails an assessment of "the things done in the body, whether good or worthless" (2 Cor 5:10).[1] While Paul is adamant that it is faith alone which justifies here and now, he is equally insistent that it is the "doers of the law," Rom 2:13, who will be justified in eschatological judgment.[2] As Cosgrove rightly stresses, *justification*, not simply judgment, belongs not only at the beginning of life in Christ but also at its final consummation: there are, in fact, two moments of justification.[3] In addressing the problem, we shall argue that it is none other than "faith's obedience" which bridges the gap between these seemingly polar opposites.

---

[1] On the problem, see Cosgrove, "Justification," 653–56. Of course, the idea of final judgment according to behavior is not unique to Romans 2, as per Matt 12:36–37; 16:27; 25:31–46; 1 Cor 9:24–27; Col 3:25; 2 Tim 4:14; 1 Pet 1:17; Rev 2:23.

[2] Faith/obedience/judgment in Paul is well-worn territory. For works devoted to faith and obedience, see my *Obedience*, 2, nn. 5, 6. The judgment motif has been canvassed, e.g., in the works of Mattern, *Verständnis*; Kertelge, *"Rechtfertigung,"* 134–43; Roetzel, *Judgment*; Cambier, "jugement;" Donfried, "Justification;" Cosgrove, "Justification;" Synofzik, *Aussagen*, esp. 78–90; Wilckens, *Römer* 1.142–46; N.M. Watson, "Justified;" F. Watson, *Paul*, 119–22; Snodgrass, "Justification;" Heiligenthal, *Werke*, esp. 165–97; Hultgren, *Gospel*, 98–111; Kreitzer, *Jesus*, 99–129; Berkouwer, *Justification*, 103–12. All these treatments approximate the present one in their recognition of the importance of "the obedience of faith" for the judgment texts in Paul.

[3] Cosgrove, "Justification," 660–61, 654, 670. This is sufficient reason to qualify Schrenk's claim that Paul never discusses justification in relation to final judgment (*TDNT* 2.208). In fact, Schrenk himself later acknowledges that Paul links δικαιόω with the last judgment (ibid., 217).

I. Paul's Dialogue with Israel in Romans 1:1–3:8

As we recall, one of Paul's prime purposes in Romans is to redefine the people of God by redrawing the boundaries which distinguish them.[4] Whereas once to be a member of the covenant people was to live within the perimeters set by the Torah, the eschatological people have assumed a new corporate identity. And since with the advent of Jesus Christ there is "no distinction" between Jew and Gentile, Paul seeks in Romans to expound the social and ethical expressions of this new entity. At the outset (1:1–7), then, he draws upon concepts evocative of Israel's relationship to Yahweh and applies them to *all* the Romans, the κλητοί of Jesus Christ. The pivotal point of the introduction is v. 5 – the obedience of faith among all the nations for Christ's name's sake – "A neat and fitting summary of his complete apologetic in Romans."[5]

The letter's opening paragraph is paralleled by 1:16–17,[6] which is normally perceived to be the letter's thematic statement. However, in distinction to many traditional approaches to Romans, I take the theme to be *the revelation of the righteousness of God in the gospel to all who believe* – the Jew first but also the Greek. As such, 1:16–17 is the functional equivalent of 1:5, "the obedience of faith among all the nations." As modern research has demonstrated, δικαιοσύνη is essentially a relational concept.[7] As predicated of God, it is his fidelity to the covenant with Israel: "God is 'righteous' when he fulfills the obligations he took upon himself to be Israel's God, that is, to rescue Israel and punish Israel's enemies."[8] As is well-known, in the Psalms and the Prophets God's righteousness is synonymous with his salvation, i.e., his deliverance of

---

[4] The redefinition motif takes us to the heart of the Roman letter. To pick up on a suggestion of R. B. Hays (*Echoes*, 53), on its most basic level Romans is a theodicy, i.e., Paul justifies the faithfulness of God to Israel, notwithstanding his reception of the Gentiles by *faith alone* and the apparent abandonment of his promises to Israel. "Romans demonstrates," according to Beker, "that the question of God's faithfulness to Israel is answered in the gospel, and the affirmation of God's faithfulness demonstrates in turn the reliability of God's act in Christ for the salvation of the Gentiles" (*Paul*, 151). Thus, by redefining the people, Paul is able to justify God, because his intention all along was to keep faith with a community newly formed after the clay (the old Israel) spoiled in the potter's hand (9:20–21 = Isa 29:16; 45:9; esp. Jer 18:1–11). In this light, Romans 9–11, as anticipated by 1:16 ("the Jew first") and 3:1–8, ought to be regarded as both the center and pinnacle of the letter. Perhaps the most succinct statement of Paul's theodicy is 3:26: God remains righteous even while justifying (καὶ δικαιοῦντα) the one who has faith (alone) in Jesus. As Davies notes, δικαιοσύνη θεοῦ accents God's faithfulness in keeping his promises (*Faith*, 36).

[5] Dunn, *Romans* 1.18.

[6] Common to both are: Jew/Gentile, the gospel, faith, obedience/righteousness, and power.

[7] See, among others, Hultgren, *Gospel*, 12–46; Käsemann "Righteousness," 172; Kertelge, *"Rechtfertigung,"* 15–24; Hill, *Words*, 85–86; Reumann, *Righteousness*, 12; Von Rad, *Genesis*, 185; McGrath, *Justification*; Wright, "Justification;" id., "Righteousness."

[8] Dunn, *Romans* 1.41. Cf. Eichrodt, *Theology* 1.241–42. Accounts of research on "the righteousness of God" are supplied, among many others, by Stuhlmacher, *Gerechtigkeit*, 11–73; Brauch, "Perspectives;" Williams, "Righteousness," 241–45; Fung, "Justification."

Israel from bondage and his vindication of it in the presence of its enemies.[9] His δικαιοσύνη (צדקה/צדק), in short, is his "act to restore his own and to sustain them within the covenant,"[10] arising out of his prior commitment to them.[11] Thus, the δικαιοσύνη θεοῦ which has *now* been manifested apart from the law (Rom 3:21) is "God's action on behalf of those to whom he has committed himself."[12] In Paul's estimation, of course, God has pledged himself equally to Gentiles as to Jews, requiring in return their commitment of faith/faithfulness as defined in terms of the new covenant rather than the old.

This dynamic or "action-oriented" understanding of righteousness (as opposed to "status" only)[13] has a twofold bearing on our particular concern. For one thing, it supports our contention that the controversy between Paul and Judaism had respect not to "grace" vs. "legalism" in the commonly accepted

---

[9] E.g., Pss 35:27–28; 72:1–4; 85:11–13; 96:13; 98:2–3, 9; Isa 9:7; 11:1–2; 45:8, 22–25; 51:5–6; 53:10b–11; 61:1–2, 11; Jer 23:5–6; Mal 4:2. See further Motyer, "Righteousness," 35–36. The equation of righteousness with vindication perhaps lies behind those passages in the DSS which ascribe the sectary's משפט to God alone, in spite of his own personal unworthiness (1QS 11:1–3, 5, 11–12, 13–15; 1QH 4:30–33; 7:30–31; 13:17; 15:12–25). While משפט is not necessarily to be translated "justification" (Fitzmyer, "Justification," 201, with other literature), it may well mean "judgment" in the sense of "vindication." In this case, the outlook of the Scrolls is not really so divergent from the Pauline perspective. More than anything else, it is a question of who may rest assured of Yahweh's saving vindication in the judgment: Is it the members of the sect or "all" – including Gentiles – who simply trust in Christ? Cf. Garlington, *Obedience*, 266–67.

[10] Dunn, *Romans* 1.41. As Käsemann ("Righteousness") argues so forcefully, in Christ God's covenant fidelity relates to all his creatures. Williams' proposal that a leading connotation of δικαιοσύνη θεοῦ (in Rom 1:16–17, Romans 4, and Galatians 3) is God's faithfulness in keeping his promise to Abraham ("Righteousness," esp. 263–70, 278–89) simply confirms the point, because, according to Romans 4, the true seed of Abraham are those who walk in the footsteps of the believing patriarch, whether circumcised or uncircumcised. Williams, then, is correct that δικαιοσύνη has to do with "God's faithfulness to his promises to Abraham, promises which focus upon the eschatological gathering of all the nations into the people of God" (ibid., 270). Paul thus "shatters the Mosaic covenant as the context of the promises of God" (p. 269). However, in wishing to distance himself from Käsemann's connection of righteousness with new covenant and new creation (*Romans*, 79–80; "Righteousness," 177–82), he simply begs the question by asserting that new covenant language is absent from Romans and that new creation ideas are never connected with "righteousness of God" (p. 269, n. 83). We shall see in chapters 4 and 5 that creation in particular forms the substructure of Romans 5–8 as a whole, of which righteousness is certainly a distinguishing feature.

[11] The familiar debate as to whether the genitive θεοῦ is subjective or objective is basically pointless, as is the dispute whether δικαιόω means "declare righteous" or "make righteous." This is so because righteousness in its substantival, adjectival, and verbal forms speaks of a relationship comprehensive of more than one idea at the same time (cf. Dunn, *Romans* 1.41–42). Nevertheless, if stress should be placed on one aspect of δικαιοσύνη θεοῦ in Rom 1:17, it would be on the subjective factor, indicative of both God's *attribute* of covenant fidelity and his consequent *action* to save Israel.

[12] Dunn, *Romans* 1.166 (on 3:22).

[13] Reumann, *Righteousness*, 15–16. In agreement with Hultgren, Paul's imagery of justification is more prophetic/apocalyptic (theological/theocentric) than forensic (anthropological/anthropocentric) (*Gospel*, 37).

sense of the terms but to Pauline ethnic inclusiveness as opposed to the Jewish restriction of God's covenant favor to Israel (though including proselytes). For Paul to draw upon a term so well-fixed by his Jewish heritage was, in effect, for him to say that Yahweh's pledge to uphold and sustain the ancient covenant people now has equal applicability to "the Greek," who is no longer obliged to become as "the Jew" in order to participate in the δικαιοσύνη θεοῦ.[14] As J. A. Ziesler puts it: "God's righteousness is his own covenant loyalty, now in Paul widened beyond a covenant with Israel and made universal. This righteousness is saving precisely in that man, Jew or Gentile, is now drawn into and lives in God's righteousness."[15] Consequently, *"God's* righteousness," according to Rom 3:21–22; 10:3 (Phil 3:9), is no longer peculiarly that of the Torah, but is now embodied in Christ, the τέλος of the law. Hence, justification in Paul is primarily concerned to answer the question, On whose behalf does the God of Israel act in the reclamation of his creation; is it Israel only or also the Gentiles?[16] I must add my voice to that of Stendahl, Fitzmeyer, and others: Paul employs justification as a tool for bringing down the "dividing wall of hostility" between Jew and Gentile (Eph 2:14).[17] Throughout Romans particularly, justification, along with other arguments, serves to buttress the proposition that "there is no distinction" between Jew and Gentile.

For another thing, because δικαιοσύνη assumes as its frame of reference the Hebrew (as contrasted with the Greco-Roman) notion of righteousness, we are alerted to the possibility that the semantic range of the verb δικαιόω is broadened by its relation to the Hebraic concept of the δικαιοσύνη θεοῦ.[18] According to Reumann's findings, righteousness/justice/justification terminology in the Hebrew scriptures is "action-oriented," not just "status" or "being" language, and *"binds together forensic, ethical and other aspects in such a way that some sort of more unified ancient Near Eastern view can readily be presup-*

---

[14] As K. Stendahl puts it: Paul's discussion of Jew/Gentile equality (in Romans 2 and 3) is carried on "in light of the new avenue of salvation, which has been opened in Christ, an avenue which is equally open to Jews and Gentiles, since it is not based on the Law, in which the very distinction between the two rests" (*Paul*, 81).

[15] Ziesler, *Righteousness*, 187. In Reumann's words, "The gospel of God's righteousness will have to do not just with his loyalty to his covenant people but with his whole creation and all peoples" (*Righteousness*, 65). Cf. Kaylor, *Community*, 60.

[16] This particular formulation of δικαιοσύνη θεοῦ recognizes that righteousness is both an attribute and an activity of Yahweh. Williams writes that δικαιοσύνη, as the other covenant terms אמונה, חסד, and אמת, designates the nature and being of the God who makes himself known in deeds ("Righteousness," 261–63): "... what God *is* determines what he *does*, even though what he is can be known only by what he does" (ibid., 261, n. 64).

[17] Stendahl, *Paul*, esp. 80–85; Fitzmeyer, "Justification," 205. Fitzmeyer notes that justification is entirely absent in a letter such as 1 Thessalonians because there is no trace of a Judaizing problem in the letter. Rather, the focus, I would add, is on the way the Thessalonians turned from idols to serve the "living and true God" (1:9). Cf. Motyer, "Righteousness," 34.

[18] Cf. Cosgrove, "Justification," 662. Williams ("Righteousness," 259–60), in my opinion, artificially distinguishes between δικαιόω, δικαιοσύνη, and δικαιοσύνη θεοῦ.

posed."¹⁹ "Justify" is an adequate translation of δικαιόω as long as we are mindful that more is at stake than a "heavenly decree." If God's righteousness is "his intervention in a saving act on behalf of his people," then the passive of δικαιόω means "to be an object of the saving righteousness of God (so as to be well-pleasing to him at the judgment)."²⁰

Given that actual Pauline paradigm of justification is the Psalms and the Prophets, "to be an object of the saving righteousness of God" is to be placed within a renewed covenant relationship and enabled to render to God an obedience commensurate with that relationship. It is just the passive of δικαιόω in Rom 5:1, 9 which finds its correspondent in 5:9−10, i.e., justification is tantamount to being "saved" and "reconciled." In 6:7, the use of δικαιόω ("justified from sin") stands in direct parallel to ἐλευθερόω ("liberated from sin") in 6:18. The parallel is preserved by rendering the former as "freed from sin." To this we may add Gal 2:15−21: those who have been justified in Christ (vv. 16−17) now live in him (vv. 19−20). Justification and life together constitute the δικαιοσύνη which has been procured by the death of Christ (v. 21).²¹ Moreover, "justified" in 1 Cor 6:11 finds its equivalent in "washed" and "sanctified" (cf. 1QS 11:14), all three pointing to the time when the Corinthians ceased to be what they once were outside of Christ (6:9−10).²²

It is this pregnant significance of δικαιόω which modern scholars have sought to preserve by the resurrection of the archaic term "rightwise."²³ Even in those instances in the LXX where δικαιόω (= the hiphil of צדק) is strongly forensic, Ziesler reminds us that it is forensic in the Hebrew sense, i.e., the verb signifies "restoration of the community or covenant relationship, and thus cannot be separated from the ethical altogether. The restoration is not merely to a standing, but to an existence in the relationship." As a result, "righteousness" in this scenario has reference to a vindicated *existence* conferred on a person by a gracious God. "What this means is that men live together in freedom, possessing their civil rights in a good society. *It is not just a vindicated status, but*

---

¹⁹ Reumann, *Righteousness*, 16 (italics mine).
²⁰ Motyer, "Righteousness," 48.
²¹ Cf. Longenecker, *Galatians*, 85.
²² Beasley-Murray (*Baptism*, 164−65) can say that the "sanctification" by the Spirit and "justification" by the Lord Jesus occurred at the same time − it is a once-for-all consecration Paul has in mind, not a process. Both he and G.D. Fee (*First Corinthians*, 246, n. 32) take ἐδικαιώθητε to be a look back to "unrighteous" (ἄδικοι) in vv. 1, 9, Paul's description of pagan judges and of some of the Corinthians' rather seamy past. Thus, there is more at stake than a changed status: those who had been dead are now alive; they are new creatures in a new creation. In this light, Paul's statement becomes an exhortation for Christians to live as those who are washed, sanctified, and justified.
²³ As Byrne puts it, the cross is an offer of final salvation on the basis of God's righteousness operative solely and exclusively through faith. "It is an offer of salvation because through faith human beings can come under the 'right-wising' verdict of God, be 'justified', 'acquitted' of their sins, found 'righteous' and thus, through God's grace and favor alone, worthy of eternal life" ("righteousness," 572). In place of "rightwise," Sanders opts for a somewhat unwieldy term of his own devising: "to righteous" (*Law*, 13−14, n. 18, passim).

a vindicated life."[24] Therefore, the one of whom δικαιοῦσθαι is predicated is regarded as δίκαιος, i.e., committed to the covenant and the God of the covenant in a household relationship.[25] If such is an adequate grasp of δικαιόω, insight is immediately provided into how Paul can move so deftly from justification by faith here and now to ultimate justification by "doing the law,"[26] although, in point of fact, he actually follows the opposite course in Romans: he first addresses himself, in 2:13, to the future justification of the "doers" and thereafter, in 3:21—4:25, to present justification by faith. It is as though he states his conclusion first and afterwards provides its premise.

These perspectives are confirmed by Paul's application of two central OT texts to his Romans readers, Hab 2:4 (1:17) and Gen 15:6 (4:3—12; cf. Gal 3:6—9). Hab 2:4 is addressed to the righteous Israelite who, through continued allegiance to Yahweh's covenant, will survive the impending judgment upon a largely apostate people and return to the land in a new exodus deliverance. This is the "righteous" person who lives "out of ["by," in the Hebrew of Hab 2:4] his faith(fulness)." In agreement with Davies and a number of commentators, ἐκ πίστεως, in the construction ὁ δίκαιος ἐκ πίστεως ζήσεται, is to be construed with ζήσεται rather than ὁ δίκαιος. Paul, as the prophet, asserts that a life of faith(fulness) characterizes the pious. "The description of such a person as 'righteous' is necessarily derived from God (cf. 5.19), indeed from God's righteousness, yet the accent of the verse falls upon that person living by faith." "In short," Davies continues, "the state of righteousness for the believer has ethical implications: the obedience of faith."[27] Notwithstanding an element of discontinuity between Habakkuk and Paul,[28] the apostle's citation of Hab 2:4 establishes that the same principle of faithful obedience has always been operative in covenant life.[29] In this regard, the faithful of Israel and the faithful of the Pauline churches are at heart one. Before Paul ever comes to his first employment of the verb δικαιόω in Romans (2:13), he has established a

---

[24] Ziesler, *Righteousness*, 20, 25 (italics mine). Cf. Kertelge, *"Rechtfertigung,"* 113—20; Beker, *Paul*, 263—64; Fitzmeyer, "Justification," 198; Reumann, *Righteousness*, 16; Longenecker, *Galatians*, 84—85. Likewise Käsemann ("Righteousness," 172), who says that in the OT and Judaism generally δικαιοσύνη has in view the relations of community members: "originally signifying trustworthiness in regard to the community, it came to mean *the rehabilitated standing of a member of the community who had been acquitted of an offense against it*" (italics mine).

[25] Cf. Schrenk, *TDNT* 2.185, 189.

[26] Cf. Motyer, "Righteousness," 51, 55.

[27] Davies, *Faith*, 38. He notes that Rabbi Simlai summarized the 613 commands of the Torah into one: "the righteous shall live by faith" (*Mak.* 23b). It is significant that Hab 2:5—17 speaks of various vices which characterize the enemies of Israel and are to be renounced by the righteous. These vices, in typical Jewish fashion, are connected with idolatry (vv. 18—19).

[28] The shock effect for the Jew of Paul's usage of Habakkuk is that πίστις (אמונה) is now detachable from the Torah. Paul thus stands in obvious juxtaposition to 1QpHab 8:1—3 (cf. CD 20:27—34), where faith in the Teacher of Righteousness as the authoritative expounder of *the law* is said to be the fulfillment of Hab 2:4. Cf. Gunther, *Opponents*, 257; Garlington, *Obedience*, 257—58, n. 22.

[29] Davies, *Faith*, 42—43.

framework for its interpretation, viz., the well-known principle that the righteous person will be delivered from his enemies by virtue of steadfast commitment to the Lord.

Indispensable to understanding Paul's employment of the other passage, Gen 15:6, is its function within its own context. At first glance (or blush), the student of Paul notices – or should notice – that Gen 15:6 is not "forensic" as postulated by Protestant theology. Rather than being Abraham's "justification" in the sense of his "conversion," this declaration serves to confirm the patriarch's already existent faith in God's promise concerning an heir. Genesis 15 is hardly the beginning of God's dealings with Abraham, because a trusting relationship between the two has been operative since Gen 12:1–9.[30] Whatever else we say about Gen 15:6, its declaration that Abraham believed Yahweh forms a climactic moment in the patriarch's sojourn of faith. It is not unexpected, then, that Reformed scholars such as Ridderbos think that Paul uses the text in a sense other than its original one.[31] However, a less expedient alternative is readily at hand.

With an adjusted conception on our part of Paul's purposes in Romans 4 and Galatians 3, his appeal to the original significance of Gen 15:6 makes perfectly good sense on its own terms. The goal of his argument in both letters is to establish that Abraham is the prototype of those who now believe in Christ, the children who "walk in the footsteps" of their progenitor (Rom 4:12). Rom 4:9–17a is thus adamant that the blessing of Abraham is in no way contingent on the patriarch's adherence to the law, in contradistinction to the pre-Christian Jewish traditions which assert that he actually kept the Torah before Sinai.[32] Abraham is to Paul the paradigm of all who look to Christ in faith alone, not to the Torah, as the source of salvation and fidelity to God. In him, *the uncircumcised believer in the promises of God*, the nations find the embodiment covenant loyalty. Along similar lines, Gal 3:1–5 adduces the Galatians' experience of the Spirit as proof positive that they have entered the new age. Immediately, in vv. 6–9, Abraham is cited not as a mere example of Christian (mainly Gentile) believers but as one who was qualitatively in the same position as they; that is, he was declared by God to be a covenant keeper, one faithful to the promise concerning the seed, quite irrespective of circumcision and the law of Moses.[33]

---

[30] "Apparently the narrator intends to represent Abraham's departure [to Canaan] as a paradigmatic test of faith" (Von Rad, *Genesis*, 166). The author of Hebrews certainly understood this to be the intention (11:8). We might say that Genesis 12, 15, and 22 are the peaks of Abraham's experience of "the obedience [perseverance] of faith."

[31] Ridderbos, *Paul*, 176–78. Paul, for Ridderbos, gives the words of Gen 15:6 a different shade of meaning by "translating" them into "the judicial-legalistic way of thinking of later Judaism" (ibid., 177).

[32] See Hansen, *Abraham*, 175–99; Siker, *Jews*, 17–27; Davies, *Faith*, 143–47; Garlington, *Obedience*, 37–40, 104, 119–120.

[33] The Hebrew idiom of Gen 15:6, חשׁב ל, as rendered by λογίζομαι εἰς, means to consider a thing to be true and thereby to allow it to stand to the credit of someone (Von Rad, "Faith"). Thus, in Rom 4:3, 5, 9, 10, faith is considered to be righteousness = covenant fidelity, i.e.,

Because the underlying issue in Genesis is Abraham's unreserved faith(fulness) in times of testing, we may infer that he is portrayed in Romans and Galatians not only as the model of the Gentiles who have turned to Christ apart from circumcision, etc., but also as the "forefather" (Rom 4:1) of all those who cling to God's promise respecting his coming salvation.[34] No wonder, by the time Paul reaches v. 17b of Romans 4, he begins to play up the persevering quality of Abraham's faith. In short, Abraham is living proof of "the obedience of faith."

Having stated his thesis that the δικαιοσύνη θεοῦ is now available to all without distinction,[35] Paul proceeds in 1:18−3:20 (including the recapitulating statement of 3:23) to eliminate Jewish superiority by a series of arguments designed to place Israel on an equal footing with the remainder of humanity.[36] Kaylor has correctly seen that although Paul does indeed address himself to the reality of universal human sinfulness, his central design is to show that there is *no real distinction between Gentile and Jew*: "This affirmation of non-distinction in sinfulness has as its larger purpose the affirmation that there is no distinction in salvation! There is one new covenant that unites Jew and Gentile as the one people of God."[37] Paul's message to Israel, then, is that the Torah is powerless to provide freedom from sin's power.[38] In so saying, he is "preparing the way for the presentation of one new covenant in Christ which will bind Jew and Gentile together as one new people of God, renewed by God's grace and empowered by the Spirit to fulfill God's will in ways that neither Gentile nor Jew has been able to accomplish."[39]

The first item of his agenda is pursued in 1:18−32, where, as we have seen, he implicates Israel in the disobedience = idolatry of Adam, thereby reducing the covenant people to the level of Greco-Roman paganism. Thereafter Rom 2:1−3:8 forms the central section of the broader division of 1:18−3:20. Considering the amount of space Paul devotes to Israel here, it would follow, as remarked above, that his actual intention is to remove the nation from a position of superiority, particularly as this segment of the letter is the outgrowth of 1:18−32 (διό, 2:1). Before turning his attention directly to the one who "calls

---

faith alone (in Christ) is accepted by God in the place of full-orbed commitment to the covenant, which, of course, for first-century Judaism was inseparable from the Torah; hence, the irony of Paul's application of the passage. Even where righteousness is said to be reckoned directly to the believer (vv. 6, 11), Paul is probably using a shorthand version of the longer "reckon faith as righteousness." In any event, δικαιοσύνη continues to bear its normal OT connotations.

[34] Gal 5:5 maintains that Christians, as Abraham, look forward to a consummation of the promise, i.e. "the hope of righteousness." In its own way, Gal 5:5 is the analogue of Rom 2:13. See Kertelge, *"Rechtfertigung,"* 147−51.

[35] "All" throughout Romans bears a strongly qualitative sense, i.e., "all God's beloved in Rome" (1:7), Jew and Gentile in Christ (as documented by Minear's *Obedience*).

[36] Kaylor (*Community*, 32) terms this section "Gentile and Jew: Alike in Covenant Breaking."

[37] Ibid., 34.

[38] Ibid., 35.

[39] Ibid., 45−46.

himself a Jew" (2:17),[40] the groundwork is laid in vv. 1–16 for the indictment of Israel. Before giving detailed consideration to 2:13, it will be useful to survey the main features of 2:1–3:8.

At the outset of chap. 2 (vv. 1–5), Paul continues to speak in broad generic terms: his adversary is humankind as such (ὦ ἄνθρωπε), vv. 1, 3. Even so, he is occupied with man as he stands in judgment on other humans. That Jewish man is in the back of his mind is evident from vv. 17–24, because it is he who charges others with sin, while not free of sin's taint himself. The Jew, who believed that God would judge the world "in righteousness" (Pss 9:8; 96:13; 98:2, 9), himself will be the object of wrath, the punitive side of righteousness,[41] because the judgment of God is "according to *truth*" (v. 2), which, like *righteousness*, is God's covenant *faithfulness*.[42] It is the Jew, who is presumptuous in his judgment of others, who must acknowledge that the goodness of God (especially in the gospel) is meant to lead *him* to repentance (v. 4);[43] it is *he* who is delinquent in his responsibility to the Creator (see below). Cambier, then, is quite right that the situation envisaged by Paul is that of the Jewish exclusivist claim to salvation, as reflected by his vocabulary of judgment (various forms of κρίνω).[44]

The principle of judgment according to works, commensurate with judgment "according to truth,"[45] introduced in vv. 6–16, becomes in Paul's hands an implement for undoing Israel's boasting in national privileges. This is ironic because a whole host of Jewish texts lie behind the proposition that "he will

---

[40] See Wilckens, *Römer* 1.147–48.

[41] Rom 1:17's declaration that the righteousness of God is revealed in the gospel alludes to Ps 98:2, 9: "The Lord has made known his salvation; before the nations he has revealed his righteousness... for he comes to judge the earth; he will judge the world in righteousness and the peoples with uprightness." Not only so, the same Psalm underlies Rom 1:18's programmatic statement that the wrath of God is being revealed from heaven. Accordingly, the wrath which Israel expected to fall on the Gentiles because of their lack of conformity to the Mosaic standards will fall on it because it refuses to render to God the obedience of faith which has Christ as its object: it, in other words, will not submit to the righteousness of God (10:3) as revealed eschatologically in the gospel. Cf. Davies, *Faith*, 75–79.

[42] The ἀλήθεια group in the LXX frequently does service for אמונה, etc., designating God's fidelity to the covenant. Particularly striking are passages in which God's ἀλήθεια represents his determination to punish Israel for breaking the covenant, e.g., Neh 9:33; Pr Azar 4–5, 8–9; Tob 3:2; Add Esth 14:6–7; 1QS 1:26. See further Williams, "Righteousness," 268; Marcus, *Law*, 3–4; Roetzel, *Judgment*, 32.

[43] The riches of God's kindness is a prominent covenant idea (cf. Rom 10:21 = Isa 65:2 [LXX]). As the Israel of old, the Israel of Paul's day remains the object of Yahweh's pleading: his goodness is still being extended to his people, this time in the preaching of Jesus Christ. Yet, in typical fashion, the nation's heart is hard and impenitent (v. 5). As a sidelight, what is known to theology as "common grace" is actually the δικαιοσύνη θεοῦ, God's commitment to his covenant and ultimately to his creation, the concrete manifestation of which is his "goodness," designed to lead the disobedient to repentance (cf. Acts 14:17).

[44] Cambier, "jugement," 189.

[45] As Cambier demonstrates ("jugement," 188), the twofold center of interest, works and truth, is established at the outset of chap. 2 in vv. 1 and 2 and then continued into vv. 6–16: works (2:6, 11) correspond to the judgment of the inner person (vv. 9–16).

render to everyone according to his works."[46] Indeed, the idea of judgment taking stock of works is one of the most basic assumptions of Judaism and appears in all strata of Jewish literature.[47] But what appears on the surface to be a riddle is explicable by Paul's consistent use of creation imagery in his definition of the "works" according to which God will judge as the quest for "glory, honor, and immortality." In other words, to those inclined to complete this original Adamic mandate will be given "eternal life" and "peace" (vv. 7, 10). Likewise, the talk of "obedience" in v. 8, as confirmed by the Adam/Christ analogy of 5:12–19, implies that the vindicating judgment of the last day is not conditioned on Jewishness but on one's commitment to be an accurate image-bearer of God the Creator, a possibility for *any* who trace their lineage back to Adam.[48] Thus, the "righteousness" in which God will judge the world predates the Torah and takes one back to the time when there was no Jew/Gentile divide. Vv. 10–11, which glance at 1:16–17, make it explicit that "glory, honor, and peace" are for *"everyone* who does good, the Jew first and also the Greek." If we may cite Luke's report of Peter's words to Cornelius: "Truly I perceive that God shows no partiality, but in every nation anyone who fears him and performs righteousness [ἐργαζόμενος δικαιοσύνην] is acceptable to him" (Acts 10:34–35).[49]

Vv. 12–16 develop the proposition that the possession of the law is in itself no guarantee against wrath in the day of judgment; what is required is obedience to the law, which Romans as a whole clarifies to be "the obedience of faith." Thus, Gentiles, who have the law written on their hearts, are qualitatively in the same position as Israel. The focus is on that law which transcends Sinai and finds its origin in creation. It is this law that the Gentiles can do "by nature" (φύσει), i. e., as the image of God. Once more, Paul levels humanity by means of creation ideas; in this instance, by the law inscribed on Adam's heart.

Rom 2:17–3:8 approaches the subject along the lines of a synagogue debate.[50] Drawing upon the perspective established in 2:1–3, 2:17–24 judges

---

[46] See Heiligenthal, *Werke*, 148–51, 172–75; Cranfield, *Romans* 1.146; Snodgrass, "Justification," 90, n. 44; Cosgrove, "Justification," 659.

[47] Snodgrass, "Justification," 77. See his assemblage of passages (ibid., 90, n. 38). Byrne adds: "Paul's grace-vision is not to injure one bit the ethical seriousness of the Jewish tradition presupposed in Romans" ("Righteousness," 563).

[48] Paul thus denies a role to the Torah in eschatological judgment by assigning that function to the primal Creator/creature relationship established in Eden. This in itself informs us that the focus of judgment is loyalty to or apostasy from God the Creator (not one's allegiance or lack thereof to the Sinai covenant).

[49] Davies reminds us that in the OT fearing God is closely linked to trusting God: "Peter here is describing the two features of faith and obedience which identify those who are in relationship with God" (*Faith*, 56, n. 3). Cf. Garlington, *Obedience*, 19–20, 187.

[50] It is common to ascribe Paul's stylistics to the Greek diatribe (e.g., Stowers, *Diatribe*; Porter, "Argument;" Moo, *Romans*, 124–25). But while diatribal elements may be present, Jeremias ("Gedankenführung," 269–71) and Ridderbos (*Romeinen*, 12–13), in my view, are closer to the mark: in Romans Paul takes us into the synagogue and allows us to witness his actual presentation of the gospel to Israel. Ridderbos (ibid., 12) says that the letter provides a

the Jew guilty of the very things of which he accuses others. We find here the reversal of those passages in Jewish literature which tie morality to Israel's segregation from the nations.[51] Then vv. 25–29 move from the realm of "morals" into that of the "boundary markers" of Israel, specifically circumcision.[52] The argument is to similar effect as in vv. 12–16, viz., circumcision in itself is no preventive against the judgment of God, because the uncircumcised person who keeps the law will be regarded as circumcised. In addition, for the first time in Romans Paul speaks of the "true Jew" as one who is identified by means of internal not external (nationalistic) realities.[53] Anticipating 7:6, where the antithesis of "Spirit" and "letter" likewise comes to the fore, 2:29 places the genuine Jew within the realm of the Spirit, i.e., the era of the Spirit's work in the eschaton. From now on, Jewishness is defined in relation to the *new creation*, and effectively to Christ, the Lord who is the Spirit (2 Cor 3:17).

Rom 3:1–8 carries the dialogue with Israel to a final step. Paul here qualifies that being Jewish does indeed have advantages, particularly as regards being entrusted with the "oracles of God" (cf. Sir 1:15; '*Abot* 1:1). Yet this is so only if Israel is faithful, which Paul denies, at least in the case of "some" (v. 3). This rejection of Israel's claim to faithfulness makes sense in light of the charge of idolatry in 2:22, i.e., his compatriots have not been loyal to the only God after all, inasmuch as they have allowed the Torah to usurp the place reserved for his Son.[54] Therefore, their peculiar glorying in the Torah is renounced by Paul (2:17, 23; 3:27), since, ironically, it is the emblem of their disobedience, not

---

clear example of διαλέγεσθαι, Luke's term to describe Paul's debates in the synagogues of the Diaspora (Acts 17:2, 17; 18:4, 19; 19:8, 9). Cf. Hengel, *Paul*, 134, n. 238. Correlative to this is Hengel's observation that Paul seeks to refute the teaching which once was obligatory for him with the very methods learned in the "Pharisaic school" (ibid., 48). The practical importance of this observation is that Paul ties into the Jewish tradition which presupposes an intrinsic link between righteousness and the gaining of eternal life (Byrne, "Righteousness," 558, 571).

[51] E.g., *Ep. Arist.* 139–43; Josephus, *Ag. Ap.* 2.169–75; Philo, *Mos.* 1.278; *Jub.* 22:16; *Pss. Sol.* 17:28; 3 Macc 3:4. The outlook articulated so clearly by these individual passages is characteristic of entire documents, such as Judith, the Additions to Esther, and the Qumran corpus.

[52] The importance of circumcision can hardly be exaggerated. To illustrate, the author of *Jubilees* (15:25, 28–29) merges the Abrahamic and Sinai covenants, with the "sign" of the former functioning as that of the latter too, which was actually the sabbath (Exod 31:12). Betz ("Beschneidung," 718–19) shows how some later authors equated circumcision with law-obedience, even to the extent of identifying "the blood of the covenant" (Exod 24:8) with "the blood of circumcision." From Stern's *Jews* it is evident that although other ancient peoples practiced circumcision, the Jews were preeminently "the circumcised." See in addition Garlington, *Obedience*, 88, 103–5, 261–62; Dunn, *Partings*, 28–29 (and n. 45 for further literature), 124–27.

[53] See Davies, *Faith*, 67–70.

[54] Gal 4:3, 8–11 draw a parallel between the Galatians' former bondage to idols and their desire to embrace the bondage of the Mosaic law; the latter is no better than the former. Moo is right that Israel, in Rom 3:1–8, is indicted for factual transgression of the law (*Romans*, 126). However, its transgression, as that of the Gentiles, is rooted in idolatry. Therefore, Paul's "main indictment" (Moo) does pertain to "covenantal nomism" and Israel's failure to live up to its commitment to Yahweh.

obedience.⁵⁵ When judged by the criterion of fidelity to the Creator (κατὰ ἀλήθειαν, 2:2), the Jew is as guilty as the Gentile. Stephen's anti-temple polemic (esp. Acts 7:39–53) is to the same effect: his executioners, in their devotion to the temple, are as guilty of idolatry as their forefathers in the wilderness!⁵⁶

The flow of thought of 1:1–3:8, as briefly surveyed here, must be allowed to provide the necessary framework for understanding the justification of "the doers" in 2:13, because of the essence of grasping the relation of works and final judgment in Paul is an awareness of the direction in which his thought moves as he pens these words (and like statements elsewhere). The upshot is that the actual subject matter of this lengthy section of the letter is Paul's response to the inbred nationalism of his Jewish contemporaries, the gist of which is his denial that they actually occupy the uniquely favored position supposed by them. Hence, the mentality against which he argues is not that of a "legalistic" works-righteousness method of salvation but one which would confine (eschatological) salvation to the members of a "private reserve" – Israel.⁵⁷

It is in view of these data that Cosgrove's analysis of justification language in Paul takes on added relevance. In the main, his study has adequately demonstrated that the apostle characteristically construes δικαιόω with prepositions indicating instrumentality, not evidential basis.⁵⁸ In his words: "The question never becomes whether one can be justified *on the basis of* the law or works but remains always whether one can be justified in the sphere of the law."⁵⁹ Most pointedly, as I attempt to adapt Cosgrove's findings, the thrust of Paul's argumentation in Romans (and Galatians) is that remaining within the sphere of the Sinai covenant has become irrelevant as regards eschatological justification. Indeed, it can be the greatest stumbling block to justification, because determined allegiance to the Torah obstructs one's view of Christ, the τέλος of the law. Hence, Israel cannot be justified *within the arena of* or, in more conventional terms, *by means of* the law (covenantal nomism), because the law thus implemented excludes one from Christ.⁶⁰

In short, because such is the real issue under debate, we are prevented from prejudging that there was in Paul's mind a necessary contradiction between doing good in this life and justification in final judgment. In other words, an attempt on Paul's part to circumvent a "legalistic" understanding of justification is simply out of accord with the aim pursued by him.⁶¹

---

⁵⁵ Cf. Davies, *Faith*, 134–35.
⁵⁶ See Kilgallen, *Speech*, 90–98; Dunn, *Partings*, 64–67.
⁵⁷ Käsemann, "Abraham," 88.
⁵⁸ Cosgrove, "Justification," esp. 654–61. Perhaps he is most vulnerable to criticism in the case of ἐξ ἔργων νόμου. It is at least plausible that ἐκ, indicative of source, can, given certain assumptions, speak of the basis of justification. However, in itself ἐκ specifies only the matrix or starting point of justification.
⁵⁹ Ibid., 662.
⁶⁰ Cf. Räisänen, *Paul*, 177.
⁶¹ Cf. Dunn, *Partings*, 123–24.

II. The Justification of the Doers of the Law: Romans 2:13

Because Rom 2:13 must be seen as part of an integral whole, it will be necessary to say something in more detail about the verses immediately preceding and following.[62]

The *entrée* into v. 13 is provided by vv. 6–12, which state the principle of judgment by works; this forms Paul's rebuttal to the presumptuous person who judges others (ὁ κρίνων, vv. 1–5).[63] In other words, this ἄνθρωπος will not escape condemnation precisely because God is an impartial judge, whose verdict is κατὰ ἀλήθειαν (v. 2): he will render to every man according to his deeds (v. 6). With Ps 62:12; Prov 24:12 in mind, Paul pens what in and of itself was a perfectly acceptable dictum to first-century Judaism. Indeed, the notion of the vindication of the faithful is one of the commonplaces of Jewish thought (e.g., 2 Macc 7:9; 4 Macc 17:11–12; Tob 4:9–11; *Pss. Sol.* 9:3–5). The Jew would have understood eschatological justification to be the inevitable outcome of his believing observance of covenant obligations and privileges, integral to which was God's provision of sacrifice to cover the sins of his people and restore them to fellowship with himself. Correspondingly, the nations are to be condemned because of their rejection of these standards.

That Paul has something else in mind, however, is indicated by the creation phraseology of v. 7: τοῖς καθ' ὑπομονὴν ἔργου ἀγαθοῦ δόξαν καὶ τιμὴν καὶ ἀφθαρσίαν ζητοῦσιν ἀποδώσει ζωὴν αἰώνιον. That is to say, consonant with 1:18–3:20, the standard of judgment is one which bypasses the Sinai covenant and roots the vindication of the individual in matters which pertain to humanity as such, not simply *Jewish* humanity.

The combination of "glory" and "honor" recalls Ps 8:5's depiction of man's (Adam's) creation (cf. Job 40:10). "Glory" stands by itself in 1:23 and 3:23: both times it designates the obverse of the quest delineated in 2:7. In the former, man outside of Christ has rejected the glory of Yahweh for the sake of idols, while in the latter he has failed to measure up to his capacity as God's image (glory).[64]

"Immortality" (ἀφθαρσία) in the LXX occurs only in Wisdom and 4 Maccabees. Wis 2:23 is particularly relevant: "God created man for immortality [ἐφ' ἀφθαρσίᾳ], and made him the image of his own eternity." This not only gives voice to the author's conception of man's reason for existence, it places in parallel the ideas of immortality and image: man is God's image by virtue of his capacity for endless life. 4 Macc 17:12, especially striking in view of Paul's present argument, makes "the prize for victory" of the Jewish martyrs "immortality in long-lasting life." If Paul in fact has such a conception

---

[62] See the analyses of Dunn, *Romans* 1.76–77, 89; Bassler, *Impartiality*, 121–66; Davies, *Faith*, 57–59.

[63] See Longenecker, *Eschatology*, 175.

[64] Most likely, Paul here ties into the equation of "glory" and "image" in Jewish theology. See Dunn, *Romans* 1.167–68; Kim, *Origin*, 319–20.

in mind, his appeal to immortality represents a reversal of the mentality of 4 Maccabees as a whole, which makes abstinence from pork of the essence of fidelity to God and thus a precondition of ἀφθαρσία (see especially 5:14–38). In the same vein, according to 2 Macc 6:18–20; 7:1, one ought to be willing to die rather than partake of swine's flesh. Particularly striking is the connection of such refusal and the prospect of resurrection (eternal life) in 2 Maccabees 7 in its entirety.

"Life" as a creation motif is exhibited by the prominence given the idea in the first two chapters of Genesis. Outside the NT, the exact phrase "eternal life" occurs only in Dan 12:2; 2 Macc 7:9; 4 Macc 15:3, where it is tantamount to resurrection, and in 1QS 4:7, where everlasting life (חיי נצח) is clearly in view. The term features prominently in Paul's delineation of the work of Christ and its effects in Rom 5:12–6:23. "Eternal life," then, is equivalent to the life of the age to come, i.e., resurrection and "immortality," and in effect a completion of the program commenced and yet interrupted with Adam.[65] Noteworthy is the phrase "the justification of life" (δικαίωσις ζωῆς) in 5:18. This is justification as it inevitably results in life and from which it is inseparable.

If we bring v. 10 into view, another creation term emerges, viz., "peace," which is employed by the Prophets in depicting the restoration of paradise. Yahweh's εἰρήνη (= שלום), in the prophetic hope, stands for his eschatological deliverance of Israel from its enemies and his recreation of all things; in short, "peace" is a return to the bliss of the Garden of Eden. From the NT's perspective generally, εἰρήνη is the promised final "salvation" which has now transpired historically through Jesus Christ.[66] A virtual synonym of "peace" is "rest."[67] In Gen 2:1–3, Yahweh's own rest provides the paradigm of Adam's rest to be enjoyed after the completion of his mandate to subdue the earth (Gen 1:28). With Adam's fall, however, "rest" undergoes a semantic shift and likewise becomes synonymous with the "salvation" (= new creation) procured by Christ.[68]

It is in light of these data that the adverbial phrase καθ' ὑπομονὴν ἔργου ἀγαθοῦ (v. 7) is to be given its obvious and straightforward meaning: "patient persistence in doing what is recognized to be good."[69] This speaks of the modality of humanity's quest to be all that it was intended to be in the design of the Creator. That actual (and expected) activity is envisaged is confirmed by the synonymous expressions "obeying the truth" (v. 8) and "doing good" (v. 10), as well as by the antitheses "disobeying the truth," "obeying wickedness" (v. 8), and "doing evil" (v. 9). Moreover, as Dunn further comments, the verb

---

[65] Cf. the comments of Dunn, *Christology*, 110–111.
[66] Von Rad/Foerster, *TDNT* 2.405–6, 412–15.
[67] See Hebert, *Throne*, 159–63.
[68] Lincoln, "Sabbath." Cf. the use of Ps 95:8–11 in Heb 3:7–4:13.
[69] Dunn, *Romans* 1.86. As we have seen and shall see again, the "good work" of 2:7 relates to the knowledge of good and evil in the Garden of Eden. Ultimately, this "good work" is allegiance to God the Creator and a refusal to be seduced by Satan's alternate explanation of the Creator/creature relationship (tantamount to idolatry).

ζητέω reinforces ὑπομονή: "what is in mind is a sustained and deliberate application... rather than a casual or spasmodic pursuit of the goal."[70] If we may state one of our major conclusions beforehand, it is just ὑπομονή, endurance in testing, that defines in large measure what is intended by "the obedience of faith" which issues in eschatological justification.

The effect of this evocation of the creation goal of man's existence is that "God shows no partiality" (v. 11).[71] This, in turn, opens up the way into the paragraph of vv. 12–16, where Paul's intentions surface even more clearly. The terms used by him to bifurcate the human race (from the Jewish point of view) are significant. V. 12 distinguishes between those who have sinned ἀνόμως and those who have sinned ἐν νόμῳ. Thereafter νόμος becomes the fulcrum of the discussion of final judgment (vv. 13, 14, 15). One's relation to the law, in other words, is reflective of the normal Jewish distinction between the people of God and outsiders: the Torah was to be the standard of the great assize, and according to it one would be vindicated or condemned. Thus, to be ἐν νόμῳ, i.e., Jewish,[72] was to be safe,[73] and to be ἀνόμως (μὴ ἔχοντες νόμον, v. 14), i.e., Gentile, was to be lost. Once again, while Paul speaks formally in terms acceptable to Jewish ears, he turns them to Israel's disadvantage. "His real point... is that judgment will *not* depend on whether the individual starts from within the people of the law or from outside. Both will be judged; sin in both cases will be condemned."[74]

The escalating argument of 2:6–3:8 reaches a climax when 2:13 enters the picture as an explanation of why remaining within the perimeters of the law is no insurance against the eschatological wrath of God. That is to say, the possession of the Torah, including its boundary markers of Jewish identity, is not enough: "For it is not the hearers of the law who are righteous before God, but the doers of the law will be justified." Paul, in other words, grounds immunity from the condemnation of the last day in one's performance of the law, not in pride of its ownership (as illustrated by Bar 4:3–4).

By now, it comes as no surprise that Paul draws on conceptions which in themselves were familiar to his contemporaries. The combination of "hearing"

---

[70] Ibid.

[71] On προσωπολημψία, see ibid., 1.89.

[72] On ἐν νόμῳ and similar phrases, see Dunn, *Jesus, Paul*, 221–22, 225–28. According to Dunn's assessment, "Paul is referring to the typical Jewish self-understanding of the people of God as circumcised and defined by the law, as characterized by practice of the law's distinctive features" (ibid., 228).

[73] As Sanders more than once affirms, "all Israelites have a share in the world to come unless they renounce it by transgression" (i.e., apostasy) (*Paul*, 147, citing *m. Sanh.* 10:1).

[74] Dunn, *Romans* 1.96. "What one finds in Romans 2," remarks Snodgrass, "is essentially a Jewish view of judgment, but one that is radicalized and applied to both Jew and Gentile." Snodgrass adds that Jewish texts normally accord mercy to Israel while condemning Gentiles according to their works. As for Jewish self-assessment: "The degree to which the Jews were automatically accorded mercy or were also judged according to works differs in the various writings and often depended on how much an author was pleased or displeased with his Jewish contemporaries" ("Justification," 78).

and "doing," as Dunn notes, was characteristic of Judaism. Indeed, as Wilckens affirms, the *shema* of Deut 6:4 – "Hear, O Israel" – has doing in view.[75] However, what would have sounded odd was Paul's *contrast* of the two here – hearing *versus* doing – because the respective appellations "hearers of the law" and "righteous" were complementary and overlapped in large measure:[76] hearing/believing and works are two ways of saying the same thing.[77] This leads us to infer that in driving a wedge between these interdependent components of Jewish self-definition Paul has in mind *a different kind of "doing the law,"*[78] a doing, as we shall see, commensurate with "the obedience of faith."

Significantly, the first occurrence of δικαιόω in the letter is here in 2:13, where it has reference to the future justification (δικαιωθήσονται) of οἱ ποιηταὶ τοῦ νόμου. To be sure, beginning with 3:21, Paul will explain that the ultimate vindication of the people of God has been secured by the "redemption which is in Christ Jesus" (3:24). Nevertheless, the future tense, appearing in this setting of last judgment, serves to underscore that justification properly speaking is yet to be. That "doers of the law" is to be taken at face value is confirmed by the "*parallelismus membrorum*" of 2:13a and b; that is, those who will be justified are the δίκαιοι παρὰ θεῷ. The latter phrase is steeped in the Jewish idea of conformity to the covenant, as confirmed by τὰ τοῦ νόμου and τὸ ἔργον τοῦ νόμου (2:14, 15), to which the consciences of the Gentiles bear witness.[79] Attempts have been made to deny that the perspective of Rom 2:13 is

---

[75] Wilckens, *Römer* 1.132. See also Beker, *Paul*, 268.

[76] Dunn, *Romans* 1.97. He cites Deut 4:1, 5–6, 13–14; 30:11–14; 1 Macc 2:67; 13:48; *Sib. Or.* 3:70; Philo, *Cong.* 70; *Praem.* 79; Josephus, *Ant.* 5.107, 132; 20.44. Cf. Dunn's comments on Rom 1:17 and 10:5.

[77] Much of my *Obedience* is devoted to arguing that in the pre-Christian materials hearing and doing (i.e., faith and obedience) are tantamount to each other. Thus, a first-century Jew offered the option of hearing *or* doing would have rejected it as a false alternative. Cf. Dunn, *Romans* 1.97–98; 2.582–83, 593, 613; Beker, *Paul*, 268–69; Schoeps, *Paul*, 202; Buber, *Faith*, 56; Mußner, *Galaterbrief*, 170; Gunther, *Opponents*, 70; MacKenzie, "Susanna," 216–17; Garlington, *Obedience*, 233; Segal, *Paul*, 175.

[78] Dunn, *Romans* 1.97.

[79] Rom 2:14–16 is problematic for many interpreters of Paul (Cranfield, *Romans* 1.155–16, and Räisänen, *Paul*, 103–6; Davies, *Faith*, 61–64, give the various views). Sanders (*Law*, 123–24) sees these verses, when compared with 1:18–32, as forming the "principal incongruity" of Romans 1 and 2 (Sanders [ibid., 123–32] and Räisänen [*Paul*, 99–108] are in agreement that Romans 2 as a whole is irreconcilable with Paul's teaching elsewhere). Yet, even though I do think the reference is to Gentiles *qua* Gentiles, there is no basis here for the justification of man outside of Christ. The γάρ of v. 14 is the last in a sequence of four such γάρ's (vv. 11–14), whose function is to buttress the impartiality of God in final judgment. In themselves, vv. 14–16 do not affirm that Gentiles or Jews can be justified by any sort of doing outside of Christ: they are simply the last link in a chain of reasoning that Jews *qua* Jews are no better off than pagans *qua* pagans, especially since the Gentiles have the functional equivalent of Israel's law as carved on tables of stone. If anything – given the backdrop of 1:18–32 – the verses teach that Jew and Gentile are equally exposed to the wrath of God because of idolatry, and both must seek "the redemption which is in Christ Jesus" (3:24). To say that Gentiles at times perform the requirements of the law (ὅταν plus the subjunctive) is not to attribute to

Paul's.[80] Ziesler, for example, takes it to be the expression of the Jewish viewpoint, "used to demonstrate to the Jews that their traditional way of justification is really no way, because while possessing and hearing the law, they do not fulfil it."[81] Along similar lines are those interpretations which effectively, if not formally, make the verse hypothetical, i.e., Paul formulates the principle of justification according to strict justice for the purpose of demonstrating that no one can be justified by the law (assuming the factor of sin).[82]

However, such interpretations falter because there is nothing in Paul's language to suggest either that the viewpoint represented is someone else's (the Jew's) exclusively or that he is speaking in hypothetical terms.[83] His pronouncement about future justification by "doing good" is as realistic as his declaration of God's wrath upon the one who "does evil." On this he and his Jewish interlocutor are in agreement. Indeed, it is just in terms of the *continuity* of Pauline and Jewish theology at this point that the genius of the argument of Romans 2 emerges. In other words, because the Judaism of Paul's day knew of a future vindication based on present fidelity to the covenant, his concern is seen to be that of calling into question the prevailing understanding of who "the righteous" are and the grounds on which they may expect to be justified.

> The difference [between Paul and Judaism] is that the dominant strands in the Judaism of Paul's time started from the presupposition of a favored status before God by virtue of membership of the covenant people, which could be characterized by the very link between "hearing the law" and "the righteous" which Paul here puts in question. Like his fellow Jews and the whole prophetic tradition, Paul is ready to insist that a doing of the law is necessary for final acquittal before God; but that doing is neither synonymous with nor dependent upon maintaining a loyal membership of the covenant people.[84]

This statement of the matter leads us to draw both a negative and a positive conclusion. Negatively, since Paul endeavors to undermine a nationalistic/ exclusivistic understanding of judgment, his purpose is not to deny a role to human activity as such in the scheme of ultimate justification: his theology displays nothing which is inimical to works.[85] Positively, as intimated above, we are informed that the specific character of "doing," in Paul's mind, is distinctive in important respects to that assumed by his Jewish counterparts. It is to this we now turn.

---

them "the obedience of faith" requisite to justification in final judgment: *man outside of Christ cannot be obedient.*

[80] The various approaches have been categorized by Snodgrass, "Justification," 73–74; Sanders, *Law*, 125–26; Räisänen, *Paul*, 103–6.

[81] Ziesler, *Righteousness*, 189. Cf. Kertelge, *"Rechtfertigung,"* 143; Michel, *Römer*, 117.

[82] E.g., Calvin, *Romans*, 47; Hodge, *Romans*, 53–54; Moo, *Romans*, 141, 464. The various interpretations are catalogued by Cranfield, *Romans* 1.15–52; Davies, *Faith*, 54–55.

[83] Cf. Cranfield, *Romans* 1.152; Murray, *Romans* 1.63; Davies, *Faith*, 55.

[84] Dunn, *Romans* 1.98.

[85] Wilckens, *Römer* 1.145.

III. The Doing of the Law as the Obedience of Faith

Foundational to an understanding of faith's obedience in Paul is a historically accurate picture of the same theology in Judaism. It hardly has to be reiterated by this time that I would endorse, for example, R.N. Longenecker's disapproval of those Christian scholars who have followed Emil Schürer's assessment of Judaism as a "fearful burden which a spurious legalism had laid upon the shoulders of the people."[86] Nevertheless, this basic attitude is still with us; and one of its most conspicuous by-products is the premise that the rank and file of the Jewish people had no concern with heart purity and internal religion. Bultmann's contention that obedience for the Jew was "formal" rather than "radical," in that the law failed to claim the allegiance of the *whole* person, is not entirely outmoded.[87]

We cannot here enter fully into the issue. Suffice it to say that the sources can be read otherwise, so as to suggest that the conception of faith's obedience in the Judaism antecedent to and contemporary with Paul was not dissimilar to his own. One cannot read such passages as 2 Macc 1:3; Sus 35, 56; *Pss. Sol.* 1:3, 7; 2:14–15; 3:7–8, 12; 4:5, 8; 8:9 without some recognition of the internal factor in Jewish religion. As for the later tannaitic literature, Longenecker's treatment of "The Piety of Hebraic Judaism" is a model handling of the materials.[88] He demonstrates, in the words of I. Abrahams, that there were both "weeds" and "flowers" in the garden of Judaism, and that the elements of nomism and spirituality must be kept in proper proportion to one other.[89] On the one side, an obedience rooted in faith is in evidence; on the other, the "weeds" of Judaism were its tendency toward "externalism," of which Buber, among other Jewish writers, was aware.[90]

However, "externalism," if it is to be retained, has to be defined. It is not, I would submit, a disregard of inward motivation or internal purity but an oversensitivity to Israel's status as a distinct society. "Externalism," phrased otherwise, is "nationalism." As Dunn remarks, such an understanding of the covenant and of the law inevitably puts too much weight on physical and national factors, on outward and visible enactments, and gives too little weight

---

[86] Longenecker, *Paul*, 65. A more recent example of Schürer's stance is Thyen, *Studien*, 76–77.

[87] Bultmann, *Christianity*, 68.

[88] Longenecker, *Paul*, 65–85. Though assuming a different stance to the one herein presented, Silva's "Reconstruction" is admirably sensitive to the necessity of balance in our approach to the sources. The same applies to Hengel (*Paul*, 46–53).

[89] Longenecker, *Paul*, 82–83. Sanders' *Paul* shows repeatedly how rabbinic authors (especially in their prayers) long for internal purity and personal communion with God. Likewise, the Qumran hymns exhibit this clearly, not surprisingly in light of Betz's findings that in the scrolls the righteousness of God takes absolute priority over human activity ("Rechtfertigung," 34). As Betz concludes, the issue at Qumran (and, I would say, in all the pre-Christian texts) is not merit but a consciousness of Israel's election stemming from membership in the community of salvation (ibid., 36). See further Schnabel, *Law*, 188–90.

[90] Buber, *Faith*, 58–59. Cf. Banks, *Law*, 180.

to elements such as love from the heart. Such an understanding of the people of God, he says, inevitably results in a false set of priorities.[91]

Paul's real polemic, then, is to be taken as a protest against an undue accent on the Torah as the "fence" between Israel and the nations (*Ep. Arist.* 139–42). It is just because remaining within the "fence" secured one's membership in the covenant community that Dunn's additional comment is much to the point: "The obedience God looked for was the obedience of faith, obedience from the heart (6:17), that is, from a commitment and a lifestyle which penetrate far below matters of race and ritual and which could be sustained and maintained independently of either."[92] It is just here that "the obedience of faith" enters the picture, whose significance may be considered under three headings: (a) the hearing of faith; (b) the primacy of love; (c) perseverance.

A. The Hearing of Faith

When Paul wished to impress upon his Galatian converts the irreducible minimum of his gospel as opposed to that of his adversaries, he asked them if they received the Spirit ἐξ ἔργων νόμου or ἐξ ἀκοῆς πίστεως (Gal 3:2). As noted in the first chapter, hearing and faith in the OT and in later Jewish thinking are virtually synonymous: to hear rightly *is* to obey.[93] Consequently, "the *obedience* of faith" and "the *hearing* of faith" depict the same activity, i.e., believing response to the gospel. In fact, the resemblance of the two phrases would be even clearer were we to translate the latter as "the *response* of faith."[94] Nevertheless, Paul juxtaposes "the hearing of faith" (Christianity) and "works of the law" (Judaism/Judaistic Christianity). Naturally, this raises the question, In what sense can such a contrast be meaningful, given the common heritage of Paul and his Jewish kinsmen? The answer is bound up with an earlier observation, viz., that in Rom 2:13 Paul, in a very un-Jewish manner, pits "hearing" against "doing," for the purpose of remonstrating with Israel that *its particular hearing and doing* are unacceptable to God in final judgment. Similarly, Gal 3:2, in context, is sufficiently clear that the hearing of faith is directed toward the gospel (= "the faith," 3:25), as opposed to the "other gospel" (= "works of the law," 3:2) of the circumcision party. What one finds in more or less seminal form in Gal 3:2 is expounded at greater length in Rom 10:14–21.

The lead-in to Rom 10:14–21 is 9:30–10:13, according to which Israel has preferred to maintain *its own* righteousness, i.e., a righteousness peculiar to itself (= national righteousness) as defined by the Sinai covenant (10:3),[95] rather than submit to the righteousness of God in *Christ*, who is the τέλος of the law (10:4). For this reason, Israel is ashamed to confess Christ as Lord

---

[91] Dunn, *Jesus, Paul*, 227. Cf. id., *Romans* 2.582–83, 593.
[92] Dunn, *Romans* 2.593 (on 9:32).
[93] Young, "Obedience," 580; Käsemann, "Righteousness," 177.
[94] Dunn, *Romans* 1.17.
[95] Ibid., 2.587–88; id., *Jesus, Paul*, 223; Sanders, *Law*, 38; Howard, "Christ," 336.

(10:9–13). It is in particular Israel's failure to confess Christ which gives rise to the assertions of 10:14–21 that its non-confession is the result of its non-hearing of the gospel. To be sure, the nation has heard in one sense: preachers have been sent (vv. 14–17), and the word has gone forth to "the ends of the earth" (v. 18). In the most meaningful sense, however, God continues to hold out his hands to "a disobedient [= non-listening] and contrary people."

Israel, then, has heard – but it has not heard. Inasmuch as it has not heard with "the hearing of faith," i.e., faith directed toward the gospel, it is incapable of "the obedience of faith" which grows out of the gospel. Since "faith comes from hearing" the word of God, i.e., the gospel (10:17), Israel's "doing" is unacceptable because it is not ἐκ πίστεως in the specifically Christian sense; and since Israel's faith is not in Christ, it must be condemned as insufficient, because it is only *in Christ* that one can become "the righteousness *of God*" (2 Cor 5:21).[96] *God's* righteousness, according to Paul, is available exclusively in Christ, meaning, in the final analysis, that the "doing" in question is the extension of Christ's doing – the starting point must be Christ. Paul's antithesis of believing and doing thus constitutes his most radical polemic against Judaism: "Faith is determined by its object and not celebrated for its own sake."[97] It is none other than faith's new object which signifies that faith itself involves a radical reorientation and commitment.[98]

If, therefore, Israel's "doing" is unacceptable, it is because its "hearing" is defective: it will listen only to God speaking *in the Torah*, not in the gospel. Starting from the eternity of the law,[99] the Jewish position was that the Hebrew Scriptures were sufficient in and of themselves to define obedience and to sustain the faithful through the tension of this waiting period until Yahweh's righteousness is apocalyptically revealed.[100] Yet the force of Paul's polemic is that Israel has misjudged the intention of the law: it has not seen it as a παιδαγωγὸς εἰς Χριστόν (Gal 3:24)[101] and has, consequently, settled for an obedience which fails to measure up to the demands of the gospel. This brings us to consider both the primacy of love and perseverance in Paul.

---

[96] Faith in Paul, as Cosgrove argues, is not faith in God per se but in him as the vindicator of the crucified Messiah ("Justification," 666). Cf. Wilckens, *Römer* 1.89; Garlington, *Obedience*, 256, n. 5.

[97] Beker, *Paul*, 268. Cf. my *Obedience*, 255–56 (with other literature).

[98] Segal, *Paul*, 121.

[99] E.g., Sir 24:9, 33; Bar 4:1; Wis 18:4; *T. Naph.* 3:1–2. Quite conspicuously, *Jubilees* promotes the doctrine of the preexistence of the law on heavenly tablets. See Banks, *Law*, 50–64, 67–85; id., "Law," 175–77; Davies, *Torah*, 84.

[100] Beker, *Paul*, 268.

[101] See Lull, "Pedagogue;" Gordon, "ΠΑΙΔΑΓΩΓΟΣ;" Braswell, "Blessing."

B. The Primacy of Love[102]

Without uncritically drawing parallels between Romans and Galatians, a comparison of the love motif common to both is in order. Because Galatians particularly is the most intense of Paul's controversial letters, it pinpoints as none of his other epistles the bone of contention between him and his opponents. Especially relevant for the present purposes is the paraenesis of Galatians 5 and 6. The conspicuous theme of this section of the epistle is Paul's depiction of Christianity as a religion of love, especially as love is set in contrast to the influence of the Jewish Christian missionaries, who to Paul, for all practical purposes, were indistinguishable from non-Christian Jews. Not only does he call them "false brethren" (2:4), disputing their claim actually to be Christians, his method of argumentation in the letter would have had equal applicability to Judaism as to the sort of Jewish Christianity represented by the circumcision party.[103]

According to his portrait, his opponents were stimulating the Galatians to "bite and devour one another" (5:15). In spite of their claims, they do not really "abide in *all things* written in the book of the law," because they have neglected the principal part – love. Over against them, "the whole law" for Paul "is fulfilled in one word, 'You shall love your neighbor as yourself'" (5:14). Love is particularly set in opposition to circumcision, which for the Judaizers was one of the acid tests of loyalty to the God of Israel. For the apostle, however, circumcision now counts for nothing: what matters in the new creation is *faith working through love* (5:6; cf. 6:15) and Christians serving one another through love (5:13). For this reason, love heads the list of the fruit of the Spirit (5:20). If one walks by the Spirit (5:25), instead of being conceited and provoking others (5:26), one will bear the brother's burden and so fulfill the law of Christ (6:1–2). Even this sketch of the love motif in Galatians informs us that the theology of the new creation was important to Paul because, from his vantage point, *the lovelessness of the Judaizers was the product of their exclusivistic theology*.

The same perspective is evident in Romans, particularly in chaps. 12–15. Having laid the salvation-historical basis for the mutual reception of Jew and Gentile in chaps. 1–11, Paul speaks directly in the final chapters of the social ramifications of believers in one church. Therefore, the practical directives of these chapters bring to the fore the apostle's conception of the Christian church as it consists of peoples of divergent backgrounds inseparably joined in the one body of Christ. In the words of H. Strohl:

---

[102] This segment of the chapter is adapted from my "Burden Bearing," 153–58. Cf. Gundry Volf, *Perseverance*, 141–54. The love theme in Paul has been treated many times, e.g., Spicq, *Agapé* 1.208–314; 2.9–305; Ridderbos, *Paul*, 293–301; Furnish, *Theology*, 181–206; id., *Command*, 91–131; Schrage, *Ethics*, 211–17; Piper, *Enemies*, 102–119.

[103] This group is designated variously: τινας ἀπὸ Ἰακώβου (Gal 2:12); οἱ ἐκ περιτομῆς πιστοί (Acts 10:45); τινες τῶν ἀπὸ τῆς αἱρέσεως τῶν Φαρισαίων πεπιστευκότες (Acts 15:5); ἡ κατατομή (Phil 3:2; cf. Gal 5:12). For literature, see Garlington, *Obedience*, 254, n. 1.

They are the charter of the new humanity. They indicate the relations which love has created among the different members of the body of Christ. Everywhere the dominant idea is that the [individual] man forms part of a whole; he never lives alone in the world, but is joined by the lines of a close solidarity to others with whom he shares in responsibilities and blessings.[104]

Paul talks explicitly of love in 13:8–10. Instead of being overcome with evil (i.e., the evil of seeking vengeance, 12:21), the Christian is to leave the debt of love outstanding, thus fulfilling the law. (That such a reminder was necessary for the Romans becomes evident in chaps. 14–15.) V. 8a is written directly in view of vv. 6–7; that is, although there are debts which are never to be left outstanding, there is one debt which is always to be left outstanding – the debt of love: we are always to owe our brethren this debt which can never be fully paid. But almost paradoxically, v. 8b explains that the unpaid debt of love is the fulfillment of the law: what from one point of view is an outstanding debt is, from another, a full payment to the law. Note how 8b is answered by 10b: the two in combination give us the essence of this phase of Paul's paraenesis. We are reminded again (from Gal 5:6, 14–15, 20, 22; 6:1–2) that love characterizes the community of the new creation and is the outgrowth of "the obedience of faith," which alone satisfies the demands of the law.[105] Both interesting and significant is the fact that the "works of the flesh" in Gal 5:19–21 are mainly attitudes and activities disruptive of the life of love and fellowship. As such, these "works of the flesh" find an important point of contact with Rom 2:8; 16:17: the ἐριθεία and διχοστασίαι characteristic of those who "disobey the truth" represent a return to chaos, a reversal of God's creation plan for his people.

It is in keeping with Paul's characterization of the new covenant as a community of love that we are to understand one of his most fundamental complaints against contemporary Judaism. To appreciate the issue at stake, it is necessary to reckon with the "theology of zeal" originating in the Hasmonean period. In lieu of a full discussion of the matter, we note simply that the "zealots,"[106] from Mattathias (1 Macc 2:19–70) onward, are consistently marked out as defenders of the Jewish way of life as embodied in the Torah.[107]

---

[104] Quoted by Feuillet, "plan," 508.

[105] Note particularly Furnish's treatment of love and the new creation (*Command*, 91–95). "Paul's preaching of love does not just stand alongside his emphasis on justification by faith but is vitally related to it. To believe in Christ means to belong to him, and to belong to him means to share in his death and in the power of his resurrection. Thereby one's whole life is radically reoriented from sin to righteousness as he is freed from bondage to himself and placed under the truly liberating dominion of God's grace" (ibid., 92).

[106] "Zealot" is being used in a non-technical (non-factional) sense to denote the Mattathias-type of attitude toward violators of the law, an attitude which cut across party boundaries. Cf. Donaldson, "Zealot," 1178–79. As Hammerton-Kelly reminds us, "zealot" does not automatically mean "revolutionary" ("Violence," 107, n. 23).

[107] Among the plethora of works devoted to zeal and Zealotism, see Garlington, *Obedience*, 112–14 (with literature); Hengel, *Zealots*, 146–228; Dunn, *Partings*, 121; Farmer, *Maccabees*; id., "Zealot;" Donaldson, "Zealot and Convert," 672–74.

They were ready not only to die for the purity of the covenant, but to kill for it as well – and they did just that.[108] To them: "In every case of serious threat to Israel's sacred blessings, either from within Israel or from outside, the use of violence became a sacred duty."[109] Philo (*Spec. Leg.* 2.253) tells us the ζηλωταὶ νόμου were merciless to any who would subvert the ancestral ways, and 1QS 9:22 characterizes the righteous man as one who is "to bear unremitting hatred towards all men of ill repute."[110] Cf. Josephus, *Ag. Ap.* 2.37 (271–72); 2.41 (292). Paul himself, as one involved in "boundary maintenance,"[111] was formerly such a "zealot" (Gal 1:13–14; Phil 3:6), who did not flinch at the use of brutal violence in his attempted annihilation of the followers of Jesus.[112] To those "zealous for the law" Christianity appeared to subvert loyalty to Judaism and was, consequently, rejected by the mass of first-century Jews.[113]

It is in opposition to such zeal for the law, and its by-product of hatred toward

---

[108] "Such a 'zealot' was unconditionally prepared to use force in order to turn God's wrath away from Israel, giving his own life to protect the sanctuary and law against the serious lawbreaker" (Hengel, *Paul*, 70). Indeed, "Anyone who wanted to impose God's will as laid down in the Torah also by political means could not be too squeamish when it came to using force" (ibid., 44–45). Dunn rightly characterizes the "zealots" of the ilk of Mattathias as "heroes of the faith who had been willing to use the sword to defend and maintain Israel's distinctiveness as God's covenant people" ("Righteousness," 221). A sampling of texts includes Sir 45:23–24; 1 Macc 2:23–28, 50, 54, 58; 4 Macc 18:12; 1QS 4:1, 4; 9:23; 1QH 14:14; *T. Ash.* 4:5.

[109] Hengel, *Zealots*, 225. He cites as applicable to the Zealots, *mutatis mutandis*, *Num. R.* 21:3 (on Num 25:13): "Everyone who sheds the blood of godless men is like one who offers a sacrifice" (ibid., 85).

[110] Regarding the Pharisees, E. Bickerman comments that "Early Pharisaism was a belligerent movement that knew how to hate" (*Ezra*, 103). Cf. Neusner, *Politics*, 51–52. Of many examples which could be cited from Second Temple literature, hatred toward the Gentiles in particular surfaces in Jdt 16:17 and throughout the LXX additions to Esther. Along these lines, Benoit ("Qumran," 13) and Schubert ("Sermon," 120) distinguish Jesus and the Dead Sea community precisely in terms of the former's love of sinners. Cf. Piper, *Enemies*, 40–41; Grundmann, "Teacher," 95; Bruce, "Scrolls," 73–75. See 1QS 1:4–11; 1QM 13:3–5. In fairness, we acknowledge Vermes' observation that given the customary gulf between belief and conduct, the convictions of the sect may have given rise to rigidity, bigotry, and hatred; but *by intention* they were a company of poor and humble men constantly attentive to the word of God and grateful for his favors (*Scrolls*, 51–52). The same applies to Pharisaism (Sanders, *Judaism*, 494).

[111] Donaldson, "Zealot and Convert," 672.

[112] See especially Hengel, *Zealots*, 177–224; id., *Paul*, 63–86; Hultgren, "Persecutions;" Donaldson, "Zealot and Convert," esp. 668–80; cf. Brandon, *Zealots*, 146–220. Hultgren states that Paul's ire was aroused not only by the Christian claim that salvation was possible apart from the law but also by the positive proclamation of "the faith" (Gal 1:23) that Jesus is the crucified and risen Messiah of Israel ("Persecutions," 102), while Donaldson stresses that Paul's own zeal stemmed from that of persecuting zeal generally, i.e., from perceived threats to the covenant community ("Zealot and Convert," 678–80).

[113] "That it was misunderstood from the Jewish side at that time as a new sect urging apostasy from the law and assimilation is indirectly the last and most grievous legacy of those Jewish renegades who, between 175 and 164 BC, attempted to do away with the law and 'make a covenant with the people round about'" (Hengel, *Judaism* 1.314). See Hengel's important discussion of "Zeal as a Typical Element of Piety in Late Judaism" (*Zealots*, 177–83).

outsiders to the covenant,[114] that Paul appeals to love not only as the ideal of the new creation but also as the actual fulfillment of Israel's own law. Hence, if we ask, What is the obedience of faith which eventuates in eschatological justification?, the answer, in part, is love, which fulfills the law. In this regard, it is certainly striking that Rom 12:19 quotes Deut 32:35 (cf. Lev 19:18): Yahweh's threat of wrath against the ancient covenant people. In Paul's application of this passage, there is heard an "echo" which is meant to resound in the ears of those members of the new covenant community who refuse to display genuine love (v. 9) and seek to avenge themselves against wrong-doing (v. 19a). It is they, who have failed to love their fellow Christians, who will be the recipients of God's wrath, not vindication, in the final judgment. In this light, love must characterize the Christian community; it is *the* indispensable boundary marker of the latter day people of God.[115]

C. Perseverance

Without entering into the entire complex of Paul's teaching on perseverance, we recall that the goal of glory, honor, peace, and eternal life is to be attained καθ' ὑπομονὴν ἔργου ἀγαθοῦ (2:7), language reminiscent of Adam in the Garden. Adam, however, failed the test and became the first apostate from Yahweh. Yet it is the creation program as commenced in the first man which is still operative for all his descendants, notwithstanding the disadvantages which he has bequeathed to them (Rom 5:12−19). Hence, for Paul the renewal of the creation mandate is embodied in the obedience of faith, i.e., *the work of endurance consequent upon entrance into Christ.* Ultimately, the issue at stake is *faith vs. unbelief.* "The difference between faith and unbelief is exactly the theme of the story of Eden. Men align themselves with

---

[114] A qualification is in order. McKnight's survey of Jewish attitudes toward Gentiles and proselytism (*Light*, 11−19, 31−33) demonstrates clearly enough that not all Jews expressed negative feelings towards their pagan neighbors. Indeed, his data suggest that in certain circles at least there was a good deal of friendliness toward outsiders. However, it is interesting that his sources are mainly from Diaspora Judaism (including Josephus, who was amply motivated not to offend unduly the Romans), while his treatment of "resistance tendencies," i.e., negative attitudes to integration with non-Jews (ibid., 19−25, 43−44), is illustrated to a larger degree by Palestinian literature. Without making hard and fast distinctions between Hellenistic and Palestinian Judaism, this is significant inasmuch as the Jews of Palestine had witnessed first-hand the devastation of their homeland by both the Syrians and the Romans, thus accounting for the kind of vitriol recorded, e.g., in *Jub.* 22:16; *Pss. Sol.* 17:21−27. McKnight's study is excellent; but I would suggest that in forming an overall impression of Jew/Gentile relations in the first century the "theology of zeal," which characterized Palestine in particular, needs to be given its due.

[115] Cf. Dunn, *Jesus, Paul*, 245; id., *Partings*, 153; Stuhlmacher, "Righteousness," 85; Braswell, "Blessing," 88. For Mußner the essence of Christianity resides in the love command (*Galaterbrief*, 399), while Deidun writes that "The holiness of the New Covenant community − that which constitutes it as such − is *agapê*" (*Morality*, 104; cf. ibid., 150). Spicq is of the same opinion (*Agapè* 2.115).

Adam, the type of the Man of wickedness [2 Thess 2:3]... or with God."[116] Or, as Stendahl states it so well: "The danger is not to get a little worse, and the hope is not to get a little better (ethically, or in terms of faith). It is sharpened in the simplified black and white of all eschatological situations: the dangers of apostasy."[117]

Cambier has assembled some illuminating parallels between Romans and the other Paulines.[118] As Rom 2:7, Col 1:10−11 links ὑπομονή with ἔργον ἀγαθόν, thus placing the terms in a distinctively Christian context. We might say that the believer's "good work" (cf. 2 Thess 2:17; 2 Cor 9:8) *is* his "perseverance," corresponding to the creation pattern evident in Romans 2. Again, confirmation is to be had from Deut 30:15: "I have set before you this day *life and good, death and evil*," an admonition integrally related to Israel's decision whether to obey or not. Cambier himself notes that ὑπομονή designates the Christian life in a manner very characteristic of Paul. In 1 Thess 1:3, the term is joined with the triad πίστις-ἀγάπη-ἐλπίς in Paul's praise of his readers' "work of faith, labor of love and endurance of hope" (cf. 2 Thess 1:4). Likewise, 2 Thess 3:5 is Paul's prayer that God would direct their hearts into the love of God and into the endurance of Christ: "The love of God in the hearts of believers is concretely the ὑπομονή of Christ which the believer lives in gentle and humble service for the benefit of his brethren."[119] Paul can epitomize his own life and ministry as existence ἐν ὑπομονῇ πολλῇ: his acceptance of obstacles and difficulties "with endurance" is his faith in action.[120] Hence, the ὑπομονὴ ἔργου ἀγαθοῦ of Rom 2:7 for Paul is nothing but "the work of faith" (1 Thess 1:3) or "faith working through love" (Gal 5:6).[121] "For every Christian the... endurance (ὑπομονή) of trials and of the limitations of our human condition is an expression of solid faith, of hope and the love which has been given him by the Holy Spirit."[122]

Of particular note in Romans is 5:1−5 − especially its conjunction of justification and the ὑπομονή which produces both δοκιμή (v. 4) and ἐλπίς (v. 5). The last mentioned does not expose us to (eschatological) shame, because God's

---

[116] Barrett, *Adam*, 14.
[117] Quoted by Donfried, "Justification," 102, n. 52. Mattern, then, justifiably underscores the primacy of faith as opposed to unbelief in Romans 2 (*Verständnis*, 138).
[118] Cambier, "jugement," 190−93.
[119] Ibid., 191. This runs counter to Sanders' claim that it is "un-Pauline to require good works" (*Law*, 129).
[120] Cambier, "jugement," 191.
[121] Moo's objection (*Romans*, 125) that faith in Rom 2:1−3:8 is conspicuous by its absence fails to appreciate that faith is implicit in the ὑπομονή of which Paul speaks. The pursuit of glory, honor, and immortality is one of *faithful* endurance. As noted above, any antithesis between faith and doing for a first-century Jew would have been considered a false alternative.
[122] Cambier, "jugement," 191−92. Sanders criticizes Mattern (as quoted above) for making the principal issue in Romans 2 faith as opposed to unbelief. However, he has not discerned the overarching significance of "the obedience of faith," which provides the conceptual framework of the letter. No wonder, then, he thinks that 1:18−2:29 is beset with numerous internal inconsistencies and is atypical of Paul (*Law*, 123, 132).

ἀγάπη has been poured into our hearts (v. 5). If one is permitted to cite James in relation to Paul (!): "Blessed is the man who *endures* trial, for when he has stood the test he will receive the crown of life which God has promised to those who *love* him" (1:12).[123] Conspicuous here is the combination of perseverance and love as the preconditions of eternal life. In short, the obedience of faith which finally justifies is for Paul, as well as James, persevering "faith working by love."[124] In line with both Paul and James, Heb 10:24 also exhorts Christians to stir one another up to *love and good works*.

Of course, the idea of perseverance is hardly unique to Paul. Even a passing acquaintance with pre-Christian Jewish literature is sufficient to inform one that *the* issue before many of its authors was precisely loyalty to the Mosaic standards in the face of widespread apostasy. But what is new in Paul is that *perseverance has changed its focus*: no longer are the people of God to obey the Torah but rather the "form of teaching," i.e., the Pauline gospel concerning God's Son, to which they have been committed (Rom 6:17 in connection with 1:1–3a; 2:16). For him perseverance is bound up with one's inclusion in Christ: only in Christ is there no condemnation (Rom 8:1); it is Christ who insures the perseverance of his people (Rom 5:12–19).[125]

From the entire foregoing discussion we may conclude that the passage from present justification by faith alone to future justification by the obedience of faith is natural enough, given the broader purview – and most notably the creation character – of Paul's theology of faith and obedience. However, practically speaking, this conclusion is sufficiently important (and controversial) that something more must be said. As Sanders and Snodgrass acknowledge concerning the Jewish doctrine of judgment,[126] what is in view is not justification by "works" in any meritorious sense but *an extension of the righteousness of God in Christ*. Snodgrass in particular speaks of the apparent incongruity for modern readers of judgment according to both God's mercy and human works. He notes that although there were abuses of both in ancient Judaism, neither

---

[123] I would submit that Paul and James are not as far apart as is commonly believed. Cf. Adamson, *James*, 203–10, 266–307; Lenski, *James*, 589; Moo, *James*, 109–10; Burtchaell, "Theology," 46–47. The essential point of Jas 2:21–26 is that Genesis 22 represents the fulfillment (complement) of Abraham's faith as recorded by Gen 15:6. Actually, both passages have to do with the patriarch's fidelity in testing situations, as supported by James' reference to "the perseverance of Job" in 5:11.

[124] In Fitzmeyer's words: "Paul certainly does not mean that human beings can be justified by love alone; *but can they be without it?*" As he continues, Paul's "last word" in Galatians (6:11–18) sums up the meaning of the cross without any explicit reference to righteousness/justification, or even to faith. This leads Fitzmeyer to conclude: "To me, at least, it shows that 'the cross' can be expressed without such recourse and that it has other aspects significant for human existence and salvation than merely justification by grace through faith" ("Justification," 209. Italics mine. Cf. O'Donovan, *Resurrection*, 253–56). What is true of love is also applicable to "mercy." See Adamson, *James*, 288.

[125] The author of Hebrews speaks to the same effect in calling Christ the "surety" of a better covenant (Heb 7:22).

[126] Sanders, *Paul*, 128; Snodgrass, "Justification," 78.

the OT nor Jewish literature sensed any anomaly between the two. Indeed, Ps 62:12, normally considered to be the source of Rom 2:6, actually says: "to you, O Lord, belongs *steadfast love*, for you requite a person *according to his work*."[127]

When both themes are kept together, there is no problem. When the two are separated, an over-emphasis on either could and did lead to perversion. Over-emphasis on judgment according to works could lead to casuistry and a strict doctrine of weighing. Over-emphasis on God's mercy could lead to presumption of his mercy and neglect of obedience.[128]

Though requiring a study in itself, it is the Christian's union with Christ and the gift of his Spirit (Rom 8:9; 2 Cor 1:22; 5:5; Eph 1:14, etc.) which are the fountainhead of the obedience of faith: it is *in Christ* that one becomes a doer of the law, not in the sense of sinless perfection but of one's commitment to God's (new) covenant, whose κύριος is Christ.[129] It is because of the obedience of Christ, the last Adam, that the people of God have become obedient in him, as once they were disobedient in the first Adam (Rom 5:12–19).[130] Paul himself puts it in a nutshell in 1 Cor 15:22: "as in Adam all die, so in Christ shall all be made alive." It is in the same comprehensive sense that the author of Hebrews can say that Christ is the source of eternal salvation to all who obey him (Heb 5:9). With these necessary christological qualifications, "doing the law," in Rom 2:13, is no different in kind than the OT's classic statement of "covenantal nomism," Lev 18:5: one continues to live within the covenant relationship by compliance with its terms, i.e., perseverance.[131]

Otherwise put, *in Christ* one becomes, according to 2 Cor 5:21, "the righte-

---

[127] As Motyer observes, in the Psalms there is a surface tension between the capacity of God's people to be righteous and the necessity of Yahweh being merciful to a still sinful people ("Righteousness," 37–38). The tension is resolved, however, by grasping the very genius of righteousness, i.e., as both the Lord's own saving activity and the stamp placed upon those who are caught up into that activity (ibid., 53–54).

[128] Snodgrass, "Justification," 78.

[129] Sanders is wrong in relegating Rom 2:13 to a category distinct from Rom 14:10; 2 Cor 5:10, in that it refers to all humanity who are judged by one standard, the law (*Law*, 126). He does not allow for the fact that when Paul pens the words of 2:13, he has in mind what he will say from 3:21 onward, viz., that people are justified and become obedient *in Christ*. The person in Christ becomes a doer of the law, i.e., one who perseveres in the covenant, and is enabled to achieve what Israel and the nations could not.

[130] "Christ is the new Adam, because as the bearer of human destiny, he brings in the world of obedience" (Käsemann, "Righteousness," 180. Cf. Snodgrass, "Justification," 81–82). Note how Phil 2:8's assertion that Christ was "obedient unto death" is evocative of the Adam motif (as it intersects with that of the Servant of Yahweh). The conjunction of v. 8 with vv. 12–13 demonstrates that for Paul Christian obedience is linked inextricably to Christ in his role as Adam/Servant, the obedient one who is to be obeyed.

[131] Moo objects that "doing the law" cannot mean this, because the choice of words is too much is like the expressions "works of the law" or "works," which, according to the apostle, cannot justify (*Romans*, 144). However, Moo leans on an assumed meaning of the latter two formulations (see at more length his "'Law'"). To be sure, Paul does deny that "works of the law" or "works" can justify, but only because such "works" represent a refusal to leave

ousness of God." This succinct statement of the believer's mode of existence flows from the foregoing words: "if anyone is in Christ, behold, the new creation" (2 Cor 5:18)! The very burden of the above exposition is that Paul depicts the obedience of faith issuing in eschatological justification as a new creation: what man in Adam has failed to obtain – glory, honor, and immortality – man in Christ has. This compels me to agree with Käsemann that the righteousness of God is his sovereign power effecting a new creation:[132] "The faithful *are* the world as it has been recalled to the sovereignty of God, the company of those who live under the eschatological justice of God, in which company, according to II Cor 5:21, God's righteousness becomes manifest on earth."[133]

IV. Summary

In Rom 2:13, Paul proposes that there is a phase of justification yet to transpire: it is the "doers of the law" (Christians), rather than the "hearers of the law" (Israel), who will be vindicated.[134] "Doing the law," however, is not to be defined as "works-righteousness" or unaided human achievement; it is, rather, "the obedience of faith," i.e., continuance in the Creator/creature relationship as articulated by Paul's christological gospel. It is *in Christ* that one becomes a "doer of the law;" and the Christian's loving obedience to God is nothing other than the extension to him/her of the righteousness of *Christ himself*. It could not be otherwise, because salvation for the apostle is God's gift from beginning to end (e.g., Rom 5:15–17; 6:22–23; Eph 2:8–10).[135]

Judaism and come to Christ: these are the "works" which exclude one from Christ. See my brief response to Moo's "'Law'" (*Obedience*, 265, n. 83).

[132] "Δικαιοσύνη θεοῦ is for Paul God's sovereignty over the world revealing itself eschatologically in Jesus" (Käsemann, "Righteousness," 180).

[133] Ibid., 181 (italics his). We recall that Kertelge similarly defines the righteousness of God as his redemptive power offsetting the sway of the old aeon (*"Rechtfertigung,"* 104).

[134] The extreme irony of applying this nomenclature to Christians, instead of Israel, is highlighted by 1 Macc. 2:67, where the exact phrase "the doers of the law" (τοὺς ποιητὰς τοῦ νόμου) designates loyalist Jews who would be vindicated against the Gentiles by devine justice. Significant also are 1QpHab 7:11, 8:1, 12:4.

[135] See further Käsemann, *Romans*, 155; Beker, *Paul*, 264, 267; Snodgrass, "Justification," 81 (who terms the "glory," "honor," and "immortality" of Rom 2:7 "eschatological gifts").

Chapter Four
The Obedience of Christ and the Obedience of the Christian

Our investigation of faith, obedience, and perseverance in Romans has thus far yielded three basic conclusions. (1) The phrase ὑπακοὴ πίστεως embodies a twin idea: the obedience consisting in faith and the obedience arising out of faith. (2) The Israel of Paul's day was incapable of rendering to Yahweh "the obedience of faith" because of its idolatrous attachment to the Torah. (3) Faith's obedience, defined in the first instance as *perseverance in Christ*, is the link between present justification "by faith" and the future-eschatological justification of the "doers of the law" (Rom 2:13). We come now to consider in more detail the role of Christ, the obedient one, who ensures the faithful obedience of his people. Our attention will be focused on Romans 5.

I. Romans 5 within the Scheme of Chapters 5–8[1]

As one reads these chapters, one cannot help but be impressed by the series of antitheses constructed by Paul, which in very broad terms may be reduced to the following elements. Chap. 5: life in Christ vs. death in Adam; 6:1–7:6: newness of life in Christ vs. death and bondage to sin and the law; 7:7–8:39: life and liberty in union with Christ and the Spirit vs. captivity to the flesh, even in spite of indwelling sin and the believer's groaning for the redemption of the body (7:14–25; 8:18–25). In each instance, the motif of the believer's once-for-all break with the past and his entrance into a new state of affairs stands out in prominent relief: an old pattern of existence is broken in order that a new mode of life may begin. The representatives of the old age – sin, death, the law, and the flesh – have been overthrown and caused to release their grip on those who are now in Christ.[2]

There is, accordingly, a pronounced christological aspect of each phase of the believer's transformation from his old condition to the new. Chap. 5 highlights

---

[1] The purpose of these remarks is to set forth a salvation-historical structuring of these chapters without pretending that this is the only way of approaching the text. On the complexity of chaps. 5–8 as a whole, see Beker, *Paul*, 84–85.

[2] Beker maintains that Paul's interpretation of the death of Christ is remarkably apocalyptic, inasmuch as the major apocalyptic forces for him are those ontological powers which determine the human situation within the context of God's created order and which comprise the field of death, sin, the law, and the flesh (*Paul*, 189).

his solidarity with Christ as he heads up the age to come, in opposition to his former union with Adam, who is the head of "the present evil age" (Gal 1:4). In 6:1–7:6, the believer has died to sin and has been raised in newness of life; because he has died to the law through the body of Christ, he is discharged from that which held him captive, so that "now," i.e., in this new phase of world history, he serves not in the oldness of the letter but in the newness of the Spirit. Chap. 8 makes explicit the connection between the sonship of Christians and the sonship of Christ: they are the sons of God because he is the Son of God. In the Son, their lives are no longer characterized by fear and bondage to the flesh; it is to the image of the Son that they are being conformed; and it is by virtue of the indwelling Spirit of the Son that they now walk after the Spirit, as formerly they walked after the flesh.

Hand in hand with the ethical and christological dimensions of these chapters there is a conspicuous time-element. Echoing 3:21, the "eschatological νῦν" is present in 5:10; 6:21; 7:6, 17; 8:1; and even when the "now" of salvation is not expressly mentioned, it is just beneath the surface of all of those passages which speak of the definitive break with the old age. From the ethical point of view, chaps. 5–8 can be viewed as Paul's delineation of the eschatological (resurrection) life of the people of God, those upon whom "the ends of the ages have come" (1 Cor 10:11). The frequent occurrence of "life" throughout the section takes us back to 1:17, where, according to Paul's use of Hab 2:4, life is the outcome of the righteous man's faith, as well as 4:17–21, according to which Abraham's faith was in the God who raises the dead. Ultimately, as we have seen, "life" is a creation concept, stemming from Genesis 1 and 2 (cf. Rom 2:7).

Therefore, from 5:1 through the end of chap. 8 Paul runs the entire course of salvation history, from old creation to new. After the transitional paragraph of 5:1–11, 5:12–21 depicts the disobedience of the old humanity in Adam and the obedience of the new in Christ. 6:1–7:6 speaks further of the inception of the new creation with the death and resurrection of Christ: the oldness of the letter has given way to the newness of the Spirit.[3] As the outgrowth of an objection raised and answered in 7:7–12, 7:13–25 articulates the overlap of the two creations, with its resultant tension in the believer's inward being. Chap. 8, finally, predicts the glories of the consummated new creation.

The substructure of Romans 5–8 can thus be viewed as Paul's announcement of the passing of the old creation and the advent of the new. It is as though this entire portion of the letter were an elaborate commentary on 2 Cor 5:17: "If anyone is in Christ, [there is] the new creation. The old things have passed away; behold, all things have become new." From a slightly adjusted perspective, we can say, with Byrne, that chaps. 5–8 are to be regarded as a unified block bound together by a common theme: "the hope of eternal life on the basis

---

[3] Romans 6 has a prophetic background: the death and resurrection of Christ correspond to those oracles concerning the captivity and restoration of Israel, the nation's own death and resurrection, e.g., Isa 26:19; Ezek 37:1–14; Hos 6:1–2. The new creation/new covenant associations of these prophecies are explicit in their respective contexts.

of justification, despite the present reality of suffering and the prospect of physical death."[4]

In this light, we see that Paul's dialogue with Judaism (and the Judaizers) is continued into the present stage of the letter. The essential difference between him and the Jewish outlook lay just in his conviction that, in Christ, the eschaton had arrived. Given the assumption of 3:21–4:25 that faith in Christ has secured both justification and the promise to Abraham of a seed, it follows that in his appearance the life of the new creation is here.[5]

II. Romans 5:1–11: Reconciliation and New Creation

Some commentators make 5:1–11 the conclusion of what has preceded (3:21–4:25), while others classify it as the beginning of a new section of the letter (chaps. 5–8).[6] Actually, it makes relatively little difference which course we follow, because these verses are essentially a transitional passage containing ideas from the previous part of the argument (faith, grace, sinners, justification, blood, enemies, wrath, and the resurrection of Christ) as well as those which pave the way for what is to follow (suffering, endurance, hope, the Holy Spirit, the love of God, and future salvation as the result of past reconciliation).[7]

The particular terms "ungodly," "sinners," "enemies," and "wrath," as compared with "justified," "saved," and "reconciled," articulate a contrast between the believer's past and his present. Kaylor is correct that this contrast is organized around the theme of reconciliation.[8] As illustrated most graphically from Hosea, reconciliation derives its meaning from Israel's covenant relationship with God: "Reconciliation implies the restoration of a previous condition and as such builds upon the idea of a covenant within which God and Israel once lived in a harmony which was subsequently disrupted.... God betrothed Israel

---

[4] Byrne, "Righteousness," 560.

[5] It is frequently noted that in 5:1–8:39 ζάω and ζωή, used some 24 times, dominate Paul's vocabulary.

[6] There are variations, of course, e.g., Kaylor, *Community*, 93; Beker, *Paul*, 85. For further literature, see Porter, "Argument," 655, n. 1. The ensuing exposition accepts that chaps. 5–8 stand as a unit, whose substructure is comprised of a theology of creation. The leading parallels between 5:1–11 and chap. 8 are listed by Dahl (*Studies*, 88–90) and Moo (*Romans*, 323). For additional literature, see Byrne, "Righteousness," 560, n. 7. Byrne notes that "hope" is one of the ligaments connecting chaps. 5 and 8 as the extremities of the literary unit comprised of 5–8.

[7] On the place of chap. 5 within Romans, see the analyses of Moo, *Romans*, 300–303; Dunn, "Analysis," 2855–58; Bornkamm, "Anakolouthe," 81–82; Martin, *Reconciliation*, 136–40; Brandenburger, *Adam*, 255–64; Elliot, *Rhetoric*, 226; Robinson, *Wrestling*, 57; de Boer, *Defeat*, 148–49. Elliot (*Rhetoric*, 226) maintains that Romans 5 *in toto* is the pivot on which the letter's argument turns, and Nygren thinks that the chapter is the "high point" of the letter, where all the lines of Paul's thinking converge (*Romans*, 209). Nygren, rightly in my view, links 5 to 6–8, as do others (see Moo, *Romans*, 300, n. 1).

[8] Kaylor, *Community*, 93–94. See further Martin, *Reconciliation*, 136–54.

in faithfulness, but though God remained faithful, Israel became 'adulterous' and pursued other lovers (gods)."⁹ Reconciliation, in keeping with this figure, is nothing less than the restoration of a broken marriage. That it is a central concept for Paul emerges from 2 Cor 5:16–21, where, like Rom 5:1–11, Paul can characterize his new covenant ministry as one of reconciliation of Jew and Gentile.

Structurally, the paragraph can be analyzed according to the "ABA" pattern so frequent in Romans.¹⁰

A: vv. 1–2, the two direct results of justification by faith;
B: vv. 3–10, the relation of these two;
A: v. 11, the two direct results of justification by faith.

A. *The Two Results of Justification by Faith, vv. 1–2*

The first is peace with God. It is peace which particularly highlights the eschatological dimension of what has transpired with the work of Christ. The term "peace" is one which characterizes the OT's messianic outlook (e. g., Isa 9:6–7; 32; 52:7; 57:19; Ezek 37:26; Hag 2:9; cf. Num 6:22–26). In the prophetic expectation, the Messiah was to be the "Prince of Peace" (Isa 9:6), in whose person Yahweh's שלום would attend the time of worldwide bliss, the new creation, when the lion and the lamb would dwell together and war would be no more. As we saw in the previous chapter, "peace" (= "rest") ultimately takes us back to the paradisiacal condition of the unfallen creation.

It is too often overlooked, however, that the direct background of Rom 5:1 is Isa 32:17–18: "And the work of righteousness shall be peace; and the effect of righteousness quietness and assurance forever. And my people shall dwell in a peaceful habitation, and in sure dwellings, and in quiet resting places."¹¹ According to the prophet, the שלום of the restored Israel is to be the result of its renewed commitment to the covenant (צדקה), an event commensurate with the outpouring of the Spirit of Yahweh (v. 15) and the appearance of a king whose own rule is characterized by righteousness (v. 1). Rom 5:1 (5:5) thus asserts that the prophecy has found its fulfillment in the rightwising of the believer in Christ, again suggesting that Paul's horizons are broader than simply justification as a past forensic act, since against the backdrop of Isaiah 32 δικαιόω broadens to include the new Israel's commitment to the covenant *in toto*.¹² The

---

⁹ Kaylor, *Community*, 94–95.

¹⁰ See throughout Feuillet's "plan," and Collins, "Pattern." From another point of view, these verses exhibit chiasmus ("ABBA"):

    A: peace, 1–2a   B: hope, 2b
    B: hope, 3–5   A: peace, 6–11

¹¹ This echoing of Isa 32:17–18 in Rom 5:1 is a prime example of intertextuality, i. e., an old voice (prior text) is heard in a new setting (à la Hays, *Echoes*).

¹² That δικαιόω, in 5:1, summarizes 3:21–4:25 is not a particular problem for this more inclusive reading of the verb, since 4:18–22 stresses the *persevering quality* of Abraham's faith.

vindication/restoration/blessing of the people of God has been procured by Christ, as attended by the effusion of the love of God into our hearts by the Holy Spirit (Rom 5:5). The long-awaited eschaton is here, because cosmic peace (שׁלום) and salvation have been proleptically manifested in Christ, disclosing themselves in our obedience to his lordship.[13]

We may add that at the other end of this overall segment of the letter, in 8:31–39, is located the counterpart. The questions of 8:33 are taken from Isa 50:8–9, which embody the challenge of the obedient Servant of Yahweh to his enemies to set forth their case in the presence of God the Judge, who, he is confident, will exonerate him from all wrongdoing. The context of this Servant-song is replete with new creation associations, signifying that the blissful future for Israel is to be secured by the obedience of the עבד יהוה. For Paul this Servant is, in the first instance, Christ, in whom eschatological vindication has been secured for the latter-day people of God. Nevertheless, the conspicuous fact is that Paul refers these rhetorical questions not to Christ directly but to Christians, who, with the same confidence of the Servant himself, can call upon God to vindicate them from the accusations of every enemy.

In view of these findings, Rom 5:1 and 8:31–39 can be looked upon as a kind of *inclusio*, signaling the commencement and conclusion of a major section of the letter. In the case of both, with their respective OT backdrops, there is an identification of the covenant community with a central covenant figure (Servant-King): his obedience forms the matrix of his people's obedience and consequent blessings. This, we shall argue, is the conceptual framework of Rom 5:12–21, which forms Paul's horizon as he develops his Adam/Christ typology.

The second effect of justification is the Christian's boasting in the hope of the glory of God. The combination of ἐλπίς and ἡ δόξα τοῦ θεοῦ is distinctively eschatological in impact. "Hope" is faith directed to the future,[14] and "the glory of God," according to 8:18–25, is the consummation of the new creation and, by implication, the rectification of Adam's failure to be God's image (3:23). Indeed, 8:18, 24–25 again combine glory and hope, as the believer is pointed forward to the renewal of the creation and the redemption of the body. Paul, then, asserts that present reconciliation has as its consequence the assurance that one may anticipate the consummate fullness of a new heavens and a new earth. The Christian, in other words, may be assured that his hope in Christ will not expose him to eschatological shame;[15] and such hope is vital because in

---

[13] Beker, *Paul*, 264. Cf. de Boer, *Defeat*, 236, n. 35; Bultmann, *Theology* 1.276, 278. Beker's treatment of "grace" is also relevant. Once grace in Paul has been loosed from its privatistic Western moorings, says Beker, and placed in its original apocalyptic setting, it is seen to refer to both a cosmic power and to the domain of our life in Christ. Hence, Beker is correct that the historic debate concerning *gratia imputata* versus *gratia infusa* bypasses Paul's basic intent (*Paul*, 265).

[14] Cf. Gundry Volf, *Perseverance*, 50 (n. 11), 55. See the excellent remarks on hope in Paul by Beker, *Paul*, 146–49, 269–71; Bultmann, *Theology* 1.319–24.

[15] Cf. Gundry Volf, *Perseverance*, 50. "Shame," particularly in the Prophets, is synonym-

between there is the reality of suffering, tension, and groaning as one anticipates the end, the peculiar emphases of 7:14–25 and 8:18–25. *Perseverance* thus becomes the keynote of Christian existence as long as the tension of the Already and Not Yet in the cosmic plan of God remains unresolved.

B. The Relation of the Two Results of Justification by Faith, vv. 3–10

In this "B" section of the paragraph, Paul correlates the two results of justification, taking them up in reverse order (thus the possibility of a chiastic ordering of the verses). To be more precise, vv. 3–5 expand on hope, and vv. 6–10 explicate peace (= reconciliation).

Anticipating 7:14–25; 8:18–25, vv. 3–5 relate that the believer's hope is alive *because of* the presence of trials. As Beker explains, these are the tribulations of the end-time (Paul's modification of the messianic woes), which Christians do not merely endure but rather glory in.[16] The very fact of suffering, in its own way, is a sign that the ages have taken a decisive turn in the cosmic purposes of God. Tribulation, however, necessitates hope, a hope produced by the love of God poured into their hearts by the Holy Spirit, in keeping with the prophetic prediction that the Spirit would be poured out in the age to come (e.g., Isa 32:15; Joel 2:28–29).

Vv. 6–10 bring to the fore the work of Christ as effecting (messianic) peace with God. We note only two of the verses' prominent features.

First of all, Paul repeatedly emphasizes the person of Jesus as he elaborates this result of justification. This is due to his insistence that the eschaton has arrived *in Christ*; and life in Christ *is* the life of a new epoch and domain. Ἐν Χριστῷ for Paul, as Beker confirms, "has essentially a participatory-instrumental meaning and signifies the transfer to the new age that has been inaugurated with the death and resurrection of Christ."[17] When we look back to 3:24, we can see that 5:6–10 is a commentary on Paul's claim that justification is through the redemption *which is in Christ Jesus*. Consequently, what differentiates Paul's conception of righteousness from Jewish apocalyptic eschatology is his christology: "this righteousness (both as God's redemptive action and as gift) finds its apocalyptic disclosure (a) in the event of the death of Jesus Christ, and thus, as Rom 3.21 radically puts it, (b) 'apart from the law'."[18]

Second, vv. 9–10 are a statement of inauguration and consummation in the saving plan of God: what Christ has done for us in the past he will bring to completion in the day of judgment. The two verses explicate each other:

---

ous with judgment. See Ellis, *Paul*, 44–45. The imagery stems from Genesis 3: the shameful nakedness of Adam and Eve was the reversal of their original glory.

[16] Beker, *Paul*, 146.

[17] Ibid., 272.

[18] de Boer, *Defeat*, 155–56. As Cosgrove rightly contends, the accent in 3:21–31 is universality: "Faith as access to redemption... is open to both Jew and Gentile" ("Justification," 665).

v. 9: if justified by his blood, then (how much more) saved from (eschatological) wrath.

v. 10: if reconciled by his death, then (how much more) saved by his (resurrection) life.

The past redemptive event in Christ has given rise to hope in the believer, a hope which has as its primary focus the future eschatological consummation of the new creation. Or, as Elliot puts it, vv. 9–10 "relocate the soteriological fulcrum in the apocalyptic future: the gracious justification and reconciliation of the impious is made the basis for sure hope in the salvation to come."[19] Paul thus polarizes past and future as the epochal stages of the salvation experience, with the assurance that although the consummation of redemption is still outstanding, the believer can take comfort that God's purposes cannot fail.

It is normally observed that the argument is akin to the rabbinic *qal wahomer* pattern, which can be viewed as either *a minori ad majus* or *a maiori ad minus*, depending on how the interpreter assesses the force of the argument.[20] While it may be misleading to talk of a "greater" and a "lesser" strictly speaking, I favor *a minori ad majus*, because, without minimizing the significance of Christ's death for Paul, his sacrifice must eventuate in the final salvation of his people in order to accomplish its goal. The salvific process is commenced with present justification (δικαιωθέντες νῦν), but it will not be consummated until we are finally saved (σωθησόμεθα).[21] And "the process of consummating the work of salvation is more like an obstacle course than a downhill ride to the finishline. For the destiny of Christians does not go unchallenged in a world opposed to God's purposes. The powers of evil in the form of afflictions and trials threaten continuity in their salvation."[22] Thus, for instance, Cranfield's remark that deliverance from eschatological wrath is, in relation to justification, "very easy" fails to appreciate the formidable nature of the "obstacle course."[23] Given the θλίψεις which attend the life of faith this side of the resurrection, the great thing, from the perspective of the present passage, is yet to be accomplished.

C. The Two Results of Justification by Faith, v. 11

V. 11's restatement of vv. 1–2 displays the genius of the "ABA" style of writing, because it is not a mere verbal repetition of vv. 1–2, but is shaped by the intervening material of vv. 3–10. Thus, there are some significant vari-

---

[19] Elliot, *Rhetoric*, 229. See further Beker, *Paul*, 176–81.

[20] E.g., Gundry Volf, *Perseverance*, 53; Moo, *Romans*, 318; Cranfield, *Romans* 1.266. See further Str-B 3.224–26; Müller, "Schluß;" Brandenburger, *Adam*, 221–24; Quek, "Adam," 67–79.

[21] The disputed last clause of 4:25, ἠγέρθη διὰ τὴν δικαίωσιν ἡμῶν, makes perfectly good sense as a reference to eschatological justification, being equivalent to σωθησόμεθα in 5:9–10, particularly as 5:10 stresses that ultimate salvation is due to the *life* of Christ.

[22] Gundry Volf, *Perseverance*, 81. Berkouwer identifies continuity in salvation as the central problem of perseverance (*Perseverance*, 12).

[23] Cranfield, *Romans* 1.266.

ations. (1) Boasting in the hope of the glory of God becomes boasting in God through Christ, the reversal of Paul's former boast in Yahweh and the Torah (2:17, 23). (2) Reconciliation becomes virtually synonymous with "justification," "peace," and "access" (v. 2), which, in salvation-historical terms, relates to man's pristine condition of dwelling in the immediate presence of God in paradise (cf. the way Rev 21:5; 22:2 correlate the renewed presence of God with access to the tree of life).[24]

In sum, as the transition from chaps. 1–4 to 5:12–8:39, 5:1–11 explicates the believer's reconciliation in such a way as to announce the arrival of the new creation (cf. 2 Cor 5:17–19, which does the same). From both the juridical and experiential points of view, a radical change has been effected in the Christian's standing before God and in his way of life: whereas once believers were "sinners" and the "ungodly" enemies of God, under his wrath, they now have been justified and reconciled and rejoice in the hope of eventual salvation.

III. Romans 5:12–21: Adam and Christ: Disobedience and Obedience[25]

A. Structure and Relation to the Preceding

Because of its connection with 5:1–11, 5:12–19 proceeds to develop a theology of the obedience of Christ, as contrasted with the disobedience of Adam. As Elliot observes, the section takes shape around Paul's "breaking and realignment of typological correlations," formed on the structure "just as ... so also" (ὡς/ὥσπερ ... οὕτως).[26] The paragraph, as is commonly known, exhibits the most conspicuous example of Pauline anacoluthon. The train of thought commences in v. 12; but because Paul felt the necessity of a justification and elaboration of this statement, he does not formalize his analogy until v. 18. The section would appear to follow the "ABA" pattern:

---

[24] "Justification or reconciliation, is, as we have already been told, the initial act of a process; but it carries with it the assurance that the process will be completed" (Dodd, *Romans*, 77). Dodd's equation of justification and reconciliation is rightly grounded in the parallel of the two in Rom 5:1–11. Barth entitles the whole of Romans 5 "The Gospel as Man's Reconciliation with God" (*Shorter*, 55).

[25] For literature on 5:12–21, see the bibliographies of Cranfield, *Romans* 1.270–71, n. 1; Käsemann, *Romans*, 140; Wilckens, *Römer* 1.305–6; Quek, "Adam," 74–75 (nn. 4–5); Dunn, *Romans* 1.244–45; Brandenburger, *Adam*, 280–85; Lombard, "'Typology'," 97–100; Johnson, "Romans 5:12," 299, n. 6; Seebass, *NIDNTT* 1.88. Access to the Jewish materials on Adam (though interpreted variously) may be had through Brandenburger, *Adam*, 15–57; Jervell, *Imago*, 15–121; Scroggs, *Adam*; Levison, *Adam*; Str-B 3.226–29; Davies, *Paul*, 36–57; Wedderburn, "Structure," 339–54; Kim, *Origin*, 162–93; Schlier, *Römerbrief*, 183–89.

[26] Elliot, *Rhetoric*, 229.

A: v. 12: the initial statement of the old humanity's solidarity with the first Adam and its consequences;
B: vv. 13–17: justification and elaboration of the proposition begun in v. 12;
A: vv. 18–19: recapitulation and formal statement of the analogous work of Adam and Christ and its consequences.
[vv. 20–21 lie outside the Adam/Christ analogy proper]

Numerous commentators are correct that the διὰ τοῦτο of v. 12 is to be connected with the whole of vv. 1–11. Yet that paragraph can be reduced to two overlapping notions. For one, there is the juxtaposition of the believer's former condition ("ungodly," "sinners," "enemies," "wrath") with his present one ("justified," "saved," "reconciled"). 5:12–21, then, takes us back to the inception of "this present evil age," with the fall of Adam, and explains to the Romans that their past existence was the result of the disobedience of the first man. At the same time, however, we are informed that their current condition is due to the work of another Adam, who by his obedience has introduced a new creation.[27] In brief, "Adam is the head of the old aeon, the age of *death*; Christ is the head of the new aeon, the age of *life*."[28] Or, as Paul expresses it to the Corinthians, "As in Adam all die, so in Christ shall all be made alive" (1 Cor 15:22), and, most pointedly, "If anyone is in Christ, [there is] the new creation. The old things have passed away; behold, all things have become new" (2 Cor 5:17).

Second, there is the Christian's assured perseverance due to the life of the risen Christ, 5:9–10. Although the new creation has been inaugurated by justification, with its immediate effects of "peace" and the "hope of glory," this new creation must be consummated, and the people of God must endure θλῖψις until their adoption is complete (8:18–24). Therefore, the Adam/Christ analogy is intended to ground the perseverance of the saints in the perseverance (obedience) of Christ himself, because the one who now lives by the power of an indissoluble life (Heb 7:16) was obedient unto death (Phil 2:8). It is just here that the perspectives of 5:1–11 merge: as once we bore the image of Adam and were compelled to repeat his disobedience, so now we bear the image of Christ and are privileged to imitate his pattern of suffering followed by glory (cf. 1 Pet 1:3–12).

These constituent elements of 5:1–11, combined with the "therefore" of 5:12, alert us that the horizon of 5:12–21 is not to be restricted to a past forensic declaration. What is at stake in Romans 5 in its entirety is salvation in the broadest sense – the new creation inaugurated and consummated – and the necessity of perseverance until the old creation is thoroughly displaced by the new. Thus, while διὰ τοῦτο remains difficult,[29] the inference drawn from vv. 1–11 is to this effect: the Christian's entrance into the new creation and his assurance of enjoying its finalized bliss depend on his union with the living Lord, the other Adam and the authentic image of God.

---

[27] See Nygren, *Romans*, 210–11; Leenhardt, *Romans*, 141.
[28] Nygren, *Romans*, 210.
[29] See the discussion of the various options by Moo (*Romans*, 328–30).

B. Paul's Creation Typology

The verses exhibit an observable swing from the personal and individual language of 5:1–11 to a different key in which "the whole sweep of human history is embraced by the two epochs instituted by Adam and Christ."[30] The perspective of vv. 12–19 thus differs from vv. 1–11 in its cosmic focus. Yet the continuity of the two paragraphs is equally noticeable by virtue of "the re-emergence of the reversal theme in explicit terms of the two men whose single acts of disobedience and obedience encapsulate and determine the character of the two epochs which together span human history." "A very effective conclusion," continues Dunn, "is thus achieved by showing how the sweeping indictment of Adamic humanity in 1.19ff., and repeated summarily in 3.23, is more than answered by the abundance of grace through Christ."[31]

It is in keeping with this cosmic/salvation-historical perspective that Paul continues to retrogress from the Torah backward in history. In chap. 4, he appealed to Abraham's priority to the law; and here he takes a further step back to Adam and the creation, thus recapitulating the argument begun in 1:18, in which he depicted the revelation of God's wrath as the outworking of the primal covenant relationship between the Creator and his creatures (the punitive side of the δικαιοσύνη θεοῦ). Paul's tendency in Romans to move back beyond the Torah, a tacit denial of its eternity, has already been illustrated (in the previous chapter) by 2:12–16, according to which creation accounts for the law shared in common by Jew and Gentile.

At the head of old and new creations respectively are the first Adam and the last. In Acts 17:26, Paul is reported to say that God made from one (ἐξ ἑνός) all men to live on all the face of the earth. This is of interest because in this place the comparison of the two Adams stresses that through "one man" (δι' ἑνός) and his singular act of disobedience or obedience the whole race has been effected for ill or for good. With all the debate on particulars, the one given of the passage is that each division of humanity is in solidarity with its leader, so that the action of the "one" has a bearing on the condition of the "many." Of course, there is no overall consensus as to the mechanics of the solidarity in question.[32] Since Paul does not say explicitly what impels his logic, the exegete is left to reconstruct from his world of thought, which can be understood variously. "Corporate personality" is a possibility, though it has not escaped criticism;[33] and while it cannot be dismissed entirely, Käsemann is correct that "Decisive in the interpretation of our text... is not the comparison of two heads

---

[30] Dunn, *Romans* 1.271. Dunn further observes that the final sentence of chap. 5, which serves as a transition into the next phase of the discussion, places side by side the two quasi-powers who dominate the old aeon (sin and death).

[31] Dunn, "Analysis," 2856. Cf. Moo, *Romans*, 326.

[32] Cf. Sanday/Headlam, *Romans*, 132; Moo, *Romans*, 340. The various attempts to relate the personal and community aspects of sin and death are discussed in full by Moo (ibid., 335–41).

[33] See Porter, "Sin," 16 (with literature). Akin to corporate personality is the "ancestor-

of a generation, but of the two figures, in sharp dualism, who alone inaugurated a world of perdition and salvation, so that they cannot be listed in a series of ancestors." In this dualistic contrast, Christ and Adam are now the bearers of destiny for the world determined by them.[34]

Thus, in interpreting Rom 5:12–21, it is vital to see that Paul's vision encompasses the whole of creation. "The spheres of Adam and Christ, of death and life, are separated as alternative, exclusive, and ultimate, and this happens in *global breadth*. An old world and a new world are at issue."[35] Consequently, given the creation focus of 5:12–19 (and chaps. 5–8 as a whole), man as the image of God springs immediately to mind. It is through the first and last Adams respectively that humanity bears either the failed or successful likeness of the Creator.[36] The identification and character of all people thus depend on Adam or Christ, the "direct" images of the invisible God. Therefore, the primal principle of creation continues: *like begets like*. The "many" and the "all" bear the likeness of the "one" in that the former derive their being and character from the latter and imitate his example. This, we shall argue, most effectively opens up Paul's intentions in this much disputed passage.

C. Paul's Dialogue with Israel

This portion of Paul's letter is more than just a teaching model to explain the nature of the new creation which has arrived in Christ; it is, in fact, integral to his interaction with the Jewish point of view. In the words of Beker: "Jew and Gentile are now subsumed under the one figure of Adam, who by his transgression sealed 'all men'... under sin and death. The subject is no longer Jew or Gentile, but 'the many.'"[37] Taken within its polemical context, Rom 5:12–19 bears witness to the radicalness of Paul's stance toward Israel. As we saw in chapter 2, some two and half centuries before Paul, Ben Sira claimed that the people of Israel and their Torah are God's new beginning and the remedy for the ills of Adam's disobedience (Sir 10:19; 17:1–17).[38] Similar ideas characterized Apocalyptic as a whole.[39] Moreover, in at least one rabbinic text, *Gen. R.* 14:6, Abraham appears as a second Adam, compensating for the failure of the original. As N.T. Wright has demonstrated, the Adam theology of Jewish literature is intended to advance a claim about *Israel* in the purposes of God. As such, it fulfills a specific purpose, i.e., to mark out this nation as God's true humanity and the realization of his creation designs. In brief,

---

descendant" motif, i.e., the descendant is affected by the actions of the progenitor (Cambier, "Péchés," 221, 225–26).

[34] Käsemann, *Romans*, 142–43, 146. Cf. Oepke, *TDNT* 2.542.

[35] Käsemann, *Romans*, 147 (italics mine).

[36] "The first Adam, like the second, imprints his likeness on those under his headship" (Goppelt, *Typos*, 134).

[37] Beker, *Paul*, 85.

[38] Cf. Garlington, *Obedience*, 58–60.

[39] de Boer, *Defeat*, 153–54.

III. Romans 5:12–21: Adam and Christ: Disobedience and Obedience

"Adam has become embodied... in Israel, the people of the Torah, and in her future hope."[40]

To reiterate from before, one may say that there is a legitimate sense in which a new beginning was made with Abraham and continued into subsequent Israelite history. However, Israel's mistake was to suppose that the world was made for it and that it alone was meant to reprise the role marked out for Adam, consonant with the fact that it was the law – the embodiment of true wisdom – which formed the charter of Israel's national life precisely as the way of God's true humanity.[41] As a result, Paul's contemporaries were insistent that participation in the new creation was possible only within the confines of the chosen people and their Torah.

For Paul, however, if Israel marked a new beginning in the saving purposes of God, it was only that in the fullness of time this new beginning might, in Christ, be extended to the ends of the earth. The role traditionally assigned to Israel has devolved on Christ: Paul now regards *him and his people* as God's true humanity.[42] As stated previously, he is bold enough to say, on the one hand, that humanity outside of Christ – including Israel – is in Adam and, therefore, still participates in the effects of his sin ("ungodly," "sinners," "enemies," "wrath"). On the other hand, with equal boldness, he asserts that everyone in Christ – regardless of ethnic identity and commitment to the Torah – has entered the new creation with its blessings ("justified," "saved," "reconciled"). In general terms, 5:1–11 addresses itself to all weak, ungodly people who have missed the way of God's covenant nation.[43] However, the real impact (scandal) of Romans 5 as a whole is the involvement of *Israel* in Adam's apostasy.

It is the role played by Rom 5:12–21 within Paul's dialogue with Israel which, at least in part, serves to inform us of his intentions; that is, Christ has succeeded where Adam and Israel have not. (The joint failure of Adam and Israel is likewise evident in 7:7–11.) The first man failed to accomplish his mandate of bringing the earth to its full potential, its "eschatological" state. Another son of God, Israel, likewise became idolatrous by exchanging the glory of the immortal God for images (Rom 1:23 = Ps 106:20; Jer 2:11).[44] In the case of Paul's contemporaries, the disobedience in question was a failure to be loyal to the God of Israel because of an idolatrous attachment to the Torah. By way of contrast, the obedience of Christ, as we shall argue, can be defined as his perseverance in faith and his consequent realization of what humanity was

---

[40] Wright, "Adam," 360–65 (quote from p. 364); id., *Climax*, 21–26. Cf. Jervell, *Imago*, 31–37.

[41] Wright, "Adam," 361–63, 365.

[42] Ibid., 365–87 (esp. pp. 370–73). Wright qualifies, however, that Christ does not simply replace Israel; he began where Adam ended, with the entail of sin, working its way out to judgment, and thus must deal with the "many trespasses" and condemnation resultant from Adam's sin (pp. 371–72). He later contrasts the redemptive work of Christ with Israel's failure to redeem the world, seeking, rather, to rule it (p. 389).

[43] Kaylor, *Community*, 100.

[44] Cf. Berkouwer, *Sin*, 274.

intended to be in the first Adam. Our treatment of the passage, then, will concentrate on those aspects of Paul's argument which stand at the forefront of his claim that the last Adam has succeeded where the first Adam fell short.

D. *The Disobedient First Adam and the Old Humanity*

1. *Adam's Sin as the Gateway of All Subsequent Sin and Death*

V. 12, the protasis of Paul's sentence, to be completed by the apodosis of vv. 18−19, is a statement of cause and effect: through one man sin and death entered into the world, so that death (has) spread to all men because all, in some sense, (have) sinned. Unlike many of his contemporaries, Paul does not speculate about the way in which sin entered the world: he is concerned with universal experience, not cosmic speculation. However, it is equally true, contrary particularly to Dodd, that he *is* concerned with origins, if for no other reason than to lay the foundation for the origin of righteousness in Christ. If, as Dodd himself affirms, in Adam humanity is corporately sinful,[45] it is because Adam was the first disobedient man. Adam, most pointedly, is the origin of sin and, consequently, death in the world: "Adam sums up and symbolizes all this humanity both in his person and in his behaviour, and the conditions of life of every individual are moulded by it."[46] As Dunn reminds us, Adam (אדם) means "man:" what can be said of Adam can be said of men in general, and what is true of men in general is true of Adam.[47] Thus, "In the fall narrative of Genesis 3 'all subsequent human history lies encapsulated'; its incidents are re-enacted in the life of the race and indeed, to some extent, of each member of the race."[48]

Of course, what Paul means exactly is a matter of both historical and contemporary debate.[49] Consequently, it is possible only to make certain proposals without entering in detail into the debate. The controversy centers chiefly around the last clause of v. 12, Paul's depiction of the plight of mankind outside of Christ: sin and death first entered the world δι' ἑνὸς ἀνθρώπου, yet, in his words, death spread to all people ἐφ' ᾧ πάντες ἥμαρτον. Käsemann identifies 12 d as the real interpretive problem, where, in his view, the motif of

---

[45] Dodd, *Romans*, 80.

[46] Leenhardt, *Romans*, 141 (see additionally his perceptive comments on pp. 140−44). Cf. Nygren, *Romans*, 213. Various Jewish authors attribute the advent of sin to Satan (e. g., Wis 2:14) and Eve (e. g., *Apoc. Mos.* 32:2), not to Adam directly. Paul himself can associate Eve with humanity's fall (Rom 7:11; 2 Cor 11:3 [2 Tim 2:13−14]), without, however, holding her responsible for it. *Deut. R.* 9 (206 a), like Paul, blames Adam. *2 Apoc. Bar.* 54:15 also formally agrees with Paul that it was Adam who sinned first and brought death upon all who were not in his own time (but see below n. 65). The Satanic seduction of the human race in Jewish literature has been treated many times. See, e. g., Kelly, "Devil," 202−14.

[47] Dunn, *Christology*, 101. Cf. Davies, *Paul*, 55.

[48] Bruce, *Romans*, 126.

[49] These have been detailed by Murray, *Imputation*; Hutchinson, *Sin*; Cranfield, *Romans* 1.274−79; id., "Problems," 330−38; Johnson, "Romans 5:12," 306−13.

destiny which dominates 12 a-c gives way to that of the personal guilt of mankind.[50] Of course, not everyone sees in these words personal guilt at all but the imputed guilt of Adam's original trespass. So, in what sense is it meaningful that πάντες ἥμαρτον, thus accounting for the dissemination of death and suffering among the human race? The various answers to the question have understandably focused on ἐφ' ᾧ and ἥμαρτον, to which we shall give some attention; yet the scope of πάντες is not irrelevant to the debate.

The Augustinian equation of ἐφ' ᾧ with *in quo* (i.e., in Adam), grammatically and lexically speaking anyway, has been discounted by modern scholars, even if theologically one accepts that mankind sinned "in Adam."[51] With some degree of confidence at least, it can be said that the expression is either idiomatic, meaning "because" or "in that," or equivalent to ἐπὶ τούτῳ ὅτι, grounding the death of mankind in the circumstance that all have sinned.[52] Either lends itself to the interpretation herein proposed.

The referent of ἥμαρτον is a much more complicated matter. For reasons to be clarified presently, the view propounded here is that the verb has to do with the human situation resultant from its union with Adam. Paul, in other words, explains the universal sway of death to be due to the sin = apostasy of mankind, as rooted in the sin = apostasy of the first Adam. Ἥμαρτον, accordingly, gives voice to mankind's repetition in principle of Adam's trespass, thus giving rise to the spread of sin and death throughout the human family. Among the commentators, the stance assumed by me is approximated by Cranfield (following the lead of Calvin), who understands ἥμαρτον in terms of "the fruit of the desperate moral debility and corruption which resulted from man's primal transgression and which all succeeding generations of mankind have inherited."[53] This is preferable, I think, to the imputation of Adam's guilt. However, even it is not precisely Paul's point.

It is not to be overlooked that in Romans 5 the apostle's thought is steeped in the creation. Thus, while it is probable that Paul envisages humanity in Adam as inheriting a "sinful nature," the most relevant thing we can say is that *man in Adam enters the world devoid of the Spirit*. It is at least arguable that Paul conceived of unfallen Adam, so to speak, as "the temple of the Holy Spirit."[54]

---

[50] Käsemann, *Romans*, 147.

[51] E.g., Murray, *Imputation*, 9, n. 10; Bruce, *Romans*, 130.

[52] Lyonnet ("ἐφ' ᾧ") as followed by numerous scholars. For example, Black (*Romans*, 89) proposes that the expression should be translated "*wherefore, from which it follows,* [= thus providing proof that] that all men, like Adam, sinned." But see Brandenburger's criticisms of Lyonnet (*Adam*, 171–72). Another alternative is proposed by Cambier ("Péchés," 242–51), who renders ἐφ' ᾧ as "those who," with ἀνθρώπους as the antecedent.

[53] Cranfield, *Romans* 1.278; id., "Problems," 335–40; Calvin, *Romans*, 111–12; id., *Institutes* 2.1.8. Cf. Leenhardt, *Romans*, 141–46; Sanday/Headlam, *Romans*, 134. "Surely there must be something inherent in being human that causes everyone, without exception, to decide to worship idols rather than the true God" (Moo, *Romans*, 335; cf. ibid., 341). Moo, however, favors the imputation of Adam's sin.

[54] Smeaton, *Spirit*, 10–17; Kline, *Images*, 13–34.

Therefore, on this construction, when he fell, he forfeited the presence of the Spirit, so that all his descendants emerge from the womb bereft of the Spirit's influence. As formed in the likeness of "the man of dust" (1 Cor 15:49), man in Adam, in Paul's words elsewhere, is a ψυχικὸς ἄνθρωπος (1 Cor 2:13), possessing, in his fallenness, an ἀδόκιμος νοῦς (Rom 1:28).[55]

Vis-à-vis Cranfield and others, Ridderbos and Berkouwer are quite right that the present context directly concerns man's immediate involvement in Adam's sin and death, not moral corruption as such.[56] This is why I have sought to emphasize that "sin" in the first instance is not so much "depravity" as a (damnation-) historical state introduced by Adam.[57] Human failing is a reality; yet, in perspective, it is but the by-product of the apostasy bequeathed by Adam, whose hallmark is the absence of the Spirit.[58] Again thinking in salvation-historical terms, confirmation is had by Paul's teaching that the impartation of the Spirit is a new creation: in becoming the renewed image of God, humankind "in Christ" is again indwelt by the Spirit. We might say that whereas the first Adam forfeited the Spirit, the last Adam, in his role as life-giver, restores the Spirit (1 Cor 15:45).[59]

It may be said, then, that Paul's intent in the latter part of v. 12, particularly evident from the words "and so death spread to all men," is *original death* rather than original sin; it is original death which furnishes the background of the actual theme of the section: the origin of life.[60] Adam's ἁμαρτία, as chaps. 5–8 clarify, is not so much this or that infraction of the divine law; it is, rather, a state of estrangement and condemnation, which can do none other than produce

---

[55] The ψυχικὸς ἄνθρωπος of 1 Cor 2:13 is the one to whom the things of the Spirit of God are foolishness. Personhood stemming from Adam is not only σῶμα ψυχικόν constitutionally (1 Cor 15:44), it has become ψυχικὸς ἄνθρωπος in the pregnant sense of the phrase, i.e., bereft of the Spirit and unable to discern the plan of God for the ages.

[56] Ridderbos, *Romeinen*, 116; Berkouwer, *Sin*, 497.

[57] Cambier points out that the epochal coming of sin into the world parallels the epochal advent of Christ as "the coming one" ("Péchés," 232–33).

[58] This interpretation does not really assume an implicit "middle term," i.e., a bridge from Adam's sin to ours (Moo, *Romans*, 337, 354; cf. Murray, *Imputation*, 67), because the birth of individuals into the world *eo ipso* guarantees immediate involvement in Adam's sin and death. But even if such a middle term is required, it is one provided by creation itself. Like begets like: as Adam sinned (apostatized), so have his progeny, who bear his image.

[59] In 1 Cor 15:45, Paul goes beyond the Adam-model of Romans 5 by ascribing to Christ the role of the Creator-Spirit of Gen 1:2; 2:7.

[60] Bultmann, "Adam," 152; Dunn, *Romans* 1.273. One can agree with Moo (*Romans*, 338, n. 39) that "original death" requires a corresponding idea of "original sin." But it is the definition of "original sin" which is the crux of the debate. In Dunn's words: "Paul could be said to hold a doctrine of *original sin*, in the sense that from the beginning everyone has been under the power of sin with death as the consequence, but not a doctrine of *original guilt*, since individuals are only held responsible for deliberate acts of defiance against God and his law" (*Romans* 1.291). The relation of "original sin" in Paul and the rabbinic doctrine of the יצר הרע is here being left an open question, except to say that the element of choice appears to figure in both (Cambier, "Péchés," 220).

III. Romans 5:12−21: Adam and Christ: Disobedience and Obedience

death in the all-embracing sense.[61] In this regard, Moo correctly surmises that sin is given an active role: it "reigns" (5:20; cf. 6:13); it can be "obeyed" (6:16−17); it pays wages (6:23); it seizes opportunity (7:8, 11); it "kills" (7:11, 13); it is a power that holds sway in the world outside of Christ, bringing disaster and death on all humanity.[62] "Paul," Käsemann adds, "is not speaking primarily of act and punishment but of ruling powers which implicate all people individually and everywhere determine reality as destiny."[63] All this suggests that sin is far more than guilt forensically considered; it is, in fact, a life-force of its own.

While individual acts of sin are the outgrowth of this ἁμαρτία, the consistent use of the singular noun throughout Romans 5−8 intimates that Paul looks upon sin as a unified and coherent whole:[64] along with death and the law, it stands for the old creation as that entity hostile to God and aligned with evil. If, as seems to be the case, Paul distinguishes between "sin" and "transgression," the latter is but the unavoidable consequence of the former, which is "an inward disposition of rebellion against God rising out of exaltation of the self."[65] To put it most pointedly, "sin" is "apostasy." Paul, therefore, can insist in 6:5−11 that the believer has died to sin, i.e., he has renounced his former condition of rebellion: his orientation is now to the new age and its ideals. This means, on the other hand, that the contrast between chap. 6 and 7:14−25 is not as stark as has been imagined, because while one can renounce in principle the values of the old life, those values still seek to reassert their previous domination, thus setting up the conflict depicted in 7:14−25.

It is in this setting that ἥμαρτον, which focuses on Adam's descendants, speaks of the race in its imitation of its forebear,[66] with the effect that death

---

[61] See Stuart, *Romans*, 206−7; Dunn, *Romans* 1.275−76; Schlier, *Römerbrief*, 160−61. Schlier writes that this is death in the sense of ἀπώλεια and ἀπόλλυσθαι, the outworking of God's ὀργή and the τέλος of sin (6:21). Brandenburger (*Adam*, 165−67) adds that θάνατος is man's radical lostness before God (κατάκριμα), as is shown by the antithesis of θάνατος-ζωὴ αἰώνιος (vv. 12, 17, 21).

[62] Moo, *Romans*, 331. Sanday/Headlam similarly describe sin as "a malignant force let loose among mankind" (*Romans*, 132). For this reason, death is also depicted in tyrant-like terms. See Black, "Perspectives," 430−31.

[63] Käsemann, *Romans*, 150 (on v. 14). Cf. Cambier, "Péchés," 233−34; Brandenburger, *Adam*, 160, passim.

[64] See Beker, *Paul*, 189−90; Moo, *Romans*, 331.

[65] Barrett, *Romans*, 112. Moo contends that "sin" (in the singular) is composed of individual acts of sin ("sins"); these, he says, are a principle or network of sin "so pervasive and dominant that the person's destiny is determined by those actions" (*Romans*, 331). Without putting too fine a point on it, I would want to say that the various actions, or "sins," are determined by the "sin" which is Adam's rebellion. To be sure, a person's actions, in Pauline perspective, have a bearing on his/her destiny. Yet, for him, in Adam one's destiny has already been fixed, until, that is, one is transferred into Christ.

[66] "The distinction between the 'one' and the 'all' is matched by the distinction between ἁμαρτία and ἥμαρτον..." (Dunn, *Romans* 1.274). Reference is frequently made to *2 Apoc. Bar.* 54:19: "Adam is, therefore, not the cause, except only for himself, but each of us has become his own Adam." In context, the statement reminds Israel that Adam's choice to

spread to all people, "taking hold of each individual man in turn, as the generations succeeded one another."⁶⁷ This is the sin whose essential traits return in every sin.⁶⁸ Not only so, the gravity of the human condition increases exponentially with the birth of every new person into the world.⁶⁹

It is in such an all-embracive sense that death εἰς πάντας ἀνθρώπους διῆλθεν: it has *permeated* (Murray) and *pervaded* (Sanday/Headlam) Adam's race *in toto*. Though it is true that several times in Romans 5 Paul points to the one man through whom sin and death became realities, there is reason to think that his concern is equally with the κόσμος or the people to whom death has penetrated.⁷⁰ Wilckens calls attention to the fact that v. 12 (vv. 18–19) does not mention Adam by name, from which he infers that Paul's interest in Adam lies primarily in his role of the portal through which the *world* became the place of death's activity. That is to say, Adam's sin is significant because it occasioned the demise of the κόσμος.⁷¹ Without, then, downplaying the repeated stress on the "one man," whose significance we shall explore below, it follows that the preposition διά should receive at least equal stress: it was *through* the one man that all have been affected for ill. When, in vv. 18–19, Paul returns to his original point, it is this preposition which will serve to underscore the instrumental significance of Christ for the new humanity's obedience and life.⁷²

---

forsake God does not have to be the choice of everyone. While death is inevitable because of his sin (v. 15), judgment is not. Hence, individuals must decide for future glory, so as to avoid the coming torment (vv. 15–16); those who choose otherwise are the unrighteous, who do not love God's law and refuse to be instructed by his creation (vv. 14, 17–18). Inasmuch as both this author and Paul highlight human responsibility, there is a formal agreement between them. However, any attempt to draw a direct parallel must take cognizance of one important qualification, viz., that in the former the faithful and the wicked both reside within the community of Israel. Throughout the apocalypse, the scribe speaks to the people and, e.g., in chaps. 41–42 he confronts the issue of apostasy from the covenant. Thus, the ability to choose assumed by the words "Adam is not the cause, except only for himself" is to be located within its covenant context, as are similar statements in, e.g., Sir 1:26; 15:15; 21:11; Tob 4:5; *Pss. Sol.* 9:7; *Testament of Asher* 1; 4 Macc 1:15; CD 3:3. In distinction, the impression left by Paul is that Adam's descendants not only willingly imitate his example, they are compelled to do so because they partake of a community of nature with him, including – quite radically – Israel, whose hardness is evident in its rejection of Christ (11:7–9, 25).

⁶⁷ Cranfield, *Romans* 1.274.
⁶⁸ Berkouwer, *Sin*, 274.
⁶⁹ See Leenhardt, *Romans*, 143. Paul's own thought is remarkably similar to 4 Ezra 3:7–11, 20–27; 4:30; 7:118. Morris observes that Paul is not simply repeating a Jewish commonplace, since no other author goes as far as he. Nonetheless, these references show that his position developed naturally from his Jewish background (*Romans*, 230, n. 47). Cf. Wright, "Adam," 370. Barrett deduces that the common element between Paul and the various Jewish writers is the disastrous effects of Adam's sin, which are ultimately cosmic in proportion (*Adam*, 8–9, 14–15). Cf. Scroggs, *Adam*, 17–20, 33–38; Wedderburn, "Structure," 344–45.
⁷⁰ On κόσμος, see Gibbs, *Creation*, 51, n. 2.
⁷¹ Wilckens, *Römer* 1.315. Dunn calls Adam an "epochal figure," i.e., he is "the one who initiated the first major phase of human history and thereby determined the character of that phase for those belonging to it" (*Romans* 1.289). Cf. Barth, *Shorter*, 61; Ridderbos, *Romeinen*, 112; Wedderburn, "Adam," 423.
⁷² The same is true of 1 Cor 15:21. Stuart (*Romans*, 204) remarks that διά designates the

III. Romans 5:12−21: Adam and Christ: Disobedience and Obedience

Thus far it has been intimated that within the cadre of the present passage the terms "sin" and "disobedience" are to be regarded specifically as "apostasy." The basis of this assumption now needs to be clarified. In a bird's eye view, not only is such a connotation appropriate because of the focus on perseverance in Romans 5 but also because of several supporting considerations: (a) the precedent established by the earlier portion of Romans; (b) Paul's Jewish heritage; (c) parallels in other NT authors. To these we now turn.

(a) According to Rom 2:12, one of the things held in common by Jew and Gentile is "sin:" ὅσοι γὰρ ἀνόμως ἥ μ α ρ τ ο ν, ἀνόμως ἀπολοῦνται· καὶ ὅσοι ἐν νόμῳ ἥμαρτον, διὰ νόμου κριθήσονται. Ἁμαρτάνω here stands over against Adam's original quest for glory, honor, and immortality, commensurate with his continued trust in the word of God and commitment to the person of his Creator. "Sin," therefore, is apostasy or mankind's failure to attain to its *raison d'être*.

Rom 3:23 epitomizes the whole of human history with the words: πάντες ἥ μ α ρ τ ο ν καὶ ὑστεροῦνται τῆς δόξης τοῦ θεοῦ. Πάντες ἥμαρτον, the precise combination of words found in 5:12, glances back to 3:9: πάντα ὑφ' ἁμαρτίαν εἶναι, Paul's conclusion from the foregoing discussion of mankind's rebellion against its Creator. In fact, 3:23 itself is a summary of 1:18−3:20 − Paul's "covenant lawsuit" against the "sin" of the human race in Adam − in which Adam/creation motifs occupied a place of some prominence. With the willing compliance of the first man, the agenda of creation was sabotaged by Satan, and all who bear Adam's likeness continue his resistance to the Creator and thus fall perpetually short (ὑστεροῦνται) of the divine image. Humanity (including Israel) in Adam is idolatrous (apostate) by definition: all his progeny bear his image in that they are born in a condition of estrangement from God (cf. Ps 51:5), with an inbuilt disposition to serve the creature rather than the Creator. Hence, 3:23, as it distills the charge of 1:18−3:20 that all are ὑφ' ἁμαρτίαν, sheds a considerable amount of light on 5:12, especially as the verse provides another point of contact with chap. 5, viz., the creation term "glory:" humanity's shortfall of the "glory" of God is its failure to be the adequate "image" of God.

In agreement with Wedderburn, this interpretation of ἁμαρτάνω is supported by the fact that Paul normally uses the verb with regard to responsible and personal sinning, particularly in the Romans passages just cited, in which, remarks Wedderburn, "Paul's whole argument would be vitiated if any mouth were not stopped by the consciousness of its own guilt before God."[73] Πάντες

---

causa principalis, not the mere secondary, instrumental, or occasional cause. Note how in vv. 18−19 δἰ ἑνός is complemented by εἰς πάντας and πάντας ἀνθρώπους, who are made either sinners or righteous.

[73] Wedderburn, "Structure," 351. He further remarks that a reference to individual guilt make the best sense in the light of Jewish parallels (ibid., 352). See the defense of this interpretation of ἁμαρτάνω and ἁμαρτία by Brandenburger (*Adam*, 175−76. See ibid., 175, n. 3, for other references); Stuart (*Romans*, 213−17, 220−27); Cambier ("Péchés," 235−41);

ἥμαρτον, therefore, in both cases is to be taken in the same sense, i.e., death has spread to all because all *have sinned*, i.e., have apostatized, because of their union with Adam. Thus interpreted, the aorist in each instance is constative and is to be translated by the English present perfect tense.[74]

(b) As to Paul's Jewish background, of obvious significance is Genesis 3's account of the fall of Adam. Without going into any real detail, the heart of the narrative is to the effect that "Adam endeavoured to set himself in the place of God... and in that moment sin was born."[75] Not content with being God's image, wherein his authentic glory resided, he aspired to be on a par with God himself. "Man was unwilling, says Barrett, to recognize a Lord; he chose to be Lord himself, and to glorify himself,"[76] all because the Serpent "twisted the instruction of the Creator given for man's good and made it sound like the legislation of a dictator fearful of losing his special status and prerogatives. Thus deceived, man clutched at a godlike life and grasped only death."[77] From that point on, the Creator/creature distinction was distorted, rendering Adam an idolater and a defector from the relationship established in the creation. Berkouwer, then, justifiably writes that although the word *fall* does not occur in Genesis 3, "sin is pictured as *apostasy from God.*"[78]

It is this Israelite sense of man's primal apostasy in Adam, as shaped by the Genesis story, that calls forth the confession of the author of Psalm 51: "Behold, I was brought forth in iniquity, and in sin my mother conceived me" (v. 5). The condition of fallen Adam, in other words, is reproduced in the birth of each individual.

Moving briefly to Second Temple Judaism, "sin" assumes the meaning of "apostasy" in Sir 24:22:

> Whoever obeys me will not be put
>   to shame,
> and those who work with my
>   help will not sin.

This is to be compared with Sir 4:15–16; 15:15:

> He who obeys her will judge the
>   nations,
> and whoever gives heed to her
>   will dwell secure.

---

and Shedd (*Romans*, 125–27). Ἁμαρτάνω is used of Adam's personal sin in v. 16a, so that the sin of his posterity matches his own.

[74] Cf. Cranfield, *Romans* 1.279; Cambier, "Péchés," 241; Robertson, *Grammar*, 833. As contra Morris (*Romans*, 231), the aorist in 5:12 no more *has* to point to "one act in the past," i.e., the sin of Adam, than in 2:12 and 3:23.

[75] Barrett, *Romans*, 111.

[76] Ibid., 36–37 (on 1:21).

[77] Dunn, *Christology*, 103.

[78] Berkouwer, *Sin*, 268 (italics mine). Likewise Calvin (*Institutes* 2.1.4) and Schlatter (*Gerechtigkeit*, 192).

> If he has faith in her he will ob-
> tain her;
> > and his descendants will remain
> > in possession of her.
> If you will, you can keep the com-
> mandments,
> > and to act faithfully is a matter
> > of your own choice.

In these several pronouncements, the scribe exhorts his students to obey wisdom or the Torah. According to the immediate context of 4:15–16 (vv. 17–19), one is to give heed to wisdom, because she is a tester of those who come forward to serve the Lord (cf. Sir 2:1–6). The author here casts his students in the role of Israel tested in the wilderness, to see if they will persevere in trials and confirm their confidence in wisdom, their guide and disciplinarian.[79] 15:15 places in parallel keeping the commandments and faithful action, which is not "legalistic perfection" but the disciple's continued allegiance to his covenant commitment.[80] It is in comparison with these kindred statements that the saying of 24:22 makes sense: "Whoever *obeys* me will not be put to shame, and those who work with my help (ἐν ἐμοί) will not *sin*." (Note how Ben Sira quite naturally associates two of the most crucial terms of Rom 5:12–19, "obedience" and "sin.") In light of the sage's encouragement to confess one's shortcomings (4:26), "sin" cannot have reference to sinless perfection, and, because of the *parallelismus membrorum* of the verse, "obey," likewise, cannot mean anything approaching this. Rather, wisdom's promise is that the obedient person will not sin so as to forsake Yahweh and incur judgment (contrast Ps 78:32; *2 Apoc. Bar.* 54:22 [in context]). This was particularly relevant for Ben Sira, given the incipient Hellenistic encroachments on Israelite religion and culture in his day.[81]

Compatible with the perspective of Ben Sira is the claim of the Wisdom of Solomon that "We will not sin, because we know that we are accounted thine" (Wis 15:2). The immediate context dictates that the "sin" in question is idolatry or apostasy. By way of parallel, Wis 14:29–31 is especially relevant. The writer condemns those who trust in and obey (προσέχω) lifeless idols and, consequently, have contempt for the holiness of God's covenant. Accordingly, there is a "just penalty for those who sin." Therefore, ἁμαρτάνω assumes in this setting the specific connotation of abandonment of Yahweh in favor of a pagan lifestyle. But because believers are accounted God's, their *perseverance* is assured. In terms of Wis 15:3, the faithful possess the knowledge of God, which is the root of their immortality, as opposed to idols, which have no power to confer eternal life. This reading of "sin" in the passage is buttressed by the motif of the testing of the righteous sons of God which permeates the book of Wisdom.[82]

---

[79] I have treated the text in *Obedience*, 26–28.
[80] See further ibid., 31–33.
[81] See ibid., 15–19, and the other literature cited.
[82] See ibid., 74–79, 84–86.

In view of the above texts, the statement of Pr Man 8 is perfectly comprehensible: "Thou therefore, O Lord, that art the God of the just, hast not appointed repentance to the righteous, to Abraham, and Isaac, and Jacob, who have not sinned against thee; but thou hast appointed repentance to me that am a sinner." A casual reading would suggest that the author is attributing sinlessness to Israel's patriarchs. To "sin," however, means "commit idolatry." The Prayer places this confession in the mouth of Manasseh, one of the most wicked of the Israelite kings, who made his own children pass through the fire of idolatrous sacrifice. So, for this author repentance has been appointed even for the worst kind of sinner, the idolater and the apostate. The "just" ("righteous"), by contrast, do not need repentance in the sense intended, because they never forsook the covenant. Cf. *Pss. Sol.* 17:36; *T. Jud.* 24:1, which predicate "sin"-lessness of the Messiah.

(c) Such a meaning of "sin" is also in evidence in NT authors other than Paul. The Epistle to the Hebrews warns its readers: "If we sin deliberately after receiving the knowledge of the truth, there no longer remains a sacrifice for sins" (Heb 10:26). The adverb "deliberately" or "willingly" (ἑκουσίως), as H. W. Attridge comments, reflects the Pentateuchal distinction between high-handed and inadvertent sins, which, he says, was widely recognized in post-biblical Judaism: "As the sequel indicates, our author has in mind a specific willful sin, that of apostasy."[83] It goes without saying that the burden of the entire letter is perseverance, which is why "sin" more than once has reference to apostasy (e. g., 4:15).[84]

1 John 3:4–9 equates sin with lawlessness (ἀνομία). The concept of lawlessness is one which, in Jewish history, comes to prominence during the Greek persecution and Maccabean revolt of the second century BCE. To make a long story very short, the "lawless" (ἄνομοι and παράνομοι) correspond to the "Sons of Belial," who, according to Deuteronomy 13, arose from the people to induce them to worship foreign gods. Lawlessness, in other words, was abandonment of "the holy covenant" (1 Macc 1:15).[85] John's own equation of sin as lawlessness fits very easily into this category, so that the ἀνομία which is ἁμαρτία, and vice versa (both subject and predicate are preceded by the article) is not to be reduced to individual infractions of the divine will; it is, rather, *the abandonment of God himself*. This is why John can identify the one who sins with the Devil, who "has sinned from the beginning" (v. 8). The apostate, in other words, imitates the one responsible for mankind's primal falling away in the Garden of Eden.

Stephen Smalley confirms that elsewhere in the NT "lawlessness" bears this technical meaning and serves as a description of the "Satan-inspired rejection of God and his law that will be manifest in the present age and will come to a

---

[83] Attridge, *Hebrews*, 292 (cf. Dunn, *Romans* 1.275). Lane adds that ἑκουσίως connotes "a conscious expression of an attitude that displays contempt for God" (*Hebrews* 2.292).

[84] See in detail McKnight, "Passages," 37–43.

[85] See Garlington, *Obedience*, 91–102, passim.

climax before Christ's second coming." "It implies," consequently, "not merely breaking God's law, but flagrantly opposing him (in Satanic fashion) by so doing."[86] I. H. Marshall concurs: "To commit sin is thus to place oneself on the side of the Devil and the Antichrist and to stand in opposition to Christ." He argues that this understanding of "lawlessness" is in keeping with John's earlier teaching on the presence of the Antichrist in the world: "One cannot hope for the appearing of Christ and at the same time persist in the sin which signifies rebellion against him. Sin is not a matter of isolated peccadillos: it is an expression of siding with God's ultimate enemy – the Devil (vv. 8–10)."[87] It is in this specific sense that John can affirm that anyone born of God does not "sin," i.e., apostatize (1 John 5:18): he is kept by Christ, and the evil one does not touch him. But because temptations to apostasy are always present, John feels compelled to remind his "little children" to keep themselves from idols (5:21), especially given that there is such a thing as a sin which is "unto death" (5:16), i.e., apostasy.[88]

In encouraging his fellow Christians to persevere through the fiery trial to which they have been called, the author of 1 Peter places before them the example of Christ, who did not sin and on whose lips no deceit was found (1 Pet 2:22). The words ὃς ἁμαρτίαν οὐκ ἐποίησεν οὐδὲ εὑρέθη δόλος ἐν τῷ στόματι αὐτοῦ are quoted from the LXX of Isa 53:9, except that ἁμαρτίαν is substituted for ἀνομίαν. The LXX translator chose ἀνομία (= חמס) because of the bitter irony involved in the rejection of the Servant of Yahweh: he is to be cut off from the people as a rebel against the covenant, although, in fact, he was not guilty of such "lawlessness." Peter's perspective is the same: he would have his readers understand that Jesus, even in the face of abusive speech insinuating his guilt (v. 23), did not repay evil with evil; rather, he continued to entrust himself to the one who judges righteously and finally finished his course.

The change of ἀνομία to ἁμαρτία in the quotation may be accounted for by its second clause. The first man on whose lips deceit was found was Adam, who sought to cover his sin (cf. Prov 28:13) by blaming his disobedience immediately on his wife and ultimately on God (Gen 3:12). For the Hebrew author (and LXX translator) the Servant's refusal to commit ἀνομία is the antipode of Adam's apostasy and attempted cover-up. Again Peter's concern is the same as the prophet's; but in substituting "sin" for "lawlessness," he draws on a synonymous term which places it beyond doubt that, unlike Adam, Jesus did not forsake his Father and then resort to deceit to excuse his rebellion.

In light of these data, the assertion of 1 Pet 2:22 is not a generalized or abstract statement of the sinlessness of Jesus: it is an assurance that the believer can endure in the midst of persecution, because his Lord, the one who refused

---

[86] Smalley, *1 John*, 155. Paul's own phrase ὁ ἄνθρωπος τῆς ἀνομίας (2 Thess 2:3) may be an allusion to Adam, the first man associated with ἀνομία or apostasy (Barrett, *Adam*, 14). It is particularly striking that the same verse connects this man with ἡ ἀποστασία.
[87] Marshall, *Epistles*, 176, 177.
[88] See Smalley, *1 John*, 297–98.

to repeat the infidelity of Adam, "did not sin." In his own way, this writer, like Paul, represents Christ as another Adam, who succeeds where his predecessor failed.

Apart from "sin," "disobedience" frequently in the OT and usually in Second Temple literature is tantamount to apostasy. The materials are too massive even to begin to canvass. I can only relate the conclusion drawn from my previous study of the Jewish materials: whereas obedience is a commitment to God's covenant as articulated by the law of Moses, disobedience is apostasy from the covenant and the God of the covenant. The same connotation is brought over into the NT, for example, in Heb 3:18–19, where "those who were *disobedient*" were unable to enter the land because of *unbelief*. It is the disobedience (= unbelief) of the first wilderness generation which in Hebrews is juxtaposed to the obedience of Christ (e.g., 5:8) and the obedience to which its readers are called (e.g., 3:7–19).

In keeping with these examples in Romans, Jewish literature, and other Christian writings, which have to do directly with ideas associated with Romans 5, I would suggest that a pattern within the letter is observable. 1:18–3:20 is Paul's indictment of the "sin" of the human race, depicted in Adam-like terms. 3:23 (preceded by 3:9) summarizes the entire first portion of letter with its declaration that "all have sinned and fall short of the glory of God." 5:1–11 similarly epitomizes the "sin" of man outside of Christ with the terms "ungodly," "sinners," "enemies," and "wrath." 5:12–19 then builds on the foundation laid in the earlier chapters by making explicit what was more or less implicit before; that is, the human race's estrangement from the Creator is traceable to the first human being, Adam, whose "sin" and "disobedience" plunged the world into grief. All this sets the stage for Paul's presentation of another Adam, who by his "righteousness" and "obedience" rectifies the apostasy of his predecessor and its consequences on his race: the divine program for man which broke down with Adam is to be run through again, this time in the person of Jesus.[89]

Finally, in our consideration of Rom 5:12, there is the scope of "all" in Paul's assertion that πάντες ἥμαρτον. It is often objected that the above interpretation fails to reckon with the reality of infant mortality, especially in light of v. 14: "death reigned from Adam to Moses, even over those who did not sin in the likeness of Adam's trespass." Suffice it to say that the objection overlooks the phenomenon that πάντες in 5:12–19 serves to obliterate the customary Jew/Gentile distinction, in keeping with the other occurrences of "all" in Romans. Likewise in 3:23, the same "all" who have fallen short of God's glory are justified by God's grace (3:24). In both 3:23 and 5:12, πάντες is *ethnically qualitative*, not quantitative: Paul's argument is that Israel, as much as the

---

[89] Dunn, *Christology*, 111.

Gentiles, is in Adam and repeats his sin. As such, the fate of infants (and the mentally deficient) simply does not fall within his horizon.[90]

2. The Reign of Death from Adam to Moses

Having stated his thesis that universal sin and death are the effect of one man's disobedience, Paul, in vv. 13–14, seems compelled to defend what he has written. These verses commence the "B" section of our passage. Very noticeable, remarks Dunn, is the speed with which Paul's thought reverts to the law – a further indication that *it* was the chief point of tension between Paul the Christian and the traditional emphases of Judaism.[91] In particular, v. 12 would have appeared to the Jewish mind to contain a puzzling proposition. Given Paul's consistent denial of the existence of the law before Sinai, How could there have been sin strictly speaking, since, ostensibly, there was no law according to which sin could be reckoned? Sin, after all, for Judaism was measured in relation to *the Torah*. It is this which Paul now seeks to clarify.

His explanation glances back at 4:15b, οὗ δὲ οὐκ νόμος οὐδὲ παράβασις, where these words are appended to the statement of the previous part of the verse, ὁ γὰρ νόμος ὀργὴν κατεργάζεται. By claiming, in 5:12, that "all" have sinned, Paul has implied that they have rejected God's law and have, therefore, been the recipients of wrath (death). This, of course, raises a historical problem: if the law (of Moses) works wrath, and if sin is not reckoned apart from the law, How could there have been sin and death before Sinai? For a sizeable segment of Judaism anyway, the answer was obvious: the Torah has existed from the dawn of history, and the nations are exposed to wrath because they have spurned the eternal Torah. As early as Ben Sira this idea is in evidence: Abraham himself kept none other than the law (of Moses) during a time of testing (Sir 44:20). Afterward, the author of *Jubilees* would make the same claim (24:11; cf. 23:10), as does *Kidd.* 4:4.[92] Even more striking in *Jubilees* is the preexistence of the law on "heavenly tablets," "the eternal books always before the Lord."[93] The eternity of the law is likewise the conviction of Sir 24:9, 33; Bar 4:1; Wis 18:4; *T. Naph.* 3:1–2).[94] The corresponding attitude toward the Gentiles (and apostate Jews) is illustrated by Ben Sira's assurance (Sir 12:6) that God hates sinners and will inflict punishment on the ungodly (ἀσεβεῖς). To this may be added Sir 36:1–10, according to which the sage's fury was called forth by the

---

[90] Cf. Calvin, *Romans*, 113; Stuart, *Romans*, 215–16; Godet, *Romans*, 207; Cranfield, "Problems," 339; Moo, *Romans*, 339 (n. 40), 343; Dunn, *Romans* 1.276; Denny, "Romans," 627; Kaylor, *Community*, 110; Wedderburn, "Structure," 351; Cambier, "Péchés," 253.

[91] Dunn, *Romans* 1.274.

[92] See Garlington, *Obedience*, 38.

[93] E.g., *Jub.* 16:29; 31:32; 32:10, 15, 21–26, 28; 33:10; 39:7. See further Banks, *Law*, 68–69; id., "Law," 176.

[94] On the eternity of the law in Jewish literature, see Banks, *Law*, 67–85 (cf. ibid., 49–64); id., "Law," 173–85; Davies, *Torah*, e.g., 84.

desecration of the temple by Gentiles (cf. 48:18; 49:6; 50:4). The same hostility is vividly present in *Jub.* 22:16; *Pss. Sol.* 17:21–27.

In rather stark contrast, Paul allows that there was an era prior to and distinguishable from that of the Torah (v. 13a). A law has been spurned, a law which functions similarly to the νόμος which works wrath. However, it is not the law of the Sinai covenant, as in 4:15; it is, rather, some law in existence before the birth of Israel's nationhood, which effectively eliminates the grounds for Israel's boasting in the Torah; it is none other than this law, preceding the Torah, which produced death in the period from Adam to Moses (v. 14). Vv. 13–14, therefore, can be plausibly interpreted as the apostle's denial of a recognized tenet of Jewish theology.[95] For him there was a period during which the Torah as such was not in existence but in which, nevertheless, "death reigned." In turn, this would be a tacit rebuff of the perspective of Sir 10:19, according to which the non-Jewish segment of the human race is unworthy of honor because it has transgressed the commandments. In other words, the Gentiles, from Paul's perspective, are not deserving of death because they have violated *the Torah*.[96] He thus appeals to the existence of this pre-Mosaic law as a great leveler of the human race. In the words of 3:23: "*All* have sinned."

His fundamental proposition is stated in v. 13b: ἁμαρτία δέ οὐκ ἐλλογεῖται, i.e., "is not entered into the ledger against" (Black), so as to hold one liable in judgment,[97] μὴ ὄντος νόμου. By focusing on the nexus of sin and the law, he states what would have been perfectly acceptable to the synagogue: since sin by definition is meaningless apart from divine law, some law must have existed in the period from Adam to Moses. However, given the conviction that the law has been in the world from the Garden of Eden, the dictum of 13a in part would have been unacceptable. While it could be agreed that sin was a reality before Sinai, it was at least questionable that there was an era ἄχρι νόμου. In making such a claim, Paul appears to proceed presuppositionally, on grounds derived from the Pentateuch itself, which gives no indication that Israel's law had any being before the establishment of its national covenant. Given the order of events in the biblical record, Paul is able to reason that the period ἄχρι νόμου (ἀπὸ Ἀδὰμ μέχρι Μωϋσέως, v. 14) witnessed sin and the consequent reign of death, and on that basis he is led further to infer that before Sinai a law was in existence, whose transgression accounts for mankind's present plight. It is what the Bible actually says, as the apostle reads it, which provides the force of the strongly adversative ἀλλά in v. 14. Far from sin not being reckoned, death is

---

[95] The doctrine of the law's eternity later developed into the rabbinic Torah-ontology. See Hengel, *Judaism* 1.171–75.

[96] Contra Jüngel ("Gesetz," 50–57).

[97] Contra Quek ("Adam," 73), ἐλλογεῖται does have to do with individual responsibility. The other Pauline occurrence of ἐλλογέω is in Phlm 18, where the apostle assumes personal accountability for the debt of Onesimus.

regarded as the reigning monarch from Adam until the giving of the law – "incontrovertible proof of the presence of sin in this period."[98]

As is true more than once in 5:12–19, Paul's logic is not made explicit, leaving us to discern his intentions from the broader setting of Romans. In one regard, his justification of v. 12 is a statement of the obvious, i.e., the reality of death from Adam to Moses; yet, in another, he appears to beg the question, viz., the existence of a law antecedent to that delivered to Israel at the time of the Exodus. However, in keeping with his procedure in Romans to bypass the Torah and return to creation, Paul is best understood as here building on presuppositions already established in 2:14–15. That is to say, by virtue of bearing the image of God, all humans are in possession of the law written on the heart, whose function was to regulate the aboriginal (creation) covenant, as seen by its present-day function of linking mankind to its Maker, in conjunction with the co-witness of the conscience (cf. 1:32). Death, therefore, was universal in the pre-Mosaic period because of the repudiation of *this* law, not the Torah.[99] We are thus taken back to 1:18 in that the rejection of the law written on the heart is tantamount to the suppression of the knowledge of God.

The force of his argument resides in the assertion that death reigned even over those who did not sin ἐπὶ τῷ ὁμοιώματι τῆς παραβάσεως Ἀδάμ. As in 8:3, ὁμοίωμα here means an "exact likeness."[100] We might say that Adam's descendants did not willfully rebuff a clearly revealed command (the normal meaning of παράβασις in Paul), as Israel was later to do. But more to the point, "the likeness of Adam's trespass" indicates that they did not do *precisely* what Adam did, i.e., eat a piece of forbidden fruit in the Garden of Eden. Even so, they die because their sin in principle is an act of apostasy from Yahweh. In suppressing the knowledge of God inscribed on the heart (1:18–23), humanity in the first Adam has rejected God himself and, as a result, suffers the fate of Adam. It is especially noteworthy that Adam and Eve ate from "the tree of the knowledge of good and evil." "Good" and "evil" mean not so much "right" and "wrong" as *the* good of acknowledging God the Creator and *the* evil of renouncing him (see esp. Deut 30:15; Isa 7:15; Rom 2:7–10; 7:13–20; 15:2; 16:19; 1 Cor 10:6–7). How this can be asserted of Israel emerges from our previous look at the idolatry motif of the early portion of Romans, climaxing at 2:22: in its rejection of the gospel, Paul is able to claim that Israel has repudiated the knowledge of God as revealed eschatologically in Christ.

---

[98] Black, *Romans*, 89.
[99] Zeller, *Römer*, 117, remarks that "In the universal history [Weltgeschichte] of sin the law is not fundamental."
[100] Dunn, *Romans* 1.276, 316–17; id., *Christology*, 111; Wilckens, *Römer* 1.318, nn. 1053, 1054.

E. The Obedient Last Adam and the New Humanity

It is by the comparison with Adam that Paul's real purpose in 5:12–19 emerges. At the very least, we can say, with Moo, that if the universal consequences of Adam's sin is the *assumption* of Paul's argument, the power of Christ's act to cancel those consequences is its *goal*.[101] But to state it more fully: corresponding to Adam's disobedience = apostasy, there is the obedience = perseverance of the last Adam, which ensures the obedience = perseverance of his people and their conformity to his image (8:29). Our attention now will be given to vv. 15–17 and thereafter to vv. 18–19, the completion of the sentence commenced in v. 12.

Vv. 15–17 are normally taken to be a qualification of the incompleted proposition of v. 12, particularly as the concluding portion of v. 14 assigns to Adam the role of typifying Christ. Therefore, on this view, in vv. 15–17 Paul labors to clarify that there are important respects in which Adam and Christ differ, notwithstanding their typological correspondence. Christ, in short, is distanced from Adam as much as possible.[102] Without, however, denying the element of contrast in these verses, as seen especially in the abundance of the grace manifested in Christ, C. C. Caragounis has argued plausibly that their function is not to deviate from the commenced comparison of v. 12 and thus preclude a misunderstanding of it. It is, rather, to draw out more particularly the *comparison* of Adam and Christ, thus laying the groundwork for the inference of v. 18, which connects not only with v. 12 but also with vv. 15–17.[103] His exegesis makes good sense, especially considering that a type, by the nature of the case, stresses the continuity of two entities. It is also supported by the "ABA" construction of vv. 12–19 as a whole, whereby the final "A" takes into account the content of the "B" section.

If we may follow Caragounis further, v. 15a is a rhetorical question: "But does not the free gift operate just like the trespass did?" The question, introduced by οὐ, implies a positive response, which is affirmed by 15b. V. 16a carries on with another rhetorical question: "And is not the free gift transmitted in the same way as sin was transmitted by the one who sinned?" The answer is again yes, as confirmed by the statement of 16b. The first question is concerned with the *effect* produced by each of the two heads of humanity, while the second focuses on the *agents* of those effects.[104] It is on the basis of these questions and answers that Paul, in v. 18, can finally complete the analogy initiated in v. 12. That he should intensify his analogy in these verses is consonant with the fact that although other OT characters serve to prefigure Christ, the typological

---

[101] Moo, *Romans*, 327.

[102] Lombard, "'Typology';" Jüngel, "Gesetz;" Cranfield, *Romans* 1.272–73; id., "Problems," 328–29; Elliot, *Rhetoric*, 230–31; Berkouwer, *Sin*, 508–9; Barth, *Shorter*, 61–63.

[103] Caragounis, "Romans 5.15–16," 142–48. Goppelt remarks that Paul places in contrast the accomplishments and consequences of the mediators, not the mediators themselves (*Typos*, 136).

[104] Caragounis, "Romans 5.15–16," 145. Cf. Porter, "Argument," 672–74.

III. Romans 5:12–21: Adam and Christ: Disobedience and Obedience

relationship between Adam and Christ is on a plane all its own, inasmuch as both have inaugurated the two decisive epochs of human history. For Paul, comments Goppelt, Adam is not merely an illustrative figure but "a prophetic personality placed in Scripture by God."[105] Given such an program of typological relations, vv. 15–17 can be summarized as making one essential point: the single acts of the two respective persons have comprehensive, all-embracing effects. Although there is an obvious qualitative difference between the acts and the effects, the operative principle is the same.[106]

These verses exhibit several conspicuous features. One is the *qal wahomer* argument (again *a minori ad majus*): if Adam's trespass has brought condemnation and death, how much more has Christ's obedience brought righteousness and life (a return to vv. 9–10 of chap. 5). Another is the repetition of the phrases "the free gift," "the free gift of righteousness," "the free gift in the grace of the one man," "the grace of God," and "the abundance of grace." Within the horizons set by the Roman letter, these expressions of the freeness of grace stress that righteousness and life do not depend on "covenantal nomism" (4:4–5) but only on faith in Christ. As Käsemann puts it, the δωρεὰ δικαιοσύνης (v. 17) is God's power which takes the concrete form of a gift: "With an epexegetical genitive the gift is defined as righteousness which is Christ's work pure and simple."[107] These affirmations of 5:15–17 are founded on the proposition of 3:24, in which the *grace* of justification is connected with the *now*-revelation of the righteousness of God *apart from the law* (3:21). And it is just this eschatological slant of "grace" in Paul which is extraordinarily relevant for our passage, because "grace" "marks a new epoch and a new dominion of power that is antithetical to that of the power of sin."[108] In other words, the presence of "grace" signals a new creation (cf. Gal 5:5; John 1:17).

Second, there is the continued stress on the "one man," Adam or Christ. Given Paul's placement of Israel in Adam in vv. 12–14, the repetition of "one man" underscores that Christ, not the Jewish nation, is wholly responsible for the new creation blessings of righteousness and life. The parallel of 1 Cor 15:45–47 informs us that just as Christ is the "last Adam," so he is also the "second man." That is to say, he is the eschatological Adam, beyond whom there is no other, and the second man, before whom there is only one, the first Adam. "He cannot, therefore, be compared with one man within Israelite

---

[105] Goppelt, *Typos*, 130; cf. Bruce, *Romans*, 131, n. 1.

[106] Paul's typology is thus inclusive of three closely related ingredients: (1) Adam and Christ inaugurate respectively the old and new creations; (2) both set a pattern for others to follow, either disobedience leading to death or obedience leading to life; (3) the effect of their work is universal in extent. On Adam as the type of Christ, see Goppelt, *Typos*, 129–36; Versteeg, *Adam*, 8–15 (with further literature); cf. Moo, *Romans*, 346; Cranfield, *Romans* 1.283.

[107] Käsemann, *Romans*, 155. The gift character of righteousness in v. 17 is underscored by λαμβάνοντες. See further Beker's remarks on "grace" in Paul (*Paul*, 264). Jüngel ("Gesetz," 63) further notes that χάρισμα and χάρις (vv. 15, 16, 17) for Paul have to do with *God's* (eschatological) act.

[108] Beker, *Paul*, 265. See as well the remarks on "freedom" (ibid., 269–71).

salvation history (such as Abraham or Moses), but can only be juxtaposed to the originator of the old humanity."[109] As Bruce notes, Moses is conspicuously bypassed, because, as Paul will explain, the law given through him was never intended to be permanent.[110] Therefore, within the whole scope of salvation history there is room for only two persons, two beginnings – and Israel, with its Torah, is not included.

Beyond Paul's interaction with Israel, his insistence on the one act of the one man, either for ill or for good, calls to mind again the principle that like begets like: Adam and Christ correspond typologically as creators of their respective races, with each community bearing the image of its creator.[111] Whereas the one trespass of the one man has brought about condemnation and death, the grace of God in the one man Jesus Christ has produced righteousness and life. The contrasting states of the two humanities correspond to those depicted in vv. 1–11 of this chapter. As in that earlier portrait, the condition of the old and new humanities respectively is not to be restricted to the realm of the forensic, for the simple reason that the categories in question are comprehensive by definition. "Condemnation" (v. 16) is qualified within this context by "sin" (vv. 12–13) and "death" (vv. 14, 17), both of which have to do with the devastating consequences of man's apostasy *in toto*. Correspondingly, on the positive side, the triad δικαίωμα/δικαιοσύνη/ζωή, derived from OT covenantal ideology, speaks of a renewed relationship with the Creator.

Hence, as we shall argue presently, just as Adam, by his disobedience/apostasy, was responsible for the disobedience/apostasy of his race, Christ, by his obedience/perseverance, has restored to his community the image of God and enables it to persevere in that capacity where the first Adam and the old humanity failed. In the words of 2:7–10, the new humanity in Christ fulfills the goal originally set before Adam: the quest for glory, honor, and immortality. These are they who do "good," the specific "good" of keeping faith with the God of the covenant. In this light, it is not irrelevant that, in the face of the threat posed by certain (Jewish?) teachers, Paul desires the Romans to be σοφοὺς εἰς τὸ ἀγαθόν, ἀκεραίους δὲ εἰς τὸ κακόν (16:19). In other words, the potential existed for church members actually to abandon Christ, if they followed the lead of the deceivers (v. 18), who play a Satan-like role (cf. 2 Cor 11:3–4, 13–15).

---

[109] Michel, *Römer*, 186.

[110] Bruce, *Romans*, 128. "In this masterful view of human history, Moses and Israel's law are only a chapter of minor importance" (Goppelt, *Typos*, 130).

[111] These communities are comprised of the "all" and the "many" (vv. 15, 18, 19). The two adjectives are used interchangeably and reflect a Semitic idiom: "many" (an inclusive term) are "all" who belong to a certain group (e.g., Dan 12:2; Mark 10:45). On the usage, see Brandenburger, *Adam*, 221; Kim, *Son*, 52–53; Meyer, "Many." In the present case, the "many" are "all" who constitute the old and new humanities respectively. Quite strikingly, in 1QS 6:11–13, "many" is a technical term for the sect as the elect community or eschatological people of God. The underlying source of the scroll, as well as of the NT, is probably Isa 53:11: the Servant of Yahweh causes "many" to be righteous.

III. Romans 5:12–21: Adam and Christ: Disobedience and Obedience

Third, v. 17, as it epitomizes the intensified analogy of the two Adams in vv. 15–16, draws on the language of kingship. In the case of the first Adam, sin became a king; but, in the case of the last Adam, those who have received his grace themselves become kings through him. Whereas death reigned *through* the one man, the new people reign in life *through* the other. The language of reigning reminds us that Adam was formed to be the king of creation (Gen 1:28; Ps 8:5). Therefore, for the people of God to reign in life means that, in Christ, they are able to achieve what the first Adam forfeited by sin (cf. Heb 2:5–9).

The thought broken off in v. 12 is finally completed in vv. 18–19. The ἄρα οὖν commencing v. 18 likely draws on two sources. The first is certainly v. 12; but, in all probability, the intervening verses contribute as well to Paul's inference, primarily because the vocabulary of vv. 18–19 is influenced by those verses (characteristic of the "ABA" schema), as confirmed by Caragounis' study. V. 18 is a very terse elliptical sentence stating the relationship between the two Adams. Its interpretation is bound up with unraveling the construction, which involves supplying the missing elements, drawn from what has been said up to this point. As BDF (§ 481) note, the verse would be unintelligible apart from the long exposition of the preceding verses. Yet within Paul's overall flow of thought its purpose is again to emphasize "the correspondence between the two contrasting causes (διά) and ultimate ends (εἰς) and in between their equivalent extension (εἰς)." It can be translated something like: "Therefore, as through one trespass sin abounded to all people so that they were condemned, so also through one act of righteousness grace has abounded to all people so that they experience the justification of life." V. 19 thereafter explains more in particular what is entailed in this contrast and comparison.

Besides the continued correlation of "one" and "all," by means of which Paul again calls to mind "a single action which inaugurated a whole epoch,"[112] the leading terms in v. 18 are παράπτωμα and δικαίωμα, predicated of Adam and Christ respectively: δι' ἑνὸς παραπτώματος εἰς πάντας ἀνθρώπους εἰς κατάκριμα is balanced by δι' ἑνὸς δικαιώματος εἰς πάντας ἀνθρώπους εἰς δικαίωσιν ζωῆς. Παράπτωμα, paralleled by παρακοή in v. 19, retains its meaning from vv. 15 and 17, i.e., Adam's breach of faith with Yahweh when, desiring to be "as God," he ate the forbidden fruit. Likewise, δικαίωμα, matched by ὑπακοή in v. 19, looks back to v. 16. Moo is right that the parallelism of v. 18 dictates that as παράπτωμα refers to something Adam did, so δικαίωμα relates to something Christ did, his "act of righteousness."[113] As Cranfield maintains, Christ's δικαίωμα for Paul is not just his death but his obedient life as a whole: "His loving God with all His heart and soul and mind and strength, and His neighbour with complete sincerity, which is the righteous conduct which God's law requires."[114]

Protestant exegesis has tended to assume that the usage of δικαίωμα in v. 18

---

[112] Dunn, *Romans* 1.283.
[113] Moo, *Romans*, 354.
[114] Cranfield, *Romans* 1.289. Cf. Leenhardt, *Romans*, 146.

is distinct from that in v. 16, where it is taken to be "justification," set within a strictly forensic frame. However, apart from assigning a different sense to the term than it bears in v. 18 (with no particular hint from Paul), the interpretation is flawed in not taking sufficiently into account the Hebraic/covenantal backdrop of the δικ- family of words.[115] What is in view in v. 16 is not merely a declaration and a resultant status but a commitment to a relationship, evidenced by the holiness of the covenant and a determination to persevere in it. It is such a wholehearted devotion to the Creator/creature relationship, in v. 16, which is the effect of God's free grace in Christ. The conclusion is reinforced by the recollection that underlying Rom 5:1 is Isaiah 32, Israel's restoration to the covenant, the result of which is *shalom*.

Therefore, seeing that the semantic field of vv. 18–19 is largely determined by vv. 15–17, the inference drawn by Paul in v. 18 is to the effect that Christ has rendered to God the δικαίωμα required of his covenant partners, offsetting Adam's παράπτωμα and its consequent κατάκριμα, which is not merely the sentence of condemnation but the rebelliousness depicted so graphically in 1:18–32 (5:6–10). This being so, the δικαίωμα of the Christian in v. 16 (paralleled by δικαιοσύνη in v. 17) matches that of Christ in v. 18: the former is the product of the latter.

Noteworthy in Paul's explanation of the effect of Christ's δικαίωμα is the phrase δικαίωσις ζωῆς. Ζωή may be taken as the "eternal life" (Rom 2:7) of "the age to come," standing for the restoration of the Creator/creature relationship enjoyed in Eden. In keeping with the apocalyptic outlook generally, ζωή in Paul is eschatological and protological at the same time: the end is a return to the beginning. Yet what is the relation of δικαίωσις to the genitive ζωῆς? I would propose that inasmuch as Paul's genitives (and datives) frequently ignore established conventions, it is plausible to see the present instance as a mingling of various types of genitive: qualitative (Käsemann), result (Cranfield, Sanday/Headlam), direction or goal (Brandenburger), and epexegetical.[116] But whatever grammatical tags are applied, Leenhardt's comments are particularly relevant. Εἰς δικαίωσιν ζωῆς speaks of "a justification which introduces us to divine life;" and given the close connection of present and future eschatological life in Paul, δικαίωσις ζωῆς "suggest equally the idea of a justification which is here and now realized in a life which concretely practises righteousness, as will shortly be said (6:11, 13, 16, 18, 19, 22, 23). It will be noted that Christ's obedience of which our text speaks becomes also the believer's obedience, an obedience which leads to the practise of righteousness (ὑπακοῆς εἰς

---

[115] Cf. Wedderburn's criticism of Bultmann ("Structure," 351, n. 5). In Rom 1:32 and 2:26, δικαίωμα is the behavior required by the law written on the heart, for which Gentiles are held accountable; in 8:4 it summarizes the obligation of the Sinai covenant as fulfilled in the believer, who, by virtue of the work of Christ and the indwelling Spirit, walks not after the flesh but the Spirit.

[116] Zerwick, *Greek*, 17; Turner, Grammar, 214; Lightfoot, *Notes*, 293.

δικαιοσύνην, 6:16)."¹¹⁷ From this perspective, δικαίωσις *is* the ζωή of the age to come, as ζωή recapitulates unfallen Adam's existence in the Garden and is set in motion in by "in Christ" experience of the Christian.

Paul's portrait of the two Adams, continues Leenhardt, leads him to stress the factual obedience of Christ as opposed to the factual disobedience of Adam, "in order to show that Christ creates a humanity of righteous men, just as Adam had created a humanity of sinners."¹¹⁸ We may observe, with Elliot, that in so saying Paul expands a sin-forgiveness typology to a "deeper death-life typology:" "Adam's transgression has made necessary not just the countervailing entry of expiation for sin in Christ: it has occasioned the cosmic dominion of Death, calling for the creation of life from the dead in Christ."¹¹⁹ In short, δικαίωσις ζωῆς is a compendious way of expressing what the δικαίωμα of Christ has accomplished in *all*: his lifetime of conformity to the covenant engenders the same in his people. Ζωή, consequently, cannot be restricted to its future eschatological manifestation,¹²⁰ because this is the life imparted at creation, whose whole *raison d'être* is the glory of God. Thus, δικαίωσις ζωῆς means the presence of the new creation.

> Disobedience is of the essence of sin, and the revelation of the new obedience in Christ is eschatological salvation. Christ has thus been exalted to be the hidden Ruler of the world.... His people, being obedient, participate for the time being in the freedom from the powers which he has won and will one day share openly in the kingdom (*basileia*, v. 17b). Even more plainly than before, the dawn of the new creation is now proclaimed.¹²¹

In a manner akin to the parallelism of 5:9–10, v. 19 complements its counterpart, v. 18, by the use of synonymous terms. Specifically, "trespass" (παράπτωμα) and "act of righteousness" (δικαίωμα) in v. 18 are replaced by "disobedience" (παρακοή) and "obedience" (ὑπακοή). Also, "condemnation" and "justification of life" in v. 18 are matched by "sinners" and "righteous." Here the focus is on what kind of people individuals have become as a result of the work of Adam and Christ respectively: by his disobedience, Adam has turned his posterity into sinners, while Christ, by his obedience, has made his people righteous. The question arises whether v. 19 is the basis or the explanation of v. 18. The two, of course, are not mutually exclusive, because the one verse could clarify the other by providing its basis. But whatever the technical relation of vv. 18 and 19 may be, it is consonant with the argument developed in this monograph to see the two destinies of condemnation and rightwising as

---

¹¹⁷ Leenhardt, *Romans*, 148.
¹¹⁸ Ibid.
¹¹⁹ Elliot, *Rhetoric*, 231. He continues: "Χάρις is not simply the cancelling of transgression... but is a cosmic power that deposes Death and restores 'righteousness', that is, the cosmic 'right' of divine will, and brings life to what was dead" (ibid., 231–32). Cf. Beker, *Paul*, 190–91.
¹²⁰ See Käsemann, *Romans*, 155, 156, 157–58.
¹²¹ Ibid., 157. Cf. Beker, *Paul*, 270–71.

based on the two conditions into which people are put – "sinners" and "righteous."[122]

That Paul should speak of the acts of Adam and Christ as "disobedience" and "obedience" and of the condition of their respective offspring as "sinners" and "righteous" comes as no surprise, especially given the connotations of apostasy and fidelity connected with the terms in the OT and Jewish literature, which themselves are rooted in Genesis 3.[123] Adam's παρακοή was his renunciation of Yahweh the Creator and thereby his identity as Yahweh's image. By signing a "declaration of independence," he chose for himself and his descendants the path of autonomy and self-determination.[124] In so doing, he brought disaster, κατάκριμα, upon those who, thanks to him, have become ἁμαρτωλοί, repudiators of the Creator/creature distinction.

By contrast, Christ's ὑπακοή, his perseverance or life-long commitment to do his Father's will, culminating in his "obedience unto death" (Phil 2:8), has turned former ἁμαρτωλοί into δίκαιοι, covenant-keepers, who now render to Jesus "the obedience of faith" (Rom 1:5; [16:26]) and reign as kings with him (5:17).[125] In short, Christ restores the divine/human family bond by rendering to God the allegiance expected of Adam: "Christ... shatters subjection to the Adamic world of sin and death by setting the world before its Creator again and by setting us in the state of creatureliness."[126] Given this specificity of ἁμαρτωλοί and δίκαιοι, the important consequence is that the Christian does not remain a "sinner." Rather than being *simul iustus et peccator*, the believer says of himself, *tunc peccator – nunc iustus* ("once a sinner, now righteous").[127]

Crucial to the interpretation of v. 19 is the verb καθίστημι. Moo, following Oepke, observes that this verb never designates a judgment or consideration which does not conform to the actual state of the individuals involved.[128]

---

[122] As suggested by Moo (*Romans*, 357), though he is disinclined to accept it himself.

[123] Cf. Käsemann, *Romans*, 157. Dunn (*Jesus, Paul*, 61–88; *Partings*, 102–7) has shown how "sinner" in particular is a factional or sectarian term, describing others from the vantage point of the members of a group, who are the "righteous" (e.g., *1 Enoch* 91–107; *Pss. Sol.* 4:1–8; *Testament of Moses* 7). Normally, the "sinners" would be deemed disloyal to God's covenant. Cf. Garlington, *Obedience*, 97–98. An illuminating usage of one of the antonyms of "sinner" is exhibited by Ps 32:6: David calls upon כל חסיד, "everyone loyal to Yahweh's covenant, to pray (Anderson, *Psalms* 1.258). It is not accidental that חסדים in subsequent Jewish history became the technical term for those who distinguished themselves by their observance of the law and determined opposition to Hellenism.

[124] See Barrett, *Adam*, 11–13. In Adam one sees the opposite of grace, self-seeking, and self-centered desire (ibid., 15. See further pp. 16–17, 20).

[125] It is artificial to restrict Christ's obedience to his death. His ὑπακοή, just as his δικαίωμα, is his perseverance in the whole of God's demand. Cf. Cranfield, *Romans* 1.291; Bruce, *Romans*, 127; Michel, *Römer*, 191; Longenecker, "Obedience," 142–52. Paul's insistence in Phil 2:5–11 that Christ was obedient *unto* death implies clearly that the cross was but the climax of a whole life of obedience. Barrett shows point for point in this passage how Christ's whole obedience corresponds positively to the disobedience of Adam (*Adam*, 16).

[126] Käsemann, *Romans*, 156.

[127] Beker, *Paul*, 216. Cf. Byrne, "Righteousness," 579.

[128] Moo, *Romans*, 358; Kertelge, *"Rechtfertigung,"* 145; Oepke, *TDNT* 3.445. According

III. Romans 5:12–21: Adam and Christ: Disobedience and Obedience

People, in other words, were really *made* sinners or righteous through the disobedience and obedience of the two men respectively. However, he contends that being *made* sinners or righteous is to be understood "in light of Paul's typical forensic categories," according to which "righteous" means "to be judged acquitted, cleared of all charges, in the heavenly courtroom."[129] The many are *made* "sinners" and "righteous" because God considers them to be such by virtue of the acts of Adam and Christ. Moo thus approves of an underlying notion of imputation in Paul's thought.[130]

But this construction evokes two questions: (1) Are Paul's categories typically forensic? (2) What would Paul have understood by "forensic?" Since it is impossible to give anything like a full reply, it must suffice to say, in addressing the first question, that Paul's thought-forms can only artificially be restricted to the forensic. They are, in fact, cosmic in breadth, as derived from the creation, in which a relationship was established between God and his creatures; or, as de Boer puts it, Paul's framework is cosmological-apocalyptic.[131] This applies not least to the vocabulary of righteousness. If righteousness by definition is a commitment to the covenant relationship, and if, as many have argued, righteousness on the divine side is ultimately God's fidelity to his creation, then the many in Christ have been *made* righteous in the sense that the primal creation bond has been renewed: the image of God has been restored, resulting in a basic change of attitude on the part of those who have been reconciled to God through the death of his Son.

As to the other question, even if the forensic features in Paul's theology – which is not at all being denied[132] – what are we to understand by "forensic?" I would submit, as intimated before, that the term is to be taken within the precincts of the Hebrew courtroom. It is true, as commonly recognized, that lying behind Paul's use of δικαιόω is the Hebrew צדק, particularly in the hiphil. Yet, if we may draw again on Ziesler's findings, while this verb is normally

---

to Oepke, "Pronounced righteous, they will then normally be righteous as well." Oepke is careful, however, not to exclude the judicial sentence of God, "which on the basis of the act of the head determines the destiny of all" (ibid., 446). Cranfield's suggestion (*Romans* 1.291, n. 1) that καθίστημι in the passive may have been chosen by Paul as the true passive equivalent of γίνομαι makes good sense in this context. Cf. Dunn, *Romans* 1.284; Käsemann, *Romans*, 157; Wilckens, *Römer* 1.328; Brandenburger, *Adam*, 233.

[129] Moo, *Romans*, 359. Cf. Berkouwer, *Sin*, 498–99; Bultmann, "Adam," 159.

[130] As do Morris, *Romans*, 240; Murray, *Romans* 1.204–6; id., *Imputation*, 86–90; Ridderbos, *Romeinen*, 122; Ellis, *Use*, 60; Hoekema, *Image*, 162–67; Versteeg, *Adam*, 23; Gaffin, "Adam," 5. I would venture to propose that such an undergirding assumption of imputation is the sort of "middle term" which Moo in particular finds objectionable about the Calvin/Cranfield, et al., approach to v. 12. See n. 58 above.

[131] de Boer, *Defeat*, 163. See further Goppelt, *Typos*, 209–37; Elliot, *Rhetoric*, 230–32; cf. Scroggs, *Adam*, 57–74. Without setting Apocalyptic over against a salvation history, our exegesis is in harmony with the heart of Beker's work, viz., that the apostle's teaching centers around the apocalyptic triumph of God in Christ. Apocalyptic categories, Beker maintains, are not a provincial idiosyncrasy of Paul's; they are, rather, interwoven with profound christological, anthropological, and ethical issues (*Paul*, 172).

[132] See Fitzmeyer, "Justification," 200.

forensic, it is forensic in the *Hebrew* sense, i.e., it gives voice to a "restoration of the community or covenant relationship," which means that it cannot be separated from the ethical altogether: "*The restoration is not merely to a standing, but to an existence in the relationship*," so that the "righteous" are those who enjoy not just a vindicated status but a vindicated life.[133] To put it in more traditional terms: "in his summing up, Paul includes in one statement both justification as a forensic acquittal from guilt, and actual salvation from sin."[134] In Byrne's words, the immense emphasis is on the grace of God, operative not only to rescue humanity from sin, but to set justified human beings on the path to eternal life.[135] In brief, we have been reconciled to God through the life and death of his Son (Rom 5:1–11), making us "righteous" in the pointedly Hebrew sense of a renewed devotion to the Lord and his covenant.

Καθίστημι is placed by Paul in both the aorist and the future tenses. The former speaks of every person born into the world "in Adam;" the latter of those who enter the new creation "in Christ." Wedderburn's observation is much to the point: "the characteristics of the old age are put in the aorist even though that old age is not wholly done away with, and the characteristics of the new age are put in the future even though the firstfruits of that age are already with us."[136] Κατασταθήσονται thus corresponds to βασιλεύσουσιν in v. 17 and to ζῳοποιηθήσονται in 1 Cor 15:22. Syntactically, the future may be taken as "logical," indicating, to adapt Murray's observation, that "this act of God's grace is being continually exercised and will continue to be exercised throughout future generations of mankind."[137] However, in light of Wedderburn's comments, the tense can be labeled "eschatological," as long as it is kept in mind that the eschaton has already begun with Christ's present reign.

To be sure, the righteousness of the people of Christ flows from their union with him. As Paul puts it neatly elsewhere, in *him* we have become the righteousness of God (2 Cor 5:21. Note how 2 Cor 5:19–20 correlates reconciliation with righteousness, as does Romans 5.). And it is just Paul's idea of believers ἐν Χριστῷ which undergirds the parallelism of 5:19 (and the whole Adam/Christ typology): as in Adam all die, so in Christ shall all be made alive (1 Cor 15:22). Because Paul contemplates a union with either Adam or Christ, it

---

[133] Ziesler, *Righteousness*, 20, 25 (italics mine). See further ibid., 160–61; Käsemann, "Righteousness," 172; Beker, *Paul*, 263–64; Reumann, *Righteousness*, 16. The argument gains in force if, as many think, Isa 53:11 stands behind the present text: the Servant of Yahweh "causes many to be righteous" (יצדיק). Cf. Ziesler, *Righteousness*, 19. As is so of all the Servant Songs, Isaiah 53 occurs in the broader setting of the restoration of the remnant of Israel to its pristine covenant (creation) relationship.

[134] Dodd, *Romans*, 83.

[135] Byrne, "Righteousness," 562.

[136] Wedderburn, "Structure," 352–53. Likewise Kertelge (*"Rechtfertigung,"* 146–47), Brandenburger (*Adam*, 234), and Porter ("Sin," 15: "Christ is the first fruit of what is still expected, hence the form of expectation – the future form – is used").

[137] Murray, *Romans* 1.206.

can be *through* their respective acts of disobedience and obedience that the "all" and the "many" become sinners or righteous. No more than in 2:13 does Paul envisage a scenario in which one attains to righteousness on one's own. If like begets like, the δίκαιοι are those in whom *Christ* has been reproduced. To state it in other terms, the condition of being δίκαιοι *is* the gift of God. 6:22–23 states it just this way: "you have *your fruit unto sanctification*, whose end is eternal life. For the wages of sin is death, but *the free gift of God* is eternal life in Christ Jesus our Lord." Eternal life, to be sure, is the eventuation of a process of fruit bearing; but it is all traceable back to God's doing; it is his gift.[138] Besides, ultimately obedience and disobedience, as we have argued before, are reducible to faith and unbelief.[139]

F. Christ, not the Torah, the Source of Life

We may round off our exposition of Romans 5 by offering some brief comments on vv. 20–21, which lie outside the Adam/Christ discussion proper and form the transition into chap. 6. In these verses, Paul returns again (from 3:19–20; 4:15; cf. Gal 3:19) to the function of the law as a revealer of sin and thereby a worker of wrath. It can be inferred that he does so to combat that aspect of Jewish theology which asserted that Sinai restored a proper relationship between God and the true humanity, Israel, through the mediation of the Torah,[140] and, accordingly, that Jewishness would insure ultimate deliverance from the effects of Adam's sin.

Various Jewish sources voice the conviction that the law *eo ipso* insures life. Ben Sira uses the actual phrase "the law of life" (Sir 17:11; 45:5), while the author of Baruch commends to his readers "the commandments of life" (Bar 3:9). These commandments are no less than the very embodiment of Israel's wisdom: "All who hold her fast will live, and those who forsake her will die" (Bar 4:1). See also 4 Ezra 14:30; *Pss. Sol.* 14:2; cf. 4 Ezra 7:129; *t. Sabb.* 5:17.[141] Hand in hand went the equally strong conviction that the law was eternal and unchangeable (e.g., Sir 24:9, 33; Bar 4:1; *Jub.* 16:29; 31:32; 32:10, 15, 21–26, 28; 33:10; Wis 18:4; *T. Naph.* 3:1–2; 4 Ezra 9:26–37).

Over against these traditions, Paul's stance is altogether conspicuous. For one thing, the verb παρεισῆλθεν, in v. 20, implies that the law is not eternal: its entrance onto the stage of history was occasioned only by the advent (εἰσῆλθεν,

---

[138] See Berkouwer, *Sanctification*, 108–13 (esp. pp. 108, 112).

[139] "The difference between faith and unbelief is exactly the theme of the story of Eden. Men align themselves with Adam, the type of the Man of wickedness [2 Thess 2:3]... or with God" (Barrett, *Adam*, 14).

[140] Scroggs, *Adam*, 38, 53; Kaylor, *Community*, 234, n. 21. de Boer notes that particularly in forensic apocalyptic eschatology the law was the divine solution to the sentence of death meted out to Adam and his descendants for repudiating God (*Defeat*, 167).

[141] See further Brandenburger, *Adam*, 248, n. 2; Cosgrove, *Cross*, 90–91.

v. 12) of sin.¹⁴² More startling yet is the law's actual function – to intensify the problem created by Adam, i.e., to cause sin to reign in death. "Trespass" (παράπτωμα) and "sin" (ἁμαρτία) are retained from the foregoing discussion, signifying that Adam's idolatry has not, as supposed, been rectified by the Torah, because it preeminently is the stimulus of "trespass" and "sin." Israel itself, therefore, continues to participate in the first man's apostasy, as evidenced most conspicuously, in Paul's view, by its rejection of the Christ. In fact, in Israel's case, it is possible to see Paul's point as quite a specific one: *it was the very possession of the Torah which engendered the spirit of idolatry*. The nation preferred to view the law as God's definitive answer to sin rather than only a means to an end, i.e., as preparation for the "coming one" (v. 14), whose act of obedience would put an end to sin forever. In Paul's mind, Israel's "sin" has abounded all the more because of its misunderstanding and misapplication of the Torah.

It is in this connection that v. 21 assures the readers that the reign of sin in death was with the eventual view that grace might reign through righteousness to eternal life through *Jesus Christ our Lord*. "Sin and death held sway both before and after the Torah; they did not originate with the Torah, nor are they solved by it. The Torah intensifies sin (and by implication death) but in a final sense it is not a decisive factor in the human equation."¹⁴³ The decisive factor is Christ, the τέλος of the law (Rom 10:4; Gal 3:21–25), whose coming is prepared by the sin intensifying function of the law itself. It was in pointing to Christ that God's grace to Israel was embodied in the law:¹⁴⁴ he, not the Torah, is the head of the cosmos;¹⁴⁵ he is the one and only source of eternal life.

IV. Summary

The obedience of Christ, according to Romans 5, is specifically his fidelity to God the Creator and his perseverance in the course set before him by his Father. Christ thus plays out the role originally assigned to Adam as the progenitor of the human race: he is the actual εἰκὼν τοῦ θεοῦ, the one who projects onto the field of space and time the likeness of the invisible God (Col 1:15). It is he who is obedient, where another son of God, Israel, failed, whose history can be characterized by Paul in 2 Cor 3:7, 9 as an era of condemnation and death.

Paul, however, does not contemplate the obedience of Christ as an end in

---

¹⁴² Cf. Jüngel: whereas the precursor of the gospel is the promise to Abraham, the forerunner of the law is sin ("Gesetz," 45–47). See Rom 4:13–15.

¹⁴³ Kaylor, *Community*, 111.

¹⁴⁴ Berkouwer, *Sin*, 509.

¹⁴⁵ Cf. Elliot, *Rhetoric*, 232–33. Heb 2:5–9 makes the same point: the world to come has not been subjected to angels, the mediators of the law (Deut 33:2 [LXX]; Ps 68:18; Acts 7:38; Gal 3:19), but to Christ.

itself, because it is *through* the one man that obedience has been disseminated *to* all. At heart, human obedience is the acceptance of one's identity as the image of God and the consequent obligation of creaturely service.[146] The obedience of the Christian is thus the antipode of his former disobedience, his rejection of Creator/creature distinction. In short, the believer has been delivered from the slavery of his former existence (Rom 6:15–23; 8:2; Eph 2:1–3) and enabled to persevere in the faith-commitment incumbent originally on the first Adam.

---

[146] See Goppelt, *Typos*, 130–36.

Chapter Five
The Obedience of Faith as Life Between two Worlds

So far, this investigation of faith, obedience, and perseverance in Romans has focused on: (1) an examination of the phrase ὑπακοὴ πίστεως; (2) Israel's disobedience; (3) the significance of the concept of faith's obedience for eschatological justification; (4) the role of Christ as the obedient one who insures the ultimate salvation of his people. We turn now to consider Rom 7:14−25 and its portrait of the perseverance of the Christian from the perspective of personal/subjective awareness. Of course, many students of Paul dispute precisely that the passage speaks of *Christian* experience. For this reason, a considerable amount of energy must be expended in defense of the interpretation which views it in such terms.

I. The Approach to Romans 7:14−25

In his Tyndale Lecture of 1974, J. D. G. Dunn prefaced his study of Rom 7:14−25 with the observation:

> Rom 7 is one of those key passages in Paul's writings which offers us an insight into a whole dimension of Paul's thought and faith. Even more important, it is one of the few really pivotal passages in Paul's theology; by which I mean that *our* understanding of it will in large measure determine our understanding of Paul's theology as a whole, particularly his anthropology and soteriology. As interpretations of Rom 7 differ, so interpretations of Paul's anthropology and soteriology markedly alter in content and emphasis. Dispute about a tense, a phrase, a half-verse in Rom 7 means in fact dispute about the whole character of Paul's gospel.[1]

Dunn's point is well-taken and, practically speaking, all-important: one's view of Romans 7 will inevitably influence one's outlook on the broader dimensions of Paul's preaching. Yet, methodologically speaking, we may reason in the opposite direction as well: one's view of Rom 7:14−25 hinges equally as much on one's assessment of its particular niche within the edifice of the Pauline theology.[2] Most relevantly, if the commentator sees in the passage the same articulation of the letter/Spirit antithesis as in Rom 2:29; 7:6; 2 Corinthians 3, then that particular aspect of Paul's teaching will serve as the larger fabric of which Rom 7:14−25 is

---

[1] Dunn, "Rom. 7,14−25," 257 (italics his).
[2] Cf. Moo, *Romans*, 470−71.

but a thread. Thus interpreted, the conflict depicted by Paul in Rom 7:14–25 would be that of a person engulfed by the power of sin and convicted by the killing letter of the law, who as yet remains within the era of condemnation with no experience of the life-giving Spirit.

However, a different framework of interpretation will result in a different evaluation of Romans 7. Dunn, for example, links the passage to the eschatological character of the believer's possession of the Spirit, i. e., the tension of the Already and the Not Yet, resulting in his/her participation in the sufferings of Christ.[3] Consequently, Dunn places this portion of Romans 7 squarely within the believer's experience of the grace of God: depicted is one who has passed from death to life and yet undergoes the painful transition from an existence wholly given over to the flesh to one wholly controlled by the Spirit. The person of Rom 7:14–25 is, most pointedly, flesh and Spirit at the same time. In his struggle with indwelling sin, he is a microcosm of the whole of salvation history, reproducing the career of Jesus himself, who was weak but became strong (2 Cor 13:4).[4]

Clearly enough, then, the exegesis of Rom 7:14–25 is directly contingent on an appreciation of the whole Pauline picture, or at least of those areas of the canvas which provide the most directly relevant control over the interpreter's approach to the problematics of the text. It is because of the place allotted to chap. 7 in the Pauline theology, not merely in the argument of the Roman letter, that such divergent approaches to the passage have been engendered.[5] These can be reduced to six:[6] (1) A person under the conviction of sin prior to conversion,[7] with Romans 7 frequently set in contrast to Romans 8.[8] Sometimes

---

[3] Dunn, "Rom. 7,14–25," 264–73; id., *Jesus*, 308–18. Dunn applies the Already/Not Yet schema to the structure of Romans 6–8 (*Romans* 1.302–3).

[4] Cf. Dunn, "Jesus," e. g., 56.

[5] Of course, the argument of Romans is important. D. H. Campbell writes: "Perhaps the most serious error one could commit in attempting to make sense of Rom 7 is to isolate it from its natural context" ("Identity," 57). In this we are in agreement with Meyer ("Worm," 62–64) and Byrne ("Righteousness," 577). The setting of chap. 7 within the letter will be one of the mainstays of our argument.

[6] Accounts of research are provided by Kuss, *Römerbrief* 2.462–85; Wilckens, *Römer* 2.101–117; Michel, *Römer*, 240–45; Dunn, "Rom. 7,14–25," 257–58; Theissen, *Aspects*, 190–91; Morris, *Romans*, 285–87; Moo, *Romans*, 450–52, 470–73; Schnackenburg, "Römer 7," 284–88.

[7] Defended in the commentaries of Sanday/Headlam, Käsemann, Kuss, Prumm, Ridderbos, Schlatter, Schlier, Wilckens, and Zeller. See as well Bultmann, "Romans 7;" Bornkamm, "Sin;" id., *Paul*, 125–29; Schnackenburg, "Römer 7;" Kertelge, "Überlegungen;" Martin, "Identity;" Theissen, *Aspects*, 179–265; Ridderbos, *Paul*, 126–30; Bandstra, *Law*, 134–49; Beker, *Paul*, 182–83, 215–18, 238–43; Hoekema, *Christian*, 61–67; Gundry, "Frustration." Largely influential has been Kümmel's *Römer 7*, though not all have accepted Kümmel's conclusions respecting the "I" of Romans 7.

[8] E.g., Ridderbos, *Romeinen*, 163; Hoekema, *Christian*, 64–65; Theissen, *Aspects*, 183; Feuillet, "plan," 390; id., "citation," 65; Brandenburger, *Fleisch*, 48–49; Beker, *Paul*, 216–17.

the person in question is specifically Adamic man.[9] (2) Supportive of the same conclusion is the "salvation-historical" approach, according to which Paul identifies himself with Israel in its reception of the Torah at Sinai, when sin was confirmed and radicalized, resulting in death.[10] (3) The normative condition of the Christian, who experiences lifelong frustration as his sin is aroused by the spiritual law of God.[11] (4) The Christian who attempts to perform the law without the full aid of the Spirit.[12] (5) The person who is in the process of becoming a Christian, but is, strictly speaking, neither "regenerate" or "unregenerate."[13] (6) "The distressing experience of any morally earnest man, whether Christian or not, who attempts to live up to the commands of God 'on his own'...."[14]

The following treatment of Romans 7 is in agreement with Dunn and others: Paul's cry of Rom 7:24, "wretched man that I am!", is the product of the overlap of two ages and, consequently, two antithetical modes of existence. This is:

> the frustration of one who has to try to follow the leading of the Spirit while still in the flesh, the anguish of trying to express the life of the Spirit through the body of death, the longing to be free of the tension between old humanity and new, the longing for the life of the Spirit to have a spiritual body as its embodiment and means of expression. In a word, it is not the cry of the non-Christian for the freedom of the Christian; rather *it is the cry of the Christian for the full freedom of Christ.*[15]

Dunn is quite right, in my view, to root the exegesis of this much disputed passage, called by Nygren the "most discussed and fought over" portion of the letter,[16] in the doctrine of the two ages. Accordingly, this look at Rom 7:14–25 is intended to take what, I believe, is a correct insight and set it within the broadest possible perimeters. That is to say, the idea of two ages, inherent in both Jewish and early Christian eschatology, is nothing other than the contrast of old and new creations. The argument of this chapter, then, is that Paul himself provides our framework of interpretation by means of a theology of

---

[9] E.g., Deidun, *Morality*, 196–201.

[10] Moo, Karlberg ("History"), Wright (*Climax*, 196–200), and others (see Moo, *Romans*, 452, n. 7). It must be clarified that the position for which I shall argue sees in Romans 7 *a* salvation history without being *the* "salvation-historical" interpretation of Moo, et al.

[11] Apart from Dunn, the view is represented by the commentaries of Barrett, Bruce, Calvin, Cranfield, Hodge, Morris, Murray, and Nygren, along with Bruce, "Law;" Packer, "Wretched;" Campbell, "Identity;" Espy, "Conscience;" Berkouwer, *Sanctification*, 55–63.

[12] Wenham, "Life;" Fung, "Impotence."

[13] See Moo, *Romans*, 473, n. 10, for representatives.

[14] Mitton, "Romans vii" (quote from p. 133b). Akin are Meyer, "Worm;" Longenecker, *Paul*, 86–97.

[15] Dunn, "Rom. 7,14–25," 268 (italics mine).

[16] Nygren, *Romans*, 284. Cf. Wilckens, *Römer* 2.97; Kuss, *Römer* 2.481. Bibliographies are provided by Dunn, Käsemann, and Kertelge ("Überlegungen," 105–6, n. 1).

creation, which serves as the substructure of Romans 5–8,[17] and that 7:14–25 takes its place within this schema of the two creations.[18]

Note on the "I" of 7:14–25

The ensuing exposition accepts that the "I" of 7:14–25 is Paul himself – the so-called autobiographical interpretation – because, to quote Dunn: "The existential anguish and frustration of vv. 15 ff. and 24 is too real, too sharply poignant to permit any reduction of the 'I' to a mere figure of style. Whatever else this is, it is surely Paul speaking from the heart of *his own experience*. I must say that it seems to me a rather convoluted process of reasoning which argues both that the 'I' does not denote Paul's personal experience but it does the experience of everyman – *everyman, except Paul!*"[19] In Phil 3:4–7, a passage reminiscent of Romans 7, the *ego* is undeniably Paul himself.[20] Our approach, accordingly, agrees with the analyses, e.g., of Kertelge and Theissen respecting the personal reference of the "I" throughout Romans 7.[21] Theissen in particular pronounces W.G. Kümmel's arguments to the contrary "methodologically unusable," inasmuch as the literary analogies forwarded by him are inappropriate to Paul.[22]

It is true, of course, that Paul does not write as a private person but as the representative of a group. One indication is the presence of οἴδαμεν in v. 14 (as opposed to οἶδα μέν).[23] As Leenhardt writes, "The statement that the law is spiritual is not a personal opinion, but the faith of all. Thus it is a question here of a credal confession with the community; hence the use of the plural."[24] Nevertheless, *he* is decidedly a member of that group.[25] In Calvin's words, Paul depicts in his own person the character and extent of the weakness of believers.[26] The "I" of the Qumran hymns presents an instructive analogy, inasmuch as the autobiographical and typical elements of the "I" cannot be separated.[27]

---

[17] The "creation and redemption" motif, therefore, is not to be confined to 5:12–21 and 8:19–23, 38–39, as is done by Gibbs, *Creation*, 33–58.

[18] The analyses of Kertelge ("Überlegungen," 112) and Schnackenburg ("Römer 7," 288–91), for example, are too restrictive. The former seizes on justification and its consequences, and the latter on the theme of the law. In a similar vein, many of Theissen's structural remarks are valid and stimulating. However, he has mainly contented himself with an analysis of the internal workings of 7:7–23 and has failed to set his interpretation within the broader salvation-historical framework of chaps. 5–8.

[19] Dunn, "Rom. 7,14–25," 260 (first italics his, second mine). Cf. Gundry, "Frustration," 229. See further the "Note on Paul's Wretchedness" below.

[20] Cf. Dodd, *Romans*, 107.

[21] Kertelge, "Überlegungen," 107–112; Theissen, *Aspects*, 190–201.

[22] Ibid., 191. Cf. Longenecker, *Paul*, 87–89.

[23] See, e.g., Ridderbos, *Romeinen*, 154–55.

[24] Leenhardt, *Romans*, 190. Barth, then, is wrong in calling the presence of οἴδαμεν here unsuitable (*Romans*, 259, n. 1).

[25] Cf. the "I" of Gal 2:19–20: Paul is clearly speaking of all Christians, of whom he is a spokesman.

[26] Calvin, *Romans*, 149.

[27] See Theissen, *Aspects*, 201, n. 37; Longenecker, *Paul*, 88–90; Wilckens, *Römer* 2.77–78; Michel, *Römer*, 225; Kuhn, "Light," 102–3. Moo, "Israel," 128–29; id., *Romans*, 455–56, 467, relates other instances in which a Jewish writer closely identifies himself with the group for which he is the mouthpiece.

II. Romans 5–8 and the Theology of Creation

For the sake of continuity in the argument, it will be necessary, in setting Rom 7:14–25 within its context in Romans, to retrace some of the steps leading up to this point.

At the heart of Paul's purposes in the Roman letter lies his design to redefine the people of God, i.e., to redraw the boundaries which distinguished that people. Once, to be a member of the covenant community was to remain within the boundaries set by the law. However, the eschatological people have now assumed a new corporate identity: instead of being the people of the law, Christians are "they of faith" (Gal 3:9), who are committed to Christ alone. In this light, Rom 1:5 is a verse of pivotal significance. In declaring that the obedience of faith is a possibility for all races by faith alone, Paul has effectively rewritten the ground rules of covenant fidelity: from now on there is "no distinction" between Jew and Gentile (1:16–17; 2:11; 10:12, etc.).

That creation features in Paul's delineation of the new people is evident from the outset of the letter. Rom 1:18–32 is modeled on the fall of Adam in Genesis 3. In fact, the polemic pursued in 1:18–3:20 as a whole is to the effect that, contrary to its claims, Israel is involved in and repeats the primal sin of Adam. Far from being the solution to the complex of problems occasioned by the first man's apostasy, Israel itself is guilty of idolatry: all, including Israel, have sinned and have fallen short of God's glory (3:23; cf. 5:12), the image of God bestowed on man in the beginning (Ps 8:5). It is in the middle of this argument that Paul pleads for Gentile equality based on God's impartial judgment (2:1–16). The nations, by virtue of creation, possess the law written on the heart, the functional equivalent of the Jewish law inscribed on tables of stone (2:14–15). Accordingly, "the doers of the law" to be justified in eschatological judgment (2:13) are defined not in terms of allegiance to the Torah but of Adam's original mandate to pursue glory, honor, and immortality (2:7). As the whole of Romans clarifies, only in union with Christ, not Israel, is it possible to persevere where the first Adam fell away, and thus be vindicated when God judges "according to truth" (2:2).

It is Paul's distinctively Christian convictions about Christ, creation, and the people of God which are elaborated in chaps. 5–8, in which he undertakes to demonstrate that the new creation has dawned in Jesus of Nazareth. God's plan to remedy the ills of the old creation has been realized not in Israel and its Torah but in Jesus Christ and his church. These chapters begin and end on the same note, viz., the vindication of the people of God in Christ. In keeping with the two-stage eschatological scheme of the NT generally, Rom 5:1–21 and 8:18–39 articulate respectively the inauguration and consummation of the prophetic expectation of a new world order. In between (6:1–8:17), as we shall argue, there is the outworking of the life of this new creation and the consequent counterattack of the old, which still seeks to assert its former dominance.

Therefore, the substructure of Romans 5–8 can be viewed as the passing of the old creation and the advent of the new.²⁸ This program particularly comes to light in the series of antitheses constructed by Paul. (1) 5:1–21: the justification of life in Christ vs. the condemnation of death in Adam. (2) 6:1–7:6: resurrection life and deliverance from sin in Christ vs. death and bondage to sin and the law. (3) 7:7–8:39: life and liberty in union with Christ and the indwelling Spirit vs. captivity to the flesh, even in spite of indwelling sin and the believer's groaning for the redemption of the body (7:14–25; 8:18–25). In each division of chaps. 5–8, the motif of the believer's definitive break with the past and his entrance into a new state of affairs stands out in prominent relief: an old pattern of existence is broken in order that a new mode of life may begin. Or, as stated in the previous chapter, from a slightly adjusted vantage point chaps. 5–8 are to be regarded as a unified block bound together by a common theme: the hope of eternal life on the basis of justification, despite the present reality of suffering and the prospect of physical death.²⁹

III. The Function of Romans 7:14–25 within the Debate of Chapters 6–7

Following the assertions of chap. 5 that Christ, not Israel, is God's new beginning after the fall of Adam, chaps. 6–7, which stand together as an internal unit of 5–8, are organized around a series of questions, corresponding to the synagogue debate style. As though he were engaged in live argument, Paul here takes up Jewish objections to the propositions of chap. 5. In every instance, Paul's theology of the new creation and the role of the law within it comes by way of his answer to the four questions posed by his interlocutor. This particular mode of writing is employed in Romans wherever Paul is engaged in direct dialogue with Israel; and since it finds its most intense expression in chaps. 6–7 (and 9–11), the implication is that the ideas therein expressed were particularly offensive to Jewish convictions. The structure of the section may be set out as follows.

---

²⁸ Contra Ridderbos (*Romeinen*, 164), this reading of the context does provide a rationale as to how Paul in 7:14–25 can speak of the new man in agreement with the organic and logical construction of chaps. 7 and 8. Without drawing on the language of creation directly, Nygren analyzes chaps. 5–8 as Paul's exposition of what it means to "live in Christ." This leads him to inquire "how Paul could suddenly turn, in that context, to a description of the anguished and discordant status of the soul of the man who is under the law" (*Romans*, 288). Dodd comments similarly, *Romans*, 108. Campbell adds that at 5:12 Paul commences his description of Christian experience. Thereafter chaps. 6–8, which come to grips with the remaining stumbling blocks to the attainment of maturity, serve to clarify how the rule of grace comes to fruition in the Christian life. These stumbling blocks are not three separate conflicts in which the Christian engages, but "one conflict described from three different perspectives" ("Identity," 57). In fairness, however, explanations feasible in themselves are offered by Ridderbos (*Romeinen*, 164), Kertelge ("Überlegungen," 112), and Schnackenburg ("Römer 7," 297).

²⁹ Byrne, "Righteousness," 560.

First round of debate: 6:1–14: Does non-allegiance to the Torah inevitably result in a pagan lifestyle?
Second round of debate: 6:15–7:6: Does the era of grace, as preached by Paul, necessitate a sinful life?
Third round of debate: 7:7–12: Is the law itself sin(ful) because it awakens the consciousness of sin?
Fourth round of debate: 7:13–25: Is the law the direct cause of death?

Since 7: (13) 14–25 is organically one with 7:7–12 in particular, it will be necessary to say something about the relationship of these two portions of the chapter. The round of debate represented by 7:7–12 is occasioned by 7:1–6, and more especially by vv. 5–6. In v. 5, Paul speaks of "the desires of sin through the law" which were at work in our members when "we were in the flesh." As in 3:20; 4:15; 5:20, he attaches to the law a negative, i.e., sin-stimulating, function. Furthermore, v. 6 (especially against the backdrop of chap. 6) identifies the law with the old realm of sin and death. Thus, the question naturally arises, "Is the law sin?" (v. 7). As Wilckens notes, Paul's interlocutor calls attention to what he sees as a contradiction in his argument: How can Paul hold to a basic dictum of Jewish theology, viz., that the law is good, and, at the same time, ascribe to it evil, i.e., the production of death?[30]

In answering this new objection, Paul has essentially one thing to say: even though the law per se is not sin, it was, nevertheless, by the law's instrumentality that he came to recognize his own idolatry. We see, then, in Paul himself the example of one who was placed under the discipline of the law, who was "shut up to sin" (Gal 3:22), in order that he might find Christ. In other words, he applies the macrocosm of this salvation-historical principle to the microcosm of his own experience, which, as we will argue, is just what he does in 7:14–25. Therefore, Paul demonstrates from his pre-Christian days that the law does indeed reveal sin and increase the trespass: he is an Israelite in whom the law has achieved its overall redemptive purpose. This in itself argues that, Gal 1:14 and Phil 3:4–6 notwithstanding, Paul the Pharisee was confronted at some point by the condemning letter of the law. When the various pieces of evidence are weighed, it makes sense to think that the encounter took place just prior to his conversion and contributed to it.

Especially interesting in Paul's depiction of the law as a revealer of sin are his allusions to Genesis 3.[31] As Käsemann informs us, "There is nothing in our

---

[30] Wilckens, *Römer* 2.84–85.
[31] See further Dunn, *Christology*, 103; Goppelt, *Typos*, 131; Theissen, *Aspects*, 202–11; Longenecker, *Paul*, 92–96; Espy, "Conscience," 169; Gundry, "Frustration," 232; Bruce, "Law," 268–69; Wedderburn, "Adam," 419–22; id., "Structure," 344–45; Lyonnet, "'Tu ne convoiteras pas';" id., "L'histoire." Theissen, as others before him, contends that in 7:7–13 Paul makes Adam the model of his own experience (*Aspects*, 208). Similarly, Bornkamm entertains the possibility that Paul's "I" is Adam as the representative of mankind ("Sin," 93). However, for reasons to be argued below, the paradigm of fallen Adam does not fit the perspective of vv. 14–25.

III. The Function of Romans 7:14–25 within the Debate of Chapters 6–7 117

verses which does not fit Adam, and everything only fits Adam."[32] Dodd agrees that it "fits like a glove,"[33] while Dunn concurs that the conviction that (Adam's) covetousness is the root of all sin was certainly well-established among Paul's contemporaries.[34]

To be specific, in v. 8, Paul hints that sin, in his experience, resembled the tactics of the Serpent. As Barrett comments, "Sin – the Serpent – was in the Garden even before man, but had no opportunity of attacking the man until the command 'Thou shalt not eat of it' (Gen. ii.17) had been given. It was precisely by means of this command, the prototype of all law and religion, that the Serpent tempted man."[35] The acknowledgment of v. 11, "through the law" sin "deceived [ἐξηπάτησεν] me," alludes to the LXX of Gen 3:13, according to which Eve protested that the Serpent "deceived [ἠπάτησεν] me."[36] In Dunn's words: "It [the Serpent] twisted the instruction of the Creator given for man's good and made it sound like the legislation of a dictator fearful of losing his special status and prerogatives. Thus deceived, man clutched at a godlike life and grasped only death."[37] Paul, therefore, describes the law in the same terms as the deceitful work of the Serpent in the garden. Qualitatively speaking, Paul was deceived as Eve was deceived: both were expecting life from something which could produce only death. In Paul's case, that something was the law. In so saying, it simply would have been impossible for him more emphatically to consign the Torah to the old creation, the era dominated by Satan's rule.

In sum, the Adam/Eve associations in this segment of the debate confirm that Paul's thought moves decidedly within the realm of creation, albeit the old creation.[38] With bold strokes of the pen, he relegates the law to the era of man's

---

[32] Käsemann, *Romans*, 196.

[33] Dodd, *Romans*, 106.

[34] Dunn, *Christology*, 103. He further remarks that the rabbinic view that Adam received the (several) commandments of the law in the single command not to eat from the tree of the knowledge of good and evil may well go back to Paul's time. For references, see ibid., 307, n. 18.

[35] Barrett, *Romans*, 143.

[36] Paul uses ἐξαπατάω similarly in 2 Cor 11:13. Contra Moo (*Romans*, 465), its occurrences in Rom 16:18 (as we have seen) and 2 Thess 2:3 do have Satanic associations. Moo's explanation of Israel's (not Paul's personal) deception at Sinai is consistent with his overall exposition, but only convincing given his underlying assumption that the law has to be kept perfectly.

[37] Dunn, *Christology*, 104.

[38] To Moo, Karlberg, et al., it is to be conceded that in 7:7–13 there is a connection with Israel under the law; it is, after, all the tenth commandment which impacted on Paul. Nevertheless, it is a mistake to downplay the primary creation focus of Paul's thought. The principle underlying the tenth commandment appears for the first time in Eden, not at Sinai. In fact, Moo acknowledges that Israel's experience of the law is parallel to and, to some extent, recapitulates Adam's experience with the commandment of God (*Romans*, 463–64). Also, particularly in reply to Karlberg, the "old man" in Paul (e.g., Rom 6:6) is fundamentally Adam, who stands in contrast to Christ, the "new man" and "last Adam." That both Adam and Israel referents should coexist in the same passage is not surprising, inasmuch as Israel, the "son of God," at Sinai represents the inception of a new creation and finds itself qualitatively in

fall and its consequent ills, likening it to the Serpent, who beguiled Eve. Not that the Torah in itself is evil, because, of course, the very burden of 7:7–12 is the exoneration of the law of God, which is holy, just, and good. Nevertheless, the law has become the instrument of sin's deceitful working and the occasion of death. When, in its sin-mirroring capacity, it exposes idolatry for what it really is, Paul can only die in the presence of the commandment.[39]

Note on Paul, Adam, and Eve

Paul probably chose Eve as his primary model because of the connotations of apostasy associated with Adam. Eve, like Paul later, gave in momentarily to idolatry, but she did not in principle renounce Yahweh the Creator. Paul, then, places himself *qualitatively* in the same position as Eve in the Garden, only with the law, not the Serpent, being the instrument of his undoing. Paul's experience is analogous to that of Eve's in that in his life-history the law has performed the same function as the Serpent in hers. Thus, the law's indictment of Paul as a covetous person (vv. 7–8) parallels the situation in Eden. As Bruce explains: "Although the prohibition of the forbidden fruit in the fall narrative is not a part of the law of Moses, it could well be regarded as an anticipatory instance of the commandment against covetousness. And it could be argued that covetousness (ἐπιθυμία) is the quintessential sin."[40] From this perspective, the command of Gen 2:17 and that of Exod 20:17 (Deut 5:21) are virtually identifiable.[41]

However, although Paul selected Eve rather than Adam as his primary model,[42] we

---

the same situation of testing as the first human couple. Cf. Kim, *Origin*, 236. Some rabbinic commentators, accordingly, viewed the golden calf incident as a new fall. See Urbach, *Sages*, 425–28; Str-B 3.237; Moo, *Romans*, 463.

[39] Gundry's main thesis is that the "lust" of which Paul was convicted was sexual desire, commencing with his bar mitzvah ("Frustration," 232–33). The same case was argued by Davies (*Paul*, 23–25). By way of alternative, however, it makes sense to think that the law convicted him, as a faithful Jew, of the sin of sins, idolatry, particularly if Col 3:5 is regarded as Pauline. And in view of Phil 4:10–13, according to which Paul had to learn contentment as regards material things, his idolatry may have had peculiar reference to earthly possessions and comforts. Another possibility is that, spurred by his zeal for the law, his covetousness may have set its sight on preeminence in the Jewish community as one of its leading lights. In any event, Gundry's purview is too confined: Paul's testimony is that the law wrought in him "all kinds of covetousness" (Rom 7:8) (πᾶσαν ἐπιθυμίαν). In addition, Gundry seems to disregard Paul's own awareness of the gift of celibacy (1 Cor 7:7). Cf. further the criticism of Davies by Porter ("Sin," 9–13).

[40] Bruce, "Law," 269. Ziesler ("Commandment"), therefore, is wrong that only the tenth commandment would work within the setting of 7:13–25. In his view, Paul's paradigm is a faulty one, since only the tenth commandment has to do with desire rather than overt performance. I would contend, on the contrary, that each of the commandments underscores to Israel the wrongness of idolatry. It must not be overlooked that the tenth and seventh commandments overlap to the degree that one of the items prohibited by the former is the desire of one's neighbor's wife. Col 3:5, in addition, tends to confirm that covetousness is "the quintessential sin" because of its association with idolatry.

[41] Moo is right that Paul does not envisage the existence of the law of Moses in Eden, for which Adam was responsible (*Romans*, 453–454). Nevertheless, "the quintessential sin" (Bruce) of idolatry lies at the heart of Yahweh's prohibitions both in the Garden and later at Sinai. The two share this in common, and Adam's idolatry anticipates that of Israel later.

[42] As rightly perceived by Gundry ("Frustration," 230).

are not to forget that Rom 1:18–32 (3:23; 5:12) depicts the condition of fallen mankind, including Israel, in Adam-like terms. 7:7–13 thus represents a kind of throwback to the letter's earlier assertions about man and his plight. Longenecker, then, justifiably writes that Paul, in one sense at least, is identifying himself with Adam: "For him the experience of Adam was an historical reality. And since he is identified with Adam, even though as a Christian also identified with Christ, the history of Adam is his irrevocable history. When Adam lived, I lived; when Adam coveted, I coveted; when Adam was deceived, I was deceived; when Adam died, I died."[43]

Hence, in view of the complex Adam/Eve associations derived from Paul's Jewish heritage, it is possible that in 7:7–13 he intends simply to place himself in the company of the progenitors of fallen humanity, without distinguishing formally between Adam and Eve as individuals. Goppelt is quite right, I would say, that there is no clear dividing line between the two personalities, "particularly since the Pauline reflection [on the Genesis story] allows the clarity of the individual relationships to be lost in configurations of ideas."[44] If we wish a more systematic formulation, if such is necessary, we might say that, like Adam, Paul was exposed as an idolater, but, like Eve, he was recoverable from the error of his way.

IV. Romans 7:13–25: Two Creations, One Person

Following the customary pattern, the issue debated in 7:13–25 is drawn from what has preceded. The question is: "Was the law, which is good in itself, the direct and immediate cause of death?" Once more, his answer is μὴ γένοιτο, with a reassertion that the law was but the instrument of sin, v. 13 (cf. v. 23).

Vv. 14–25 are organically linked to v. 13, which introduces this last round of debate. Whatever else may be said by way of the interpretation of these verses, they must be seen as part of Paul's total answer to the objection raised in v. 13.[45] Indeed, once this connection is grasped, it follows that vv. 14–25 are an application to his present experience of the law's capacity to mirror sin. In other words, both before his entrance into the new creation (vv. 7–12, 13) and afterward (vv. 14–25), the law acts as God's instrument to expose sin and maintain the standard of his holy will. This intimate connection of vv. 14–25 with vv. 7–12 strengthens the conviction that the former is indeed autobiographical, because, as G. Lyons observes, Paul makes autobiographical references when he has been provoked to do so by his opponents.[46]

---

[43] Longenecker, *Paul*, 93–94 (cf. ibid., 96).

[44] Goppelt, *Typos*, 132–33.

[45] V. 16 ("the law is good") reminds us that the principal thrust of the section is to clarify Paul's teaching on the law vis-à-vis the false impression received by his Jewish peers. Kertelge ("Überlegungen," 108–9) correctly points out that it is only from v. 13 onwards that Paul lays the real blame for death at the door of sin.

[46] Lyons, *Autobiography*, 75 (see n. 1, for literature). Besides Lyon's book, see Gaventa, "Autobiography." Both studies establish that Paul normally talks about himself in order that his readers may imitate his example. If the pattern holds true here, Rom 7:14–25 describes both a condition in which the apostle finds himself as he pens Romans and which he deems desirable for others.

The substructure of vv. 13–25, then, may be set out as follows:

v. 13: the issue to be debated is raised and answered with respect to Paul's past.

vv. 14–20: Paul's answer is substantiated by his present experience of the law. The argument is pursued in two parallel statements:

14	18a
15a	18b
15b	19
16–17	20

vv. 21–25: summary and conclusion.

A. *The Law and Paul's Awareness of Sin, v. 13*

As is characteristic of the debate format of chaps. 6–7, each successive question posed by the interlocutor represents a nuanced rephrasing of the previous question. Thus, the objection of 7:13, "Did that which is good bring death to me," is a spin-off of the one voiced in 7:7: "Is the law sin?" Indeed, the answer to both questions is the same: the law is neither sin in itself nor the cause of death in Paul; it is only the instrument through which sin is revealed. This is not to minimize the law's powerful salvation-historical function of making sin "exceedingly sinful," for, instead of assuring Paul that his standing before God was secure because of his membership in the covenant people, the law realized in him "God's fuller and deeper strategy to bring out the character of sin,"[47] i.e., sin as idolatry, to the end that he might gain *Christ* (Phil 3:9) and become in *him* the righteousness of God (2 Cor 5:21).

B. *The Law and Paul's Continuing Struggle with Sin, vv. 14–20*

Whether one locates vv. 14–25 within Paul's pre- or post-Christian experience, the conspicuous feature of these verses is his *struggle*. Yet, I would submit, it is the very presence of strife which argues forcefully that this segment of Romans is the product of Paul's Christian consciousness. Whereas in vv. 7–13 Paul is simply dead because of the sin-revealing law, in vv. 14–20 (21–25) he is actively resistant to the impulses of indwelling sin in that he *wills* to do what is right – in itself a sign of life.[48] Paul's awareness of covetousness (=

---

[47] Dunn, *Romans* 1.387. Rom 7:7, 13 and like statements can be read as Paul's response to the Jewish conviction that fidelity to the law is *eo ipso* to possess life. Perhaps adapting Ben Sira's phrase "the law of life" (Sir 17:11; 45:5), the author of Baruch commends to his readers "the commandments of life" (3:9; 4:1. Cf. 4 Ezra 14:30; *Pss. Sol.* 14:2. As Kneucker comments, "they are called 'the laws of life' inasmuch as, when they are followed, they promise long life" (*Baruch*, 277). See further Cosgrove, *Cross*, 90–91; Brandenburger, *Adam*, 248, n. 2. These commandments are no less than the very embodiment of Israel's wisdom: "All who hold her fast will live, and those who forsake her will die" (4:1). Paul may have Bar 3:9; 4:1 in mind when in Rom 7:10 he writes of ἡ ἐντολὴ ἡ εἰς ζωήν. To be sure, Paul repeatedly stresses that the law is both good and spiritual; but left to itself, it can only arouse "the passions of sins" (v. 5) – life must come from some other source.

[48] Cf. Dunn, "Rom. 7,14–25," 271–73.

idolatry, Col 3:5) was a death experience: all he could do, as it were, was lie down and die before the law's accusation. But now, because he delights in the law of God in the inner person, he strives to do what he knows is acceptable according to the law's prescriptions.[49] In this regard, though not decisive in itself, the movement from the past tense of the verbs in 7–13 to the present tense in 14–25 is not to be downplayed. The γάρ of v. 14 is easily enough explained even with this shift from the past to the present, because vv. 14–25 are meant to say that the law performs qualitatively the same function after his conversion as before, by reminding him of the ideals of the new age and exposing his shortfall of those standards. Thus, the γάρ, as combined with οἴδαμεν, supports the contention of v. 13 by an appeal to the joint experience of Paul and the Romans.[50] In other words, the present sin-exposing activity of the law is a testimony to its similar role in Paul's past.

Note on the Present Tenses of 7:14–25

Wilckens takes v. 13 as the superscription to vv. 14–23, which, he says, accounts for the change of tense at v. 14. In other words, vv. 14–25 describe Paul's on-going condition resultant from the event of sin's power-grip (v. 13).[51] Schlier, Kuss, Kertelge, and Schnackenburg also assess the latter part of chap. 7 as descriptive of the situation of the man sold under sin.[52] Theissen similarly divides Paul's experience of sin and the law in 7:7–23 into a "narrative part" (7–13) and a "descriptive part" (14–23).[53] Certainly, these readings of the text are plausible in themselves and, given certain presuppositions, internally consistent.[54] However, given the framework of interpretation assumed by me, Dunn's analysis of the tenses is especially telling. He refers back to v. 7: "I would not have known (οὐκ ᾔδειν) what it was to covet had the law not said, 'You shall not covet.'" By the use of the imperfect, "Paul probably intends... to describe the beginning of a *continuing experience*; he still experiences lust. The covetousness which, as he now recognizes, characterized his pre-Christian past... is still a feature of his Christian present. Consequently 7:7–13 is not an interruption to the flow of thought through 6 to 8... since it in fact describes the beginning of an experience which continues for the believer – one aspect of Paul's experience even as a Christian. Even as a Christian there is still a sense in which he can and must say, 'I died and am dead because of sin'."[55] Thus, it

---

[49] *Mutatis mutandis*, Michel is right that Paul's "inner man" is the pious one of Israel, who has insight into the commandments of God and consents to them with his whole heart. But this one also experiences the sinfulness of fallen mankind and undergoes the tension of those need to offer sacrifice in order to hold to Yahweh's covenant (*Römer*, 235).

[50] Cranfield, *Romans* 1.355.

[51] Wilckens, *Römer* 2.85. Likewise Moo (*Romans*, 478).

[52] Schlier, *Römer*, 228; Kuss, *Römerbrief* 2.451; Kertelge, "Überlegungen," 108; Schnackenburg, "Römer 7," 292.

[53] Theissen, *Aspects*, 185, 195–97.

[54] They would seem to provide an adequate answer to Packer ("Wretched," 266–67). Gundry points to Phil 3:4–6, which employs an implied present tense in its review of Paul's former career as a Pharisee ("Frustration," 228–29). However, v. 7 recapitulates with the imperfect ἦν.

[55] Dunn, "Rom. 7,14–25," 261 (italics his). On the tenses of v. 7, cf. Cranfield, *Romans* 1.348; Barrett, *Romans*, 142, n. 17; Dunn, *Romans* 1.379.

is actually vv. 7–13 which initiate the thought of a continuing state resultant from a historical encounter with the law, and vv. 14–25, with their shift to the present tense, draw a line of continuity from Paul's primal confrontation with the law (v. 7) through its on-going killing effects (vv. 8–13) to his Christian experience of the same sin-revealing law. "The fact that Paul does not make much of the transition [i.e., from past to present tenses], that his thought moves from past to present almost unconsciously, underlines the degree of continuity which Paul recognizes between his pre-Christian experience and his experience as a Christian. But there is a difference. In vv. 7–13 there was no resistance: sin launched its attack, struck him down, and left him for dead with no fight in him. But in vv. 14–25 we see battle joined – we see Paul with a resistance and firmness of purpose which was lacking in vv. 7–13. He is still defeated, but he is now fighting. Where the strength of the counter attack comes from we will not learn till chapter 8, but the suggestion is already implicit that it is the Spirit joining battle in Paul with the flesh."[56]

Paul's struggle results from the antipathy of the "spiritual" law to his "carnal" self. The designation of the law as "spiritual" has led some to affirm a rather radical inconsistency on Paul's part, since in chaps. 5 and 6 the law was linked with the old creation entities of sin, flesh, bondage, and death.[57] However, Dunn rightly discerns that the law partakes of a duality (law-sin and law-Spirit), as does Paul himself as a "typical" believer (flesh-sin and mind-Spirit). These dualities are complementary (flesh-law-sin; mind-law-Spirit), allowing Paul to retrieve the law from a straightforward identification with sin and death.[58] This insight is, in fact, pivotal to an appreciation of the character of Rom 7:14–25; that is, the very genius of the passage is the conflict within Paul's psyche stemming from the dualism inherent in his experience of overlapping and competing ages. As the law itself can be joined with either flesh or Spirit, so can Paul, whose *ego* is divided between the epochs of Adam and Christ: "The 'I' is split and the law is split in complementary fashion because each belongs to both epochs at the same time in this period of overlap between the epoch of Adam and the epoch of Christ, between the era of the flesh and the era of the Spirit."[59]

In calling the law "spiritual," Paul, I would maintain, identifies it with the Holy Spirit and, therefore, with the age of the Spirit's manifestation and working, i.e., the new creation as foretold by the Prophets.[60] Specifically, the law is derived from the Spirit and is the expression of God's will as conveyed

---

[56] Dunn, "Rom. 7,14–25," 262. Gundry's criticism ("Frustration," 241, n. 4) that Dunn has not maintained the difference between vv. 7–13 and 14–25 necessary to argue from the present tense is unclear. Certainly, Dunn has accounted for the difference in this statement. We might add, ironically, that Gundry has missed the particular *continuity* of these two segments of chap. 7 stressed by Dunn.

[57] Sanders, *Law*, 76–81; Räisänen, *Paul*, 142.

[58] Dunn, *Romans* 1.387.

[59] Ibid., 1.388. Dunn clarifies later that the "I" is not completely schizoid or split in two: it is the same "I" each time which is either fleshly or willing to perform the law (p. 390).

[60] Cf. Schlier, *Römerbrief*, 229. Πνευματικός in 1 Cor 2:15 designates the "spiritual person," and in 15:44–46 the "spiritual body" of the resurrection, one created and fully indwelt by the Holy Spirit.

IV. Romans 7:13–25: Two Creations, One Person

through the Spirit.[61] The law is thus clearly associated with the Spirit; and since "Spirit" throughout these chapters is a synonym of the new era, *Paul places the law as a sin-revealer within the new creation.* For him this is not an exclusively old creation phenomenon, because when he is convicted of sin by the law, he yearns all the more for the ideals of the age to come and groans for the liberation of the sons of God (8:23). In a sense related to though distinct from his pre-Christian days, the law still points Paul to *Christ.* By its very "spirituality," i. e., as the product and mirror-image of God's will through the Spirit, the law makes Paul feel "carnal, sold under sin." Therefore, although sin no longer has dominion over Paul as it did when he was in Adam, in view of what he longs to be in the last Adam, he must confess that he is nothing less than "carnal." And it is just the presence of the "good and perfect" law of God in this "day of salvation" (2 Cor 6:2) which serves as a constant reminder that he has not yet been ushered into the consummate phase of his redemption.

In the presence of the "spiritual" law, Paul can only admit that he is "carnal, sold under sin." Linguistic affinities with πεπραμένος ὑπὸ τὴν ἁμαρτίαν can be found in the LXX, almost half of whose usages pertain to slavery.[62] Apart from that, the language is accounted for by the imagery of slavery in 6:16–19, to which Paul here reverts. This is consonant with the figure of captivity (v. 23), inasmuch as in antiquity captive soldiers were normally sold as slaves. Particularly noteworthy is the perfect tense, πεπραμένος, which commonly indicates a present condition resultant from a past action. In the instance before us, the past action is the event(s) of vv. 7–11: "what is in view is the consequence of the archetypal 'I''s capture and subjection to death at the hands of sin, the condition of the 'I' within the epoch of sin and death."[63] But taking into account the more distant background, it also makes sense to see an allusion to Adam's sin as the occasion when all in union with him became "sold under sin."[64] The case is particularly compelling when Paul's depiction of his idolatrous past in 7:7–11 is connected with 5:12–19. If, therefore, "sin" is the complex of idolatry/apostasy inherited from Adam, Paul blames his present tendencies to idolatry on his aboriginal connection with the first man: the same forces characteristic of Paul's Adamic existence still seek to lead him into the paths of "sin" and away from God in Christ. While Paul is no longer *willingly* a bond slave of "sin" (6:15–18, 22), "sin," nevertheless, continues to oppress him.

However, the starkness of the language does not of necessity preclude Paul *the believer*, even in view of the aorists of 7:4–6, because, as in chap. 6, the early aorists (6:1–11) are qualified later by the exhortations for the Christian to become what he already is. In fact, it is characteristic of chaps. 6–8 for Paul to state a proposition in seemingly absolute terms and then qualify. Theologically

---

[61] Cf. Cranfield, *Romans* 1.355–56.
[62] Moo, *Romans*, 481.
[63] Dunn, *Romans* 1.388.
[64] Moo, *Romans*, 481. He rightly points to 3:9, which summarizes the plight of Adamic mankind as ὑφ' ἁμαρτίαν εἶναι (ibid., 482).

speaking, this is due to the salvation-historical fact that a new beginning has been made in Christ without the total obliteration of "the present evil age" (Gal 1:4). In other words:

> Paul makes an in-principle statement in clear-cut unequivocal terms at the start of each chapter only to go on immediately to qualify it and to blur the clean-cut lines by showing that the reality of the believer's experience is more ambivalent. The "Already" has to be qualified by the "Not Yet"; the indicative of a salvation process begun has to be qualified by the imperative of a salvation process as yet incomplete.[65]

Paul, then, even as one who has entered the new creation, still feels the effects of his past existence in Adam.[66] To be sure, "flesh" and "fleshly" are synonyms of the old creation, the former life in Adam.[67] However, that epoch runs until the end of this age when finally it gives way to a new heavens and earth – and believers are not exempt from its powerful influence from the present till the conclusion of history.

King Ahab, who "sold himself to do that which is evil in the sight of the Lord" (1 Kgs 21:20, 25), is frequently made the paradigm of Paul's admission that he is "sold under sin." However, there is a vital difference. As Berkouwer explains, Paul says that he *has been* sold under sin, whereas Elijah throws into Ahab's teeth the fact that he has *sold himself*.

> In the case of Ahab we have simon-pure hostility to God and an unconditional surrender to the Evil one. In the case of Paul we have sin as an overpowering force which makes him cry out against it – granted that he is not exempt from responsibility to it. But to say as Paul does that he finds himself doing what he really loathes is impossible for Ahab. Ahab does the evil he relishes and rejects the clear commandment of God. He pursues his career in single-minded dedication to evil. Even in his being sold under sin, in the daily experience of being overpowered, Paul is not a slave to sin. Servants of sin – that is what believers used to be; now they are servants of righteousness (Rom. 6:17–18).[68]

In view of these considerations, one is not forced to the position that Paul means *categorically* that he is σάρκινος, "sold under sin," and can never perform the will of God.[69] This is to press the language further than its intended

---

[65] Dunn, *Romans* 1.302–3.

[66] Cf. Karlberg, "History," 73.

[67] As Barrett puts it, "flesh" is "human nature living in and for this age" (*Romans*, 151). Cf. Michel, *Römer*, 230.

[68] Berkouwer, *Sanctification*, 59–60.

[69] Cf. Cranfield, *Romans* 1.357; Morris, *Romans*, 291. "The thesis of the paragraph, 'I am carnal, sold under sin', is stated categorically and without qualification, not because this is the whole truth about Paul the Christian, but because it is the only part of the truth about himself that *the law* can tell him" (Packer, "Wretched," 269. Italics mine.). It is because Schlatter (*Gerechtigkeit*, 240–41) failed to see Paul's own qualification that he pressed the preposition ὑπό, thus making Paul the powerless slave of sin (cf. 6:17, 20). Similarly, Ridderbos, referring to 1 Kgs 21:20, contends that "sold under sin" expresses total subjugation to a foreign ruler, under which a slave is brought (*Romeinen*, 153). He assumes that the "I" of chap. 7 is powerless and, therefore, cannot be the new man in Christ (ibid., 157, 165, 168). The same line

meaning,[70] particularly given a context heavily laden with eschatological qualifications.[71] He is "carnal" in the sense that he still lives in the flesh (this creation) and participates in its condition.[72] As he relates to the law, *which is nothing but spiritual*, and anticipates the life of the age to come, he is forced to recognize that in his flesh dwells much that is at variance with this law which is good in the unqualified sense. The law, in other words, articulates ideals which will be realized perfectly in the consummate phase of salvation. But until then, Paul must view himself as one who falls far short of the ideal.

In company with certain of his contemporaries,[73] Paul's confession should serve as a reminder that it is precisely the saint who is most conscious of his sinfulness.[74] Longenecker is right that Rom 7:14−25, except for the christologi-

---

is taken by Kuss (*Römerbrief* 2.452, 459: "The 'I' is absolutely lost"). Zeller, commenting on v. 17, goes further: "It [sin] possesses the 'I' as a demon" (*Römer*, 141).

[70] Σάρκινος is a relative term. Moo concedes that since Paul can call the Corinthians σάρκινοι (1 Cor 3:1), the adjective in itself does not require that the "I" of Romans 7 be unregenerate (*Romans*, 481).

[71] Theissen's juxtaposition of Romans 7 and 8 is, therefore, oversimplified (*Aspects*, 183). For the same reason, Wenham thinks that 7:14−25 describes a state from which we have been delivered ("Life," 88). Gundry likewise thinks that the "I" of Romans 7 is powerless and imprisoned ("Frustration," 232, 238). Likewise Ridderbos (*Romeinen*, 157, 158, 165, 168) and Kertelge ("Überlegungen," 112).

[72] Nygren, *Romans*, 299.

[73] Charlesworth rightly remarks that the awareness of sin did not originate with Paul. See Charlesworth's preface to the reissue of *Paul and the Dead Sea Scrolls*, xii-xiii; id., *OTP* 2.628−30. Among the most relevant references are 1QS 11:9−10; 1QH 1:21−27; 4:29−33; 7:16−18; 12:24−31; 13:13−16. Käsemann points out that in the DSS awareness of sin did not lead to despair, but caused the saints "to arm themselves more firmly for further warfare under the banner of the Torah." However, he wrongly juxtaposes this attitude to Paul, who, in his view, "depicts the situation of the pious [before Christ] as objectively a desperate one" (*Romans*, 203). On the Dead Sea materials in relation to Paul, see Longenecker, *Paul*, 115; Michel, *Römer*, 243−45; Grundmann, "Justification," 87−88; Bruce, "Scrolls," 69−73; Braun, "Römer 7:7−25," though, in my judgment, Braun incorrectly sets at loggerheads grace (in Paul) and works (in Qumran) (ibid., 15). Kuhn ("Light," 103−4) contends that the universe of discourse assumed by both Qumran and Paul is the same, viz., *peirasmos* as the situation of the believer in the world, who is beset by the "two-power system" of sin and the flesh. The link is strengthened if the community, as Beker argues, celebrated the presence of the eschatological Spirit in its midst, thereby setting up a tension not dissimilar to that of early Christianity (*Paul*, 159, 281). He cites 1QH 12:11−12; 13:19; 14:13; 16:9, 11−12. Of course, the conspicuous difference between Paul and the scrolls respects their divergent attitudes toward the law. As Braun puts it, "For Paul salvation is liberation *from* the Torah, but for Qumran it is liberation *to* the Torah" ("Römer 7:7−25," 16. Italics his.). In this sense, Longenecker's remark that Qumran parallels Romans 7 and 8 in piety but not in theology is appropriate (*Paul*, 96).

[74] Dunn, *Romans* 1.389. Cf. Berkouwer, *Sanctification*, 66−67. See in addition Ezra 9:6−15; Neh 9:6−37; Psalm 44; Dan 9:3−19; Prayer of Azariah; Tob 3:1−6; 1 Esd 8:74−90; Bar 1:15−3:8; 1QS 1:24b−2:1; CD 20:28−30. As Morris comments, sin is always a problem for the servant of God, and "Paul is concentrating on the problem area" (*Romans*, 292). Morris' criticism of Stendahl (ibid.) is appropriate. In propounding his thesis that Augustine, not Paul, was the first "introspective man of the West," Stendahl was forced to argue that Paul's admissions of imperfection are merely metaphorical for the holiness of the law, not an

cal emphasis of v. 25, could also have been composed by a Jewish reactionomist.[75] However, it remains that the intensity of *Paul's* testimony is distinguished by his christology (or "christological eschatology"): the new creation has arrived with the first advent of Jesus Christ, though it has not come in its fullness. Paul stakes a claim to distinctiveness from his Jewish counterparts in that he has been raised with Christ and made to sit with him in the heavenly places (Rom 6:4–10; Eph 2:1–7; Col 3:1–3); and it is through Christ that God will finally deliver him from "the body of this death."

If v. 14 introduced the principal combatants of the warfare, the spiritual law and Paul's fleshly self, vv. 15–20 portray the battle itself. It is exegetically important to recognize that the γάρ of v. 15 introduces the qualification of what it means to be "sold under sin," i.e., it is "not an abject, unquestioning servitude, but a slavery under protest, the frustrated impotence of one who has to live 'in newness of Spirit' while still 'in the flesh'."[76] Therefore, the condition of "sold under sin" does not imply total defeat with no hope of release from captivity. Despite the vividness of the phrase, it is not intended absolutely but relatively. Being "sold under sin" does, in point of fact, entail a positive dimension, because integral to this state is the resistance of the will (the "I") to evil.

Of foremost importance is Paul's desire to do what is right according to the "good" law of God. Repeatedly and emphatically in vv. 15–20, he assures the Romans that he wills to do God's will and that he agrees (σύμφημι) with the law (v. 16) and rejoices (συνήδομαι) in it (v. 22). One cannot read such adulations of the law without thinking, e.g., of Ps 19:7–14 and Psalm 119 in its entirety, particularly vv. 16, 24, 47, 70, 77, 97, 111, 127, 143, 159, 165, 167, 174, in which David gives voice to his delight in and love for the commandments of the Lord. Paul shares this in common with David.[77] However, lying behind *his* willing *ego* is also the new covenant/new creation promise of Jer 31:33 and Ezek 36:26 that God will give his people a heart to do his will.[78] The writing of the law on the

---

index to his own awareness of sin ("We look in vain for a statement in which Paul would speak about himself as an actual sinner," *Paul*, 91). Wenham ("Life," 82) and de Lacey ("Question," 160) have similar convictions. Dodd's approach is diametrically opposite: Augustine is the greatest interpreter of Paul (*Romans*, 109)! Likewise Käsemann: "Paul's view of salvation history does not differ from Augustine's. Salvation history is the battle field of the *civitas dei* and the *civitas terrena*" ("Justification," 67). I must say that it seems to me that the distinction between the "introspective man of the West" and any other man is artificial at best. For a detailed critique of Stendahl, see Espy, "Conscience," 163–67.

[75] Longenecker, *Paul*, 97.

[76] Dunn, *Romans* 1.389. Ridderbos (*Romeinen*, 155) recognizes that vv. 15–20 describe more precisely what being sold under sin consists of; but he plays down the importance of Paul's "willing I" and his delight in the law, which, as we shall see presently, actually puts Paul within the era of salvation.

[77] Moo (*Romans*, 489) is right that many instances of Jewish delight in the law can be cited from the sources. However, such individuals conceive of themselves as in covenant relationship with Yahweh, not as lost and condemned by the law. Cf. n. 74 above.

[78] Baruch likewise draws on the Jeremiah prophecy. He promises that God's mercy to a

heart (Jeremiah) and the impartation of a heart of flesh in place of the former heart of stone (Ezekiel) are ways of saying that the renewed people of God will desire to obey his law from the heart and will delight in it, in Paul's words, κατὰ τὸν ἔσω ἄνθρωπον (v. 22).[79]

At the base of these prophecies is the expectation that the redeemed Israel will come to love God with all its heart and soul, when its heart is circumcised by the Lord (Deut 30:1–10). Along with Jeremiah 31; Ezekiel 36–37, Deuteronomy 30 envisages the time when Israel would put away its idols and worship Yahweh alone. This has extraordinary relevance for Paul, because it was his own involvement in the idolatry of the first human couple, repeated by Israel, which was condemned by the law. Therefore, when the apostle speaks of doing "good" (vv. 19, 21), he means not "good" in the abstract but "good" as devotion to the God of the covenant. For Paul Deuteronomy 30 has been fulfilled with the preaching of the word of faith (Rom 10:6–10): he now serves the creator rather than the creature (Rom 1:25). That such a specific connotation is attached to "good" is confirmed by our previous findings on "good" and "evil" elsewhere in Romans (2:7, 9, 10; 16:19; cf. 12:9, 21; Deut 30:15), i.e., the terms signify *the* good of serving the creator, as opposed to *the* evil of aligning oneself with Satan.[80] The overall case is strengthened if the νυνί of 7:17 is Paul's characteristic "eschatological now." In other words, *in this era of salvation*, "I no longer do it [i.e., sin] but sin which dwells in me."

As observed above, one can envisage in Paul a pattern as respects the law of God and the human heart. According to 2:15, "the work of the law" is "written on the heart" of the Gentiles by virtue of their existence as God's creatures. Using this as a point of departure, we might say that God's will was "written" on the heart of Adam; and as long as Adam remained unfallen, he complied spontaneously and cheerfully with that will. When he apostatized, however, he ceased to delight in the will of God, thus bequeathing to his posterity an internally written law marred by his own disobedience and accompanied by an unawareness of the reality of God.[81] This, in turn, necessitated the writing of the law once again on the heart of Adam's progeny in a new act of creative

---

disobedient people will take the form of a new covenant (2:35), in which Yahweh himself will guarantee the obedience of the nation: "I will give them *a heart that obeys and ears that hear*" (2:31 and the entire paragraph 2:27–35; cf. *Jub.* 1:22–25). See the remarks of Moore (*Additions*, 289) and Kneucker (*Baruch*, 256). Over against Paul, however, the new covenant for Baruch was inseparable from renewed loyalty to the Torah.

[79] Gundry disregards this covenantal context in making the "mind" of 7:14–25 a "moral monitor such as even pagans have" ("Frustration," 236). At the outset of his essay (p. 22), Gundry commits himself to the proposition that "Everyman's biography is the autobiography of Paul" (reversing a dictum of T. W. Manson). This is essentially an abstraction.

[80] Bultmann ("Romans 7," 152), as seconded by Meyer ("Worm," 75, 78), has seen that "good" and "evil" are more than labels for conventional moral values. His proposal that the terms stand for the two eschatological possibilities of "life" and "death," I would say, relate to our proposed interpretation by being the final outcome of the service of God or Satan respectively.

[81] Leenhardt, *Romans*, 146.

power (Jer 31:33). Hence, when, in the new covenant, the law is definitively written on the heart, there is, at least in principle, a return to the paradisiacal condition of Adam before his fall, the restoration of the image of God, a new creation.

It is within this schema that Paul's profession of delight in the law of God makes sense. He has entered the new covenant/new creation, the evidence of which is his delight in and consent to the commandment which is holy, just, and good (7:12), the "spiritual" law of God (7:14). In this, Paul stands in decided contrast to the "mindset of the flesh," which is hostile to God and cannot please him (8:7).[82] Because he serves *with his mind* the law of God (7:25b), he is not to be classified with those who live according to the flesh and *set their minds* on the things of the flesh (8:6). The negative side of the same attitude is that Paul hates his sin (7:15b) and is actually incapable of understanding his own actions when he sins (7:15a), given that his mind serves the law of God (7:25).[83]

It is Paul's love of the law and his hatred of his sin which constitute the hostilities within and eventuate in the agonized cry of frustration, "Wretched man that I am!" (v. 24). As he himself succinctly puts it, "The desires of the flesh are against the Spirit, and the desires of the Spirit are against the flesh; for these are opposed to each other to prevent you from doing what you would" (Gal 5:17).[84] If we may hear Dunn again: "In Paul we are confronted with the

---

[82] See Murray's remarks (*Romans* 1.257–58). Reflecting on 8:5, 7, Packer deduces: "Unless we are to suppose that Paul had reversed his anthropology within the space of less than ten verses, we are surely forced by this to conclude that in Rom 7:14–25 Paul is not, after all, describing a man in Adam, but a man in Christ" ("Wretched," 268). See also Espy, "Conscience," 174. Ridderbos' argument to the contrary is not compelling (*Romeinen*, 167).

[83] Cranfield, Dunn, Moo, and others prefer to take γινώσκω in 7:15a in the sense of "acknowledge," i.e., Paul does not "approve" or "condone" what he does. Murray opts for the frequent biblical sense of "know" as "love" or "delight in" (*Romans* 1.261); Paul, in other words, hates his actions. If these commentators, especially Murray, are correct, then Wright's appeal (*Climax*, 228) to the LXX of Gen 4:9–10 (ὁ δὲ εἶπεν Οὐ γινώσκω... καὶ εἶπεν ὁ θεός Τί ἐποίησας), Cain's professed ignorance of the significance of his sin, as a fitting parallel to Paul's use of γινώσκω is invalid. In any event, Wright's attempt to uncover a reference to Cain in 7:13–15 is objectionable because it is one-dimensional. Two factors have been overlooked. (1) Cain's ignorance represents a minimizing (excusing) of what he had done, while Paul conveys precisely the opposite impression: Rom 7:14–25 is his agonized *maximization* of the significance of sin and his assumption of full responsibility for it. (2) Paul delights in the law of God – hardly a trait of Cain's character!

[84] Barclay rightly maintains that the flesh and Spirit antithesis in Galatians takes us to the heart of Paul's ethics in a particularly direct way: "It reveals the situation of believers transformed by the power of the new age and enlisted in the service of the Lord and yet required to live out that service in the midst of the lures and temptations of the old age by a constant renewal of their obedience to the truth in faith" (*Truth*, 215).

Wenham ("Life," 83) denies that Gal 5:17 has any bearing on the thesis herein defended. For him the context tells against the assumption that Paul is describing a state of moral frustration. Gundry ("Frustration," 239), assuming that the "I" of Romans 7 inevitably suffers defeat, also denies that Gal 5:17 is parallel: the former is a "dismal defeat," while the latter is a "confident exhortation." Likewise Ridderbos (*Romeinen*, 163). Admittedly, Paul's aim in Galatians 5 is not to describe a state of frustration: his exhortation is a confident one.

IV. Romans 7:13–25: Two Creations, One Person

sharpness and frustration of the eschatological tension – that is, a tension which even if present elsewhere is rendered all the sharper and more poignant by the fact that the individual (believer) has already begun to experience the possibilities and promise of a wholly Spirit-directed life."[85] Furthermore, without this eschatological tension the parallel with the rabbinic "evil inclination" (יצר הרע) is incomplete.[86]

Cranfield concurs that in the Christian two factors are simultaneously operative: the revelation of God's will in the law and the activity of the Holy Spirit, who clarifies, interprets and applies the law.

It is where these two are present, that is, in the Christian believer, that the corruption of fallen human nature appears conspicuously. Here battle is joined in earnest *in a way that it is not possible before a man is sanctified by the Holy Spirit*. For in the Christian there is a continual growth in understanding of the will of God and therefore also an ever-deepening perception of the extent to which he falls short of it; and this growing knowledge and the deepening hatred of sin which accompanies it are not merely phenomena of the Christian's human psychology but *the work of the Spirit of God*.[87]

Nevertheless, the context is descriptive not only of "a confident call to live by the Spirit" (Wenham) but also of a warning that one may actually engage in the "works of the flesh." V. 17 then buttresses the exhortation to walk by the Spirit and not gratify the desire of the flesh (v. 16). Moreover, Wenham's attempt to make the ἵνα clause of v. 17 final rather than consecutive carries little conviction because, at best, his distinction between "the tendency of the tension between flesh and Spirit" and "the actual and necessary results of the tension" is artificial, at least in practical terms. Fung (*Galatians*, 250; "Impotence," 36) argues for the consecutive ἵνα (though Fung thinks that Gal 5:17 raises the question whether the "unequal conflict" of Romans 7 is the normal outcome of the Spirit/flesh struggle in the believer). In any event, final or consecutive, the *prima facie* reading of 5:17 is that there is a conflict between flesh and Spirit: "The human body is a battlefield on which the powers of the flesh and the Spirit fight against each other, so that the human will is disabled from carrying out its intentions" (Betz, *Galatians*, 280–81).

[85] Dunn, *Romans* 1.389.

[86] Ibid., 1.391. On the rabbinic doctrine of the יצר הרע as the impulse in man to sin, see, e. g., Davies, *Paul* 20–35; Porter, "Sin," 3–8; Moore, *Judaism* 1.479–96; Schechter, *Aspects*, 242–92; Montefiore/Loewe, *Anthology*, §§ 757–811; Urbach, *Sages*, 471–83; Str-B 4.1.466–83. For the tradition that the Torah was given to counteract the evil *yetzer*, see Montefiore/Loewe, *Anthology*, §§ 326–32. Beker observes that in Apocalyptic "The Torah is the ontological-moral counterpart [of the *yetzer harah*] that enables one to resist the evil powers, and obedience to it is the exclusive condition for participation in the kingdom of God" (*Paul*, 188). The earliest occurrence of יצר in extant Jewish literature is Sir 15:15 (as translated by διαβούλιον), where it means "free will" or one's decision to be obedient (cf. 1:26; 21:11; *Testament of Asher* 1). The closest verbal parallel to Sir 15:15a is *Pss. Sol.* 9:7 (cf. 4 Macc 1:15; CD 3:3; Tob 4:5). On this meaning of יצר, see Hadot, *Penchant*, 103; Maier, *Mensch*, 97; Murphy, "Yeser," 337; Skehan/Di Lella, *Ben Sira*, 81–83, 272; Hengel, *Judaism* 1.140–41; Büchler, "Sin," 33. This is of interest because Ben Sira has in view not free will in the abstract but that of Jewish man in covenant relationship with Yahweh, an idea not dissimilar to Paul's in Rom 7:14–25.

[87] Cranfield, *Romans* 1.359 (italics mine). Moreover, as Dunn suggests, the dualism of sin's reality and believing man's desire to do God's will is like that of Apocalyptic, in which the glory to come clashes with the negative features of the present age (*Romans* 1.390–91). Cf. Russell, *Apocalyptic*, 266–69.

It is at this juncture that a phenomenon of the Pauline anthropology enters the picture, i.e., Paul's distinction between the "outer person" and the "inner person" (2 Cor 4:16).[88] This is the person in his basic bipartition. However, both of these components can be analyzed further and designated variously.

The Outer Person	The Inner Person
σῶμα	ψυχή
σάρξ	πνεῦμα
μελή	νοῦς, φρόνημα
	καρδία
	θέλημα

It is important, however, to remember that Hebrew anthropology does not divide the person into so many compartments, like slices of a pie; it is, rather, *aspectival*, i.e., the whole human can be contemplated from various points of view, whether the specific terms employed, strictly speaking, have to do with the "inner" or "outer" person. It is this Hebrew aspectival anthropology which is carried over into Rom 7:14−25: the words and phrases used by Paul to depict his self-conflict have to do with him as a whole ἄνθρωπος, who experiences simultaneously the influences of old and new creations.[89] Hence, the personal pronouns ἐγώ and (ἐ)μοί are used by Paul in his identification with both aeons. On the one hand, "me" is identified with the "flesh" (v. 18), while, on the other, Paul denies that it is "I" who sins but rather sin dwelling in him (v. 19). Cf. v. 25.

It is necessary, though, to introduce a modification into this broad scheme. In at least four instances in chap. 7, Paul clearly depicts the "inner person" as aligned with the law of God (vv. 18, 22, 23, 25). In 8:6−7, it is the "thought processes" (φρόνημα) of the Christian which are in tune with the Spirit, as opposed to the "thought processes" of the flesh, which are at enmity with God. It is just the inner man, as comprised of the φρόνημα τοῦ πνεύματος, which is being renewed day by day (2 Cor 4:16). To put it another way, the ἔσω ἄνθρωπος belongs to the age to come, while the ἔξω ἄνθρωπος belongs to this age and is doomed to perish (cf. Rom 8:10).[90] It is true that the outer man is involved in the process of death to sin (Rom 6:13, 19; 8:13; 12:1; 2 Cor 7:1): our "members" are to be presented to God as the implements of righteousness

---

[88] See Jewett, *Terms*, 391−401. It is possible, as Leenhardt (*Romans*, 193) and others maintain, that the terminology of "outer" and "inner" personhood was current among Paul's Hellenistic contemporaries. But if so, he "remoulds it to modes of expression of his own anthropology which is Christian, and determined on soteriological-eschatological lines" (J. Behm, quoted by Barrett, *Romans*, 150).

[89] Dunn, "Rom. 7,14−25," 265. Cf. Scroggs, *Adam*, 60−61.

[90] Barrett, *Romans*, 150. The phrase ἔσω ἄνθρωπος occurs also in 2 Cor 4:16; Eph 3:16. It is arguable that in itself the phrase is only anthropological, not specifically soteriological (Moo, *Romans*, 490). Nevertheless, in the former passage it is the ἔσω ἄνθρωπος, as opposed to the ἔξω ἄνθρωπος, which is the subject of daily renewal; and in the latter the inner person of the Christian is strengthened by the Holy Spirit. In terms of actual usage, then, the referent of ἔσω ἄνθρωπος is to the believer.

IV. Romans 7:13–25: Two Creations, One Person

(Rom 6:13). Even so, the "body," "flesh," and "members" of the believer are never unambiguously identified with the new creation; only the consummate phase of redemption will place the ἔξω ἄνθρωπος into a position of nonambivalence with respect to the age to come, when the believer becomes σῶμα πνευματικόν (1 Cor 15:44–46).

This is not to dichotomize rigidly the constituent elements of human nature; sin, to be sure, has done its damage in the renewed believer's inner being (e. g., 2 Cor 7:1). Nevertheless, the characteristic Pauline view is that the "inner person" is unambiguously devoted to the new creation, while the "outer person" is caught up in the ambivalence of the overlapping ages. This is why "flesh" in Paul almost always has negative connotations and why in 7:18 the flesh is said to be the "me" in which no good thing dwells.[91] "Body" likewise exhibits a similar usage.[92] Although the flesh/body of the believer will be resurrected and then take its place in the consummated new creation, until that time, ambivalence still attaches itself to his flesh/body, and, for that reason, σάρξ/σῶμα (etc.) is never used in a manner which is unambiguous with regard to the new creation.

These data of the Pauline anthropology go far in arguing that the subject matter of Rom 7:14–25 is that of man in Christ who experiences the most radical cleavage of his humanity possible, the wresting of the constituent elements of his personhood.[93] On the one side, the flesh in particular has become the "headquarters" of sin;[94] on the other, the inward man, though willing to do the will of God as a participant in the new creation/new covenant,[95] is prevented by the counteraction of his flesh. Such a man divided can only cry out: "Wretched man that I am, who shall deliver me from the body of this death!"[96]

---

[91] Dunn ("Jesus," 44–48) contends that "flesh" in Paul always bears negative connotations. However, in Rom 1:4; 9:5; 11:14 it simply means Jewish humanity.

[92] As Dunn ("Rom. 7,14–25," 266) points out, although "body" in itself is a more or less neutral term, it can become negative by virtue of qualifying phrases such as "body of sin." See further his remarks on the relation of "flesh" and "body" (*Romans* 1.391). We note, however, Gundry's qualification that Paul never uses σῶμα as a synonym for σάρξ in a hamartiological sense (*Soma*, 43).

[93] Cf. P. Althaus, as quoted by Kertelge ("Überlegungen," 110), though Althaus places the man of Romans 7 within the old aeon. Moo (*Romans*, 486) concedes that Paul's anthropology is essentially monistic rather than dualistic. But, he thinks, there is an undeniable element of dualism which is more to the fore in this passage than anywhere else in Paul, thus accounting for Paul's divided state. I would reply that the anthropology of Romans 7 is not inherently dualistic, but rather underscores Paul's holistic approach to human nature. In other words, the great irony of the passage is that the integrity of his humanity has been split by the disparate loyalties of the Spirit and the flesh respectively.

[94] Gundry (*Soma*, 139) remarks that in Romans 7 Paul uses "flesh," "body," and "members" interchangeably: "Consequently, in this passage flesh does not represent sin, but the physical body, or members, which sin occupies and uses as an instrument for the performance of evil." See further ibid., 37–50; Jewett, *Terms*, 157–60, 290–99.

[95] It is to be kept in mind that new covenant and new creation in the Prophets are coterminous. This is why particularly in Isaiah, Jeremiah, and Ezekiel new creation and new covenant are intertwined in the prophecies of Israel's future salvation.

[96] Cf. Berkouwer, *Sanctification*, 60.

Some further attention must be given to Paul's admission that he is "fleshly." "Flesh" in Paul's anthropology, of course, has been explored many times. Our particular interest is in its salvation-historical associations as they have a bearing on the interpretation of Rom 7:14−25. From the vantage point of such a salvation history, "flesh," as a generalization, is concerned with the individual, but the individual as he relates to the old creation.[97]

> The force of σάρξ is precisely that it denotes an unavoidable attachment and tie to this age which must perish before redemption can be complete (Rom 8:11, 23), and which therefore denotes not merely a pre-Christian state.... It is precisely this inextricable attachedness to this age concerning which Paul makes the judgment "no good thing."[98]

Paul, as one born of woman, has entered the present creation dominated by Adam's headship (Rom 5:12−19). By birth, he is "flesh" and must remain so until his glorification in the image of Christ; until he is revealed as one of the sons of God (Rom 8:19), he "groans inwardly" as he anticipates the redemption of his body (8:23). Since he has participated in this creation, his body is dead because of sin (8:10). Thus, Paul's confession that he is "fleshly, sold under sin," and that in his flesh dwells no good thing is an avowal that he, along with those he represents, is a victim of sin and must continue to experience sin's ravages as long as this era of human history continues. Therefore, during the period of concurrent ages, "flesh" characterizes Paul and all like him. Rather than being a sign of his pre-Christian state, "flesh" within the present setting is indicative of Paul's continued belongingness − as a whole person − to the present evil age, which has not yet been superseded by the age to come in its fullness.[99] This is why he can affirm that good, i.e., the good of serving the creator rather than the creature, does not dwell in his "flesh" (v. 18), because that aspect of his personhood is allied more closely to Adam than Christ.

But Paul is not only flesh, he is also a man of the Spirit. It is, of course, this claim which is the bone of contention in the interpretation of our passage. It is true that Paul does not say in so many words that he is "spirit." However, his self-awareness which surfaces throughout Rom 7:14−25 is that of one squarely within the era of the Spirit; he has been enrolled in the new covenant, proof of which is his delight in the law of God, his desire to do God's will, and his hatred of sin. Such data are particularly compelling if we allow Rom 7:14−25 its legitimate place within the overall flow of thought of Romans 5−8. That is to say, in commitment Paul has left the old creation. Once he was "ungodly," a "sinner," an "enemy" of God, and under "wrath," but now he has been reconciled to God through the death of his Son and rejoices in the hope of sharing the glory of God (5:1−11). Formerly he was in union with the first Adam, but now he has embraced another, the last Adam (5:18).

Consequently, the same Paul has been raised in newness of life, and his

---

[97] Dunn, "Jesus," 45; id., "Rom. 7,14−25," 266; Ridderbos, *Paul*, 65−66.
[98] Dunn, *Romans* 1.391.
[99] Cf. Dunn, "Rom. 7,14−25," 266.

former *willing* bondage to sin has been terminated (6:1–23). At one time he was bound to the law and obliged to obey *it*. Now, however, he is married to Christ and is free from the law; he no longer serves in the oldness of the letter, i.e., the Torah as representative of the old creation, but in the newness of the Spirit (7:1–6). To be sure, the full manifestation of God's new creative purposes lies in the future; the sons of God are yet to be revealed, and the creation itself is to be set free from its bondage to decay (8:18–25). Until then, Paul must undergo the tension resultant from the side-by-side existence of two creations (7:14–25), with the law continuing to perform the same function in Paul as it did when he lived exclusively in the old creation (7:7–12).

It is because Paul is "spirit" as well as "flesh" that our approach to Rom 7:14–25 receives an important qualification. As encapsulated by the parallel of Gal 5:16–24, he indeed affirms that the two dimensions of his being run counter to each other and prevent his living wholly in one or the other, with the consequence that "the believer finds himself torn in two by conflicting desires and impulses, and his experience as a man of Spirit in the flesh is one of continuing frustration."[100] However, the impression perhaps has been left that this passage, thus interpreted, voices the totality of what it means to be a Christian; hence, the view herein proposed has been rejected because, as the assumption goes, it gives rise to an inadequate Christian self-image.[101]

It is in this circumstance that the connection of 7:14–25 with 8:1–17 must be given its due weight. On the heels of 7:25, 8:1 declares that there is no condemnation for those in Christ. In other words, it is the presence of the struggle – not its absence – which is indicative of life within an individual; such a one is not abandoned entirely to the flesh where death only reigns.[102] "*Therefore*," i.e., *because there is warfare within*, "there is no [eschatological] condemnation for those who are in Christ Jesus."[103] However, as one reads the opening paragraphs of chap. 8, it becomes equally evident that the promise of no condemnation is valid only for those who walk by the Spirit and put to death the deeds of the body; it is only the mind which is set on the things of the Spirit which can please God. Thus, says Paul, we are debtors not to the flesh but the Spirit. The Christian is led by the Spirit and is the son of God; he anticipates the glory of God as a fellow heir of Christ. It is, then, the overflow of Paul's thought from 7:14–25 into chap. 8 which places a safeguard over our conclusions respecting the character of Christian existence this side of the eschaton.[104] To

---

[100] Ibid., 268.

[101] E.g., Wenham ("Life," 89) implies that such a life is substandard in view of what is available in Christ. Likewise Hoekema (*Christian*, 67; cf. Fung, "Impotence," 45).

[102] Bultmann's conjecture of a gloss in 7:25b–8:1 ("Glossen," 199) misses this inner connection of Paul's logic.

[103] Contra Bornkamm ("Sin," 100), 8:1 is not to be juxtaposed to 7:25. Although 8:1 does glance back to past justification, 8:33 (= Isa 50:8–9) gives "no condemnation" (v. 23) a decidedly future dimension as well. This "Already" and "Not Yet" of "no condemnation" fits exceedingly well into the scenario of 7:14–25.

[104] Cranfield is convinced, rightly in my view, that we can do justice to the text of Paul "only

adapt Barrett's observation, 7:14–25 does not tell the whole story of what it means to be a Christian, but is written from within the Christian life to account for the role of Christianity in our experience.[105] It must be remembered that utterances such as Rom 7:24 and Jas 3:2 are confessions of sin, not excuses for sin.[106]

Gal 5:24, "those who belong to Christ Jesus have crucified the flesh with its passions and desires," is likewise directly relevant, coming, as it does, at the conclusion of the paraenesis of Gal 5:16–26.[107] V. 16 is an exhortation to walk by the Spirit and not gratify the desires of the flesh. Such an admonition is necessary because of the unceasing conflict of flesh and Spirit during the course of this age: "For the desires of the flesh are against the Spirit, and the desires of the Spirit are against the flesh; for these are opposed to each other, to prevent you from doing what you would" (v. 17). This is followed by a renewed reminder that the Christian is led by the Spirit and is not under the law, i.e., "the elements of the world" which continue to govern the old creation (4:3, 9; Col 2:8, 20).[108]

Hence, the believer possesses *the* crucial advantage in his "struggle with sin" (Heb 12:4). Thereafter Paul enumerates the "works of the flesh" as over against the "fruit of the Spirit"[109] and completes his series of "indicatives" with the salvation-historical dictum that those who belong to Christ have crucified the flesh, or, as he says earlier, their very persons have been crucified with Christ, and Christ lives in them (2:20).[110] For Paul, then, the clash of Spirit and flesh is

---

if we resolutely hold chapters 7 and 8 together ... and see in them not two successive stages, but two different aspects, two contemporaneous realities, of the Christian life, both of which continue so long as the Christian is in the flesh" (*Romans* 1.356). Regarding the expression "carnal, sold under sin," Cranfield remarks that understood in isolation from the teaching of chaps. 6, 8, and 12–16, these words would certainly leave a thoroughly wrong impression of the Christian life. But, he says, "taken closely together with it, they bring out forcefully an aspect of the Christian life which we gloss over to our undoing" (ibid., 357–58). Cf. Berkouwer, *Sanctification*, 63.

[105] Barrett, *Romans*, 153.
[106] Berkouwer, *Sanctification*, 49.
[107] In agreement with Gundry, "Frustration," 240. "Paul's teaching here is not intended to provide an easy excuse for persistent moral defeat – only an excuse for defeat experienced as *defeat*, as a wretched captivity and slavery to sin" (Dunn, *Romans* 1.412. Italics his.). Cf. Espy, "Conscience," 176.
[108] I would submit that "the world" in this phrase has reference to the old creation, which is consistent with Bandstra's conclusion that τὰ στοιχεῖα τοῦ κόσμου "refers to the fundamental forces inherent in the world, by which Paul specifically means the law and the flesh as operative in the world of humanity before and outside of Christ" (*Law*, 173. See his exposition of pp. 77–94). In broadest terms, what Bandstra calls "old age"/"new age" is the "old creation," stemming from Adam, as opposed to the "new creation," which owes its existence to the last Adam. Κόσμος, then, would underscore the solidarity of Israel and its Torah with the rest of humanity – a rather startling proposition to a first-century Jew.
[109] "The fruit of the Spirit" is primarily love and its attendant attitudes, which distinguish the Christian particularly from the circumcision party. See my "Burden Bearing."
[110] Rom 6:5–11 is directly parallel in that the believer, as Christ, has died to "sin," i.e., the old creation as ravaged by sin.

not grounds for despair and defeat but *perseverance*. As Fung comments, "This conditional sentence [v. 18] clearly shows that Paul does not regard the believer simply as a helpless spectator or an unwilling pawn in the fierce battle between the flesh and the Spirit; the assumption is rather that the Christian can overcome the flesh by siding with the Spirit."[111]

If it be objected that these are irreconcilable polar opposites, the reply must be that such is the paradox of the Christian, who is weak and strong at the same time (2 Cor 12:10).[112] *This paradox is the genius of Romans 7:14–25: the Christian is flesh and Spirit at the same time.*[113] Equally important, however, is the recognition that Paul's confession of carnality, his inability to do what he desires, and the resultant cry of frustration in 7:24, must be understood in relative, not absolute, terms. His outpouring of soul, dramatic though it is, cannot be construed as objective evidence that he has not and cannot attain to measures of victory over sin. His orientation is to *the future*; he longs for total conformity to the image of Christ (8:29), when his body is redeemed (8:23).[114] But until that time arrives, he can only lament that he falls far short of the "good" and "spiritual" law. That Paul is looking forward is confirmed by the question of 7:24b: "Who shall deliver me from the body of this death?" The answer, of course, is that God will do so through Christ (v. 25a), when Paul's adoption is complete (8:23).

---

[111] Fung, *Galatians*, 251. "How can one who exists temporally in 'the present evil age' nevertheless enjoy deliverance from it and live here and now the life of the age to come? By the aid of the indwelling Spirit, who not only makes effective in the believer the saving benefits of Christ's passion but also secures to him in advance the blessings of the age to come" (Bruce, "Law," 274). Hoekema's objection that Romans 7 makes no mention of the Spirit (*Christian*, 63–64) does not make due allowance for the sweep of Romans 5–8.

[112] "This is the enigmatical in the Christian life. The Christian is at the same time 'free from sin,' and yet subject to the condition of sin. He is not 'carnally minded,' and yet the flesh sets its mark on all that he does. No corresponding enigma rests on the natural man. There is a natural concurrence between will and action. The natural man is 'carnally minded;' and, in agreement therewith, his conduct is also carnal" (Nygren, *Romans*, 299).

[113] "God's power does not drive out human weakness; on the contrary, it only comes to its full strength through weakness. The paradox of Already/Not Yet, of Spirit and flesh, is not surmounted. The tension dare not be abandoned or slackened, for therein lies disaster. For it is only when I am weak that I am strong" (Dunn, "Rom. 7,14–25," 270). Luther spoke in like terms (see Berkouwer, *Sanctification*, 74). In disallowing this perspective, Gundry ("Frustration," 236–37) and Ridderbos (*Romeinen*, 155, 162) absolutize the contrast of flesh and Spirit. As noted several times by now, Paul provides his own qualifications to statements which, taken on their own, would seem to be categorical. Kertelge is more nuanced. He recognizes that the man of the Spirit in chap. 8 never forgets his negative past ("Überlegungen," 113, 114; cf. Moo, *Romans*, 476–77). Schnackenburg ("Römer 7," 297–98), Bornkamm ("Sin," 98–99), and Prumm (*Botschaft*, 100–1) reason along similar lines.

[114] Dunn, "Rom. 7,14–25," 265, 268.

C. Paul's Summary and Conclusion, vv. 21–25

These verses are perhaps the most problematic portion of chap. 7, because of the difficulty of determining what is meant by the repeated use of νόμος.[115] According to v. 21, Paul finds τὸν νόμον, which is his will to do to "the good," with "the evil" lying close at hand. In v. 22, it is clear enough that νόμος is the law of God. However, v. 23 speaks of the ἕτερος νόμος in Paul's members which wages war against the νόμος of his mind, taking him captive to the νόμος of sin. V. 25, in its epitome of 7:14–25, poses Paul's essential tension as the service of the νόμος of God with his mind vs. the service of the νόμος of sin with his flesh.

Two options are open: either Paul intends νόμος as the law of God consistently or he juxtaposes God's law with the "principle" of sin. Dunn argues for the former.[116] When in v. 21 Paul concludes εὑρίσκω τὸν νόμον, says Dunn, he means: "this is what I find the law to be in experience," i. e., "willing alone is not enough: I still am unable to translate what the law defines as good into practice."[117] Accordingly, both the law of Paul's mind and the "other law," which assails it (= "the law of sin") (v. 23), are the Torah as experienced differently.[118] In so describing the law, Paul purposely uses provocative language "in order to make clear the two-sidedness of the law in the epoch of overlap between sin and grace."[119] Others, however, argue for νόμος in vv. 21, 23, 25 as a working principle, observed regularity, or binding authority,[120] with the result that God's law is in conflict with the "law" of indwelling sin. In this case, it is possible that he uses (νόμος) ironically, i. e., the law of God and the "law" of sin both command him and demand obedience.[121]

Whichever view of νόμος one opts for, the main point emerges with clarity: Paul's will and mind are joined together in mortal combat with sin (or "the law of sin") and the flesh. As in the preceding verses, old and new creations are pitted against each other, with Paul's true self aligned with the latter, while sin and his flesh are allied to the former. As a man divided, Paul is confronted with competing and conflicting forces and must remain so until God in Christ delivers him from "the body of this death."

That he contemplates himself as a man who has entered the eschatological era is supported by a consideration of the alternative interpretation. Which

---
[115] Cf. Wilckens, Römer 2.88; Barrett, Romans, 148–49. The same problem crops up again in 8:2.
[116] Dunn, Romans 1.392–95.
[117] Ibid., 1.393.
[118] Likewise Wilckens (Römer 2.89) and Barrett (Romans, 149).
[119] Dunn Romans 1.395 (see also p. 398).
[120] E.g., Cranfield, Sanday/Headlam, Murray, Moo, Black, Schlier, Lietzmann, Zeller, Ridderbos; BAGD, 542; Bruce, "Law," 259; Fung, "Impotence," 44.
[121] "'The law of sin' may be conceived of as not only impelling to action that is antithetical to the law of God but also as dictating such action" (Murray, Romans 1.265). Cf. Moo, Romans, 492; Deidun, Morality, 200. Kuss calls the "other law" a "Herrschaftssystem" (Römerbrief 2.456).

IV. Romans 7:13–25: Two Creations, One Person

ἄνθρωπος, according to that approach, is intended: Gentile or Jewish? As a rule, the former was not well-informed about the Jewish law. At most, one can argue only for the condemnation of conscience as it bore witness to the law written on the heart (Rom 2:14–16).[122] Yet this is improbable, because in Romans 7 locutions are used for the law which would have been unfamiliar to Gentile ears and yet very familiar to Jewish ones: his dialogue is with Israel.[123] As for Jewish man himself, there is indeed evidence that he experienced what Paul articulates in Rom 7:14–25; but in every instance it is *the righteous, who have been faithful to Yahweh's covenant*. See Ezra 9:6–15; Neh 9:6–37; Dan 9:3–19; Psalm 44; Prayer of Azariah; Tob 3:1–6; 1 Esd 8:74–90; Bar 1:15–3:8; 1QS 1:24b–2:1; 11:9–10; 1QH 1:21–27; 4:29–33; 7:16–18; 12:24–31; 13:13–16; CD 20:28–30.[124]

In this conflict between the two laws (however interpreted), Paul acknowledges defeat: "I see in my members another law at war with the law of my mind and making me captive to the law of sin which dwells in my members" (v. 23). Admittedly, his figure is strong, even extreme, because it speaks not simply of battle but also of capture (αἰχμαλωτίζομαι). As such, the starkness of the metaphor corresponds to that of v. 14b. However, there are counterbalancing considerations. As noted above, throughout chaps. 6–8 a pattern is observable: propositions are initially stated in categorical terms and then later qualified. As the salvation-historical indicatives of 6:2–4 are matched by the imperatives of 6:12–23; 8:1–17, likewise the indicatives of 7:1–6 are qualified by the realism of 7:14–25. This means, to reiterate from before, that Paul's intentionally stark language does not have to be taken in absolute terms: "What is in view is not ... a final state, any more than in v. 14b, but an ongoing experience of warfare and defeat (note the tenses) in which the final outcome of the war in which the individual finds himself is by no means yet settled."[125] From

---

[122] Cranfield, Dunn, Barrett, Wilckens, Theissen, Zeller, and others cite classical authors who admit to internal struggles of mind and conscience. Bornkamm even refers to Herman Melville's *Billy Budd* ("Sin," 103, n. 29). However, Romans 7 has the Jewish law specifically in view, so that while these testimonies are interesting and to some degree helpful (see below), they are not directly parallel. The most relevant non-Pauline sources are Qumran and Apocalyptic.

[123] As seen by Moo (*Romans*, 453, 469): "the topic of Romans 7 is the law – not just 'law' in general, but the Mosaic law" (ibid., 453).

[124] Cf. Zeller's further references (*Römer*, 143–44). One looks virtually in vain in both pre and postdestruction Judaism for evidence of Jewish man condemned by the law who comes to recognize his lostness. The only possible exception is the Prayer of Manasseh; but even it is written from the perspective of one within the covenant who desires to return to the worship of Yahweh alone. For such there is the provision of repentance, followed by forgiveness and restoration (vv. 7, 8, 13, 14). Besides, in keeping with most of the literature of this genre, "Manasseh" probably stands for Jewish loyalists who are compelled to confess their shortcomings. 4 Ezra 7:116–26 is sometimes cited, but inappropriately in view of the document's historical setting. Cf. further Sanders, *Paul*, 397; Bruce, "Law," 271. To be sure, from the Jewish perspective all Gentiles and non-observant Jews were lost; but this is the judgment of the "righteous" evaluating "sinners," not the confession of observant Jews themselves.

[125] Dunn, *Romans* 1.396.

the perspective of the mark to which Paul presses (Phil 3:12), i.e., consummated resurrection life, the series of defeats and frustrations experienced by him can quite legitimately be called "captivity," because on every occasion on which he falls he is "taken captive." Moreover, as Dunn continues, the relative character of αἰχμαλωτίζομαι is confirmed by another consideration: "were defeat the only outcome of every battle, or were defeat not experienced and recognized as *defeat*, the speaker could have none of the hope which Paul goes on to express" [in v. 24].[126]

The paradox of Paul's existence is highlighted by the most dramatic outcry of the chapter: "Wretched man that I am! Who shall deliver me from the body of this death? Thanks be to God through Jesus Christ our Lord" (vv. 24−25a). From one perspective, he is a "wretched man." Ταλαίπωρος is a term whose nuances are varied, as attested by the usages in the LXX,[127] Josephus,[128] and Philo.[129] It can refer to a condition of hopelessness and futility, as in Wis 3:11; 13:10 (referring to those who reject wisdom and engage in idolatry). But it can also describe the state of a person who is pulled in two directions, because the power of the flesh compels him to idolatrous courses, in spite of his commitment to God the Creator.[130] Interestingly, Epictetus uses the phrase ταλαίπωρον ἀνθρωπάριον ("wretched paltry man") to express the two-sidedness of everyman, i.e., his reason and his flesh.[131] The parallel is worthy of notice because, in so speaking, Epictetus does not despair of life, but is the more determined to resist negative influences. For Paul also "wretched man that I am!" is not the cry of despair but of frustration, the frustration of falling short of the new creation ideals embodied in the "spiritual" law.[132] Yet it must be qualified that Paul's conflict, as distinct from that of Epictetus (and Ovid), is not vaguely anthropological;[133] it is pointedly *eschatological*, i.e., "the eschatological tension of being caught between the two epochs of Adam and Christ, of death

---

[126] Ibid.

[127] Judg 5:27 (A); Ps 136:8; Isa 33:1; Tob 7:7; 2 Macc 4:47; 3 Macc 5:5, 22, 47; 4 Macc 16:7.

[128] Josephus, *J. W.* 2.295; 6.194, 348; *Ant.* 1.204; 9.226; 10.157; 11.1; 14.61.

[129] Philo, *Cong.* 174; *Mut.* 189; *Legat.* 274.

[130] Cf. Dunn, *Romans* 1.396. Cranfield (*Romans* 1.366) and Fung ("Impotence," 38) point out that ταλαίπωρος can indicate distress without the implication of hopelessness.

[131] Epictetus, *Discourses* 2.26.4 (cited by Dunn, *Romans* 1.396). Moo also cites Ovid, *Metamorphoses* 7.21: "I see and approve the better course, but I follow the worse." I prefer not to press these analogies too far, as does Theissen (*Aspects*, 195−96), who is liable to the same charge he himself lays at the feet of Kümmel, viz., that the parallels are not altogether appropriate. Similarities are present; but what distinguishes Paul is an experience of *Christ* impinging on his psyche and creating a tension within his inner being.

[132] Dunn, "Rom. 7,14−25," 268; id., *Romans* 1.410. Cf. Murray, *Romans* 1.266, 268, 273. Says Murray: "The 'heart-rending cry' [of v. 25] cannot... be construed as one of despair; it must never be dissociated from the sequel of confident hope" (ibid., 1.269).

[133] As per Moo, *Romans*, 484.

IV. Romans 7:13–25: Two Creations, One Person

and life,"[134] "the tension necessarily set up when one lives 'between the times' – in two aeons simultaneously."[135]

The wretchedness of the "wretched man" thus springs from the discovery of his continuing sinfulness, and the knowledge that he cannot hope to be rid of indwelling sin, his troublesome inmate, while he remains in the body. He is painfully conscious that for the present his reach exceeds his grasp, and therefore he longs for the eschatological deliverance through which the tension between will and achievement, purpose and performance, plan and action, will be abolished.[136]

Paul's belongingness to the era of Adam and his consequent wretchedness is localized in "the body of this death," in which he is trapped for the time-being. In chaps. 6–7, this phrase is paralleled by "the body of sin" (6:6), "this mortal body" (6:12), "my flesh" (7:18), and "my members" (7:23). In each instance, what is in view is the σῶμα ψυχικόν (1 Cor 15:44) as conditioned by the old creation. This is the body which is dead on account of sin (8:10).[137]

Nevertheless, from another perspective, there is hope. In "Who shall deliver me from the body of this death?," we hear in audible tones Paul's longing to be free from the main obstacle to his performance of the will of God.[138] Yet he answers his own question: "Thanks be to God through Jesus Christ our Lord!" Given both the present eschatological context and the close parallel of 1 Cor 15:57 ("Thanks be to God who gives us the victory through our Lord Jesus Christ"), Paul's hope is not that of deliverance from the law (as one under its condemnation) but from "the body of this death" – the channel of sin to Paul's inner person – at the resurrection (cf. Phil 3:21).[139] It is the resurrection which

---

[134] Dunn, *Romans* 1.396. Though assuming a different stance than ours, Ridderbos (*Romeinen*, 169) and Kertelge ("Überlegungen," 114) are aware of the salvation-historical arena of Paul's tension. Gundry, on the other hand, plays down the eschatological in favor of the ambiguity arising from false profession and the possibility of apostasy ("Frustration," 238). Yet it is just the eschatological factor which gives rise to the necessity of perseverance: *one must endure until the time of tension is over*. Cf. Dunn, *Romans* 1.369. Ironically, Käsemann's comments on Rom 5:17 (*Romans*, 156) are perfectly applicable here!

[135] Bruce, "Law," 273–74.

[136] Packer, "Wretched," 269–70.

[137] Note that "*If Christ is in you*, the body is dead because of sin, but the Spirit is life because of righteousness." The effect of the believer's participation in the old creation is that he too must submit to death as the wages of sin (Cranfield, *Romans* 1.389). Notwithstanding Christ's presence within the Christian, his former union with Adam continues to have devastating consequences. Gundry, wishing to deny the connection of 7:24 with 8:10, falsely distinguishes between the death of the body in its moral and physical dimensions ("Frustration," 239. Similarly Moo, *Romans*, 495). Against the backdrop of 5:12–19 (Gen 2:17), death for Paul is comprehensive. Cf. Dunn, *Romans* 1.273 (on 5:12); Beker, *Paul*, 224.

[138] Moo's objection (*Romans*, 495) that a Christian would not have to inquire into the identity of his deliverer falters simply because the question is rhetorical, on the same order as the questions of 8:31–35.

[139] See Murray, *Romans* 1.269–70; Nygren, *Romans*, 301; Packer, "Wretched," 268–69. This is recognized by Gundry, "Frustration," 239. Contra Wilckens (*Römer* 2.95, n. 390), who asserts that the problem of 7:24 is other than that of 8:23: groaning for the redemption of the body. In like manner, Leenhardt is right that Paul cries for a savior, but wrong in denying that

will bring to an end the present evil age and usher in the new creation in its climactic phase; it is the resurrection which will terminate the period of overlapping ages, when the old creation will give way to a new heavens and a new earth. This is, to borrow the language of Titus 2:13, Paul's "blessed hope." Leenhardt, then, appropriately reminds us that standing behind Paul's longing for resurrection is the new covenant (new creation) promise of Ezekiel 37, according to which new life will be breathed into the dry bones of Israel.[140]

Note on Paul's Wretchedness

Scholars who assign Paul's sense of wretchedness to his pre-Christian days frequently appeal to Phil 3:4–7 in order to offset the *prima facie* impression left by Rom 7:7–12 that Saul the Pharisee, at least at some point in his life, had a keen awareness of sin. In Stendahl's phrase, Paul was not for such interpreters an "introspective man of the West." However, this raises a rather disconcerting question, *When was Paul ever wretched?* According to this construction, he was, in point of fact, a "wretched man" neither before nor after the Damascus Road because of a thoroughly positive relation to the law, both as a Pharisee and later as a Christian. Yet the Paul of Rom 7:24 exclaims that he is such a person.

It is not to be overlooked that Phil 3:4–7 is the Christian Paul's evaluation of Pharisaic life in relation to his experience of Christ (note the imperfect ἦν in v. 7). His point is that he came to recognize, in the words of Rom 10:4, that the risen Christ is the τέλος of the law; and by comparison with Christ, Torah-observance is σκύβαλα (v. 8), a particularly scathing term, inasmuch as it represents a radical reassessment of his former loyalties. As a Pharisee he was zealous to maintain daily purity on the level required only of the priests in the temple. But now he views his erstwhile devotion to purity *in toto* as one of the impurest items of all! Whatever else is said, Phil 3:4–6 must be seen in light of the punch line of 3:8, whose function is to denounce covenantal nomism as a viable alternative to Christ. To be sure, Paul does relate that he lived "a good life according to the rules," when he saw the Torah as the unchangeable expression of Yahweh's will for his people.[141] Nevertheless, his remarks simply do not preclude the possibility that the tenth commandment could have convicted him of idolatry at some point prior to his conversion. And what is true of the tenth is true in principle of all the commandments.[142]

---

he knows such a savior (*Romans*, 195). Rather, Paul's expectation is that Christ will complete his salvation with the resurrection of his body.

[140] Leenhardt, *Romans*, 194. Bruce ("Law," 275) calls to mind that 8:1–4 likewise echoes the new covenant oracles of Jer 31:31–34; Ezek 36:22–32. Thus, another indication of the continuity of chaps. 7 and 8, as argued above.

[141] Saldarini, *Pharisees*, 136. "Adequately socialized, Paul knew what was expected of him, and he lived accordingly..." (Neyrey, *Paul*, 26).

[142] Some have postulated a contradiction between Romans 7 and Phil 3:4–6 (e.g., Theissen, *Aspects*, 234–43). The contradiction, however, is predicated on the assumption that, in the latter text, Paul's blamelessness with regard to the law is a profession of virtual perfection. However, "blameless" means no more here than it does in, say, Luke 1:6. In other words, Paul depicts himself as a covenant-keeping Pharisee ("covenantal nomist"), one especially zealous for Israel, the Torah, and the Pharisaic purity laws (cf. Josephus, *J. W.* 1.110; *Ant.* 17.41). See Espy, "Conscience," 165–66. Again, he did live "a good life according to the rules" (Saldarini, *Pharisees*, 136); but to postulate that he had no awareness of sin as a Pharisee makes for historical nonsense. Cf. Kim, *Origin*, 53; Bruce, "Scrolls," 69–73 (on Qumran).

IV. Romans 7:13–25: Two Creations, One Person   141

The "salvation-historical" approach, according to which Paul identifies himself with Israel's condition under the law, entails a difficulty of its own. Moo takes the opening portion of Philippians 3 to be indicative of Paul's satisfaction with the righteousness of the law right up until he exchanged that righteousness for the righteousness given by Christ.[143] On the other hand, Rom 7:14–25 depicts the condition of all Jews under the law, which was Paul's own condition.[144] On the surface, this is self-contradictory, for the simple reason that whereas Philippians 3 is a wholly positive outlook on the law, Romans 7 is dominantly negative. How can it be both at the same time? Moo recognizes the problem and responds that whereas Philippians 3 is Paul's description of his *status* from a Jewish perspective, Romans 7 is his appraisal of his *experience* from a Christian perspective.[145] With this explanation the contradiction is formally removed; yet it only introduces other difficulties. First, as noted above, Philippians 3 is very much Paul's *Christian*, not Jewish, assessment of his past Pharisaic career. Second, the distinction between status and experience is at best an artificial one. Surely Paul's zeal for the law (Phil 3:6), with all that implies, was an intense experiential factor. Finally, there is a further improbability: are we to believe that when Paul deems himself to be a "wretched man" (Romans 7), he is the mouthpiece for others who have no real consciousness of their own plight (Philippians 3)? To be consistent with the terms of this construction, it must be concluded that not only does Paul's present "existential anguish"[146] have in view a company of which he is no longer actually a member, he voices feelings about his past which he did not actually have when he was under the law![147]

His position, moreover, is beset with its share of historical problems. For one, Israel is supposed to have died at Sinai. Yet we find indications from Second Temple sources that the law was considered to be the source of life (Sir 17:11; 45:5; Bar 3:9, 14; 4:1; cf. *Pss. Sol.* 14:2; 4 Ezra 14:30).[148] In fact, in all stands of Jewish literature, the giving of the law at Sinai was looked upon not as the death of the nation but its birth. Second, his thesis is predicated on the assumption that Israel was expected to keep the law perfectly. But the sources nowhere display such a consciousness. Quite the contrary, there is everywhere the undergirding assurance that provision for imperfection has been made in the sacrificial system. Even a foundational text like Lev 18:5 does not have in view sinless perfection, but perseverance within the standards of the covenant.

Paul's conclusion is the most succinct summary of the whole:[149] "I myself with

---

[143] Moo, *Romans*, 455.

[144] Ibid., 474.

[145] Ibid., 477. Cf. Beker, *Paul*, 238, 240; Ladd, *Theology*, 495, 508; Guthrie, *Theology*, 688.

[146] Dunn, "Rom. 7,14–25," 260. Moo's acknowledgment that the pre-Christian Paul experienced "some degree of frustration" in not fulfilling the divine standard (*Romans*, 477) hardly does justice to the intensity of Rom 7:14–25.

[147] In spite of Beker, *Paul*, 242. One may argue in the abstract that the Jew's true condition is known only in Christian perspective. But again, Paul's present tenses get in the way. He does not write: "I now perceive how wretched I once *was*." He is, rather, wretched *as he writes Romans*.

[148] Note Moo's own citation of Sir 17:11; *t. Sabb.* 15:17, and other texts (*Romans*, 464). Unfortunately, his understanding of them is colored by his premise that "the law would have given life *had it been perfectly obeyed*" (italics his). On p. 476, he concedes that Jews delighted in the law; but how this squares with Israel's "death" at Sinai is not explained.

[149] "It sums up with clear-sighted honesty – an honesty which is thoroughly consonant both with the urgency of the longing for final deliverance expressed in v. 24 and also with the

my mind serve the law of God, but with my flesh [I serve] the law of sin" (v. 25 b). Paul is a man divided; and that division is epitomized by the cleavage of his humanity, as he serves simultaneously both the law of God and the law of sin.

This ambiguous personal position reflects the eschatological situation. The Age to come has dawned, in the life, death, and resurrection of Jesus; but the present evil age has not passed. The two exist uneasily side by side, and Christians still look earnestly for the redemption of the body (8:23), knowing that they have been saved in hope (8:24).[150]

To be sure, Paul's "real self" (αὐτὸς ἐγώ), i. e., the man aligned with the new creation, takes the side of the law of God.[151] Yet this makes his conflict all the more poignant.

The emphatic αὐτὸς ἐγώ, "I, even I", expresses Paul's sense of how painfully paradoxical it is that a Christian man like himself, who desires so heartily to keep God's law and do only good, should find himself under the constant necessity of breaking the law and doing what in effect is evil. But such is the state of the Christian till his body is redeemed.[152]

Whatever precise construction is placed on νόμος, it is the two laws vying for Paul's service,[153] setting in motion "a conflict between two normative orientations,"[154] which create the dichotomy characteristic of his experience of Christ

---

confidence that God will surely accomplish that deliverance in His good time reflected in v. 25 a – the tension, with all its real anguish and also all its real hopefulness, in which the Christian never ceases to be involved so long as he is living this present life" (Cranfield, *Romans* 1.369).

[150] Barrett, *Romans*, 152. Cf. Nygren, *Romans*, 293–95. It is just here that Espy's observation on Rom 7:1–6 is so apropos. He submits that the analogy between the death of the husband and the death of the Christian to the law is deliberately left incomplete: "For it is only at the end of the world, when the 'husband' sin itself dies, that the Christian will be wholly free from it and from its Law." Sin still lives, and the analogy leaves room for a time when this will not be the case. This reading, he remarks, agrees with the eschatological orientation of chaps. 5–8, inasmuch as Paul's words of encouragement and exhortation are not allowed to obscure the fact that the consummation still lies beyond the believer's grasp ("Conscience," 168).

[151] Αὐτὸς ἐγώ is synonymous with Paul's "will," his "delight" in the law, and his "mind" which serves the law of God. Attempts have been made to render αὐτὸς ἐγώ as something like "I by myself, apart from Christ." For Kürzinger, for instance, this is the key to the understanding of Romans 7 ("Schlüssel"). Likewise Bandstra (*Law*, 147). However, the words themselves do not mean this and can be so construed only by a prior interpretation of Romans 7 *in toto*. Also such a usage of αὐτὸς ἐγώ is apparently unprecedented. See Packer, "Wretched," 267; Fung, "Impotence," 39–40.

[152] Packer, "Wretched," 269. Cf. S. Greijdanus, as cited by Ridderbos (*Romeinen*, 160). Contra Wenham ("Life," 89).

[153] Δουλέω reappears from 6:18, 22, where it was a variant of δοῦλοι (6:16, 17, 20). It is true that 6:15–19 represents in black and white terms the bondservice of sin vs. that of righteousness; but as we have seen, Paul provides his own qualification of what here is stated categorically. One of those qualifications is 7:25: the Christian's bondservice is simultaneously to the law of sin and the law of God. "There are two laws; there are two parts of human nature. The mind recognizes the law of God, the flesh – human nature living in and for this age – recognizes the law which sin has fashioned for this age" (Barrett, *Romans*, 151).

[154] Theissen, *Aspects*, 188.

this side of the eschaton. Far from signaling a preconversion outlook, "The eschatological tension is itself a proof that identification with Christ in his death has begun to combat the power of sin."[155] Struggle is a sign of life, not death; and only those who thus struggle may be assured that there is no condemnation (8:1). Moreover, according to 8:17, there is a precondition to glorification with Christ – suffering with him. As 8:18–25 goes on to clarify, the Christian's suffering resides primarily in his groaning as he awaits the redemption of his body.[156] In their own way, therefore, not only 8:18–27 but also 8:1–17 form an analogue to 7:14–25.[157] Were the Spirit/flesh conflict not a reality for the Christian, Paul would not have to exhort the Romans to resist the flesh and side with the Spirit.[158]

V. Summary

Writing as a believer in Jesus the Christ, Paul's testimony to the conflict of flesh and Spirit is to be situated within the antithesis of the two creations. This means that ultimately his struggles with the flesh and his consequent dissatisfaction with "the present distress" (1 Cor 7:26) are cosmic in proportion.[159] It is this cosmic conflict which imparts a specific character to salvation history and the believer's incorporation into it. That is to say, in his/her own person the Christian is the microcosm of world history as that history has now taken a new turn in Christ. The old has passed away, but the new has not come in fullness. During the interim, the person in Christ reproduces in his/her own body the simultaneous existence of two antithetical ages. The believer thus finds himself/ herself living in two worlds at the same time.

Paul anticipates one day being delivered from "the body of this death" at the resurrection. But until then, though tension and frustration are far from being the whole of what it means to be a Christian, they are integral to the life of faith this side of the eschaton. To be sure, God is in the process of making his people what Adam, his image, should have been. Yet until the process is complete, the Christian must labor and persevere amidst circumstances which are far from favorable. In view of what he longs to be hereafter, with Paul he can only cry out, "Wretched man that I am." Nevertheless, his ultimate confidence is that God in Christ *will* deliver him from his wretchedness.

---

[155] Dunn, *Romans* 1.412.

[156] Contra Gundry ("Frustration," 244, nn. 34, 35) and Ridderbos (*Romeinen*, 165), who maintain that the struggle of chaps. 6 and 8 is not that of chap. 7, which is fought on a different basis and out of a different power.

[157] As Brandenburger notes, the semantic field of 8:1–11(17) is determined by 7:14–25 (*Fleisch*, 48).

[158] Cf. Barrett, *Romans*, 146. Ridderbos recognizes this (*Romeinen*, 154). In its own way, Rom 12:1–2 delineates the conflict in terms of this age as opposed to the believer's renewed mind (the same νοῦς of 7:25).

[159] See Beker, *Paul*, 364–67.

Chapter Six
Reflections

With the exegetical portion of our study at an end, it is time to draw final conclusions and reflect on their theological and practical implications.

I. "The Obedience of Faith"

Lying at the base of these reflections is Paul's intentionally ambiguous ὑπακοὴ πίστεως. The words are crucial to a grasp of his missionary enterprise in that they contain a world of thought, for in them is encapsulated God's eschatological design for a new humanity, a new Israel. Thus, there could be no higher commendation of Paul's Christian readers than that voiced by Rom 1:8, "Your faith is proclaimed in all the world," and Rom 16:19, "Your obedience is known to all," both of which take their point of origin from "the obedience of faith." Moo quite rightly, then, says that ὑπακοή and πίστεως are mutually interpreting: obedience always involves faith, and faith always involves obedience. Thus, faith and obedience should not be compartmentalized or turned into separate stages of Christian experience.

> Paul called men and women into a faith that was always inseparable from obedience – for the savior in whom they believe is nothing less than our Lord – to an obedience that could never be divorced from faith – for we can only obey Jesus as Lord when we have given ourselves to Him in faith. Viewed in this light, the phrase captures the full dimension of Paul's apostolic task, a task that was not confined to initial evangelization but that included also the building up and firm establishment of churches.[1]

Berkouwer speaks to the same effect. "The obedience of faith" is an expression which gives us a hint as to the nature of faith. At first glance, he says, the phrase may seem to water down *sola gratia*. However, "This obedience cannot be abstracted from Him to whom the believer subjects himself. We cannot close our eyes to the element of obedience in faith, but if we see it aright we shall realize that it serves to show us *how completely faith is directed to its object*."[2]

The call to obedience, as Leenhardt discerns, is actually a call *back* to obedience, for the purpose of offsetting humanity's present condition of dis-

---
[1] Moo, *Romans*, 44–45 (quote from p. 45). See further Leenhardt, *Romans*, 39–40; Mundle, *Glaubensbegriff*, 29–34.
[2] Berkouwer, *Justification*, 195 (italics mine).

obedience in the first Adam (Rom 5:12–19).³ As we have seen, Paul employs πίστις and particularly ὑπακοή in contexts reminiscent of Genesis 1–3. Consequently, his summons of the nations to "the obedience of Christ" (2 Cor 10:5) is a recall of mankind back to its roots as the image of God. "In the person of the Messiah himself, and then in the company of all who are united with him and recipients of his Spirit (i.e. all who are 'justified'), there is to be found a new principle of life, a new 'faith' or 'faithfulness' (the Greek word *pistis* means both), a new obedience towards God."⁴ Paul's gospel, then, is nothing less than the proclamation of a new creation.

Therefore, although the phrase "the obedience of faith" occurs but twice (or once) in the whole Pauline corpus, it comprises the beginning, the middle, and the end of Paul's preaching. As viewed within this context of his missionary outreach, "the obedience of faith" is a compendious way of calling to mind the necessity of initial faith, persevering faith, and the faith which justifies in the last judgment. In this light, ὑπακοὴ πίστεως forms the complement of "the righteousness of God" as revealed ἐκ πίστεως εἰς πίστιν (Rom 1:17).⁵ In short, "the obedience of faith" concentrates into one short sequence of words the essence of Paul's gospel of salvation for the world.

In articulating such a self-awareness for the new people of God, the phrase takes on a decidedly polemical dimension. Over against Israel, which is unbelieving and disobedient, the nations have responded in faith to the gospel of Christ and have become, in contrast to what they once were (e.g., Rom 1:18–32; 6:16; Eph 2:1–3; 4:17–20; Col 3:5–9), the faithfully obedient covenant partner of Yahweh. The phrase thus neatly summarizes Paul's apologetic in this most famous of his missionary epistles.⁶ It is just so that his accusation that Israel is disobedient or idolatrous (Rom 2:22; 10:19–20; Gal 4:8–9) makes sense. By clinging, in lieu of Christ, to the Torah as the God-given source of eternal life, the ancient people, ironically enough, have failed to keep pace with the Gentiles, who have turned from idols to serve "the true and living God" (1 Thess 1:9–10).⁷ "The obedience of faith," consequently, can no longer be defined in terms of Jewish nationalistic interests. Rather, "The obedience God looked for was the obedience of faith, obedience from the heart (6:17), that is,

---

³ Leenhardt, *Romans*, 40.

⁴ Motyer, "Righteousness," 51. Motyer is in accord with our own understanding of "the obedience of faith" and rightly sets the phrase in parallel with a new love for God.

⁵ Of course, ἐκ πίστεως εἰς πίστιν is one of the many disputed phrases in Paul. However, in keeping with the basic idiom ἐκ... εἰς... (e.g., Ps 83:8 [LXX]; 2 Cor 3:18) and the parallel of 1:5 with 1:17, it is not farfetched to take it as a declaration of the multi-functional character of faith in its initial, intermediate, and ultimate phases. If this is Paul's meaning, perseverance in faith is certainly on his agenda by this choice of words, whether or not he also has in mind growth in faith. The latter, I must say, is likely, given the existence of such exhortations to his churches (e.g., 2 Cor 10:15). See below.

⁶ Dunn, *Romans* 1.18.

⁷ To add to the irony, the phrase "the living God," as Nickelsburg points out, is frequent in Jewish polemics against pagan idols ("Stories," 39). See Bel 5; *Jub.* 21:3; 4 Macc 5:24; *Sib. Or.* 3:763.

from a commitment and a lifestyle which penetrate far below matters of race and ritual and which could be sustained and maintained independently of either."[8]

II. The Obedience of Faith and the Doers of the Law

Consistent with the ideology contained in ὑπακοὴ πίστεως, obedience for Paul is all-embracing. We are compelled to agree with Barrett that it was important to the apostle to show that obedience has a place in the system of grace and faith.[9] Or, as Nygren puts it: "Obedience is always required of man in his relation with God. It was so in the Old Testament. There it was particularly obedience to God's law, obedience to the covenant. But obedience is also necessary in the new Aeon ushered in by Christ."[10] In the same vein, Reumann, taking a clue from Cranfield, rightly comments that in Rom 6:16 the phrase "slaves of righteousness" underscores *obedience*, which, he says, is "*a Pauline definition of faith* (1:5), thus stressing that in the Christian life 'faith-obedience' must be its characteristic mark until the work of God's justifying righteousness is complete, at the final judgment."[11] In other words, *faith and works are two ways of saying the same thing*. Mundle agrees:

> Since... acceptance of the gospel is an act of faith, the apostle in this sense can also speak of the obedience of faith... and all the more as recognition of the gospel contains within itself the resolution to be baptized and become a member of the Christian church. It is, therefore, not a matter of a change of mind which has no effect on the rest of one's life, but a decision which entails the weightiest practical consequences.[12]

Berkouwer's analysis of the relation of faith and sanctification ("works") is to the same effect. Israel's sanctification, says Berkouwer, resided in its belongingness to God. Because Israel was chosen and sanctified to be the people of God, *therefore* it had no other task than to live *as* the people of God. The command, "Be holy, for I am holy," is the epitome of the entire OT revelation inasmuch as the foundation of Israel's life in all its manifestations is this belonging to God. Berkouwer, then, can say that the sanctification initiated by

---

[8] Dunn, *Romans* 2.593 (on 9:32).

[9] Barrett, *Romans*, 131 (on 6:16). Cf. again Cranfield, *Romans* 1.66; Murray, *Romans* 1.13–14.

[10] Nygren, *Romans*, 55. The biblical notion of "righteousness," which, for all intents and purposes, is synonymous with "obedience," likewise entails a comprehensive assessment of one's place in God's covenant (note how ὑπακοή in 1:5 is paralleled by δικαιοσύνη in 1:17). Neither the OT nor Paul know of a righteousness which is only forensic, i.e., one abstracted from a quality of life concomitant to a righteous status.

[11] Reumann, *Righteousness*, 83 (italics mine). To the same effect is Berkouwer, *Justification*, 108–9. We cannot discuss James and Paul on faith and works (see, among many, Adamson, *James*, 195–227; 266–307). However, I would say, with Berkouwer, that for both "The whole of life of Abraham was *lived* in faith" (*Justification*, 136. Italics his.).

[12] Mundle, *Glaubensbegriff*, 30 (cf. ibid., 39).

II. The Obedience of Faith and the Doers of the Law

God has "self-evident" consequences: "On every occasion and in every sector of its existence Israel must give expression to the unique relationship established by God."[13]

For the sake of balance, however, it must be stressed that although the obedience in question entails specific and concrete acts of a lifestyle pleasing to God,[14] it is equally important that we not miss the wood for the trees. That is to say, the future justification of God's people is not made to hinge on, say, 51% (or more!) of law-keeping,[15] because *obedience itself is the product of faith; and where true faith and love exist, there must be ultimate vindication.*[16] When cause and effect are thus kept in proper sequence, any initial anxiety at the notion of justification by "doing" should be ameliorated, if not quelled altogether.

It is not necessary to recoil from this idea in fear of some theory of "works righteousness" or in fear of diminishing the role of Christ in the purposes of God. Nor is there any idea of a "natural theology" in the pejorative sense of the term. The witness of all the Biblical traditions and much of Judaism is that none stands before God in *his or her own righteousness*. There is no thought in Romans 2 of a person being granted life because he or she was a moral human being, independent of God. The whole context of 1.18f. assumes the necessity of recognizing God as God and honouring him with one's life. The description of those who work the good in 2.7, 14–15, and 29 shows that the obedience is a direct result of the activity of God.[17]

---

[13] Berkouwer, *Sanctification*, 24–25. Berkouwer goes on to remind us that the Reformers generally and Luther in particular were opposed only to the *meritoriousness* of "good works." Once it had been established that salvation is by grace through faith, good works were assumed to be the inseparable companion of faith (ibid., 27–36).

[14] Cf. Cosgrove, "Justification," 660–61.

[15] In keeping with the Jewish model, perfection is not required for covenant-standing and eventual salvation. Cf. Snodgrass, "Justification," 79 (see n. 53 for references), Dunn, *Jesus, Paul*, 262, n. 44). In spite of Silva ("Reconstruction," 120), neither the Prophets nor Jesus demanded perfection; they demanded, rather, fidelity to God and a treatment of one's fellow human beings consistent with the covenant bond. Silva's assumptions are shared by Hübner (*Law*), Schreiner (the various articles), and Moo (*Romans*, 177, 464). One helpful corrective to this insistence on sinless perfection is La Rondelle's study, which concludes that the biblical notion of "perfection" does not stand for the state of sinlessness or ethical blamelessness, but for "the cultic relationship, i. e., the living righteous covenant relationship with Yahweh and the fellow Israelite" (*Perfection*, 137. See the whole discussion of pp. 109–58).

[16] "The final criterion at the last judgment is, for Paul, not how many good works man has performed – this is irrelevant since it is the Spirit which enables man to do those deeds of love – but whether man has held fast and remained obedient to this new life in Christ. It is the criterion of the obedience of faith..." (Donfried, "Justification," 102–3). An apt illustration is provided by Hab 2:5–17, which enumerates certain vices to be renounced by the righteous person who lives by faith (v. 4). It is vital, however, that these vices are viewed as the outgrowth of idolatry (vv. 18–19), the converse of living by faith. We may add to this that Paul's warnings of judgment are directed not at those who, out of weakness and vulnerability, commit sins, but are puffed up, guilty of presumption, and living in a state of illusion (Watson, "Justified," 216).

[17] Snodgrass, "Justification," 80–81 (italics mine). "Judgment according to works is not the contradiction of justification by faith, but its presupposition. The significance of faith and participation in Christ for obedience are assumed for Paul" (ibid., 86). See further Berkouwer, *Sanctification*, 108–13; Schrenk, *TDNT* 2.208.

Ethical obedience, in a word, is but the outgrowth of *believing perseverance "in Christ;"* it is the fruition of God's "seed" abiding in one (1 John 3:9) and the immediate effect of "the Holy Spirit of the promise" (Eph 1:13), God's gracious gift to his latter-day people.[18] The Spirit-led life is nothing other than this people's response to the law written on their hearts, the great provision of the new covenant (Jer 31:33) and the proof positive that the Spirit has been poured into their hearts as the power of the new creation (Joel 2:28–29; Rom 5:5; cf. Acts 2:17–18; 1 John 2:20, 27). Such obedience, in brief, is "the fruit of the Spirit" (Gal 5:22).

One should, then, be no more alarmed at the call to obedience than at the confession of Christ as the precondition of eschatological salvation, insisted on by Paul in Rom 10:9–10 (cf. Mark 8:38 = Luke 9:26/Matt 10:32–33 = Luke 12:8–9). To be sure, since perseverance pertains to the covenant, it is the standard of the covenant which is to be maintained. Nevertheless, there is in all this a necessary cause and effect sequence: faith in Christ and faithful commitment to him must be the source of his people's conformity to his image. A text such as 2 Cor 5:10 is crucial. Here Paul summarizes the totality of the life in the flesh as either a "good" or a "worthless" (φαῦλον) thing.[19] The very terminology reminds us of his usage of "good" and "evil," particularly in Romans. That is to say, while ethics are clearly involved,[20] the bedrock issue is whether one has worshipped and served the Creator rather than the creature (the obverse of Rom 1:25). In a word, the *only* sin that can separate the believer from final salvation is the sin of apostasy.[21]

Moreover, anything resembling "works-righteousness" is further excluded by two important data. (1) The salvation outworked by us is *God's doing* (Rom 5:15–17; 6:23; Eph 2:8–10; Phil 2:13), in keeping with the genius of righteousness as God's gift as well as his demand.[22] Justification present or future,

---

[18] See Berkouwer, *Sanctification*, 81–83.

[19] See Hughes, *2 Corinthians*, 181, n. 58.

[20] "In the judgment the empirical reality of one's life before God as 'works' will be revealed and evaluated. This is the understanding of future judgment that we meet in 1 Cor 4:3–5; Rom 2:10; 2 Cor 5:10; Rom 2:13; and Rom 8:33. The expectation of the believer is that judgment according to works will mean *justification*" (Cosgrove, "Justification," 660–61. Italics his.). Moo writes to similar effect, but prefers to speak of works as confirming the believer's justification in this life (*Romans*, 177).

[21] McKnight, "Passages," 58.

[22] While I agree with Watson that judgment by works is an integral part of Paul's theology (*Paul*, 120–21), he has overstated the case: "*the idea that salvation occurs solely through God's grace represents a deep misunderstanding of Paul*" (ibid., 120. Italics his.). It should go without saying by now that the human element is indispensable; but, contrary to Watson, it is none other than the grace of God which gives rise to and then sustains human obedience. "The free gift is not like the trespass," says Paul, "for if many died through one man's trespass, much more have *the grace of God and the free gift in the grace of the one man Jesus Christ* abounded for many" (Rom 5:15). This is why "*the free gift of God* is eternal life in Christ Jesus our Lord" (Rom 6:23). As Berkouwer so aptly pens: "faith knows the prevenience of God's grace and *the gift of perseverance*, which is identical with the act of *God's preservation*, because through grace the transition from death unto life is irreversible" (*Perseverance*, 237–38 [italics mine];

III. The Obedience of Christ and the Obedience of the Christian

Cosgrove rightly stresses, remains at every point God's prerogative; it is that which no person can do for himself/herself.[23] (2) Our perseverance is motivated by love, the appropriate response of those who have been delivered from bondage and caused to walk in newness of life (Rom 6:1–7:6; 8:1–17).

Because the judgment of God "according to truth" (Rom 2:2) envisages the obedience of faith, it was of utmost importance to Paul that *faith and its growth should receive the primacy*. Believers in Christ are characterized by him as οἱ ἐκ πίστεως (Gal 3:9), and everything they do in service to God proceeds ἐκ πίστεως (Rom 14:23). Thus, in warning the Corinthians against possible falling away, Paul exhorts them to examine themselves to see whether they are holding to their *faith* (2 Cor 13:5). It is to this end that he refuses to be the lord of their *faith*, choosing instead to be the helper of their joy, because they stand by *faith* (2 Cor 1:24).

Accordingly, faith is the indispensable element in the consummation of eternal life, not only in its inauguration.[24] Or, in Berkouwer's words, *sola fide* is at the heart of justification, but no less at the heart of sanctification. "In the bond between faith and sanctification we perceive, no less than in the bond between faith and justification, the pulsebeat of the gospel. If faith will but lift its blossoms to catch the sunlight of God's grace, the fruit will be a life imbued with holiness.... With this marriage of faith and works in view, it is clear that all works done in this life are subjected to God's judgment, and that everything hinges on whether they are done in faith."[25] In a nutshell, Paul's logic of "getting in" and "staying in" Christ is "the logic of faith."[26] "Thus faith," writes Williams, "which is both the fruit of and response to the gospel, actually contributes to the carrying through of God's eschatological plan, even as faith – the sign and seal of the new humanity God is creating – is also the goal."[27]

---

cf. ibid., 225). Elsewhere, Berkouwer is insistent that sanctification is initiated by God (*Sanctification*, 25).

[23] Cosgrove, "Justification," 670.

[24] "The perseverance of the saints is unbreakably connected with the assurance of faith, in which the believer faces the future with confidence – not with the idea that all dangers and threats have been removed, but rather with the assurance that they shall be conquered indeed" (Berkouwer, *Perseverance*, 11). Important is Berkouwer's treatment of "Sola Fide and Sanctification" (*Sanctification*, 17–44).

[25] Berkouwer, *Sanctification*, 33, 193; *Justification*, 108 (cf. ibid., 33, 188–89). "And in teaching this the Reformation stood foursquare on Holy Scripture. Because the Sola-fide of the Reformation was not one-sided sectarianism or a weakening of the reality of salvation but a confession of 'By grace alone are we saved' – *therefore* the Sola-fide is the only sound foundation for sanctification" (Berkouwer, *Sanctification*, 43. Italics his. Cf. further id., *Justification*, chap. 7 [esp. pp. 188–201]).

[26] Dunn, *Partings*, 133. Dunn says elsewhere: "Ongoing praxis must be a continuing expression of the faith by which his readers [in Galatians] first began to function within God's covenant promise and purpose..." (*Jesus, Paul*, 247).

[27] Williams, "Righteousness," 256.

III. The Obedience of Christ and the Obedience of the Christian

In the movement from present justification by faith to future justification by the obedience of faith, the most vital link of all is the obedience of Christ. Rom 5:12–19 represents him as the realization of true humanity and, therefore, its mediator (cf. 1 Tim 2:5).[28] Over against the first Adam and all his progeny, Christ alone is incomparable; he is the last Adam, the second man, and the preeminent one of all creation. Henceforth it is his imprint which is placed on the new world created in his image.

His obedience, as chapter 4 concluded, is his commitment to the relationship (covenant) between Yahweh and Israel (Gal 4:4). Consequently, his "obedience" is nothing other than his "righteousness," i. e., his loyalty to his God. This is his δικαίωμα (Rom 5:18) or the "doing of the law" commended by Lev 18:5. In thus "doing the law," Christ has assumed the mandate of fallen Adam and has attained to glory, honor, and immortality (Rom 2:7–10). Paul's last Adam christology, then, as that of the Gospels and Hebrews, sets forth Jesus as *the man of faith par excellence*, who learned obedience through what he suffered.[29]

Christian obedience, as a result, is an impossibility apart from Christ. "In Paul's view," writes M. D. Hooker, "Christians owe everything to the fact that they are in Christ: they are nothing and they have nothing, except by virtue of being in him. Christian faith is always the response to what God has done in Christ and to what Christ is. It seems, then, that they need the faithfulness of Christ – for how are they to have even faith, except by sharing in his?"[30] The bottom line, therefore, is *Christ*. If the Christian's righteousness is a δικαιοσύνη ἐκ πίστεως, his must be a πίστις which sets its sights exclusively on Jesus Christ, the last Adam and Creator of a new, obedient humanity (Phil 2:1–16).

> Christ... shatters subjection to the Adamic world of sin and death by setting the world before its Creator again and by setting us in the state of creatureliness. Since the Adamic world is present and seems to prevail, this has to be continually reaccepted in faith. Received blessing brands us but it also sets us in conflict... and contradiction. It places us before the need to persevere and in the possibility of relapse.[31]

As we have argued, in Rom 7:14–15; 8:18–25 Paul contemplates the "conflict and contradiction" to which the believer is exposed as a result of his deliverance from the Adamic world and presses upon his readers the need of

---

[28] Scroggs, *Adam*, 100–111.

[29] While I think that Paul's phrase πίστις Ἰησοῦ Χριστοῦ does *not* signify the faith(fulness) of Christ himself, many of the points made by recent writers about his covenant fidelity are well-taken in themselves. I refer simply to Hays, *Faith* (with literature); Williams, "Righteousness," 272–76; Hooker, "ΠΙΣΤΙΣ;" Davies, *Faith*, 107–8.

[30] Hooker, "ΠΙΣΤΙΣ," 337–38. "The core of the doctrine of justification is not expressed in the tag 'by faith' (important as that may be) but in the *solus Christus*, 'that *in him* we might become the righteousness of God' (2 Cor. 5:21)" (O'Donovan, *Resurrection*, 255. Italics his.).

[31] Käsemann, *Romans*, 156.

the renewal of faith. Nevertheless, the Christian in principle possesses an entirely new disposition and outlook on life, the evidence of which is his transformation by the renewal of his mind (Rom 12:2) and the putting to death of the deeds of the body, commensurate with his walk by the Spirit (Rom 8:2–14).

To state it again in specifically covenantal categories, the people of Christ have been made *righteous* (Rom 5:19). The ideal of covenant fidelity embodied in Christ's righteousness is imparted to those who are joined with him: he is the righteous king who brings to pass the new Israel's devotion to the covenant (Isaiah 32). From a slightly different point of view, righteousness is perseverance, inasmuch as perseverance in biblical/Pauline thinking entails two elements: (1) reliance on the person of the God of the covenant; (2) a resolution to do his will, although, during the course of this "present evil age," that will is imperfectly performed. Thus, the righteousness of the covenant has reference to both a personal relationship and the ethical standards ("house rules") demanded by that relationship.

Particularly with respect to the latter, we are not to forget that outside Romans 5 ethical conformity to the image of Christ is integral to Paul's last Adam christology. Believers not only have put off the "old man," i.e., Adam with his corrupt (apostate) practices, they have put on the "new man," i.e., Christ, the last Adam (Eph 4:22; Col 3:10; cf. Rom 13:14; Gal 3:27). It is these newly created ones – God's elect, holy, and beloved – who are depicted in Col 3:12–17 as a community of love and harmony: in them is to be seen the realization of the creation ideal, because "Jesus Christ has restored 'those who receive the abundance of grace and the gift of righteousness' to their proper role as truly human beings."[32] By virtue of being clothed with the image of Christ, who himself is the image of the invisible God (Col 1:15), those who were once wholly characterized by the vices catalogued, e.g., in Col 3:5–9 are now those in whose hearts the peace of Christ reigns. Or, in the words of Rom 5:17, they themselves have been made to "reign in life through the one man Jesus Christ."

Believers in their own persons, then, are the microcosm of God's new creation plan for the universe, i.e., the restoration of what was damaged in Adam. When the sons and daughters of God are finally redeemed (Rom 8:23), they will be enabled to pick up where the old Adam left off, when their lowly bodies are conformed to the glorious body of Christ (1 Cor 15:42–57; Phil 3:21).

IV. Justification and Sanctification

The whole of this investigation has witnessed an interplay between God's initiative in saving a people and the response of that people to his grace and

---

[32] Wright, "Adam," 372.

mercy in Christ. The standard way of designating this interplay is to speak of a dialectic of (soteriological) "indicative" and (ethical) "imperative" in Paul.[33] Accordingly, we must make some attempt to address the issues of "justification" and "sanctification" in Christian theology.

To begin, we must decide what is the appropriate model of justification in Paul. I would submit that the model is none other than that to which the apostle himself appeals, viz., the Psalms and the Prophets. In chapter 3, we saw that Paul fashions his very language of the revelation of God's righteousness after passages such as Pss 35:27–28; 72:1–4; 85:11–13; 96:13; 98:2–3, 9; Isa 9:7; 11:1–2; 45:8, 22–25; 51:5–6; 53:10b–11; 61:1–2, 11; Jer 23:5–6; Mal 4:2. In fact, Rom 1:17 (δικαιοσύνη γὰρ θεοῦ ἐν αὐτῷ ἀποκαλύπτεται) takes up Ps 98:2, 9 (LXX 97:2, 9): "The Lord has made known his salvation; before the nations he has revealed his righteousness.... For he comes to judge the earth; he will judge the world in righteousness and the peoples with uprightness." In his mind also must have been such Psalm texts as 9:8; 96:13. His immediate design is the same as the Psalmists': God's righteousness is to be revealed to *the nations* and no longer restricted to Israel; the Gentiles as well as the chosen people are to be the recipients of the Lord's saving deed (δικαιοσύνη), and both without distinction are to be regarded as Yahweh's special possession. The ensuing quotation of Hab 2:4, a conspicuous instance of God's saving deed, serves to confirm the point. Thus, there is in justification a dynamic commensurate with the revelation of the "righteousness of God," inasmuch as justification *is* the Lord's activity to save his people, in order that they may resume the life of the covenant and dwell in his presence forever.

In all this, as we have repeatedly stated, there is a decided (apocalyptic-) forensic element. However, in Paul's "eschatological courtroom" it is Yahweh who vindicates the faithful from the charges of their enemies, who assume that he is unable to deliver his people and suppose that their faith in him is in vain. Hence, "the righteousness of God," on this construction, is not "retributive justice" but the Lord's salvation, his coming to the aid of his own and his fidelity in keeping his promises.[34] And when he intervenes to save his covenant partners, he plants them again in the newly created land, never to be removed.[35] This is "salvation" in the pregnant sense of the term: deliverance from evil and the bestowal of "peace" (שָׁלוֹם) on a redeemed people. Motyer, in my view, is right on target when he asserts that "the righteousness of God" is actively directed at the rescue of the creation. And

---

[33] E.g., Ridderbos, *Paul*, 253–58; Kertelge, *"Rechtfertigung,"* 251–63.

[34] See, e.g., Motyer, "Righteousness," 35–36; Davies, *Faith*, 36–37; Stuhlmacher, *Gerechtigkeit*, 98. In agreement with Davies and in distinction to Stuhlmacher, there is a negative side of righteousness, viz., God's faithfulness in judging the disobedient, in keeping precisely with the terms of the covenant. The wrath of God is not, as Stuhlmacher maintains, antithetical to righteousness; it is the "flip side" of the coin.

[35] Cf. my comments on 1 Esd 8:78 (*Obedience*, 231).

I would second his motion that although this is plain to see in the OT, its significance for Paul has only recently been explored and does not form part of the traditional Protestant doctrine.[36]

Assuming such perspectives, including Motyer's observation that there is in the NT no doctrine of justification as such but a doctrine of righteousness,[37] under which justification is subsumed, we may press on to speak more particularly of the relation of righteousness to the last judgment. Our thesis is the same as Byrne's. Paul, in line with the Jewish tradition with which he dialogues in Romans, presupposes an intrinsic link between righteousness and the gaining of eternal life: "It is through living out, or rather, allowing Christ to live out this righteousness within oneself that eternal life is gained."[38] Byrne concedes that such a view involves a return to an "ethical" understanding of righteousness. However, he is careful to qualify that "the totally christological base of such righteousness – the fact that it remains always the righteousness of *God* communicated in Christ – excludes... any sense of a righteousness held by human beings over against the operation of God."[39]

Because God's righteousness is communicated in Christ, it is vital that one participate in Christ. Byrne is quite right, vis-à-vis the work of E. P. Sanders, to insist that we are not forced to choose between righteousness (defined by Sanders as a transfer term in Paul) and participationist categories. Rather, he says, it is a matter of seeing that the nub of Paul's distinctiveness lies in the way in which participationist categories are placed in the service of righteousness.[40] In other words, How is righteousness brought about in the eschatological era? Byrne answers, and I would agree, that Paul does not introduce a new conception (definition) of righteousness; rather, he differs from Jewish tradition in that he entertains a totally divergent view of the present state of the relations between God and human beings (Israel).[41] In a nutshell, God's righteousness is "now" available only in Christ (e. g., Rom 3:22, 26; 2 Cor 5:21); he, not the Torah, is the divinely appointed way of salvation.

Paul's teaching on righteousness, then, can be contrasted with Jewish apocalyptic traditions, whereby God's final vindication of his people was still an object of hope in the completely futuristic sense. He and other Christians came

---

[36] Motyer, "Righteousness," 55.

[37] Ibid., 34.

[38] Byrne, "Righteousness," 558. See his references (n. 2). I differ with Byrne, however, in making baptism a means by which one is drawn into the righteousness of God. In my view, to make baptism or any other ceremony the way into the people of God is to overlook Paul's strategy in the battle over circumcision, the Jewish requisite for "getting in" the covenant.

[39] Ibid., 558 (italics his). Besides Phil 2:12–13, an instructive example is 1 Cor 6:11. Paul allows that his readers "had themselves washed," perhaps an allusion to baptism as symbolizing their conversion experience. Yet lying behind this voluntary action on their part (note the middle voice ἀπελούσασθε) are the divine passives "you were sanctified" (ἡγιάσθητε) and "you were justified" (ἐδικαιώθητε). This is in keeping, notes Conzelmann, with the prevailing schema of tracing everything back to God (*1 Corinthians*, 107).

[40] Byrne, "Righteousness," 571. Cf. my own criticism of Sanders (*Obedience*, 265).

[41] Byrne, "Righteousness," 571. Cf. Motyer, "Righteousness," 51, 53.

to believe that God in Christ had already ushered in the eschaton, summoning the entire world to judgment and inaugurating the end. The cross, the great divide of salvation history, has thus become the provision of salvation; therefore, salvation is offered to all on the basis of God's righteousness operative solely and exclusively through faith (Rom 3:24–26). "It is an offer of salvation because through faith human beings can come under the 'right-wising' verdict of God, be 'justified,' 'acquitted,' of sins, found 'righteous' and thus, through God's grace and favor alone, worthy of eternal life."[42]

Byrne, moreover, makes the justification of the believer organically one with that of Christ, who was vindicated when God raised him from the dead, after he had taken the place of sinners (Rom 1:4; 4:25). "The justification of Christians comes about through their association with the total 'career' of Christ, a just man fully vindicated by God. The association is possible because Christ was not simply one just man amongst many, but a man of universal significance, the 'Last Adam,' patriarch of a new humanity."[43] At the end of the day, the question about the continuing obedience required of the Christian and the relationship of this obedience to justification and ultimate salvation comes down to this: one's justification/obedience is but the extension of God's one act of vindicating Jesus. The Christ-event, precisely because it is *the* eschatological act, spans the gap between the cross and the final judgment.[44]

Hence, "Christians do not appropriate to themselves the righteousness of God [à la the traditional Protestant view]. Rather, in Christ they are taken up into it and in this way share 'the covenant loyalty that has hitherto been God's alone' . . . the righteousness of God communicated to Christians is nothing more or less than the ongoing righteousness of Christ, the continuing obedience of the one just man, lived out now in Christians and forming the basis of their destiny to eternal life."[45]

> The basis of the whole life of the people of God is his righteousness – his outreaching, saving mercy which rescues his creation for himself. This righteousness has now been supremely expressed in Christ. But as men are grasped by it, "justified" and made acceptable to God, so they are stamped with the image of their righteous saviour, and summoned to live in imitation of him as his people.[46]

An important corollary of this christocentric emphasis in justification is a renewed appreciation of the "indicative"/"imperative" approach to Paul – with one adjustment. Beker appropriately insists that a simple indicative-imperative scheme must be dismantled in favor of one which moves from the *indicative* of the Christ-event to the *imperative* of Christian obedience in order to reach its goal in *the final indicative* of the glory of God. Only then, he says, will the

---

[42] Byrne, "Righteousness," 572.
[43] Ibid., 573–74. Cf. Käsemann, "Righteousness," 180.
[44] Byrne, "Righteousness," 578. See his criticisms of Donfried (ibid., 577–78).
[45] Ibid., 574–75, quoting Ziesler, *Righteousness*, 160.
[46] Motyer, "Righteousness," 53–54.

mission and work of Christ be fully realized in the celebration of *Deus Victor*. "Although the indicative of the Christ-event is not the full but the proleptic realization of the future indicative of God's final glory, the imperative does not relativize God's action in Christ. It underscores our activity and necessary participation in the gospel of God's coming glory."[47]

To return, finally, to the original question, all of the above has a decided bearing on the justification/sanctification question. To put it forthrightly, I agree with Käsemann that no support can be found for distinguishing between the righteousness of the beginning and the righteousness of the end, between the righteousness of faith and the righteousness of life. I would further agree with him that "justification" and "sanctification" coincide, provided that the former is defined as the power of Christ taking over our life,[48] so that justification is seen to be coextensive with new creation.[49] Consequently, what is customarily termed "sanctification" is actually the extension of "justification," or, better, "rightwising." Among other things, any rigid distinction between "justification" and "sanctification" seems to be ruled out of court by the actual usage of "sanctification" in the NT, which normally has reference to the inception of the believing life.[50] By way of correlation, we may point to a similar linguistic phenomenon, i.e., Protestantism's preference to translate the same Greek word, δικαιοσύνη, by the separate terms "justification" and "sanctification" in order to preserve its distinction between the legal and moral status of the believer. This practice, however, as O'Donovan contends, can have exactly the opposite effect and may serve to obscure the connection of the two, leading Protestantism back into "the very uneschatological moralism" from which it sought to deliver us: "The correlate of a 'justification' which has nothing to do with 'righteousness' is a righteousness which has nothing to do with justification, and this soon presented itself to Protestant thought under the heading of 'sanctification'."[51]

None of this is meant to call into question that Paul and other NT authors could speak of a process of growth in faith, grace, and conformity to the image of Christ (e.g., Rom 8:29; 2 Cor 10:15; Eph 4:20−24; Col 3:1−17; 2 Thess 1:3; 2 Pet 1:5−11; 3:18).[52] But it is to say that the process in question is, in strictly Pauline terms, to be regarded as the extension of "justification," which is commensurate with what Murray calls "definitive sanctification," i.e., a per-

---

[47] Beker, *Paul*, 277−78.
[48] Käsemann, "Righteousness," 171, 175. See also Hooker, "ΠΙΣΤΙΣ," 342; Motyer, "Righteousness," 54−56; Furnish, *Theology*, 153−57 (but note Byrne's criticism, "Righteousness," 576, n. 54).
[49] Cf. Kertelge, *"Rechtfertigung,"* 159.
[50] Murray, "Sanctification;" Gaffin, *Resurrection*, 124−26; Hoekema, *Saved*, 202−6.
[51] O'Donovan, *Resurrection*, 254.
[52] See Berkouwer, *Sanctification*, esp. 107−13. Note, however, Berkouwer's observation on the relation between Romans 1−11 and 12, as well as Hebrews 1−12 and 13: "Nowhere can we find a break between justification and sanctification. There is only the relationship in which the grace of God admonishes the progressing believer" (ibid., 108).

son's incorporation into Christ and separation from the guilt and power of the old creation.

It is just the dynamic of justification as the power of Christ taking over our lives which informs us that in the act of rightwising we have actually *become righteous* (Rom 5:19) in that our commitment is now to the new age inaugurated with the coming of Christ, a commitment commensurate with a change of attitude toward God and his revealed will. Ours is no longer the "mindset of the flesh" (φρόνημα τῆς σαρκός) but the "mindset of the Spirit" (φρόνημα τοῦ πνεύματος), whose fruit is the life and peace of the new creation (Rom 8:6; cf. 5:1 = Isa 32:15–18). Or, according to C.F.D. Moule, there is in Paul's justification theology an analysis of the way a person's position vis-à-vis God's law corresponds to his position vis-à-vis God himself. In other words, since justification represents a reversal of Adam in the Garden, it entails the exact relationship of self-surrender to God and his law which the Spirit of Christ brings.[53] What is at stake in justification, therefore, is an effective declaration resulting in an "eschatologically transformed existence."[54] Without deprecating what Luther intended by his famous phrase,[55] we are not, again in strictly Pauline terms, *simul iustus et peccator* but rather *tunc peccator – nunc iustus* ("once a sinner, now righteous").[56] The believer has died to "sin," i.e., age of apostasy as dominated by the flesh, and been raised in newness of life that he might "live to God" (Rom 6:1–11).[57]

It is justification as a new beginning, a radical adjustment of thought and values, which opens up the pivotal significance of Rom 2:13. To apply Ziesler's observation on the verse: "Men are righteous before God, in the Jewish scheme, because they have obeyed the law. Thus the verb is forensic, yet based on the realities of the situation, viz. law-fulfilment."[58] It is true that Ziesler himself distances Paul from this scheme. But, in agreement with Snodgrass and others, I would maintain, as argued in chapter 3, that Paul is entirely in line with his Jewish heritage in making law-fulfillment the basis of future justification, as long as "law-fulfillment" is taken to be: "the obedience of faith" (Rom 1:5; 16:26); the "doing of the law" required of Israel of old (Lev 18:5); obedience to the truth (Rom 2:8); the desire to do "good" as opposed to "evil" (Deut 30:15; Rom 2:9–10) in the quest of eternal life (Rom 2:7). Given, therefore, that the very act of rightwising turns one from a "sinner" into a "righteous" person, Rom 2:13 (8:33) is as integral to a Pauline understanding of justification as any passage in his letters.

---

[53] Moule, "'Justification'," 185, 186.

[54] Reumann, *Righteousness*, 76–77; Fitzmeyer, "Justification," 211–12 (following Käsemann).

[55] See Berkouwer, *Sanctification*, 71–76.

[56] Beker, *Paul*, 216. See in addition Byrne, "Righteousness," 579; Cosgrove, "Justification," 668. Barrett (*Romans*, 75–76) comes close to this, but appears to stop short.

[57] On living to God, see Thüsing, *Per Christum*, 67–114.

[58] Ziesler, *Righteousness*, 190.

IV. Justification and Sanctification

It is here that Cosgrove's insights are extraordinarily apposite.[59] He remarks that although Paul never lets the thought arise that believers are somehow left to their own resources between the warring powers of the Spirit and the flesh (Rom 8:12–17), he nonetheless envisages the suffering obedience of the Christian as the basis of eschatological justification. In Romans 8, those whom God ultimately vindicates walk according to the Spirit in obedience to Christ, as they share in his sufferings. As he notes, this motif, especially evident in 8:31–39, bristles with traditional Jewish conceptions of the suffering righteous. In keeping with our own analysis of these verses, Cosgrove points out that vv. 33–34 echo the Suffering Servant's triumphal cry before his coming vindication, and Ps 44:22, cited in v. 36, belongs squarely in the same tradition. Particularly striking, I would say, is the former citation, because Paul takes the cry of the Servant from the Servant's own mouth and places it in the mouth of the Christian, who awaits his own final vindication by Yahweh.

The judgment scene of Rom 8:23–24, 31–39 thus envisions the vindication of those who share in Christ's sufferings. These suffering righteous, Cosgrove rightly maintains, are not the righteous poor of, say, *1 Enoch*, nor are they Israel seeking victory over its enemies:[60] they are those who, having been conformed to the image of God's crucified Son, find themselves sharing his sufferings. While their faith appears disconfirmed by their situation in the world, they know that just here their share in the future is manifested: ultimately, cruciform existence will have its vindication.[61] This, in Paul's words, is the justification of the "doers of the law."

As a final caution, in assessing these matters, balance is all-important. On the one side, the possibility of "righteousness by works," moral achievement, and boasting is excluded by the gift-character of God's righteousness (Rom 5:15–17; 6:23). Yet, on the other, "The same Lord who calls us to his service enables us for it and requires us to render it in such a way as to ensure that his gift is passed on."[62] Thus, while conceding that the justification/sanctification model is unsurpassed in its insistence that salvation is all of God,[63] what has been termed "sanctification" is actually the outworking of "the righteousness of God," commencing with the vindication/rightwising of the believer in Christ and eventuating in eternal life.[64]

---

[59] Cosgrove, "Justification," 667–69.

[60] Cf. the way the doxology of Rom 11:33–36 ties into but effectively reverses the apocalyptic thirst for vengeance against Israel's enemies. On the apocalyptic background of the doxology, see Dunn, *Romans* 2.700; Johnson, *Traditions*, 164–74.

[61] Cosgrove, "Justification," 669.

[62] Käsemann, "Righteousness," 175.

[63] Motyer, "Righteousness," 54.

[64] Murray's "Sanctification" has demonstrated that the NT usage of "sanctification" normally pertains not to a process but a once-for-all act (ibid., 277, passim). In this light, it is difficult to think that "justification" and "sanctification" are radically distinct, inasmuch as both, in their dominant NT employment, have reference to the same event. Cf. Motyer, "Righteousness," 54–55.

Because these conclusions are at variance in some regards with the customary Protestant theology, it will be well to offer some comment on the notion of the *ordo salutis* undergirding that theology by adding my voice to those who, in recent days, have taken issue with the sort of "order of salvation" propounded in Protestant dogmatics.[65] We proceed, however, with an awareness that the underlying motivation of the *ordo salutis* is entirely laudable, viz., the maintenance of the sovereignty of God's grace and the preservation of *sola fide*.[66]

R.B. Gaffin, for one, has criticized the traditional *ordo salutis* on several fronts,[67] of which two are relevant for our purposes. The first is that it is devoid of the exclusively eschatological air which pervades the entire Pauline eschatology. Put otherwise, the *ordo salutis* represents a de-eschatologization of Paul's outlook, because for the apostle soteriology *is* eschatology. All soteric experience, he remarks, derives from solidarity in Christ's resurrection and involves existence in the new creation inaugurated by his resurrection. Thus, this understanding of present Christian existence as an eschatological tension between resurrection realized and resurrection yet to be is totally foreign to the *ordo salutis*, for which the categories of justification, adoption, sanctification, and regeneration are *deprived of any eschatological significance and any really integral connection with the future*.

Second, the *ordo salutis* is distinguished by its insistence that justification, adoption, and sanctification, which occur at the inception of the application of redemption, are separate acts. Yet, says Gaffin, Paul views them not as distinctive acts but *as distinct aspects of a single act*. Most basic, in this regard, is the fact that the *ordo salutis* is confronted with the insoluble difficulty of trying to explain how these acts are related to the act of being joined *existentially* to Christ (italics his). If at the point of the inception of salvation union with Christ is prior to these acts (not vice versa) and, therefore, involves the possession in the inner person of all that Christ is as resurrected, *what need is there for other acts?* To say it the other way around, if these other acts are in some sense prior to union with Christ, then that union is improperly subordinated to them and its *biblical* significance severely attenuated.

More recently, A.A. Hoekema has subjected the *ordo salutis* to the same kind of reevaluation.[68] Hoekema's objections are: (1) the terms employed in constructing an *ordo salutis* (regeneration, conversion, renewal, and the like) are not used in the Bible itself in the same way they are used in systematic theology; (2) the order in which the various steps in the process of salvation are said to occur are not always the same in the Bible, e.g., 1 Cor 6:11; (3) Rom 8:30, often used as a basis for the *ordo salutis*, does not have as its primary purpose the provision of steps in the order of salvation; (4) faith should not be

---

[65] See Gaffin, *Resurrection*, 137–38, nn. 6, 9, for literature.
[66] Berkouwer, *Justification*, 26, 33. Cf. Motyer, "Righteousness," 54.
[67] Gaffin, *Resurrection*, 137–43. Except where noted, I have added the italics throughout this summary of Gaffin's discussion.
[68] Hoekema, *Saved*, 11–17. Again, italics have been added, except where noted.

thought of as only one of the stages in the order of salvation, because faith is to be exercised throughout the believer's life; (5) *justification and sanctification are not successive stages in the Christian life, but are simultaneous*; (6) the order suggested by various writers is normally not complete: *love and hope* are not mentioned, though both are as essential in the process of salvation as faith.

Like Gaffin, Hoekema considers that categories such as regeneration, justification, and sanctification are distinct and separate entities and, for that reason, are discussed in his book separately. Nevertheless, he insists that we must never forget that the latter two particularly always occur together. He thus concludes that we should not think of an *order of salvation* with successive steps or stages but of a work of grace, a *way of salvation* within which we may distinguish various aspects. Especially refreshing is his shifting of the "way of salvation" from a series of successive steps along a straight line (regeneration, conversion, justification, sanctification, perseverance) to a pentagonal building whose five walls are constructed of experiences which begin and continue simultaneously.

In drawing out the implications of this revised "way of salvation," Hoekema calls to mind three sets of facts. (1) Although regeneration occurs at the beginning of the Christian walk, its effects continue inasmuch as the believer lives a regenerate life. Although faith and repentance take place at the beginning, they must continue to be exercised for a lifetime. Though justification occurs as soon as one accepts Christ by faith, it is followed by a lifelong appropriation of its benefits. Sanctification continues throughout the Christian's life and is not completed until after death, so that perseverance in the faith is a lifelong activity.

(2) These aspects of *the process of salvation* are not only simultaneous, they are also interactive. Regeneration reveals itself in faith and repentance and is the beginning of sanctification. Faith is necessary throughout the Christian life as the means of appropriating the blessings of justification, making progress in sanctification, and of persevering fellowship with Christ; indeed, *regeneration already implies perseverance*. It is impossible to be justified without being sanctified, just as it is impossible to be converted without persevering in the faith.

(3) The process of salvation is not completed during this present life. As long as believers are in the way, they are caught up in the tension of the Already and Not Yet: they are already in Christ, but they are not yet perfect. While they are on the path which leads to glory, they are still far from the goal. They, in his words, are *genuinely* new persons but not yet *totally* new (italics his).

In addition to Gaffin and Hoekema, J. A. Fitzmeyer, while not discussing the *ordo salutis* as such, is in essential agreement. Fitzmeyer considers that one can look upon justification as "the same thing" as regeneration, renewal (*vivificatio*), reconciliation, salvation, and the forgiveness of sins, since "all these aspects of the relationship between God and human beings come ultimately from God himself (who is the sole origin of that relationship) through the work of Christ and his Spirit/grace...." In brief, "justification" for Fitzmeyer is one of the ways of describing the effects of the Christ-event. However, he is not reluctant, nor are we, to distinguish between these various aspects of God's action in us, "recognizing that they are *biblical images that describe different formalities of one complex whole (viz., the relationship itself).*"[69]

This study, I believe, is simply buttressed by these reappraisals of the *ordo salutis*, and little more needs to be said by way of supplementing the perspectives expressed so excellently by these several scholars. While one may speak of an "orderliness" determined by salvation in Christ,[70] an inflexible series of events is ruled out of court by the biblical data themselves. In this light, I wish to raise one question: If justification and sanctification are not successive but simultaneous stages in the Christian experience, is it appropriate to divide them into "forensic" and "ethical" categories, as though they occupied separate compartments? It would seem that both accomplish the same purpose, i.e., to "rightwise" the believer by *both* the forgiveness of sins *and* the placement of him/her on the "way of salvation" which eventuates in eternal life. And because both are simultaneous and lead to the same end, it appears pointless – not to say unpauline – to perpetuate a cut-and-dried distinction between them for the sake of polemics arising from church-historical controversies. The problematics of the traditional classification, once more, are underscored by a recognition that the NT's own usage of "justification" and "sanctification" proceeds not from an *ordo salutis* but a *historia salutis*, whereby individuals are vindicated eschatologically as the people of God and caused to inherit, ultimately, the new creation in its finalized manifestation.

Rom 8:29–30, for some a mainstay of the *ordo salutis*,[71] argues, ironically, in favor of its elimination. Berkouwer, in agreement with the other Reformed theologians Gaffin and Hoekema, maintains that it is not possible to deduce a fixed *ordo salutis* from the words of Scripture and their order. A case in point is Rom 8:30, in which Paul characterizes salvation in Christ, "the salvation which arises from the depths of the Father's heart and reaches out into time with an eternal blessing." The context thus suggests that the apostle does not have a sequence in mind.[72] Most conspicuously, a sequential "order of salvation" is precluded by the absence of sanctification from the list of v. 30.[73]

Berkouwer, in my estimation, has hit the mark, especially by removing Rom 8:30 from the *ordo salutis* and placing it within the *historia salutis* – where it belongs! Yet I want to press further and suggest that the precise reason why "sanctification" does not receive separate mention by Paul is because it is comprehended within "justification." The genius of δικαιόω, in other words,

---

[69] Fitzmeyer, "Justification," 197, 202 (italics mine). Cf. Berkouwer, *Justification*, 27–28; Byrne, "Righteousness," 576.
[70] Berkouwer, *Justification*, 29 (speaking of Calvin's theology, which did not formulate an *ordo salutis* as such).
[71] E.g., Murray, *Redemption*, 100–2.
[72] Berkouwer, *Justification*, 31.
[73] Ibid., 31–32.

comes to the fore just in its ability to gather both concepts into an integrated whole.[74] This is why, in v. 30, it can stand alone between calling and glorification, as forming the vital link between the two. At the same time, the fact that δικαιόω is flanked by the sovereign salvation-historical action of God is indicative that the "rightwising" of the believer is all *God's* doing.

V. The Obedience of Faith as Life Between Two Worlds

Without diminishing the impact of the definitive new beginning in Christ and the power of faith's obedience which stems from the believer's union with him, the above conclusions must not be represented as the whole story. The age to come has arrived, but it has not been consummated. Consequently, any appraisal of the life of faith this side of the eschaton must take into account the factor of human failure due to "indwelling sin," which has made the flesh its "headquarters." And it is none other than Rom 7:14–25 which stands as a witness to the counterattack of the old creation against the influence and leading of the Spirit. Such an assault can only produce tension, a tension which will be resolved at last when the sons and daughters of God are revealed (Rom 8:19).

> The process [of justification] is not complete. Though they [believers] stand acquitted in a forensic sense, the obedience of Christ is yet to run its full course in them; they yet hang with him upon the cross (Gal 2:19). The process of justification will only be complete in them, as it is in him, when it finds public, bodily expression in the resurrection-existence, the "revelation of the sons of God" (Rom 8:18–21).[75]

If, as we have just said, the Christian is the microcosm of God's new creation plan for the universe, he is, by the same standard, the microcosm of the *totality* of salvation history – a history comprised of the overlap of old and new in the unfolding cosmic drama of redemption, with its resultant toll of grief and suffering on the believer.

Admittedly, Rom 7:14–25 is singular in its *detailed* witness to Paul's conflict with sin.[76] Nevertheless, it does not stand on its own: it forms part and parcel of the overall Pauline schema of the new creation as commenced but not consummated. So, we should not think that the struggle is confined to sin in the narrowest sense; it embraces as well the Christian's total experience of simultaneous peril and deliverance, weakness and strength, life and death, themes which permeate particularly 2 Corinthians.[77] The strife with indwelling sin is only one aspect of the eschatological/cosmic conflict inaugurated by the coming of Christ. Faith, therefore, goes beyond one's initial commitment to

---

[74] Cf. Dunn, *Romans* 1.485.
[75] Byrne, "Righteousness," 578.
[76] Wenham gives some possible reasons ("Life," 94, n. 41).
[77] Cf. Hughes, *2 Corinthians*, 135–46.

Christ and encompasses "the ability to sustain the contradiction between present reality and future hope and to live out of that tension."⁷⁸

From another point of view, this "contradiction between present reality and future hope" boils down to the problem of remaining sin in the believer. The Christian is bound to acknowledge that justification and the exhortation to holiness are compatible. But one equally senses, as Berkouwer does, that there seems to be a contradiction between the teaching of justification/sanctification, on the one hand, and "the awful truth about the lives actually led by believers," on the other. He exhorts us to recall that the same Paul who could address the Corinthians as "those who are sanctified in Christ Jesus" (1 Cor 1:2) could, in the same letter, passionately expose their sins. "What," says Berkouwer, "is the awful truth we are here confronting? What is the place of sin and lustfulness, not in the tumultuous breast of Luther this time, but in the Church of Paul's day to which he said that Christ gave himself for their sins?" These things are hard to understand, especially in the light of Rom 6:2: "We who died to sin, How shall we live any longer therein?" This verse compels us to ask, "Where is this freedom, this sensational release from the past, this 'erstwhile' of sin, and where is the proof of transfer into the kingdom?"⁷⁹ And in the very act of asking, we are caused to lament that the solution is not immediately forthcoming. We must wait a while longer.

At bottom, then, it is "indwelling sin" (Rom 7:20) or the Christian warfare which causes the perplexity. If we press the question, Why should continued warfare be necessary after the achievement of victory?, the straightforward answer is that, in Paul's vision, the victory has not been finally won: Christ is yet to be revealed from heaven; he is yet to put all his enemies under his feet, the last of which is death; he is yet to reign over the kingdom of God in its finalized eschatological form and receive to himself his "holy and blameless" bride. "Holy and blameless," as Berkouwer relates, frequently has an "eschatological accent," i.e., "this admonition touches all of human life until, and in the interest of, the return of Christ. Hearts are established in order that they may be 'unblamable in holiness before our God and Father, at the coming of our Lord Jesus with all his saints' (1 Thess. 3:13)."⁸⁰

Until then, the believer speaks in the language of the Christian warfare – "Not that I have already obtained, or am made perfect; but I press on to make it my own because Christ Jesus has made me his own" (Phil 3:12) – and wages war with the incentives provided by Romans 7: humility and gratitude.⁸¹ It is because the Christian life this side of the eschaton *is* warfare that we run into the idiom of struggle throughout the word of God.

---

[78] Beker, *Paul*, 356.
[79] Berkouwer, *Sanctification*, 47–48.
[80] Ibid., 64–65.
[81] Ibid., 63, 66.

And confession of guilt is especially common with those who know the fellowship of God.... To speak of the church is to speak of the struggle to remain children of God in communion with him and to live gratefully in virtue of the forgiveness of sin. This life of sanctification proceeds in weakness, temptation, and exposure to the powers of darkness. Hence, the life of the believer is fenced in with admonitions....[82]

It is none other than the reality of persistent conflict and periodic defeat which rules out of court any notion of achievement in salvation, let alone perfection.[83] In the end, we are more than conquerors *through him who loved us* (Rom 8:37); and it is just Christians' continued sense of innate weakness and vulnerability which reminds them that they need the one who already has justified them by his blood and will hereafter save them by his life (Rom 5:9). All this underscores yet again that "righteousness" is not sinless perfection or anything approaching it – it is, rather, but *responsible covenant behavior*.[84] The comfort of Romans 7, accordingly, is this: notwithstanding our many failures, there is no condemnation as long we desire to remain within the covenant bond, true to Christ the Lord.[85]

It is the resolve to keep faith with Jesus, the κύριος of the new covenant, which brings us full circle in this study of Romans. We began by examining the range of the phrase ὑπακοὴ πίστεως (chapter 1). Thereafter we focused on the disobedience of the old Israel, consisting in its particular brand of idolatry (chapter 2), and the obedience of the new Israel "in Christ," which has succeeded in the pursuit of glory, honor, and immortality (chapter 3). This latter-day people have been enabled to resume and fulfill the mandate of the first Adam by virtue of the obedience of the last Adam, who, by investing them with the renewed image of God, has caused them to replicate his own obedience (chapter 4). It is none other than his obedience (perseverance) in the midst of adversity (à la Rom 5:3–5; 8:18–25) which paves the way for Rom 7:14–25, Paul's agonized confrontation with "indwelling sin," until his deliverance from "the body of this death" at the resurrection, when, like Christ (Rom 6:4–10), he will die definitively to sin and rise in newness of life (chapter 5). In a singular manner, Romans 7 encapsulates the "obedience of faith" experience from beginning to end by concretizing the terms of faith's obedience in everyday life. *Faith, obedience, and perseverance*, in other words, are not separate entities but three aspects of the same entity. The faith with which the Christian walk commences is unreserved trust in Jesus the Son of God. This faith, however, does not exist in the abstract; its quality as trust is put to the test in the trials and exigencies which attend "this present evil age." Thus tested, "faith" becomes the "obedience" which is "perseverance." In short, *faith, obedience, and perseverance are one and the same.*

---

[82] Ibid., 66.

[83] See ibid., 48–58, 64–67. Beker adds that Paul does not respond to the dynamic struggle of faith in daily life with "static perfectionistic rigidity" (*Paul*, 219).

[84] Ziesler, *Righteousness*, 25–26; Garlington, *Obedience*, 117.

[85] It is in this sense that Paul, like his Jewish contemporaries, can be said in principle to embrace a "covenantal nomism" (see Garlington, *Obedience*, 265).

Bibliography

Adamson, James B., *James: The Man and His Message*, Grand Rapids: Eerdmans, 1989.
Anderson, A. A., *The Book of Psalms*, NCB; London: Paternoster, 1972.
Arenhoevel, Diego, *Die Theokratie nach den 1. und 2. Makkabäerbuch*, Mainz: Matthias-Grünewald, 1967.
Attridge, Harold W., *The Epistle to the Hebrews*, Hermeneia; Philadelphia: Fortress, 1989.
Bandstra, Andrew J., *The Law and the Elements of the World: An Exegetical Study in Aspects of Paul's Teaching*, Kampen: Kok, 1964.
Banks, Robert, "The Eschatological Role of Law in Pre- and Post- Christian Jewish Thought," in *Reconciliation and Hope: New Testament Essays on Atonement and Eschatology Presented to L. L. Morris on His 60th Birthday*, ed. Robert Banks; Grand Rapids: Eerdmans, 1974, 173–85.
– *Jesus and the Law in the Synoptic Tradition*, SNTSMS 28; Cambridge: Cambridge University Press, 1975.
Barclay, J. M. G., *Obeying the Truth: A Study of Paul's Ethics in Galatians*, SNTW; Edinburgh: T. & T. Clark, 1988.
Barrett, C. K., *A Commentary on the Epistle to the Romans*, HNTC; Harper & Row, 1957.
– *From First Adam to Last: A Study in Pauline Theology*, London: A & C Black, 1962.
Barth, Karl, *The Epistle to the Romans*, Oxford: Oxford University Press, 1933.
– *A Shorter Commentary on Romans*, London: SCM, 1959.
Bartsch, Hans-Werner, "The Concept of Faith in Paul's Letter to the Romans," *BR* 13 (1968), 41–53.
Bassler, Jouette M., *Divine Impartiality: Paul and a Theological Axiom*, SBLDS 59; Chico: Scholars Press, 1982.
Beardslee, W. A., *Human Achievement and Divine Vocation in the Message of Paul*, SBT 1/31; London: SCM, 1961.
Beasley-Murray, G. R., *Baptism in the New Testament*, London: MacMillan, 1962.
Beker, J. Christiaan, *Paul the Apostle: The Triumph of God in Life and Thought*, Philadelphia: Fortress, 1980.
Benoit, Pierre, "Qumran and the New Testament," in *Paul and the Dead Sea Scrolls*, eds. J. Murphy-O'Connor and James H. Charlesworth; New York: Crossroad, 1990, 1–30.
Berkouwer, G. C., *Faith and Sanctification*, SD; Grand Rapids: Eerdmans, 1952.
– *Faith and Justification*, SD; Grand Rapids: Eerdmans, 1954.
– *Faith and Perseverance*, SD; Grand Rapids: Eerdmans, 1958.
– *Sin*, SD; Grand Rapids: Eerdmans, 1971.
Betz, Hans Dieter, *Galatians: A Commentary on Paul's Letter to the Churches in Galatia*, Hermeneia; Philadelphia: Fortress, 1979.

Betz, Otto, "Rechtfertigung in Qumran," in *Rechtfertigung: Festschrift für Ernst Käsemann zum 70. Geburtstag*, eds. Johannes Friedrich, Wolfgang Pöhlmann, and Peter Stuhlmacher; Tübingen: Mohr, 1976, 17–36.
- and Dexinger, Ferdinand, "Beschneidung" (II, III), *TRE* 5.716–25.
Bickerman, Elias, *From Ezra to the Last of the Maccabees: Foundations of Post-Biblical Judaism*, New York: Schocken, 1962.
Binder, Hermann, *Der Glaube bei Paulus*, Berlin: Evangelische Verlagsanstalt, 1968.
Black, C. Clifton, "Pauline Perspectives on Death in Romans 5–8," *JBL* 103 (1984), 413–33.
Black, Matthew, *Romans*, NCB; London: Marshall, Morgan & Scott, 1973.
Boer, Martinus C. de, *The Defeat of Death: Apocalyptic Eschatology in 1 Corinthians 15 and Romans 5*, JSNTSup 22; Sheffield: Sheffield Academic Press, 1988.
Bornkamm, Gunther, "Paulinische Anakolouthe," in *Das Ende des Gesetzes: Paulusstudien*, BEvT 16; Münich: Kaiser, 1960, 76–92.
- "Sin, Law and Death: An Exegetical Study of Romans 7," in *Early Christian Experience*, London: SCM, 1969, 87–104.
- *Paul*, London: Hodder & Stoughton, 1971.
Brandenburger, Egon, *Adam und Christus: Exegetisch-religionsgeschichtliche Untersuchungen zu Röm. 5,12–21 (1 Kor. 15)*, WMANT 7; Neukirchen: Neukirchener Verlag, 1962.
- *Fleisch und Geist: Paulus und die Dualistische Weisheit*, WMANT 29; Neukirchen: Neukirchener Verlag, 1968.
Brandon, S. G. F., *Jesus and the Zealots: A Study of the Political Factor in Primitive Christianity*, New York: Scribner, 1967.
Brasswell, Joseph P., "'The Blessing of Abraham' Versus 'The Curse of the Law': Another Look at Gal 3:10–13," *WTJ* 53 (1991), 73–91.
Brauch, Manfred T., "Perspectives on 'God's Righteousness' in Recent German Discussion," in E. P. Sanders, *Paul and Palestinian Judaism: A Comparison of Patterns of Religion*, Philadelphia: Fortress, 1977, 523–42.
Braun, Herbert, "Römer 7:7–25 und das Selbsverständnis des Qumran-Frommen," *ZTK* 56 (1959), 1–18.
Brown, Raymond E., *The Semitic Background of the Term "Mystery" in the New Testament*, Philadelphia: Fortress, 1968.
Bruce, F. F., *The Epistle of Paul to the Romans*, TNTC; London: Tyndale Press, 1963.
- "Paul and the Law of Moses," *BJRL* 57 (1974–75), 259–79.
- "The Dead Sea Scrolls and Early Christianity," in *A Mind for What Matters: Collected Essays of F. F. Bruce*, Grand Rapids: Eerdmans, 1990, 49–64.
Bruegemann, Walter, *Genesis*, Interpretation; Atlanta: John Knox Press, 1982.
Buber, Martin, *Two Types of Faith*, London: Routledge & Kegan Paul, 1951.
Büchler, Adolph, "Ben Sira's Conception of Sin and Atonement," *JQR* ns 13 (1922–23), 303–35, 461–502; 14 (1923–24), 53–83.
- *Sin and Atonement in the Rabbinic Literature of the First Century*, London: Humphrey Milford, 1928.
Bultmann, Rudolf, "Glossen im Römerbrief," *TLZ* 72 (1947), 197–202.
- *Theology of the New Testament*, 2 vols.; London: SCM, 1952.
- *Primitive Christianity in Its Contemporary Setting*, London: Thames & Hudson, 1956.

- "ἔλεος," etc., *TDNT* 2.477–87.
- "Adam and Christ According to Romans 5," in *Current Issues in New Testament Interpretation: Essays in Honor of Otto A. Piper*, eds. William Klassen and Graydon F. Snyder; London: SCM, 1962, 143–65.
- "Romans 7 and the Anthropology of Paul," in *Existence and Faith*, London: SPCK, 1964, 147–57.

Burtchaell, James, "A Theology of Faith and Works: The Epistle to the Galatians – A Catholic View," *Int* 17 (1963), 39–47.

Byrne, Brendan, "Living Out the Righteousness of God: The Contribution of Rom 6:1–8:13 to an Understanding of Paul's Ethical Presuppositions," *CBQ* 43 (1981), 557–81.

Calvin, John, *The Institutes of the Christian Religion*, ed. John T. McNeill; 2 vols.; LCC; Philadelphia: Westminster, 1960.

- *The Epistles of Paul to the Romans and to the Thessalonians*, eds. David W. Torrance and Thomas F. Torrance; Grand Rapids: Eerdmans, 1973.

Cambier, J.-M., "Péchés des hommes et péché d'Adam en Rom. V.12," *NTS* 11 (1964–65), 217–55.

- "Le jugement de touts les hommes par Dieu seul, selon la vérité, dans Rom 2:1–3:20," *ZNW* 67 (1976), 187–213.

Campbell, D. H., "The Identity of ἐγώ in Romans 7:7–25," in *Studia Biblica 1978. III: Papers on Paul and Other New Testament Authors*, ed. Elizabeth A. Livingstone; JSNTSup 3; Sheffield: JSOT Press, 1980, 57–64.

Caragrounis, Chrys C., "Romans 5.15–16 in the Context of 5.12–21: Contrast or Comparison," *NTS* 31 (1985), 142–48.

Collins, John J., "Chiasmus and the 'ABA' Pattern of the Text of Paul," in *Studiorum Paulinorum Congressus Internationalis Catholicus*; 2 vols.; AnBib 17–18; Rome: Biblical Institute Press, 1963, 2.575–83.

Conzelmann, Hans, *1 Corinthians: A Commentary on the First Epistle to the Corinthians*, Hermeneia; Philadelphia: Fortress, 1975.

Coppens, Joseph, "'Mystery' in the Theology of Saint Paul and Its Parallels at Qumran," in *Paul and the Dead Sea Scrolls*, eds. J. Murphy 0'Connor and James H. Charlesworth; New York: Crossroad, rep. 1990, 132–58.

Cosgrove, Charles H., "Justification in Paul: A Linguistic and Theological Reflection," *JBL* 106 (1987), 653–70.

- *The Cross and the Spirit: A Study in the Argumentation and Theology of Galatians*; Macon: Mercer University Press, 1988.

Cranfield, C. E. B., "On Some of the Problems of the Interpretation of Romans 5.12," *SJT* 22 (1969), 324–41.

- *A Critical and Exegetical Commentary on the Epistle to the Romans*, 2 vols.; ICC; Edinburgh: T. & T. Clark, 1975, 1979.
- "'The Works of the Law' in the Epistle to the Romans," *JSNT* 43 (1991), 89–101.

Dahl, Nils Alstrup, *Studies in Paul*, Minneapolis: Augsburg, 1977.

Davies, Glenn N., *Faith and Obedience in Romans: A Study in Romans 1–4*, JSNTSup 39; Sheffield: Sheffield Academic Press, 1990.

Davies, W. D., *Torah in the Messianic Age and/or the Age to Come*, SBLMS 7; Philadelphia: SBL, 1952.

- *Paul and Rabbinic Judaism: Some Rabbinic Elements in Pauline Theology*, London: SCM, ³1955.

– *Jewish and Pauline Studies*, Philadelphia: Fortress, 1984.
Deichgräber, Reinhard, "Gehorsam und Gehorchen in der Verkündigung Jesu," *ZNW* 52 (1961), 119–22.
Deidun, T. J., *New Covenant Morality in Paul*, AnBib 89; Rome: Biblical Institute Press, 1981.
Denny, James, "St. Paul's Epistle to the Romans," in *The Expositor's Greek New Testament*, ed. W. Robertson Nicoll; Grand Rapids: Eerdmans, rep. 1970, 2.555–725.
Dobbeler, Axel von, *Glaube als Teilhabe: Historische und semantische Grundlagen der paulinischen Theologie und Ekklesiologie des Glaubens*, WUNT 2/22; Tübingen: Mohr, 1987.
Dodd, C. H., *The Epistle of Paul to the Romans*, MNTC; London: Hodder & Stoughton, 1932.
Donaldson, Terence L., "Zealot," *ISBE* 4.1175–79.
– "Zealot and Convert: The Origin of Paul's Christ-Torah Antithesis," *CBQ* 51 (1989), 655–82.
Donfried, K. P., "Justification and Last Judgment in Paul," *ZNW* 67 (1976), 90–110.
Dunn, James D. G., "Jesus – Flesh and Spirit: An Exposition of Romans 1.3–4," *JTS* ns 24 (1973), 40–68.
– *Jesus and the Spirit: A Study of the Religious and Charismatic Experience of Jesus and the First Christians as Reflected in the New Testament*, London: SCM, 1975.
– "Rom. 7,14–25 in the Theology of Paul," *TZ* 31 (1975), 264–73.
– *Unity and Diversity in the New Testament*, London: SCM, 1977.
– *Christology in the Making: An Inquiry into the Origins of the Doctrine of the Incarnation*, London: SCM, 1980.
– "Romans 13:1–7 – A Charter for Political Quietism?," *ExA* 2 (1986), 55–68.
– "'Righteousness from the Law' and 'Righteousness from Faith:' Paul's Interpretation of Scripture in Romans 10:1–10," in *Tradition and Interpretation in the New Testament: Essays in Honor of E. Earle Ellis for His 60th Birthday*, eds. Gerald F. Hawthorne and Otto Betz; Grand Rapids: Eerdmans, 1987, 216–28.
– "Paul's Epistle to the Romans: An Analysis of Structure and Argument," *ANRW* (1987), 2.25.4, 2842–90.
– "Was Jesus a Liberal? Was Paul a Heretic?," in *The Living Word*, Philadelphia: Fortress, 1987, 44–64.
– *Romans*, 2 vols.; WBC 38 a, b; Dallas: Word, 1988.
– *Jesus, Paul, and the Law: Studies in Mark and Galatians*, Louisville: Westminster/John Knox Press, 1990.
– *The Partings of the Ways: Between Christianity and Judaism and Their Significance for the Character of Christianity*, London/Philadelphia: SCM/Trinity Press International, 1991.
Eichrodt, Walther, *Theology of the Old Testament*, 2 vols.; OTL; Philadelphia: Westminster, 1967.
Elderen, Bastiaan van, "The Purpose of Parables According to Matthew 13:10–17," in *New Dimensions in New Testament Studies*, eds. Richard N. Longenecker and Merrill C. Tenney; Grand Rapids: Zondervan, 1974, 180–90.
Elliot, Neil, *The Rhetoric of Romans: Argumentative Constraint and Strategy and Paul's Dialogue with Judaism*, JSNTSup 45; Sheffield: Sheffield Academic Press, 1990.
Ellis, E. Earle, *Paul's Use of the Old Testament*, Edinburgh: Oliver & Boyd, 1957.

– *Paul and His Recent Interpreters*, Grand Rapids: Eerdmans, 1961.
– *Prophecy and Hermeneutic in Early Christianity*, Grand Rapids: Eerdmans, 1978.
Espy, John M., "Paul's 'Robust Conscience' Re-examined," *NTS* 31 (1985), 161–88.
Farmer, William R., *Maccabees, Zealots, and Josephus: An Inquiry into Jewish Nationalism in the Greco-Roman Period*, New York: Columbia University Press, 1957.
– "Zealot," *IDB* 4.936–39.
Fee, Gordon D., *The First Epistle to the Corinthians*, NICNT; Grand Rapids: Eerdmans, 1987.
Feuillet, André, "Le plan salvifique de Dieu d'apres l'Épître aux Romains," *RB* 57 (1950), 336–87, 489–529.
– "La citation d'Habacuc 2.4 et les huit premiers chapitres de l'Épître aux Romains," *NTS* 6 (1959–60), 52–80.
Fitzmyer, Joseph A., "The Semitic Background of the New Testament *Kyrios*-Title," in *A Wandering Aramean: Collected Aramaic Essays*, SBLMS 25; Chico: Scholars Press, 1979, 115–42.
– "The Biblical Basis of Justification by Faith: Comments on the Essay of Professor Reumann," in John Reumann, *Righteousness in the New Testament: "Justification" in the United States Lutheran-Roman Catholic Dialogue, with Responses by Joseph A. Fitzmyer and Jerome D. Quinn*, Philadelphia: Fortress, 1982, 193–227.
Fohrer, Georg, *Glauben und Leben in Judentum*, UTB 885; Heidelberg: Quelle & Meyer, ²1985.
Friedrich, Gerhard, "Muß ὑπακοὴ πίστεως Röm 1:5 mit 'Glaubensgehorsam' übersetz werden?," *ZNW* 72 (1981), 118–23.
Fung, Ronald Y. K., "The Impotence of the Law: Toward a Fresh Understanding of Romans 7:14–25," in *Scripture, Tradition, and Interpretation: Essays Presented to Everett F. Harrison by Students and Colleagues in Honor of His Seventy-fifth Birthday*, eds. W. Ward Gasque and William Sanford LaSor; Grand Rapids: Eerdmans, 1978, 34–48.
– "The Status of Justification by Faith in Paul's Thought: A Brief Survey of a Modern Debate," *Them* 6 (1981), 4–11.
– *The Epistle to the Galatians*, NICNT; Grand Rapids: Eerdmans, 1988.
Furnish, Victor Paul, *Theology and Ethics in Paul*, Nashville: Abingdon, 1968.
– *The Love Command in the New Testament*, Nashville: Abingdon, 1972.
Gaffin, Richard B. Jr., *Resurrection and Redemption: A Study in Paul's Soteriology*, Phillipsburg, NJ: Presbyterian & Reformed, ²1987.
– "Adam," *NDT*, 3–5.
Garlington, Don B., *'The Obedience of Faith': A Pauline Phrase in Historical Context*, WUNT 2/38; Tübingen: Mohr, 1991.
– "Burden Bearing and the Recovery of Offending Christians (Galatians 6:1–5)," *TrinJ* ns 12 (1991), 151–83.
Gaston, Lloyd, "Paul and the Law in Galatians 2–3," in *Anti-Judaism in Early Christianity. Volume 1: Paul and the Gospels*, eds. Peter Richardson and David Granskou; Waterloo, Ont: Wilfrid Laurier University Press, 1986, 37–57.
Gaventa, Beverly R., "Galatians 1 and 2: Autobiography as Paradigm," *NovT* 28 (1986), 309–26.
Gibbs, John G., *Creation and Redemption: A Study in Pauline Theology*, NovTSup 26; Leiden: Brill, 1971.
Godet, Frederick Louis, *Commentary on Romans*, Grand Rapids: Kregel, rep. 1977.

Goppelt, Leonhardt, "τύπος," etc., *TDNT* 8.246–59.
- *Typos: The Typological Interpretation of the Old Testament in the New*, Grand Rapids: Eerdmans, 1982.
Gordon, T. David, "The Problem at Galatia," *Int* 41 (1987), 32–43.
- "A Note on ΠΑΙΔΑΓΩΓΟΣ in Galatians 3.24–25," *NTS* 35 (1989), 150–54.
Grundmann, Walther, "The Teacher of Righteousness of Qumran and the Question of Justification by Faith in the Theology of the Apostle Paul," in *Paul and the Dead Sea Scrolls*, eds. J. Murphy-O'Connor and James H. Charlesworth; New York: Crossroad, 1990, 85–131.
Gundry, Robert H., *Soma in Biblical Theology*, SNTSMS 29; Cambridge: Cambridge University Press, 1976.
- "The Moral Frustration of Paul Before His Conversion: Sexual Lust in Romans 7:7–25," in *Pauline Studies: Essays Presented to Professor F.F. Bruce on His 70th Birthday*, eds. Donald A. Hagner and Murray J. Harris; London/Grand Rapids: Paternoster/Eerdmans, 1980, 228–45.
- "Grace, Works, and Staying Saved in Paul," in *The Best in Theology*, eds. J.I. Packer, et al; Carol Stream: Christianity Today, n. d., 1.81–100 (= *Bib* 66 [1985], 1–38).
Gundry Volf, Judith M., *Paul and Perseverance: Staying In and Falling Away*, Louisville: Westminster/John Knox Press, 1990.
Gunther, John J., *St. Paul's Opponents and Their Background: A Study of Apocalyptic and Jewish Sectarian Teachings*, NovTSup 35; Leiden: Brill, 1973.
Guthrie, Donald, *New Testament Theology*, Leicester: Inter-Varsity, 1981.
Hadot, J., *Penchant mauvais et volonté libre dans la sagesse de Ben Sira*, Brussels: Presses universitaires de Bruxelles, 1969.
Hammerton-Kelly, R. G., "Sacred Violence and the Curse of the Law (Galatians 3.13): The Death of Christ as a Sacrificial Travesty," *NTS* 36 (1990), 98–118.
Hansen, G. Walter, *Abraham in Galatians: Epistolary and Rhetorical Contexts*, JSNTSup 29; Sheffield: Sheffield Academic Press, 1989.
Hays, Richard B., *The Faith of Jesus Christ: An Investigation of the Narrative Substructure of Galatians 3:1–4:11*, SBLDS 56; Chico: Scholars Press, 1983.
- *Echoes of Scripture in the Letters of Paul*, New Haven: Yale University Press, 1989.
Hebert, A.G., *The Throne of David: A Study of the Fulfilment of the Old Testament in Jesus Christ and His Church*, London: Faber, 1941.
Heiligenthal, Roman, *Werke als Zeichnen: Untersuchungen zur Bedeutung der menschlichen Taten im Frühjudentum, Neuen Testament und Frühchristentum*, WUNT 2/9; Tübingen: Mohr, 1983.
Hendriksen, William, *Romans*, 2 vols.; NTC; Grand Rapids: Baker, 1980.
Hengel, Martin, *Judaism and Hellenism: Studies in Their Encounter in Palestine During the Early Hellenistic Period*, 2 vols.; London: SCM, 1974.
- *The Zealots: Investigations into the Jewish Freedom Movement in the Period from Herod I until 70 A.D.*, Edinburgh: T. & T. Clark, 1989.
- *The Pre-Christian Paul*, London/Philadelphia: SCM/Trinity Press International, 1991.
Hill, David, *Greek Words and Hebrew Meanings*, SNTSMS 5; Cambridge: Cambridge University Press, 1967.
Hodge, Charles, *A Commentary on Romans*, Edinburgh: Banner of Truth, rep. 1975.
Hoekema, Anthony A., *The Christian Looks at Himself*, Grand Rapids: Eerdmans, 1975.
- *Created in God's Image*, Grand Rapids: Eerdmans, 1986.

- *Saved By Grace*, Grand Rapids: Eerdmans, 1989.
Hooker, M. D., "Adam in Romans I," *NTS* 6 (1959–60), 297–306.
- "ΠΙΣΤΙΣ ΧΡΙΣΤΟΥ," *NTS* 35 (1989), 321–42.
Howard, George, "Christ the End of the Law: The Meaning of Romans 10:4," *JBL* 88 (1969), 331–37.
Hübner, Hans, "Pauli Theologiae Proprium," *NTS* 26 (1980), 445–73.
- *Law in Paul's Thought*, Edinburgh: T. & T. Clark, 1984.
- "Was heißt bei Paulus 'Werke des Gesetzes'?," in *Glaube und Eschatologie: Festschrift für Werner Georg Kümmel zum 80. Geburtstag*, eds. Erich Grässer and Otto Merk; Tübingen: Mohr, 1985, 123–33.
Hughes, Philip Edgcumbe, *Paul's Second Epistle to the Corinthians*, NICNT; Grand Rapids: Eerdmans, 1962.
Hultgren, Arland J., *Paul's Gospel and Mission: The Outlook from His Letter to the Romans*, Philadelphia: Fortress, 1985.
- "Paul's Pre-Christian Persecutions of the Church: Their Purpose, Locale, and Nature," *JBL* 95 (1976), 97–111.
- "The *Pistis Christou* Formulation in Paul," *NovT* 22 (1980), 248–63.
Hutchinson, George P., *The Problem of Original Sin in American Presbyterian Theology*, Philadelphia: Presbyterian & Reformed, 1972.
Jeremias, Joachim, "Zur Gedankenführung in den paulinischen Briefen," in *Abba: Studien zur Neutestamentlichen Theologie und Zeitgeschichte*, Göttingen: Vandenhoeck & Ruprecht, 1966, 269–76.
Jervell, Jacob, *Imago Dei: Gen 1,26f. im Spätjudentum, in der Gnosis und in den paulinischen Briefen*, FRLANT 58; Göttingen: Vandenhoeck & Ruprecht, 1960.
Jewett, Robert, *Paul's Anthropological Terms: A Study of Their Use in Conflict Settings*, AGJU 10; Leiden: Brill, 1971.
- "Romans as an Ambassadorial Letter," *Int* 36 (1982), 5–20.
Johnson, E. Elizabeth, *The Function of Apocalyptic and Wisdom Traditions in Romans 9–11*, SBLDS 109; Atlanta: Scholars Press, 1989.
Johnson, S. Lewis, "Romans 5:12 – An Exercise in Exegesis and Theology," in *New Dimensions in New Testament Study*, eds. Richard N. Longenecker and Merrill C. Tenny; Grand Rapids: Zondervan, 1974, 298–316.
Jüngel, Eberhard, "Das Gesetz zwischen Adam und Christus: Eine theologische Studie zu Röm 5,12–21," *ZTK* 60 (1963), 42–74.
Käsemann, Ernst, "'The Righteousness of God' in Paul," in *New Testament Questions of Today*, Philadelphia: Fortress, 1969, 168–82.
- "The Faith of Abraham in Romans 4," in *Perspectives on Paul*, Philadelphia: Fortress, 1971, 79–101.
- *Commentary on Romans*, Grand Rapids: Eerdmans, 1980.
Karlberg, Mark W., "Israel's History Personified: Romans 7:7–13 in Relation to Paul's Teaching on the 'Old Man'," *TrinJ* ns 7 (1986), 65–74.
Kaylor, R. David, *Paul's Covenant Community: Jew and Gentile in Romans*, Atlanta: John Knox Press, 1988.
Kelly, H. A., "The Devil in the Desert," *CBQ* 26 (1964), 190–220.
Kertelge, Karl, *"Rechtfertigung" bei Paulus: Studien zur Struktur und zum Bedeutungsgehalt des paulinischen Rechfertigungsbegriffs*, NTAbh 3; Münster: Aschendorff, ^{2}1967.

– "Exegetische Überlegungen zum Verständnis der paulinischen Anthropologie nach Römer 7," *ZNW* 62 (1971), 105–114.

Kilgallen, John, *The Stephen Speech: A Literary and Redactional Study of Acts 7,2–53*, AnBib 67; Rome: Biblical Institute Press, 1976.

Kim, Seyoon, *The Origin of Paul's Gospel*, WUNT 2/4; Tübingen: Mohr, 1981.

– *"The 'Son of Man'" as the Son of God*, WUNT 1/30; Tübingen: Mohr, 1983.

Kittel, Gerhard, "ἀκούω," etc., *TDNT* 1.216–25.

Kline, Meredith G., *Images of the Spirit*, Grand Rapids: Baker, 1980.

Kneucker, J. J., *Das Buch Baruch*, Leipzig: Brockhaus, 1879.

Kreitzer, L. Joseph, *Jesus and God in Paul's Eschatology*, JSNTSup 19; Sheffield: Sheffield Academic Press, 1987.

Kümmel, Werner Georg, *Römer 7 und die Bekehrung des Paulus*, rep. in *Römer 7 und das Bild des Menschen im Neuen Testament*, TBü 53; Munich: Kaiser, 1974.

Kürzinger, Josef, "Der Schlüssel zum Verständnis von Röm 7," *BZ* nf 7 (1963), 270–74.

Kuhn, K. G., "New Light on Temptation, Sin, and Flesh in the New Testament," in *The Scrolls and the New Testament*, ed. Krister Stendahl; New York: Harper, 1957, 94–113.

Kuss, Otto, *Der Römerbrief*, 3 vols.; Regensburg: Pustet, 1959.

Lacey, D. R. de, "The Sabbath/Sunday Question and the Law in the Pauline Corpus," in *From Sabbath to Lord's Day*, ed. D. A. Carson; Grand Rapids: Zondervan, 1982, 159–95.

Ladd, George E., *A Theology of the New Testament*, Grand Rapids: Eerdmans, 1974.

Lane, William L., *Hebrews*, 2 vols.; WBC 47 a, b; Dallas: Word, 1991.

La Rondelle, Hans Karl, *Perfection and Perfectionism: A Dogmatic-Ethical Study of Biblical Perfection and Phenomenal Perfectionism*, Kampen: Kok, 1971.

Leenhardt, Franz J., *The Epistle to the Romans*, Cleveland: World, 1961.

Lenski, R. C. H., *The Interpretation of St. Paul's Epistle to the Romans*, Minneapolis: Augsburg, 1961.

– *The Interpretation of the Epistle to the Hebrews and the Epistle of James*, Minneapolis: Augsburg, 1961.

Levison, John Robert, *Portraits of Adam in Early Judaism: From Sirach to 2 Baruch*, JSPSup 1; Sheffield: Sheffield Academic Press, 1988.

Lietzmann, Hans, *Einführung in die Textgeschichte der Paulusbriefe: An die Römer*, HNT; Tübingen: Mohr, ⁴1933.

Lightfoot, J. B., *Notes on the Epistles of St. Paul*, Grand Rapids: Zondervan, rep. 1957.

Limbeck, Meinrad, *Die Ordnung des Heils: Untersuchungen zum Gesetzesverständnis des Frühjudentums*, KBANT; Düsseldorf: Patmos, 1971.

Lincoln, Andrew T., "Sabbath, Rest, and Eschatology in the New Testament," in *From Sabbath to Lord's Day: A Biblical, Historical, and Theological Investigation*, ed. D. A. Carson; Grand Rapids: Zondervan, 1982, 197–220.

Lombard, H. A., "The Adam-Christ 'Typology' in Romans 5:12–21," *Neot* 15 (1981), 69–100.

Longenecker, Bruce W., *Eschatology and the Covenant: A Comparison of 4 Ezra and Romans 1–11*, JSNTSup 57; Sheffield: Sheffield Academic Press, 1991.

Longenecker, Richard N., *Paul: Apostle of Liberty*, New York: Harper & Row, 1964.

– "The Obedience of Christ in the Theology of the Early Church," in *Reconciliation and Hope: New Testament Essays on Atonement and Eschatology Presented to L. L.*

Morris on His 60th Birthday, ed. Robert Banks; Grand Rapids: Eerdmans, 1974, 142–52.
- "The Nature of Paul's Early Eschatology," *NTS* 31 (1985), 85–95.
- *Galatians*, WBC 41; Dallas: Word, 1990.

Lührmann, Dieter, "Pistis im Judentum," *ZNW* 64 (1973), 19–38.
- *Glaube im Frühen Christentum*, Gütersloh: Gerd Mohn, 1976.

Lull, David John, "'The Law was Our Pedagogue:' A Study in Galatians 3:19–25," *JBL* 105 (1986), 481–98.

Lyonnet, S., "Le sens de ἐφ' ᾧ en Rom 5,12 et l'exégèse des Péres grecs," *Bib* 36 (1955), 436–56.
- "'Tu ne convoiteras pas' (Rom. vii 7)," in *Neotestamentica et Patristica: Eine Freundesgabe, Herrn Professor Dr. Oscar Cullmann zu seinem 60. Geburtstag Überreicht*, NovTSup 6; Leiden: Brill, 1962, 157–165.
- "L'histoire du salut selon le chapitre vii de l'Épître aux Romains," *Bib* 43 (1962), 117–51.

Lyons, George, *Pauline Autobiography*, SBLDS 73; Atlanta: Scholars Press, 1985.

MacKenzie, R. A. F., "The Meaning of the Susanna Story," *CJT* 3 (1957), 21–18.

McGrath, Alistair E., *Justification by Faith*, Grand Rapids: Zondervan, 1988.

McKnight, Scot, *A Light Among the Gentiles: Jewish Missionary Activity in the Second Temple Period*, Minneapolis: Fortress, 1991.
- "The Warning Passages of Hebrews: A Formal Analysis and Theological Conclusions," *TrinJ* ns 13 (1992), 21–59.

Maier, Gerhard, *Mensch und freier Wille: Nach den jüdischen Religionsparteien zwischen Ben Sira und Paulus*, WUNT 1/12; Tübingen: Mohr, 1971.

Marcus, Ralph, *Law in the Apocrypha*, CUOS 16; New York: AMS Press, 1966.

Marshall, I. Howard, *The Epistles of John*, NICNT; Grand Rapids: Eerdmans, 1978.

Martin, Brice L., "Some Reflections on the Identity of ἐγώ in Rom. 7:14–25," *SJT* 34 (1979), 39–47.

Martin, Ralph P., *Reconciliation: A Study of Paul's Theology*, NFTL; Atlanta: John Knox Press, 1981.

Mattern, Lieselotte, *Das Verständnis des Gerichtes bei Paulus*, ATANT 47; Zürich: Zwingli, 1966.

Meyer, B. F., "Many (= All) are Called, but Few (= Not All) are Chosen," *NTS* 36 (1990), 89–97.

Meyer, Paul W., "The Worm at the Core of the Apple: Exegetical Reflections on Romans 7," in *The Conversation Continues: Studies in Paul and John in Honor of J. Louis Martyn*, eds. Robert T. Fortna and Beverly R. Gaventa; Nashville: Abingdon, 1990, 62–84.

Michel, Otto, *Der Brief an die Römer*, MeyerK; Göttingen: Vandenhoeck & Ruprecht, [14]1978.

Milne, D. J. W., "Genesis 3 in the Letter to the Romans," *RTR* 39 (1980), 10–18.

Minear, Paul, *The Obedience of Faith: The Purposes of Paul in the Epistle to the Romans*, SBT 2/19; London: SCM, 1971.

Mitton, C. L., "Romans vii Reconsidered," *ExpT* 65 (1953–54), 78–81, 99–103, 132–35.

Montefiore, C. G. and Loewe, H., eds., *A Rabbinic Anthology*, New York: Schocken, rep. 1974.

Moo, Douglas J., "'Law,' 'Works of the Law,' and Legalism in Paul," *WTJ* 45 (1983), 73–100.
- *The Letter of James: Introduction and Commentary*, TNTC; Leicester: Inter-Varsity, 1985.
- "Israel and Paul in Romans 7.7–12," *NTS* 32 (1986), 122–35.
- *Romans 1–8*, WEC; Chicago: Moody, 1991.
Moore, Carey A., *Daniel, Esther and Jeremiah: The Additions*, AB 44; Garden City: Doubleday, 1977.
Moore, George Foote, *Judaism in the First Centuries of the Christian Era*, 3 vols.; Cambridge, Mass: Harvard University Press, rep. 1966.
Morris, Leon, *The Epistle to the Romans*, Grand Rapids/Leicester: Eerdmans/Inter-Varsity, 1988.
Motyer, Steve, "Righteousness by Faith in the New Testament," in *Here We Stand: Justification by Faith Today*, London: Hodder & Stoughton, 1986, 33–56.
Moule, C.F.D., "'Justification' in Its Relation to the Condition κατὰ πνεῦμα (Rom. 8:1–11)," in *Battesimo e Giustizia in Rom 6 e 8*, ed. Lorenzo De Lorenzi; SMB 2; Rome: Abbazia S. Paolo fuori le mura, 1974, 177–87.
- "Jesus, Judaism, and Paul," in *Tradition and Interpretation in the New Testament: Essays in Honor of E. Earl Ellis for his 60th Birthday*, eds. Gerald F. Hawthorne and Otto Betz; Grand Rapids: Eerdmans, 1987, 43–52.
Müller, Heinrich, "Der rabbinische Qal-Wachomer-Schluß in paulinischer Typologie: Zur Adam-Christus-Typologie in Rm 5," *ZNW* 58 (1967), 73–92.
Mundle, Wilhelm, *Der Glaubensbegriff des Paulus: Eine Untersuchung zur Dogmengeschichte des ältesten Christentums*, Darmstadt: Wissenschaftliche Buchgesellschaft, rep. 1977.
- "Hear, Obey," *NIDNTT* 2.172–80.
Murphy, Roland E., "Yeser in the Qumran Literature," *Bib* 39 (1958), 334–44.
Murray, John, *Redemption – Accomplished and Applied*, Grand Rapids: Eerdmans, 1955.
- *The Epistle to the Romans*, 2 vols.; NICNT; Grand Rapids: Eerdmans, 1959, 1965.
- *The Imputation of Adam's Sin*, Nutley, NJ: Presbyterian & Reformed, rep. 1977.
- "Definitive Sanctification," in *Collected Writings of John Murray*, 4 vols.; Edinburgh: Banner of Truth, 1977, 2.277–84.
Mußner, Franz, *Der Galaterbrief*, HTKNT 9; Freiburg: Herder, 1981.
Neusner, Jacob, *From Politics to Piety: The Emergence of Pharisaic Judaism*, Englewood Cliffs: Prentice-Hall, 1973.
Neyrey, Jerome H., *Paul, in Other Words: A Cultural Reading of His Letters*, Atlanta: John Knox Press, 1990.
Nickelsburg, George W.E., "Stories of Biblical and Early Post-Biblical Times," in *Jewish Writings of the Second Temple Period: Apocrypha, Pseudepigrapha, Qumran Sectarian Writings, Philo, Josephus*, ed. Michael E. Stone; CRINT; Philadelphia: Fortress, 1984, 33–87.
Nygren, Anders, *Commentary on Romans*, Philadelphia: Fortress, 1949.
O'Donovan, Oliver, *Resurrection and Moral Order: An Outline for Evangelical Ethics*, Leicester/Grand Rapids: Inter-Varsity/Eerdmans, 1986.
Oepke, Albrecht, "ἐν," *TDNT* 2.537–43.
- "καθίστημι," etc., *TDNT* 3.444–47.
Packer, J.I., "The 'Wretched Man' in Romans 7," in *Keep in Step with the Spirit*,

Tappan: Revell, 1984, 263–70 (= "The 'Wretched Man' of Romans 7," *SE* II [1964], 621–27).
Parke-Taylor, G. H., "A Note on 'εἰς ὑπακοήν πίστεως' in Romans i.5 and xvi.26," *ExpT* 55 (1943–44), 305–6.
Pathrapankal, J., *Metanoia, Faith, Covenant: A Study in Pauline Soteriology*, Bangalore: Dharmaram College, 1971.
Perry, Edmund, "The Meaning of '*emuna* in the Old Testament," *JBR* 21 (1953), 252–56.
Piper, John, *'Love Your Enemies': Jesus' Love Command in the Synoptic Gospels and the Early Christian Paraenesis*, SNTSMS 38; Cambridge: Cambridge University Press, 1979.
Pobee, John S., *Persecution and Martyrdom in the Theology of Paul*, JSNTSup 6; Sheffield: JSOT Press, 1985.
Porter, Stanley E., "The Pauline Concept of Original Sin, in Light of Rabbinic Background," *TynBul* 41 (1990), 3–30.
– "The Argument of Romans 5: Can a Rhetorical Question Make a Difference?," *JBL* 110 (1991), 655–77.
Prumm, Karl, *Die Botschaft des Römerbriefes: Ihr Aufbau und Gegenwartswert*, Freiburg: Herder, 1960.
Przybylski, Benno, *Righteousness in Matthew and His World of Thought*, SNTSMS 41; Cambridge: Cambridge University Press, 1980.
Quek, Swee-Hwa, "Adam and Christ According to Paul," in *Pauline Studies: Essays Presented to F. F. Bruce on His 70th Birthday*, eds. Donald A. Hagner and Murray J. Harris; Grand Rapids: Eerdmans, 1980, 67–79.
Rad, Gerhard von, *Genesis: A Commentary*, OTL; Philadelphia: Westminster, ²1972.
– "Faith Reckoned as Righteousness," in *The Problem of the Hexateuch and Other Essays*, London: SCM, rep. 1984, 125–30.
– and Foerster, Werner, "εἰρήνη," etc., *TDNT* 2.400–20.
Räisänen, Heikki, "Legalism and Salvation by the Law: Paul's Portrayal of the Jewish Religion as a Historical and Theological Problem," in *Die Paulinische Literatur und Theologie*, ed. S. Pedersen; Aarhus: Forlaget Aros, 1980, 63–83.
– *Paul and the Law*, WUNT 1/29; Tübingen: Mohr, 1983.
Renaud, B., "La Loi et les lois dans les livres des Maccabées," *RB* 68 (1961), 39–67.
Reumann, John, *Righteousness in the New Testament: "Justification" in the United States Lutheran-Roman Catholic Dialogue, with Responses by Joseph A. Fitzmeyer and Jerome D. Quinn*, Philadelphia: Fortress, 1982.
Ridderbos, Herman N., *Aan de Romeinen*, CNT; Kampen: Kok, 1959.
– *Paul: An Outline of His Theology*, Grand Rapids: Eerdmans, 1975.
– and Aalders, G. Ch. *Israël*, The Hague: Van Keulen, 1955.
Robertson, A. T., *A Grammar of the Greek New Testament in the Light of Historical Research*, Nashville: Broadman, 1934.
Robinson, J. A. T., *Wrestling with Romans*, London: SCM, 1979.
Roetzel, Calvin J., *Judgment in the Community: A Study of the Relationship Between Eschatology and Ecclesiology in Paul*, Leiden: Brill, 1972.
Russell, D. S., *The Method and Message of Jewish Apocalyptic*, Philadelphia: Westminster, 1964.
Saldarini, Anthony J., *Pharisees, Scribes and Sadducees in Palestinian Society*, Wilmington: Glazier, 1988.

Sanday, William and Headlam, A.C., *A Critical and Exegetical Commentary on the Epistle to the Romans*, ICC; Edinburgh: T. & T. Clark, 1895.
Sanders, E.P., *Paul and Palestinian Judaism: A Comparison of Patterns of Religion*, Philadelphia: Fortress, 1977.
– *Paul, the Law, and the Jewish People*, Philadelphia: Fortress, 1983.
– *Judaism: Practice and Belief 63BCE-66CE*, London/Philadelphia: SCM/Trinity Press International, 1992.
Schechter, Solomon, *Aspects of Rabbinic Theology*, New York: Schocken, 1961.
Schlatter, Adolf, *Gottes Gerechtigkeit: Ein Kommentar zum Römerbrief*, Stuttgart: Calwer, 1935.
Schlier, Heinrich, *Der Römerbrief*, HTKNT 6; Freiburg: Herder, 1977.
Schnabel, Eckhard J., *Law and Wisdom from Ben Sira to Paul: A Tradition-Historical Inquiry into the Relation of Law, Wisdom, and Ethics*, WUNT 2/16; Tübingen: Mohr, 1985.
Schnackenburg, Rudolf, "Römer 7 im Zusammenhang des Römerbriefes," in *Jesus und Paulus: Festschrift für Werner Georg Kümmel zum 70. Geburtstag*, eds. E. Earle Ellis and Erich Gräßer; Göttingen: Vandenhoeck & Ruprecht, 1975, 283–300.
Schoeps, H.J., *Paul: The Theology of the Apostle in the Light of Jewish Religious History*, Philadelphia: Westminster, 1961.
Schrage, Wilhelm, *The Ethics of the New Testament*, Philadelphia: Fortress, 1988.
Schreiner, Thomas R., "Is Perfect Obedience to the Law Possible? A Reexamination of Galatians 3:10," *JETS* 27 (1984), 151–60.
– "Paul and Perfect Obedience to the Law: An Evaluation of the View of E.P. Sanders," *WTJ* 47 (1985), 245–78.
– "'Works of Law' in Paul," *NovT* 33 (1991), 217–44.
– "Israel's Failure to Attain Righteousness in Romans 9:30–10:3," *TrinJ* ns 12 (1991), 209–20.
Schrenk, Gottlob, "δίκαιος," etc., *TDNT* 2.182–225.
– "ἱερός," etc. *TDNT* 3.221–83.
Schubert, Kurt, "The Sermon on the Mount and the Qumran Texts," in *The Scrolls and the New Testament*, ed. Krister Stendahl; New York: Harper, 1957, 118–28.
Scroggs, Robin, *The Last Adam: A Study in Pauline Anthropology*, Oxford: Blackwell, 1966.
Seebass, Horst, "Adam, Eve," *NIDNTT* 1.84–88.
Segal, Alan F., *Paul the Convert: The Apostolate and Apostasy of Saul the Pharisee*, New Haven: Yale University Press, 1990.
Shedd, William G.T., *A Critical and Doctrinal Commentary on the Epistle of St. Paul to the Romans*, Minneapolis: Klock & Klock, rep. 1978.
Siker, Jeffrey S., *Disinheriting the Jews: Abraham in Early Christian Controversy*, Louisville: Westminster/John Knox Press, 1991.
Silva, Moisés, "The Place of Historical Reconstruction in New Testament Criticism," in *Hermeneutics, Authority, and Canon*, eds. D.A. Carson and John Woodbridge; Grand Rapids: Zondervan, 1986, 109–33.
– "The Law and Christianity: Dunn's New Synthesis," *WTJ* 53 (1991), 339–53.
Skehan, Patrick and Di Lella, A.A., *The Wisdom of Ben Sira*, AB 39; Garden City: Doubleday, 1987.
Smalley, Stephen, *1, 2, 3 John*, WBC 51; Waco: Word, 1984.

Smeaton, George, *The Doctrine of the Holy Spirit*, Edinburgh: Banner of Truth, rep. 1958.

Snodgrass, Kline R., "Justification by Grace – to the Doers: an Analysis of the Place of Romans 2 in the Theology of Paul," *NTS* 32 (1986), 72–93.

Spicq, Ceslau, *Agapè dans le Nouveau Testament: Analyse des textes*, 3 vols.; Ebib; Paris: Gabalda, 1958–59.

Stendahl, Krister, *Paul Among Jews and Gentiles*, London: SCM, 1977.

Stern, Menahem, *Greek and Latin Authors on Jews and Judaism*, 3 vols.; Jerusalem: Israel Academy of Sciences and Humanities, 1976–83.

Stowers, Stanley, *The Diatribe and Paul's Letter to the Romans*, SBLDS 57; Chico: Scholars Press, 1981.

Stuart, Moses, *A Commentary on the Epistle to the Romans*, London: William Tegg, 1857.

Stuhlmacher, Peter, *Gottes Gerechtigkeit bei Paulus*, FRLANT 87; Göttingen: Vandenhoeck & Ruprecht, ²1966.

– "The Apostle Paul's View of Righteousness," in *Reconciliation, Law, and Righteousness: Essays in Biblical Theology*, Philadelphia: Fortress, 1986, 68–93.

Synofzik, Ernst, *Die Gerichts-und Vergeltungsaussagen bei Paulus*, GTA 8; Göttingen: Vandenhoeck & Ruprecht, 1977.

Tannehill, Robert, *Dying and Rising with Christ*, BZNW 32; Berlin: de Gruyter, 1967.

Theissen, Gerd, *Psychological Aspects of Pauline Theology*, Philadelphia: Fortress, 1987.

Thüsing, Wilhelm, *Per Christum in Deum: Studien zum Verhältnis von Christozentrik und Theozentrik in den paulinischen Hauptbriefen*, NTAbh 1; Münster: Aschendorff, 1965.

Thyen, Hartmut, *Studien zum Sündenvergebung im Neuen Testament und seinen alttestamentlichen und jüdischen Voraussetzungen*, FRLANT 96; Göttingen: Vandenhoeck & Ruprecht, 1970.

Turner, Nigel, *A Grammar of New Testament Greek. Volume III: Syntax*, Edinburgh: T. & T. Clark, 1963.

Urbach, Ephraim, *The Sages: Their Concepts and Beliefs*, Cambridge, Mass: Harvard University Press, 1987.

Vermes, Geza, *The Dead Sea Scrolls in English*, Harmondsworth: Penguin, ²1975.

Versteeg, J.P., *Is Adam a "Teaching Model" in the New Testament?*, Nutley, NJ: Presbyterian & Reformed, 1977.

Watson, Francis, *Paul, Judaism and the Gentiles*, SNTSMS 56; Cambridge: Cambridge University Press, 1986, 119–22.

Watson, Nigel M., "Justified by Faith, Judged by Works – an Antinomy?," *NTS* 29 (1983), 209–21.

Wedderburn, A.J.M., "The Theological Structure of Romans V.12," *NTS* 19 (1972–73), 339–54.

– "Adam in Paul's Letter to the Romans," in *Studia Biblica 1978. III. Papers on Paul and Other New Testament Authors*, ed. Elizabeth A. Livingston; JSNTSup 3; Sheffield: JSOT Press, 1980, 413–30.

Weiser, Artur and Bultmann, Rudolf, "πιστεύω," etc., *TDNT* 6.174–228.

Wenham, David, "The Christian Life: A Life of Tension? – A Consideration of the Nature of Christian Experience in Paul," in *Pauline Studies: Essays Presented to*

Professor F. F. Bruce on His 70th Birthday, eds. Donald A. Hagner and Murray J. Harris; London/Grand Rapids: Paternoster/Eerdmans, 1980, 80–94.

Westerholm, Stephen, *Israel's Law and the Church's Faith: Paul and His Recent Interpreters*, Grand Rapids: Eerdmans, 1988.

Wilckens, Ulrich, *Der Brief an die Römer*, 3 vols.; EKK 6; Zürich/Neukirchen: Benziger/Neukirchener, 1978–82.

Williams, Sam K., "The 'Righteousness of God' in Romans," *JBL* 99 (1980), 241–90.

Wright, Nicholas Thomas, "The Messiah and the People of God: A Study in Pauline Theology with Particular Reference to the Argument of the Epistle to the Romans," D. Phil. thesis, Oxford University, 1980.

– "Justification: The Biblical Basis and its Relevance for Contemporary Evangelicalism," in *The Great Acquittal*, ed. G. Reed; London: Collins, 1980, 13–37.

– "Adam in Pauline Christology," SBLSP 1983, ed. K. H. Richards; Chico: Scholars Press, 1983, 359–89.

– "Righteousness," *NDT*, 590–92.

– *The Climax of the Covenant: Christ and the Law in Pauline Theology*, Minneapolis: Fortress, 1991.

Young, F. W., "Obedience," *IDB* 3.580–81.

Zeller, Dieter, *Der Brief an die Römer*; RNT; Regensburg: Pustet, 1985.

Zerwick, Maximilian, *Biblical Greek: Illustrated by Examples*, Rome: Scripta Pontificii Instituti Biblici, ^{4}1963.

Ziesler, J. A., *The Meaning of Righteousness in Paul: A Linguistic and Theological Enquiry*, SNTSMS 20; Cambridge: Cambridge University Press, 1972.

– "The Role of the Tenth Commandment in Romans 7," *JSNT* 33 (1988), 41–56.

Index of Passages

I. Old Testament

Genesis
1–3	34, 145
1–2	57, 73
1:2	86 n. 59
1:28	57, 101
2:1–3	57
2:7	86 n. 59, 117, 118
2:17	139 n. 137
3	23, 77 n. 15, 90, 114
3:12	93
3:13	117
3:15	23
4:9–10	128 n. 83
12	50 n. 30
12:1–9	50
15	50, 50 n. 30
15:6	49, 50, 50 nn. 31, 33, 69 n. 123
22	50 n. 30, 69 n. 123
49:10	12

Exodus
20:17	118
21–23	36 n. 19
24:8	54 n. 52
31:12	54 n. 52

Leviticus
18:5	36 n. 18, 70, 141, 150, 156
19:18	67

Numbers
6:22–26	75
24:17–24	12

Deuteronomy
4:1	59 n. 76
4:5–6	59 n. 76
5:21	118
6:4	59
7:25–26	33
13	92
30	127
30:1–10	127
30:11–20	36 n. 18
30:11–14	59 n. 76
30:15	23, 97, 127, 156
32:4–5	39
32:15–18	39
32:21	39
32:35	67
33:32 (LXX)	108 n. 145

Judges
5:27 (A)	138 n. 127

1 Kings
21:20	124, 124 n. 69
21:25	124

Ezra
9:6–15	125 n. 74, 137

Nehemiah
9:6–37	125 n. 74, 137
9:33	52 n. 42

Job
40:10	56

Psalms
2:8–9	12
8:5	56, 101, 114
9:8	52, 152
32:6	104 n. 123
35:27–28	46 n. 9, 152
44	125 n. 74, 137
44:22	157
51:5	89, 90

62:12	56, 70	51:5–6	46 n. 9, 152
68:18	108 n. 145	53	26, 106 n. 133
69:9	25	53:9	25, 93
72:1–4	46 n. 9, 152	53:10b-11	46 n. 9, 152
78:32	91	53:11	100 n. 111, 106 n. 133
83:8 (LXX)	145 n. 5	57:19	75
85:11–13	46 n. 9, 152	61:1–2	46 n. 9, 152
95:8–11	57 n. 68	61:10	19 n. 50,
96:13	46 n. 9, 52, 152	61:11	46 n. 9, 152
97:2 (LXX)	152	65:1–16	39
97:9 (LXX)	152	65:1–2	39
98:2–3	152	65:2	52 n. 43
98:2	46 n. 9, 52, 52 n. 41, 152	65:5	52 n. 43
98:9	52, 52 n. 41, 152		
106 (LXX 105):20	35, 83	Jeremiah	
119	126		127
119:7–14	126	2:11	35, 83
119:16	126	18:1–11	45 n. 4
119:24	126	23:5–6	46 n. 9, 152
119:47	126	31	127
119:70	126	31:31–34	140 n. 140
119:77	126	31:33	126, 128, 148
119:111	126	36:26	126
119:127	126		
119:143	126	Ezekiel	
119:159	126		127
119:165	126	36–37	127
119:167	126	36:22–32	140 n. 140
119:174	126	37	140
136:8	138 n. 127	37:1–14	73 n. 3
		37:26	75
Proverbs		Daniel	
24:12	56	9:3–19	125 n. 74, 137
28:13	93	12:2	57, 100 n. 111
Isaiah		Hosea	
7:15	97	6:1–2	73
9:6–7	75		
9:6	75	Joel	
9:7	46 n. 9, 152	2:28–29	77, 148
11:1–2	46 n. 9, 152		
26:19	73 n. 3	Habakkuk	
29:16	45 n. 4	2:4	49, 49 n. 28, 73, 147
32	75, 102, 151		n. 16, 152
32:1	75	2:5–17	49 n. 27, 147 n. 16
32:15–18	156	2:18–19	49 n. 27, 147 n. 16
32:17–18	75, 75 n. 11		
32:15	75, 77	Haggai	
33:1	138 n. 127	2:9	75
45:8	46 n. 9, 152		
45:9	45 n. 4	Malachi	
45:22–25	46 n. 9, 152	4:2	46 n. 9, 152
50:8–9	76, 133 n. 103		

II. Jewish Literature

A. Apocrypha and Pseudepigrapha

Additions to Esther

	54 n. 51
11:11	42 n. 45
14:6–7	52 n. 42

2 Apocalypse of Baruch

41–42	88 n. 66
48:22	38 n. 24
54:14	88
54:15–16	88 n. 66
54:15	84 n. 46, 88 n. 66
54:17–18	88 n. 66
54:19	87 n. 66
54:22	91

Baruch

1:15–3:8	125 n. 74, 137
2:27–35	127 n. 78
2:31	127 n. 78
2:35	127 n. 78
3:9	41, 107, 120 n. 47, 141
3:14	41, 141
4:1–4	36 n. 18
4:1	36, 40, 41, 63 n. 99, 95, 107, 120 n. 47, 141
4:3–4	58

Bel and the Dragon

5	145 n. 7

1 Enoch

	157
91–107	104 n. 123

Epistle of Aristeas

139–42 (43)	41, 42 n. 47, 54 n. 51, 62

1 Esdras

8:74–90	125 n. 74, 137
8:78	152 n. 35

4 Ezra

3:7–11	88 n. 69
3:20–27	88 n. 69
3:33–36	36
4:30	88 n. 69
7:37	36
7:116–26	137 n. 124
7:118	88 n. 69
7:129	107
9:26–37	107
14:30	107, 120 n. 47, 141

Jubilees

1:22–25	127 n. 78
15:25	54 n. 52
15:28–29	54 n. 52
16:29	95 n. 93, 107
21:3	145 n. 7
22:16	54 n. 51, 67 n. 114, 96
31:32	95 n. 93, 107
32:10	95 n. 93, 107
32:15	95 n. 93, 107
32:21–26	95 n. 93, 107
32:28	95 n. 93, 107
33:10	95 n. 93, 107
39:7	95 n. 93

Judith

	54 n. 51
10:8	42 n. 45
13:4	42 n. 45
14:10	6, 42
16:17	66 n. 110

1 Maccabees

1:15	92
2:19–70	65
2:23–28	66 n. 108
2:50	66 n. 108
2:54	66 n. 108
2:58	66 n. 108
2:59	38 n. 24
2:61	38 n. 24
2:64	38 n. 24
2:67	59 n. 76, 71 n. 134
13:48	59 n. 76

2 Maccabees

	37 n. 22
1:3	61
2:39	32 n. 2
2:42	32 n. 2
4:47	138 n. 127
6:18–20	57
7	41, 57
7:1	57
7:9	56, 57
9:2	32 n. 2

3 Maccabees

	37 n. 22
3:4	54 n. 51
5:5	138 n. 127
5:22	138 n. 127
5:47	138 n. 127

4 Maccabees

	37 n. 22, 57
1:15	88 n. 66, 129 n. 86
5:14–38	57
5:24	145 n. 7
15:3	57
16:7	138 n. 127
17:11–12	56
17:12	56
18:12	66 n. 108

Prayer of Azariah

	125 n. 74, 137
4–5	52 n. 42
8–9	52 n. 42

Prayer of Manasseh

7	137 n. 124
8	92, 137 n. 124
13	137 n. 124
14	137 n. 124

Psalms of Solomon

1:3	61
1:7	61
1:8	33
2:14–15	61
3:7–8	61
3:12	61
4:1–8	104 n. 123
4:5	61
4:8	61
8:9	61
8:11	33
9:3–5	56
9:7	88 n. 66, 129 n. 86
14:2	107, 120 n. 47, 141
17:21–27	67 n. 114, 96
17:28	54 n. 51
17:36	92

Sibylline Oracles

3:70	59 n. 76
3:763	145 n. 7

Sirach

1:15	36, 43, 54
1:26	88 n. 66, 129 n. 86
2:1–6	91
4:15–16	90, 91
4:17–19	91
4:26	91
10:19	35, 36, 82, 96
12:6	95
15:15	88 n. 66, 90, 91, 129 n. 86
15:15a	129 n. 86
16:24–28	36
16:29–30	36
17	35, 36
17:1–17	82
17:1–10	36
17:11–12	36
17:11	36, 107, 120 n. 47, 141
17:14	36 n. 19
17:15	36
17:17	36
21:11	88 n. 66, 129 n. 86
23:10	95
24:9	63 n. 99, 95, 107
24:11	95
24:22	90, 91
24:23	36 n. 19
24:33	63 n. 99, 107
28:7	36 n. 19
32:24–33:3	39 n. 24
36:1–10	95
39:1–8	36 n. 19
42:2	36 n. 19
42:5	36 n. 19
44:20	95
45:5	36 n. 18, 107, 120 n. 47, 141
45:23–24	66 n. 108
50:22	42 n. 45

Susanna

35	61
36	61

Testament of Asher

1	88 n. 66, 129 n. 86
4:5	66 n. 108

Testament of Judah

24:1	92

Testament of Levi

14:5	33

Testament of Moses

7	104 n. 123
9	41
32:2	84 n. 46

Testament of Naphtali

3:1–2	63 n. 99, 95, 107

Tobit

3:1–6	125 n. 74, 137
3:2	52 n. 42
4:5	88 n. 66, 129 n. 86
4:9–11	56
7:7	138 n. 127
14:7	42 n. 45

Wisdom of Solomon

2:14	84
2:23	56
3:8	42 n. 45
3:11	138
13:10	138
14:29–31	91
15:2	91
15:3	91
18:4	40, 63 n. 99, 95, 107
18:8	42 n. 45
19:22	42 n. 45

B. Dead Sea Scrolls

	54 n. 51, 125 n. 73

CD

3:3	88 n. 66, 129 n. 86
6:16	33
20:27–34	49 n. 28
20:28–30	125 n. 74, 137

1QH

	61 n. 89
1:21–27	125 n. 73, 137
2:13–19	13 n. 18
4:29–33	125 n. 73, 137
4:30–33	46 n. 9
7:16–18	125 n. 73, 137
7:30–31	46 n. 9
12:11–12	125 n. 73
12:24–31	125 n. 73, 137
13:13–16	125 n. 73, 137
13:17	46 n. 9
13:19	125 n. 73
14:13	125 n. 73
14:14	66 n. 108
15:12–25	46 n. 9
16:9	125 n. 73
16:29–33	125 n. 73

1QpHab

	13 n. 18
7:11	71 n. 134
8:1–3	49 n. 28
8:1	71 n. 134
12:4	71 n. 134

1QM

13:3–5	66 n. 110

4Qp Ps

	13 n. 18

1QS

1:4–11	66 n. 110
1:24b-2:1	125 n. 74, 137
1:26	52 n. 42
4:1	66 n. 108
4:4	66 n. 108
4:7	57
6:11–13	100 n. 111
9:22	66
9:23	66 n. 108
11:1–3	46 n. 9
11:5	46 n. 9
11:9–10	125 n. 73, 137
11:11–12	46 n. 9
11:13–15	46 n. 9
11:14	48

C. Josephus

Antiquities

1.204	138 n. 128
4.8.10 (207)	33 n. 6
5.107	59 n. 76
5.132	59 n. 76
9.226	138 n. 128
10.157	138 n. 128
11.1	138 n. 128
14.61	138 n. 128
17.41	140 n. 142
20.44	59 n. 76

Jewish War

1.110	140 n. 142
2.295	138 n. 128
6.194	138 n. 128

Against Apion
1.249	33 n. 6
1.310–11	33 n. 6
1.318–19	33 n. 6
2.37 (271–72)	66
2.41 (292)	66
2.169–75	54 n. 51

D. Philo

De Confusione Linguarum
163	38 n. 25

De Congressu quaerendae
70	59 n. 76
174	138 n. 129

De Legatione ad Gaium
274	138 n. 129

De Mutatione Nomimum
189	138 n. 129

De Praemiis et Poenis
79	54 n. 51

De Specialibus Legibus
2.13	38 n. 25
2.253	66
4.87	38 n. 25

De Vita Mosis
1.278	54 n. 51

E. Rabbinic

Sabbat
15:17	107, 141

Sanhedrin
10:1	58 n. 73

Genesis Rabbah
14:6	36 n. 19, 82

Numbers Rabbah
21:3	66 n. 109

Deuteronomy Rabbah
9 (206 a)	84 n. 46

Kiddushin
4:4	95

Makkot
23b	49 n. 27

Pirke Aboth
1:1	43, 54

III. Greco-Roman Literature

Epictetus, *Discourses*
2.26.4	138 n. 131

Ovid, *Metamorphoses*
7.21	138 n. 131

IV. New Testament

Matthew
5:21–30	38 n. 25
10:32–33	148
12:36–37	44 n. 1
16:27	44 n. 1
20:1–6	7
25:31–46	44 n. 1

Mark
8:38	148
10:45	100 n. 111

Luke
1:6	140 n. 142
9:26	148
12:8–9	148

John
1:17	99
3:36	16, 20

Acts
2:17–18	148
7:38	108 n. 145

7:39–53	55	1:18	52 n. 41, 81, 97
10:34–35	53	1:21	90 n. 76
10:45	64 n. 103	1:23	35, 56, 83
13:45	40	1:25	127, 148
14:17	52 n. 43	1:28	86
15:5	64 n. 103	1:32	97, 102 n. 115
17:2	54 n. 50	2	3, 27 n. 75, 37, 44 n. 1, 47 n. 14, 58 n. 74, 59 n. 79, 60, 68, 68 n. 117, 147
17:17	54 n. 50		
17:26	81		
18:4	54 n. 50	2:1–3:8	51, 52, 68 n. 121
18:19	54 n. 50	2:1–16	37, 52, 114
19:8	54 n. 50	2:1–5	52, 56
19:9	54 n. 50	2:1–3	53
19:37	33 n. 6	2:1	37, 51, 52, 52 n. 45
		2:2	52, 52 n. 45, 55, 114, 149
Romans		2:3	37, 52
1–11	64, 155 n. 52	2:4	52
1–8	19	2:6–3:8	58
1–4	79	2:6–16	52, 52 n. 45
1	27 n. 75, 59 n. 79	2:6–12	56
1:1–3:8	45–55	2:6–9	37
1:1–7	11, 45	2:6	52 n. 45, 56
1:1–4	12	2:7–10	97, 100, 150
1:1–3a	69	2:7	1, 53, 56, 57, 57 n. 69, 67, 68, 71 n. 135, 73, 102, 114, 127, 147, 156
1:1	11		
1:2–4	11		
1:2	12 n. 13	2:8	19 n. 50, 29, 57, 65, 156
1:4	131 n. 91, 154	2:9–16	52 n. 45
1:5–7	6	2:9–10	156
1:5–6	20	2:9	57, 127
1:5	2, 5, 10–31, 45, 146, 146 n. 10, 104, 114, 156	2:10–11	53
		2:10	53, 57, 127, 148 n. 20
1:6–7	12	2:11	11, 52 n. 45, 58, 114
1:6	12, 20	2:12–16	53, 54, 58, 81
1:7	12	2:12	89, 90 n. 74
1:8	16, 24, 20, 144	2:13	1, 2, 4, 29, 44, 49, 51 n. 34, 52, 55, 56–60, 62, 70, 70 n. 129, 71, 72, 107, 114, 148 n. 20, 156
1:10–15	20		
1:11–12	29 n. 80		
1:11	28		
1:12	29	2:14–16	59 n. 79, 137
1:13	20	2:14–15	97, 114, 147
1:16–17	11, 20 n. 54, 24, 45, 46 n. 10, 53, 114	2:14	58, 59, 59 n. 79
		2:15	58, 59, 127
1:16	45 n. 4	2:16	69
1:17	19, 46 n. 11, 49, 59 n. 76, 73, 145, 146, 146 n. 10, 152	2:17–3:8	38, 53
		2:17–29	37
		2:17–24	29, 52, 53
1:18–3:20	56, 89	2:17–20	32
1:18–2:29	68 n. 122	2:17	8, 37, 38, 41, 52, 54, 79
1:18–32	29, 34, 35, 37, 38, 51, 59 n. 79, 81, 94, 102, 114, 119, 145, 147	2:21–22	34, 38
		2:22	2, 32, 34, 37, 43, 54, 97, 145, 149
1:18–23	97	2:23–27	38

Index of Passages

2:23	8, 38, 41, 54, 56, 79		n. 24, 80, 85, 86 n. 59, 88, 89, 94, 106, 107, 108, 114, 115, 122
2:25–29	29, 54		
2:26	102 n. 115		
2:28–29	38	5:1–11	73, 74, 74 n. 6, 75, 79, 79 n. 24, 80, 81, 83, 94, 100, 106, 132
2:29	110, 147		
3	47 n. 14		
3:1–8	45 n. 4, 54, 54 n. 54	5:1–5	68
3:2	43	5:1–2	75–77, 78
3:3	29, 54	5:1–2a	75 n. 10
3:8	37	5:1	48, 73, 75, 75 n. 11, 76, 102, 156
3:9	89, 94, 123 n. 64		
3:19–20	41, 107	5:2	41, 79
3:20	116	5:2b	75 n. 10
3:21–4:25	49	5:3–10	75, 77–78
3:21–4:5	74, 75 n. 11	5:3–5	75 n. 10, 77, 163
3:21–31	77 n. 18	5:4	68
3:21–22	47	5:5	68, 69, 75, 76, 148
3:21	13 n. 14, 19, 20 n. 54, 46, 59, 70 n. 129, 73, 77, 99	5:6–11	75 n. 10
		5:6–10	77, 102
3:22	19 n. 48, 46 n. 12, 153	5:9–10	48, 78, 78 n. 21, 80, 99, 103
3:23	51, 76, 81, 89, 90 n. 74, 94, 96, 114, 119, 153		
		5:9	13 n. 14, 48, 163
3:24–26	154	5:10	73, 78 n. 21
3:24	59, 59 n. 79, 77, 94, 99	5:11	75, 78–79
3:25–26	43	5:12–8:39	79
3:26	45, 153	5:12–6:23	57
3:27	54	5:12–21	26, 67, 76, 79–108, 113 n. 17, 115
4	7, 46 n. 10, 50, 81		
4:1	51	5:12–19	19, 23, 34, 35, 36, 37, 38, 53, 69, 70, 73, 79, 82, 94, 97, 98, 123, 132, 139 n. 137, 145, 150
4:3–12	49		
4:3	50 n. 33		
4:4–5	6, 7 n. 15, 99		
4:4	6	5:12–14	99
4:5	7 n. 15, 50 n. 33	5:12–13	100
4:6	51 n. 33	5:12	79, 80, 84, 86, 87 n. 61, 88, 89, 90 n. 74, 91, 94, 95, 97, 98, 101, 108, 114, 115 n. 28, 119, 139 n. 137
4:9–17a	50		
4:9–12	6		
4:9	50 n. 33		
4:10	50 n. 33	5:12a-c	85
4:11	51 n. 33	5:12d	84
4:12	50	5:13–14	95, 96
4:13–15	108 n. 142	5:13a	96
4:15	41, 107, 116	5:14	87 n. 63, 94, 96, 100, 108
4:15b	95	5:15–17	71, 98, 99, 102, 148, 157
4:17–21	73	5:15–16	101
4:17b	51	5:15	99 n. 107, 100 n. 111, 101, 148 n. 22
4:18–22	75 n. 11		
4:25	78 n. 21, 154	5:15a	98
5–8	2, 19, 46 n. 10, 72–74, 82, 86, 87, 113, 113 n. 18, 114–15, 115 n. 28, 132, 135, 142 n. 150	5:15b	98
		5:16	99 n. 107, 100, 102
		5:16a	98
		5:16b	98
5	2, 3, 72, 74 nn. 6, 7, 79	5:17	87 n. 61, 99, 99 n. 107,

Index of Passages

	100, 101, 102, 104, 106, 139 n. 134, 151		n. 10, 115 n. 28, 121, 122 n. 56, 124 n. 69, 125 nn. 71, 73, 129 n. 84, 130, 131 n. 93, 135, 136, 137, 137 nn. 122, 123, 140 nn. 140, 142, 141, 142 n. 151, 143 n. 156, 162, 163
5:17b	103		
5:18–19	84, 88, 98, 101, 102		
5:18	79, 98, 100 n. 111, 101, 102, 103, 132, 150		
5:19	19 n. 50, 49, 100 n. 111, 101, 103, 104, 106, 151, 156	7:1–13	41
5:20–21	107	7:1–6	116, 133, 137, 142 n. 150
5:20	41, 87, 107, 116	7:4–6	123
5:21	81 n. 30, 87 n. 61, 108	7:5–6	116
6–8	11, 74 n. 7, 111 n. 3, 115 n. 28, 121, 123, 137, 139	7:5	116, 120 n. 47
		7:6	13 n. 14, 54, 73, 110, 116
6–7	115, 120	7:7–8:39	72, 115
6	35, 73, 87, 116, 122, 123, 133, 134 n. 104, 143 n. 156	7:7–23	113 n. 18, 121
		7:7–13	116 n. 31, 117 n. 38, 119, 120, 121, 122, 122 n. 56
6:1–8:17	114	7:7–12	73, 116, 118, 119, 133, 140
6:1–7:6	72, 73, 115, 149		
6:1–14	116	7:7–11	83, 123
6:1–11	123, 156	7:7–8	118
6:1–3	34, 145	7:7	116, 120, 120 n. 47, 121, 121 n. 55
6:2–4	137		
6:2	162	7:8–13	122
6:4–10	126, 163	7:8	87, 117, 118
6:5–11	87, 134 n. 110	7:10	120 n. 47
6:6	139	7:11	23 n. 64, 84 n. 46, 87
6:7	48	7:12	128
6:11	102	7:13–25	73, 116, 118 n. 40, 119–143
6:12–23	137		
6:12	19 n. 50, 139	7:13–20	97
6:13	87, 102, 130, 131	7:13–15	128 n. 83
6:15–7:6	116	7:13	119, 119 n. 45, 120, 121
6:15–23	109	7:14–25	2, 72, 77, 87, 110–143, 150, 161, 163
6:15–18	123		
6:16–19	123	7:14–23	121
6:16–17	87	7:14–20	120–35
6:16	19 n. 50, 102, 103, 117 n. 38, 142 n. 153, 145, 146, 146 n. 9	7:14	120, 120 n. 47, 121, 126, 128
		7:14b	137
6:17–18	124	7:15–20	126, 126 n. 76
6:17	14, 19, 19 n. 50, 22, 25, 69, 142 n. 153, 145	7:15	126
		7:15a	120, 128, 128 n. 83
6:18	48, 102, 142 n. 153	7:15b	120, 128
6:19	102, 130	7:16–17	120
6:20	142 n. 153	7:16	119 n. 45, 126
6:21	73, 87	7:17	13 n. 14, 125 n. 69, 127
6:22–23	71, 107	7:18	130, 131, 132, 139
6:22	102, 123, 142 n. 153	7:18a	120
6:23	87, 102, 123, 148 n. 22, 157	7:18b	120
		7:19	120, 127, 130
7	3, 110, 111, 112, 112	7:20	120, 162

Index of Passages

7:21–25	120, 136–43	8:30	158, 160, 161
7:21	127, 136	8:31–39	76, 157
7:22	127, 130, 136	8:31–35	139 n. 138
7:23	119, 130, 136, 137, 139	8:33–34	157
7:24–25a	138	8:33	76, 133 n. 103, 156
7:24	112, 113, 128, 134, 135, 138, 139 nn. 137, 139, 140, 141 n. 149	8:36	157
		8:37	163
		9–11	12, 45 n. 4, 115
7:24b	135, 142	9:4–5	39
7:25	126, 128, 130, 133 n. 103, 136, 138 n. 132, 142 n. 153, 143 n. 158	9:5	131 n. 91,
		9:16	7 n. 15
		9:20–21	45 n. 4
7:25a	135, 142 n. 149	9:25	39
7:25b-8:1	133 n. 102	9:30–10:13	62
7:25b	128, 142	9:30b	10 n. 6
8	73, 74 n. 6, 111, 115 n. 28, 122, 125 nn. 71, 73, 133, 134 n. 104, 135 n. 113, 140 n. 140, 143 n. 156	10:2–3	7 n. 15
		10:2	41
		10:3	14, 16, 47, 52 n. 41, 62
		10:4	62, 108, 140
		10:5	59 n. 76
8:1–17	133, 137, 143, 143 n. 157, 149	10:6–10	127
		10:9–13	63
8:1–11	143 n. 157	10:12	11, 114
8:1	2, 69, 73, 133 n. 103, 143	10:14–21	62, 63
8:1–4	140 n. 140	10:14–17	63
8:2–14	151	10:16	14, 20, 29, 30
8:2	109, 136 n. 115	10:16a	16
8:3	97, 148 n. 20	10:16b	16
8:5	128 n. 82	10:17	63
8:6–7	130	10:18	63
8:6	128, 156	10:19–20	39, 145
8:7	128, 128 n. 82	10:19	39
8:9	70	10:21	16, 20, 29, 52 n. 43
8:10	130, 132, 139, 139 n. 137	11:6	7 n. 15
8:11	132	11:7–9	88 n. 66
8:12–17	157	11:11–16	39
8:13	130	11:12	28
8:17	143	11:14	131 n. 91
8:18–39	114	11:23	16, 20, 30
8:18–27	143	11:25	88 n. 66
8:18–25	72, 76, 77, 115, 133, 143, 150, 163	11:26	28
		11:30–31	29
8:18–24	80	11:30	16, 20, 30
8:18–21	161	11:31	16, 30
8:18	76	11:33–36	157 n. 60
8:19	132, 161	12–16	11, 134 n. 104
8:23–24	157	12–15	64
8:23	123, 132, 133 n. 103, 135, 139 n. 139, 142	12	155 n. 52
		12:1–2	27, 27 n. 75, 143 n. 158
8:24–25	76	12:1	25, 27, 130
8:24	142	12:2	27, 151
8:29–30	160	12:3	27 n. 73
8:29	98, 135, 155	12:9	67, 127

Index of Passages 189

12:19	67	16:19a	16, 23
12:19a	67	19:19b	23
12:21	65, 127	16:20a	23
13:6–7	65	16:25	12, 13
13:8–10	65	16:26	2, 2 n. 1, 10, 10 n. 1, 12,
13:8	65		13, 13 n. 14, 25, 30, 104,
13:8b	65		156
13:10b	65		
13:14	151	**1 Corinthians**	
14–15	65		
14:1–15:13	23	1:2	162
14:1–15:7	25	1:10–17	22
14:1	25	2:13	86, 86 n. 55
14:2–4	41	2:15	122 n. 60
14:9	31	3:1	125 n. 70
14:10	70 n. 129	4:3–5	148 n. 20
14:23	149	6:1	48 n. 22
15	26, 28	6:9–10	48
15:2	97	6:9	48 n. 22
15:3	25, 26	6:11	48, 153, 158
15:5–6	25	7:7	118 n. 39
15:5	25	7:19	41
15:5a	26	7:26	143
15:7–13	28 n. 78	9:21	41
15:7	25, 26	9:24–27	44 n. 1
15:8–13	26	10:6–7	23, 97
15:8	26, 28	10:11	73
15:9–12	12, 26	14:34	19 n. 50
15:7–12	6	15:10	27
15:13	26	15:18–19	89 n. 72
15:14–21	28, 28 n. 78	15:18	11 n. 9
15:14–16	28	15:21	88 n. 72
15:14	26	15:22	80, 106
15:15b-16	26	15:42–57	151
15:15	27 n. 73	15:44–46	131
15:16	27	15:44	86, 139
15:17–21	27, 28, 28 n. 78	15:45–47	99
15:17	22, 22 n. 62, 27	15:45	86, 86 n. 59
15:18c-19	27	15:49	86
15:18	16, 25, 25 n. 69, 27, 28,	15:57	139
	29, 30		
15:19	27	**2 Corinthians**	
15:20	20		161
15:22–33	28	1:22	70
15:22–29	28	1:24	149
15:22	70	2:9	19 n. 50
15:29	28	3	41, 110
15:30–33	29	3:6–7	41
15:31	16, 20, 29	3:7	108
16:17–20	22, 26	3:9	108
16:17	26, 65	3:18	145 n. 5
16:18	23, 100, 117 n. 36	4:6	40 n. 30
16:19	16, 20, 24, 26, 97, 100,	4:16	130, 130 n. 90
	127, 144	5:5	70

5:10	44, 70 n. 129	3:22	116
5:16–21	75	3:23–25	40, 43
5:17–19	79	3:23	14 n. 23
5:17	41, 43, 73, 80	3:24	63
5:18	71	3:25	62
5:19–20	106	3:27	151
5:21	63, 70, 71, 106, 120, 150 n. 30, 153	4:3	40, 41, 54 n. 54, 134
6:2	123	4:4	37, 150
7:1	130, 131	4:8–11	54 n. 54
7:15	19 n. 50	4:8–9	39, 40, 145
9:8	68	4:9	41, 134
10:5	19 n. 50, 145, 145 n. 5	4:10	41
10:6	19 n. 50, 22	5–6	64
10:15	155	5	128 n. 84
11:3–4	100	5:3	6
11:3	23, 84 n. 46	5:5	51 n. 34, 99
11:13–15	100	5:6	41, 64, 65, 68
11:13	117 n. 36	5:10	148, 148 n. 20
11:14–15	23	5:12	64 n. 103
12:10	135	5:14–15	65
13:4	111	5:14	64
13:5	149	5:15	64
13:17	54	5:16–26	134
		5:16–24	133
Galatians		5:16	129 n. 84
		5:17	14, 128, 128 n. 84, 129 n. 84, 134
1:4	2, 35, 72, 124		
1:13–14	41, 66	5:18	135
1:14	37, 40 n. 30, 42, 116	5:19–21	65
1:23	66 n. 112	5:20	22, 64, 65
2:4	64	5:22	148
2:5	41	5:24	134
2:14	41	5:25	64
2:15–21	48	5:26	64
2:15	42 n. 47	6:1–2	64, 65
2:16–17	48	6:2	41
2:16	8 n. 20	6:11–18	69 n. 124
2:17	42 n. 47	6:13	8
2:18	43	6:14	8, 41
2:19–20	48, 113 n. 25	6:15	41, 64
2:19	161		
2:20	134	Ephesians	
2:21	48	1:13	148
3–4	39, 40	1:14	70
3	46 n. 10, 50	2:1–7	126
3:1–5	50	2:1–3	145, 109
3:2	62	2:8–10	71, 148
3:6–9	49, 50	2:12–13	13 n. 14
3:9	114, 149	2:14	47
3:10	8 n. 20	3:16	130 n. 90
3:19	107, 108 n. 145	4:17–20	145
3:21–25	108	4:20–24	155
3:21	40	4:22	151

Index of Passages

6:1	19 n. 50	2:3	68, 93 n. 86, 107, 117 n. 36
6:5	19 n. 50	2:8	40
Philippians		2:17	68
2:1–16	150	3:5	68
2:5–11	104 n. 123	3:14	14
2:8	70 n. 130, 104	1 Timothy	
2:12–13	70 n. 130, 153 n. 39	2:5	150
2:12	19 n. 50		
2:13	148	2 Timothy	
3	141	2:13–14	84 n. 46
3:2	64 n. 103	4:14	44 n. 1
3:3	8, 41	Titus	
3:4–7	113, 140	2:5	19 n. 50
3:4–6	41, 116, 121 n. 54, 140, 140 n. 142	2:9	19 n. 50
3:5–14	41	2:13	140
3:6	40, 40 n. 30, 41, 66, 141	3:1	19 n. 50
3:7	121 n. 54, 140	3:3	22
3:8	140	Philemon	
3:9	47, 120	18	96 n. 97
3:12	138, 162	21	19 n. 50, 22
3:21	139, 151	Hebrews	
4:10–13	118 n. 39	1–12	155 n. 52
Colossians		2:5–9	101, 108 n. 145
1:10–11	68	3:7–4:13	57 n. 68
1:15	108, 151	3:7–19	94
1:26–27	13 n. 14	3:18–19	16, 20, 94
2:8	134	4:15	92
2:16–17	41	5:8	94
2:20	41, 134	5:9	70
3:1–17	155	7:16	80
3:1–3	126	7:22	69 n. 125
3:5–9	145, 151	10:24	69
3:5	118 nn. 39, 40, 121	10:26	92
3:10	151	12:4	134
3:12–17	151	13	155 n. 52
3:18	19 n. 50	James	
3:20	19 n. 50	1:12	69
3:22	19 n. 50	2:18–26	20
3:25	44 n. 1	2:21–26	69 n. 123
1 Thessalonians		3:2	134
1:3	68	5:11	69 n. 123
1:9–10	145	1 Peter	
1:9	47 n. 17	1:3–12	80
3:13	162	1:10–12	13 n. 18
2 Thessalonians		1:17	44 n. 1
1:3	155	2:22	25, 93
1:4	68	2:23	93
1:8	14, 16, 29, 40		

2 Peter
1:5–11   155
1:19–20   13 n. 18
3:18   155

1 John
2:20   148
2:27   148
3:4–9   92
3:8–10   93
3:8   92
3:9   148
5:16   93
5:18   93
5:21   93

Revelation
2:23   44 n. 1
21:5   79
22:2   79

Index of Authors

Abrahams, I., 61
Adamson, J. B., 69 nn. 123, 124, 146 n. 11
Althaus, P., 131 n. 93
Anderson, A. A., 104 n. 123
Arenhoevel, D., 6 n. 13
Attridge, H. W., 92

Bandstra, A. J., 111 n. 7, 134 n. 108, 142 n. 151
Banks, R., 43 n. 50, 61 n. 90, 63 n. 99, 95 nn. 93, 94
Barclay, J. M. G., 29 n. 85, 30 n. 89, 41 n. 33, 128 n. 84
Barrett, C. K., 15 n. 25, 25, 33 n. 7, 34 n. 12, 38 n. 25, 68 n. 116, 87 n. 65, 88 n. 69, 90 nn. 75, 76, 93 n. 86, 104 nn. 124, 125, 107 n. 139, 112 n. 11, 117, 121 n. 55, 124 n. 67, 130 nn. 88, 90, 134, 136 nn. 115, 118, 137 n. 122, 142 nn. 150, 153, 143 n. 158, 156 n. 56
Barth, K., 79 n. 24, 88 n. 71, 98 n. 102, 113 n. 24
Bartsch, H.-W., 18 n. 42
Bassler, J. M., 34 nn. 12, 13, 56 n. 62
Beardslee, W. A., 12 n. 11
Beasley-Murray, G. R., 48 n. 22
Behm, J., 130 n. 88
Beker, J. C., 2 n. 2, 8 n. 17, 12 n. 11, 41, 41 n. 32, 43, 45 n. 4, 49 n. 24, 59 nn. 75, 77, 63 n. 100, 71 n. 135, 72 nn. 1, 2, 76 nn. 13, 14, 77, 78 n. 19, 82, 87 n. 64, 99 nn. 107, 108, 103 nn. 119, 121, 104 n. 127, 105 n. 131, 106 n. 133, 111 nn. 7, 8, 125 n. 73, 129 n. 86, 139 n. 137, 141 nn. 145, 147, 143 n. 159, 154, 155 n. 47, 156 n. 56, 162 n. 78, 163 n. 83
Benoit, P., 66 n. 110
Berkouwer, G. C., 3, 5, 44 n. 2, 78 n. 22, 83 n. 44, 86, 88 n. 68, 90, 98 n. 102, 105 n. 129, 107 n. 138, 108 n. 144, 112 n. 11, 124 n. 68, 125 n. 74, 131 n. 96, 134 nn. 104, 106, 135 n. 113, 144, 146, 146 n. 11, 147 nn. 13, 17, 148 nn. 18, 22, 149, 149 n. 22, 155 n. 52, 156 n. 55, 158 n. 66, 160, nn. 69, 70, 162, 163 nn. 82, 83

Betz, H. D., 129
Betz, O., 54 n. 52, 61 n. 89
Bickerman, E., 66 n. 110
Binder, H., 12 n. 11
Black, C. C., 87 n. 62
Black, M., 10 n. 6, 14, 15, 16 n. 29, 21, 25 n. 70, 33, 33 n. 8, 85 n. 52, 96, 97 n. 98, 136 n. 120
Boer, M. C., 2 n. 2, 74 n. 7, 76 n. 13, 77 n. 18, 82 n. 39, 105 n. 131, 107 n. 140
Bornkamm, G., 74 n. 7, 111 n. 7, 116 n. 31, 133 n. 103, 135 n. 113, 137 n. 122
Brandenburger, E., 74 n. 7, 78 n. 20, 79 n. 25, 85 n. 52, 87 nn. 61, 63, 89 n. 73, 100 n. 111, 102, 105 n. 128, 106 n. 136, 107 n. 141, 111 n. 8, 120 n. 47, 143 n. 157
Brandon, S. G. F., 66 n. 112
Brasswell, J. P., 63 n. 101, 67 n. 115
Brauch, M. T., 45 n. 8
Braun, H., 125 n. 73
Brown, R. E., 13 nn. 16, 17
Bruce, F. F., 15 n. 24, 66 n. 110, 84 n. 48, 85 n. 51, 99 n. 105, 100, 104 n. 125, 112 n. 11, 116 n. 31, 118, 118 n. 41, 125 n. 73, 135 n. 111, 136 n. 120, 137 n. 124, 139 n. 135, 140 n. 142
Bruegemann, W., 7 n. 15
Buber, M., 59 n. 77, 61
Büchler, A., 18 n. 44, 129 n. 86
Bultmann, R., 12 n. 11, 17, 61, 76 nn. 13, 14, 86 n. 60, 102 n. 115, 105 n. 129, 111 n. 7, 127 n. 80, 133 n. 102
Burtchaell, J., 69 n. 123
Byrne, B., 18 n. 45, 48 n. 23, 53 n. 47, 54 n. 50, 73, 74 n. 6, 104 n. 127, 106 n. 135, 111 n. 5, 115 n. 29, 153, 154, 155 n. 48, 156 n. 56, 160 n. 69, 161 n. 75

Calvin, J., 15 n. 25, 85, 60 n. 82, 90 n. 74, 95 n. 90, 105 n. 130, 112 n. 11, 113
Cambier, J.-M., 44 n. 2, 52, 52 n. 45, 68, 68 nn. 119, 120, 122, 85 n. 52, 86 nn. 57, 60, 87 n. 63, 89 n. 73, 90 n. 74, 95 n. 90

Campbell, D. H., 111 n. 5, 112 n. 11, 115 n. 28
Caragrounis, C. C., 98
Charlesworth, J. H., 125 n. 73
Collins, J. J., 75, n. 10
Conzelmann, H., 153 n. 39
Coppens, J., 13 n. 16
Cosgrove, C. H., 44, 44 nn. 1, 2, 47 n. 18, 53 n. 46, 55 n. 58, 63 n. 96, 107 n. 141, 120 n. 47, 147 n. 14, 148 n. 20, 149, 156 n. 56, 157
Cranfield, C. E. B., 8 n. 20, 13 n. 15, 14 n. 19, 15, 15 n. 25, 16, 16 n. 30, 20, 21 n. 58, 25 n. 69, 29 n. 81, 32 n. 1, 33, 38 n. 25, 53 n. 46, 59 n. 79, 60 nn. 82, 83, 78, 78 n. 20, 79 n. 25, 84 n. 49, 85, 86, 88 n. 67, 90 n. 74, 95 n. 90, 98 n. 102, 99 n. 106, 101, 102, 104 n. 125, 105 nn. 128, 112 n. 11, 121 nn. 50, 55, 123, 124 n. 69, 128 n. 83, 129, 130, 133–34 n. 104, 136 n. 120, 137 n. 122, 138 n. 130, 139 n. 137, 142 n. 149, 146

Dahl, N. A., 74 n. 6
Davies, G. N., 2 n. 2, 4, 6 n. 12, 8 n. 18, 16 n. 29, 20 n. 54, 34 n. 12, 45 n. 4, 49, 49 n. 29, 50 n. 32, 52 n. 41, 53 n. 49, 54 n. 53, 55 n. 55, 56 n. 62, 60 nn. 82, 83, 150 n. 29, 152 n. 34
Davies, W. D., 10 n. 6, 43 n. 50, 63 n. 99, 79 n. 25, 84 n. 47, 95 n. 94, 118 n. 39, 129 n. 86
Deichgräber, R., 18 n. 43
Deidun, T. J., 67 n. 115, 112 n. 9, 136 n. 121
Denny, J., 95 n. 90
Dobbeler, A., 18
Dodd, C. H., 21 n. 58, 79 n. 24, 84, 106 n. 134, 113 n. 20, 115 n. 28, 117, 126 n. 74
Donaldson, T. L., 7 n. 16, 65 nn. 106, 107, 66 nn. 111, 112

Donfried, K. P., 44 n. 2, 68 n. 117, 147 n. 16
Dunn, J. D. G., 5, 6 n. 11, 8, 9 n. 21, 10, 11 nn. 7, 8, 13 n. 18, 23 n. 64, 26 n. 71, 27 nn. 74, 76, 30 n. 87, 32 n. 3, 34 n. 12, 41 nn. 34, 36, 37, 42 n. 46, 45 nn. 5, 8, 46 nn. 10, 11, 12, 54 n. 52, 55 nn. 56, 61, 56 nn. 62, 64, 57, 57 nn. 65, 69, 58 nn. 70, 71, 72, 74, 59 nn. 76, 77, 78, 60 n. 84, 61, 62, 62 nn. 91, 65 n. 107, 66 n. 108, 67 n. 115, 94, 95, 74 n. 7, 79 n. 25, 81, 81 n. 30, 84, 86 n. 60, 87 nn. 61, 66, 88 n. 71, 90 n. 77, 92 n. 83, 94 n. 89, 95 nn. 90, 91, 97 n. 100, 101 n. 112, 104 n. 123, 105 n. 128, 110–11, 112, 113, 116 n. 31, 117, 120 nn. 47, 48, 121, 122, 122 nn. 58, 59, 123 n. 63, 124 n. 65, 125 n. 74, 126 n. 76, 128, 128 n. 83, 129, 129 n. 85, 86, 87, 130 n. 89, 131 nn. 91, 92, 132 nn. 97, 98, 99, 133 n. 100, 134 n. 107, 135 n. 114, 136, 137 nn. 122, 125, 138 nn. 130, 131, 132, 139 nn. 134, 137, 141 n. 146, 143 n. 155, 145 n. 6, 147 n. 15, 149 n. 26, 157 n. 60, 161 n. 74

Eichrodt, W., 45 n. 8
Elderen, B., 13 n. 16
Elliot, N., 74 n. 7, 78, 79, 98 n. 102, 103, 105 n. 131, 108 n. 145
Ellis, E. E., 77 n. 15, 105 n. 130
Espy, J. M., 112 n. 11, 116 n. 31, 126 n. 74, 128 n. 82, 134 n. 107, 140 n. 142, 142 n. 150

Farmer, W. R., 65 n. 107
Fee, G. D., 48 n. 22
Feuillet, A., 75 n. 10, 65 n. 104, 111 n. 8
Fitzmyer, J. A., 31, 46 n. 9, 47, 49 n. 24, 69 n. 124, 156 n. 54, 159, 160 n. 69, 105 n. 132
Foerster, W., 57 n. 66

Fohrer, G., 18
Friedrich, G., 18 n. 43
Fung, R. Y. K., 45 n. 8, 112 n. 12, 129 n. 84, 133 n. 101, 135, 136 n. 120, 138 n. 130, 142 n. 151
Furnish, V. P., 16, 18, 19 n. 51, 27 n. 75, 64 n. 102, 65 n. 105, 155 n. 48

Gaffin, R. B. 105 n. 130, 155 n. 50, 158–59
Garlington, D. B., 1, 5, 6 nn. 11, 8 n. 17, 10 nn. 1, 2, 11 n. 8, 12 n. 11, 14, 17 nn. 35, 36, 18 n. 44, 32 n. 3, 35 n. 17, 39 n. 27, 40 nn. 29, 30, 41 n. 33, 42 n. 39, 43 n. 49, 46 n. 9, 49 n. 28, 50 n. 32, 53 n. 49, 54 n. 52, 59 n. 77, 63 nn. 96, 97, 64 nn. 102, 103, 65 n. 107, 82 n. 38, 91 nn. 79–82, 92 n. 85, 104 n. 123, 134 n. 109, 152 n. 35, 153 n. 40, 163 nn. 84, 85
Gaston, L., 41 n. 37
Gaventa, B. R., 119 n. 46
Gibbs, J. G., 88 n. 70, 113 n. 17
Godet, F. L., 21 n. 58, 95 n. 90
Goppelt, L., 19 n. 53, 82 n. 36, 98 n. 103, 99, 99 n. 106, 100 n. 110, 105 n. 131, 109 n. 146, 116 n. 31, 119
Gordon, T. D., 7 n. 16, 8 n. 20, 63 n. 101
Greijdanus, S., 142 n. 152
Grundmann, W., 66 n. 110, 125 n. 73
Gundry, R. H., 8 n. 20, 111 n. 7, 113 n. 19, 116 n. 31, 118 nn. 39, 42, 121 n. 54, 122 n. 56, 125 n. 71, 127 n. 78, 128 n. 84, 131

Index of Authors

nn. 92, 94, 134 n. 107, 135 n. 113, 139
nn. 134, 137, 139, 143 n. 156
Gundry Volf, J. M., 3, 64 n. 102, 76 nn. 14, 15, 78 nn. 20, 22
Gunther, J. J., 49 n. 28, 59 n. 77
Guthrie, D., 141 n. 145

Hadot, J., 129 n. 86
Hammerton-Kelly, R. G., 65 n. 106
Hansen, G. W., 50 n. 32
Hays, R. B., 45 n. 4, 75 n. 11, 150 n. 29
Hebert, A. G., 57 n. 67
Heiligenthal, R., 44 n. 2, 53 n. 46
Hendriksen, W., 15 n. 24
Hengel, M., 41 n. 37, 42, 54 n. 50, 61 n. 88, 65 n. 107, 66 nn. 108, 109, 112, 113, 96 n. 95, 129 n. 86
Hill, D., 17, 45 n. 7
Hodge, C., 21, 25 n. 70, 60 n. 82, 112 n. 11
Hoekema, A. A., 105 n. 130, 111 nn. 7, 8, 133 n. 101, 135 n. 111, 155 n. 50, 158−59
Hooker, M. D., 34, 35, 150, 150 n. 29, 155 n. 48
Howard, G., 62 n. 95
Hübner, H., 8 n. 20, 41 n. 36, 147 n. 15

Hughes, P. E., 148 n. 19, 161 n. 77
Hultgren, A. J., 19 n. 48, 27 n. 74, 44 n. 2, 45 n. 7, 46 n. 13, 66 n. 112
Hutchinson, G. P., 84 n. 49

Jeremias, J., 53 n. 50
Jervell, J., 79 n. 25, 83 n. 40
Jewett, R., 27 n. 74, 29, n. 80, 130 n. 88, 131 n. 94
Johnson, E. E., 157 n. 60
Johnson, S. L., 79 n. 25, 84 n. 49
Jüngel, E., 96 n. 96, 98 n. 102, 99 n. 107, 108 n. 142

Käsemann, E., 2 n. 2, 14 n. 21, 15 n. 25, 18 n. 44, 21, 24, 25, 27 nn. 74, 77, 45 n. 7, 46 n. 10, 49 n. 24, 55 n. 57, 62 n. 93, 70 n. 130, 71, 71 n. 135, 79 n. 25, 81, 82 nn. 34, 35, 84, 85 n. 51, 87, 99, 102, 103 nn. 120, 121, 104 nn. 123, 126, 105 n. 128, 106 n. 133, 111 n. 7, 112 n. 16, 116, 125 n. 73, 126 n. 74, 139 n. 134, 150 n. 31, 154 n. 43, 155, 156 n. 54, 157 n. 62
Karlberg, M. W., 112 n. 10, 117 n. 38, 124 n. 66
Kaylor, R. D., 47 n. 15, 51, 51 n. 36, 74, 74 nn. 6, 8, 75 n. 9, 83 n. 43, 95 n. 90, 107 n. 140, 108 n. 143

Kelly, H. A., 84 n. 46
Kertelge, K., 44 n. 2, 45 n. 7, 49 n. 24, 51 n. 34, 60 n. 81, 71 n. 133, 104 n. 128, 106 n. 136, 111 n. 7, 112 n. 16, 113, 113 n. 18, 115 n. 28, 119 n. 45, 121, 125 n. 71, 131 n. 93, 135 n. 113, 139 n. 134, 152 n. 33, 155 n. 49
Kilgallen, J., 55 n. 56
Kim, S., 13 n. 17, 56 n. 64, 79 n. 25, 100 n. 111, 118 n. 38, 140 n. 142
Kittel, G., 18 n. 44
Kline, M. G., 85 n. 54
Kneucker, J. J., 120 n. 47, 127 n. 78
Kreitzer, L. J., 44 n. 2
Kümmel, W. G., 111 n. 7, 113, 138 n. 131
Kürzinger, J., 142 n. 151
Kuhn, K. G., 113 n. 27, 125 n. 73
Kuss, O., 111 nn. 6, 7, 112 n. 16, 121, 125 n. 69, 136 n. 121

Lacey, D. R., 126 n. 74
Ladd, G. E., 141 n. 145
Lane, W. L., 92 n. 83
La Rondelle, H. K., 147 n. 15
Leenhardt, F. J., 21 n. 58, 25 n. 69, 33, 33 n. 8, 80 n. 27, 84 n. 46, 85 n. 53, 88 n. 69, 101 n. 114, 102, 103, 113, 127 n. 81, 130 n. 88, 139 n. 139, 140, 144, 144 n. 1, 145 n. 3
Lenski, R. C. H., 15 n. 24, 25 n. 70, 69 n. 123
Levison, J. R., 79 n. 25
Lietzmann, H., 136 n. 120
Lightfoot, J. B., 102 n. 116
Limbeck, M., 42 n. 46
Lincoln, A. T., 57 n. 68

Lombard, H. A., 79 n. 25, 98 n. 102
Longenecker, B. W., 8 n. 20, 34 n. 12, 37 n. 21, 40, 40 n. 30, 56 n. 63
Longenecker, R. N., 8 n. 17, 48 n. 21, 49 n. 24, 61, 104 n. 125, 112 n. 14, 113 nn. 22, 27, 116 n. 31, 119, 125, 125 n. 73
Lührmann, D., 38 n. 24
Lull, D. J., 40 n. 28, 63 n. 101
Lyonnet, S., 85 n. 52, 116 n. 31
Lyons, G., 119

MacKenzie, R. A. F., 59 n. 77
McGrath, A. E., 45 n. 7
McKnight, S., 3, 67 n. 114, 92 n. 84, 148 n. 21
Maier, G., 129 n. 86
Manson, T. W., 127 n. 79
Marcus, R., 52 n. 42
Marshall, I. H., 93

Martin, B. L., 111 n. 7
Martin, R. P., 74 nn. 7, 8
Mattern, L., 44 n. 2, 68 nn. 117, 122
Meyer, B. F., 100 n. 111
Meyer, P. W., 111 n. 5, 112 n. 14, 127 n. 80
Michel, O., 5, 12, 15, 16 n. 29, 21, 24, 29, 32 n. 2, 33 n. 8, 41 n. 37, 60 n. 81, 100 n. 109, 104 n. 125, 111 n. 6, 113 n. 27, 121 n. 49, 124 n. 67, 125 n. 73
Milne, D. J. W., 34 n. 12
Minear, P., 19 n. 52, 43 n. 51, 51 n. 35
Mitton, C. L., 112 n. 14
Montefiore, C. G./Loewe, H., 129 n. 86
Moo, D. J., 38 n. 25, 53 n. 50, 60 n. 82, 70 n. 131, 71 n. 131, 74 nn. 6, 7, 78 n. 20, 80 n. 29, 81 nn. 31, 32, 85 n. 53, 54 n. 54, 68 n. 121, 69 n. 123, 86 nn. 58, 60, 87, 87 nn. 64, 65, 95 n. 90, 98 n. 101, 99 n. 106, 101 n. 113, 104 nn. 122, 128, 105, 105 n. 130, 110 n. 2, 111 n. 6, 112 n. 10, 113 n. 27, 117 nn. 36, 38, 118 nn. 38, 41, 121 n. 51, 123 nn. 62, 64, 125 n. 70, 126 n. 77, 128 n. 83, 130 n. 90, 131 n. 93, 135 n. 113, 136 nn. 120, 121, 137 n. 123, 138 nn. 131, 133, 139 nn. 137, 138, 141, 141 nn. 146, 148, 144 n. 1, 147 n. 15, 148 n. 20
Moore, C. A., 127 n. 78
Moore, G. F., 129 n. 86
Morris, L., 90 n. 74, 105 n. 130, 111 n. 6, 112 n. 11, 124 n. 69, 125 n. 74
Motyer, S., 2 n. 2, 47 n. 17, 48 n. 20, 70 n. 127, 145 n. 4, 152 n. 34, 153, 153 n. 41, 154 n. 46, 155 n. 48, 157 nn. 63, 64, 158 n. 66
Moule, C. F. D., 19 n. 49, 40, 156
Müller, H., 78 n. 20
Mundle, W., 7 n. 15, 18 n. 44, 29, 144 n. 1, 146
Murphy, R. E., 129 n. 86
Murray, J., 15 n. 25, 16, 17, 21, 33, 33 n. 8, 60 n. 83, 84 n. 49, 85 n. 51, 86 n. 58, 88, 105 n. 130, 106, 112 n. 11, 128 nn. 82, 83, 136 nn. 120, 121, 138 n. 132, 139 n. 139, 155, 155 n. 50, 157 n. 64, 160 n. 71
Mußner, F., 59 n. 77, 67 n. 115

Neusner, J., 66 n. 110
Neyrey, J. H., 112, 112 n. 11, 140 n. 141
Nickelsburg, G. W. E., 145 n. 7
Nygren, A., 25 n. 69, 38 n. 24, 74 n. 7, 80 nn. 27, 28, 84 n. 46, 112, 125 n. 72, 135 n. 112, 139 n. 139, 142 n. 150, 146

O'Donovan, O., 69 n. 124, 150 n. 30, 155
Oepke, A., 104 n. 128, 105 n. 128

Packer, J. I., 112 n. 11, 121 n. 54, 124 n. 69, 128 n. 82, 139 nn. 136, 139, 142 nn. 151, 152
Parke-Taylor, G. H., 14, 31 n. 90
Pathrapankal, J., 12 n. 11, 17
Perry, E., 17
Piper, J., 64 n. 102, 66 n. 110
Pobee, J. S., 41 n. 35
Porter, S. E., 74 n. 6, 81 n. 33, 98 n. 104, 106 n. 136, 118 n. 39, 129 n. 86
Prumm, K., 111 n. 7, 135 n. 113
Przybylski, B., 30, n. 86

Quek, S.-H., 78 n. 20, 79 n. 25, 96 n. 97

Rad, G., 45 n. 7, 50 nn. 30, 33, 57 n. 66
Räisänen, H., 7 n. 15, 38 n. 25, 41 n. 36, 43 n. 50, 55 n. 60, 59 n. 79, 60 n. 80, 122 n. 57
Renaud, B., 6 n. 13
Reumann, J., 45 n. 7, 46 n. 13, 47 n. 15, 106 n. 133, 146, 156 n. 54
Ridderbos, H. N., 13 n. 17, 15 n. 25, 19 n. 49, 25 n. 69, 30 n. 87 40 n. 30, 49 n. 24, 50, 53 n. 50, 86, 64 n. 102, 88 n. 71, 105 n. 130, 111 nn. 7, 8, 113 n. 23, 115 n. 28, 124 n. 69, 125 n. 71, 126 n. 76, 128 nn. 82, 84, 132 n. 97, 135 n. 113, 136 n. 120, 139 n. 134, 142 n. 152, 143 nn. 156, 158, 152 n. 33
Robertson, A. T., 90 n. 74
Robinson, J. A. T., 74 n. 7
Roetzel, C. J., 44 n. 2, 52 n. 42
Russell, D. S., 129 n. 87

Saldarini, A. J., 41 n. 36, 140 nn. 141, 142
Sanday, W./Headlam, A. C., 15 n. 25, 22 n. 62, 24 n. 65, 81 n. 32, 85 n. 53, 87 n. 62, 88, 102, 111 n. 7, 136 n. 120
Sanders, E. P., 6, 8, 18 n. 45, 19 n. 52, 42 nn. 42, 46, 48 n. 23, 58 n. 73, 59 n. 79, 60 n. 80, 61 n. 89, 62 n. 95, 66 n. 110, 68 nn. 119, 122, 69, 70 n. 129, 122 n. 57, 153, 137 n. 124
Schechter, S., 129 n. 86
Schlatter, A., 21 n. 58, 25 n. 69, 26, 34 n. 10, 90 n. 78, 111 n. 7, 124 n. 69
Schlier, H., 14, 15 n. 25, 16, 24, 29 n. 81, 33 nn. 8, 9, 79 n. 25, 87 n. 61, 111 n. 7, 121, 122 n. 60, 136 n. 120
Schnabel, E. J., 41 n. 33, 61 n. 89
Schnackenburg, R., 111 nn. 6, 7, 113 n. 18, 115 n. 28, 121, 135 n. 113
Schoeps, H. J., 59 n. 77
Schrage, W., 64 n. 102
Schreiner, T. R., 8 n. 20, 147 n. 15

Schrenk, G., 32 n. 2, 33 n. 8, 44 n. 3, 49 n. 25, 147 n. 17
Schubert, K., 66 n. 110
Scroggs, R., 79 n. 25, 88 n. 69, 105 n. 131, 107 n. 140, 130 n. 89, 150 n. 28
Seebass, H., 79 n. 25
Segal, A. F., 59 n. 77, 63 n. 98
Shedd, W. G. T., 90 n. 73
Siker, J. S., 50 n. 32
Silva, M., 8 n. 20, 61 n. 88, 147 n. 15
Skehan, P., 129 n. 86
Smalley, S., 92, 93 nn. 86, 88
Smeaton, G., 85 n. 54
Snodgrass, K. R., 44 n. 2, 53 nn. 46, 47, 60 n. 80, 69, 70 nn. 128, 130, 71 n. 135, 147 nn. 15, 17, 156
Spicq, C., 64 n. 102, 67 n. 115
Stendahl, K., 47, 47 n. 14, 125 n. 74, 140
Stern, M., 54 n. 52
Stowers, S., 34 n. 10, 53 n. 50
Strack, H. L./Billerbeck, P., 78 n. 20, 118 n. 38, 129 n. 86
Strohl, H., 64
Stuart, M., 87 n. 61, 88 n. 72, 89 n. 73, 95 n. 90
Stuhlmacher, P., 45 n. 8, 67 n. 115, 152 n. 34
Synofzik, E., 44 n. 2

Tannehill, R., 19 n. 52
Theissen, G., 111 nn. 6, 7, 8, 113, 113 n. 27, 116 n. 31, 121, 125 n. 71, 137 n. 122, 138 n. 131, 140 n. 142, 142 n. 154
Thüsing, W., 156 n. 57
Thyen, H., 61 n. 86
Turner, N., 30 n. 88 102 n. 116

Urbach, E., 118 n. 38, 129 n. 86

Vermes, G., 66 n. 110
Versteeg, J. P., 99 n. 106, 105 n. 130

Watson, F., 32 n. 3, 33 n. 8, 37 nn. 21, 23, 38 n. 25, 44 n. 2, 148 n. 22
Watson, N. M., 44 n. 2, 147 n. 16
Wedderburn, A. J. M., 34 n. 12, 79 n. 25, 88 nn. 69, 71, 89, 95 n. 90, 102 n. 115, 106, 116 n. 31
Wenham, D., 112 n. 12, 161 n. 76, 126 n. 74, 128 n. 84, 129 n. 84, 133 n. 101, 142 n. 152
Westerholm, S., 8 n. 20, 37 n. 21, 41 n. 36
Wilckens, U., 15 n. 25, 18 n. 46, 32 n. 3, 33 n. 8, 34 n. 10, 44 n. 2, 52 n. 40, 59, 60 n. 85, 79 n. 25, 63 n. 96, 88, 97 n. 100, 105 n. 128, 111 nn. 6, 7, 112 n. 16, 113 n. 27, 116, 121, 136 nn. 115, 118, 137 n. 122, 139 n. 139
Williams, S. K., 13 n. 16, 21 n. 60, 27 n. 75, 45 n. 8, 46 n. 10, 47 nn. 16, 18, 52 n. 42, 149, 150 n. 29
Wright, N. T., 10 n. 4, 35 n. 16, 37 n. 21, 38 n. 26, 45 n. 7, 82, 83 nn. 40, 41, 42, 88 n. 69, 112 n. 10, 128 n. 83, 151

Young, F. W., 18, 62 n. 93

Zeller, D., 33 n. 8, 34 n. 11, 97 n. 99, 111 n. 7, 136 n. 120, 137 nn. 122, 124
Zerwick, M., 102 n. 116
Ziesler, J. A., 47, 48, 49 n. 24, 60, 105, 106 n. 133, 118 n. 40, 154 n. 45, 156, 163 n. 84

Index of Subjects

Abraham, 10 nn. 6, 37, 46 n. 10, 50–51, 54 n. 52, 69 n. 123, 72, 74, 75 n. 12, 81, 83, 108 n. 142, 146 n. 11

Adam
– first, 23, 26, 34–37, 51, 53, 57, 67, 68, 70, 71, 73, 76, 79–109, 112, 114, 115, 116 n. 31, 117, 118–119, 122–24, 127–28, 132, 134 n. 108, 138, 139 n. 137, 143, 145, 150–51, 156, 163
– last, 2, 23, 26, 19, 53, 70, 79–109, 132, 150–151, 154, 163

Anthropology (Pauline), 110, 113, 122, 126, 128–33, 136, 138, 141–42, 143 n. 158

Apocalyptic, 72 n. 2, 76 n. 23, 77–78, 105, 129 n. 87, 137 n. 122, 153, 157 n. 60

Baptism, 153 nn. 38, 39

Boasting, 8, 38–39, 41, 52, 54, 58, 76–77, 79, 157

Boundary/Identity Markers, 5, 6, 7, 8, 10–11, 42, 45, 54, 58, 64, 66, 67, 114

Christology (Pauline), 1, 5, 6, 7, 10–13, 17, 19, 20–21, 24, 25–26, 30, 31, 34, 37, 39, 40–43, 44, 45, 48, 50–51, 54, 55, 56, 57, 59, 62–63, 67, 69, 70, 71, 72–77, 79–109, 114, 115, 119, 122–23, 125–26, 132–33, 138, 139 n. 137, 140–41, 143, 145, 147, 150–151, 153, 155–57, 163

Circumcision, 5, 6, 26, 41, 42, 50, 54, 58 n. 72, 64, 127, 153 n. 38

Confession, 3, 41 n. 32, 62–63, 148

Corporate personality, 81–82

Covenant, 4, 7, 8, 10–12, 17–18, 19, 20, 26 n. 71, 41–42, 45, 46–52, 53 n. 48, 54 n. 52, 55, 56, 59, 60, 62, 65, 66 n. 108, 67, 69 n. 125, 70, 74–76, 81, 89–92, 96, 100, 102, 105–6, 114, 126, 128, 129 n. 86, 131 n. 95, 132, 137, 140, 146, 147 n. 15, 148, 149 n. 26, 150 n. 29, 150–152, 153 n. 38, 163

Creation, 2, 19, 41, 46 n. 10, 47 n. 15, 52 n. 43, 53, 56–58, 65, 67, 68, 71, 72, 74–109, 112–113, 114–115, 117, 119–43, 145, 148, 150–52, 154–56, 160–61

Death, 23, 48, 68, 84–97, 111, 115, 116, 117, 118, 119 n. 45, 121, 122, 126, 133, 139 n. 137, 141, 142, 143

Eschatology (Pauline), 2, 3, 4, 7, 10–13, 18 n. 45, 19, 20 n. 54, 21 n. 60, 27 n. 74, 35, 37, 40–41, 43, 44, 46, 49, 52 n. 41, 54, 55, 57, 58, 67, 68, 71, 72–78, 79–108, 111, 112, 113 n. 18, 114, 119, 121, 122–25, 126, 127, 129, 130–35, 136, 138–40, 141 n. 149, 142–43, 144, 148, 149, 150, 152, 153–155, 156–60, 161–62

Eve, 23, 97, 117, 118–119

Evil inclination, 86 n. 60, 129

Faith(fulness)/Obedience/Perseverance, 1–8, 10–31, 38, 42, 44–71, 72–109, 110–43, 144–63

Flesh, 2, 65, 72–73, 102 n. 115, 111, 112, 116, 122, 123, 124–25, 126, 128–29, 130–35, 136, 138, 142 n. 153, 143, 148, 156–57, 161

Free will, 87–88 n. 66, 129 n. 86

Gentiles/Nations, 4, 7 n. 15, 10–13, 17, 20, 25, 26–28, 29–30, 33 n. 8, 34–43, 45, 46–47, 49–55, 56, 58 n. 74, 62, 64, 67 n. 114, 75, 77 n. 18, 81–82, 91, 95–96, 102 n. 115, 114, 127, 137, 145, 152

Glory/Honor, 1, 35, 53, 56, 67, 71 n. 134, 76, 77 n. 15, 79–80, 89–90, 94, 114, 100, 129 n. 87, 132, 143, 150, 155, 159, 163

"Good" and "Evil", 21, 23, 44, 57, 60, 68, 97, 127, 148, 156, 117 n. 34, 136, 142

Gospel (Pauline), 4, 10–13, 14, 16, 17, 20, 21, 22, 24, 25, 27–28, 29–30, 41, 43, 47 n. 15, 51, 52, 53 n. 50, 62, 63, 66 n. 112, 69, 71, 97, 145–46, 149, 155

Grace/Mercy/Gift, 6, 7, 8 n. 17, 43, 46, 48 n. 23, 51, 53 n. 47, 65 n. 105, 69, 69 n. 124, 70, 70 n. 127, 71, 74, 76 n. 13, 81, 94, 99–102, 106–8, 111, 115 n. 28, 116, 136, 144, 146, 147 n. 13, 148–49, 151–157, 159

Index of Subjects

Hope, 26, 68, 73–74, 76–78, 80, 115, 132, 138, 140, 142, 153, 159, 162

Idolatry/Sacrilege, 2, 23, 32–43, 47 n. 17, 49 n. 27, 51, 53, 54 n. 54, 55, 56, 57 n. 69, 59 n. 79, 72, 83, 85 n. 53, 89, 91–92, 97, 108–9, 114, 116, 118, 120, 121, 123, 127, 138, 140, 145, 147 n. 16, 163
Image (of God/Christ), 53, 56, 76, 80, 82–83, 89, 90, 97, 100, 108, 114, 128, 132, 135, 143, 145, 148, 151, 154–55
Imputation (of Adam's sin), 85, 105
Indicative/Imperative, 20, 152, 154–55

James (and Paul), 69, 146 n. 11
Jews/Judaism/Israel, 2, 4, 5, 6, 7, 8, 10–12, 14, 16, 17–19, 20, 23, 26, 27–28, 29–30, 32–43, 45, 46–47, 49, 50–55, 56, 58–60, 61–67, 69–70, 71, 73 n. 3, 74, 75, 77 n. 18, 81–83, 88 n. 66, 94–96, 99–100, 102, 107–8, 112, 114, 115, 116, 119 n. 45, 120 n. 47, 121 n. 49, 125 n. 73, 126, 137, 140–41, 145–47, 152, 156, 157 n. 60, 163
Judgment, 1, 29, 44, 49, 52–53, 56–60, 62, 67, 69, 70, 76, 76–77 n. 15, 77, 91, 95, 114, 145–46, 147 nn. 16, 17, 148 n. 20, 149, 152–54, 157
Justification/Vindication, 1–2, 4, 7 n. 15, 19–20, 44, 45 n. 4. 46 nn. 9, 13, 47–50, 55, 56–60, 65 n. 105, 67, 68, 69, 71, 72, 74–79, 80, 83, 94, 99, 101–2, 105–6, 114, 115, 145–46, 147–63

Law/Torah/Tradition, 5, 6, 7, 8, 10 n. 6, 17, 21, 36, 38, 40–43, 44, 47, 49–55, 56–60, 61–62, 64–67, 69, 70, 71, 72, 77, 81–83, 86, 90–93, 95–97, 99–100, 102 n. 115, 107–8, 110, 112, 113 n. 18, 114, 116, 117–118, 119, 120–35, 136–37, 138, 140–41, 142, 145–48, 150, 153, 156–57
Legalism/Merit/Works-Righteousness, 6, 7, 8, 42 n. 46, 46, 55, 61, 69, 71, 91, 147–48, 153, 157, 163
Life/Resurrection/Immortality, 1, 6–7, 14, 18 n. 45, 19, 23, 40, 48, 49, 54 n. 50, 56–57, 65 n. 105, 67, 68, 69, 70, 71 n. 134, 72–74, 77, 79, 80, 82, 86, 88–89, 91, 99, 100–3, 106–8, 111, 114, 115, 117, 120, 132, 133, 138, 140, 141, 142–43, 145–153, 154, 156–58, 159, 161–63
Love
– of God, 8 n. 17, 74, 77, 163
– human, 64–67, 68, 69, 70, 71, 126, 128, 147, 151, 159

Mission/Commission (Paul), 4, 10–13, 15, 17, 20, 21 n. 60, 26, 27–28, 31, 32 n. 3, 40, 144–45

New people of God, 5–6, 10–11, 19, 27 nn. 74, 75, 45, 49, 51, 59, 65, 67, 69, 70, 71, 75–76, 80, 83, 88, 100, 101, 112, 114, 126, 127, 144, 145, 148–50, 152, 154, 163
Nomism (Covenantal), 5, 6, 7, 8, 54 n. 54, 55, 61, 70, 99, 140, 163 n. 85

"Obedience of faith", 1–6, 10–31, 42–43, 44, 45, 49, 52 n. 41, 53, 59, 60 n. 79, 62, 63, 65, 67, 68 n. 122, 69, 70, 71, 72, 114, 144–46, 163
Ordo Salutis, 4, 158–61

Peace, 26, 53, 57, 67, 75–77, 79, 80, 102
Perfection, 70, 91, 117 n. 36, 140 n. 142, 141, 147 n. 15, 159, 162–63

Reconciliation, 48, 74–80, 83, 105–6, 132
Reformers/Reformation/Protestantism, 4, 101–2, 147 n. 13, 153–56, 158, 160
Righteousness/Righteous, 4, 10 n. 6, 14, 16, 18 n. 45, 19, 20 n. 54, 45–50, 51, 52, 53, 54 n. 50, 59, 60, 61 n. 89, 62–63, 69, 70 n. 127, 70–71, 73, 75, 77, 81, 91–94, 99, 100–3, 105–7, 120, 130, 137, 141, 142 n. 153, 145–48, 150–57, 163
Roman Catholicism, 4
Roman Letter (purpose of), 10–11, 45

Sabbath/Feast Days, 5, 41
Salvation/Deliverance/Redemption, 3, 6, 7, 45–46, 47 n. 14, 48, 48 n. 23, 49–51, 52, 55, 57, 61 n. 89, 66 n. 112, 70, 71, 73–74, 76–80, 82–83, 100, 106–7, 109, 110, 115, 116, 123, 125, 127, 132, 135, 139–40 n. 139, 142, 143, 145, 147 nn. 13, 15, 141 n. 149, 143, 148, 150, 152–54, 157, 159–61, 163
Sanctification, 4, 48, 107, 146–47, 149, 151–63
Sin, 2, 11, 35, 38, 41, 42 n. 47, 48, 51, 52, 56, 58, 60, 72, 81 nn. 30, 31, 84–97, 114, 115, 116, 117, 119, 122, 120–35, 136, 137, 138, 139 n. 137, 140, 141, 142–43, 150, 156, 161, 162–63
Sinner/Ungodly/Lawless, 4, 42 n. 47, 66 nn. 109, 110, 74, 79–80, 83, 91–95, 103–4, 106, 132, 154, 156
Spirit/Spiritual, 2, 26, 27, 28, 51, 54, 64, 68,

70, 72–77, 85–86, 102 n. 115, 110–111, 112, 115, 122–23, 125, 126, 128–29, 130–35, 136, 138, 139 n. 137, 143, 145, 148, 151, 156–57, 159, 161

Typology, 27 n. 74, 79, 81–82, 98–100, 103, 107 n. 139, 119

Unbelief/Disobedience/Apostasy, 2–4, 16, 20, 22–23, 25, 29–30, 32–43, 44, 48 n. 22, 49, 52 n. 43, 53 n. 48, 54–55, 62–63, 67–68, 69, 73, 79–109, 114, 118, 127, 139 n. 134, 145, 148–49, 151, 156, 163

Union with Christ, 19, 44, 46–47, 51, 58 n. 73, 65, 65 n. 105, 66 n. 113, 69, 70, 71, 72–73, 77, 79–81, 83, 87 n. 65, 88, 103, 106–7, 114, 115, 120, 132–35, 136, 143, 150–51, 153–56, 158, 160–61, 163

Works, 4, 6–7, 20, 21, 52–53, 55, 56–71, 146–47, 148 n. 20
"Works of the Law", 5–6, 8, 16, 62, 70–71 n. 131, 127

www.ingramcontent.com/pod-product-compliance
Lightning Source LLC
Chambersburg PA
CBHW060608230426

43670CB00011B/2026